The Edinburgh History of the Greeks, 1768 to 1913

D1615587

The Edinburgh History of the Greeks
Series Editor: Thomas W. Gallant

Titles available
The Edinburgh History of the Greeks, c. 500 to 1050: The Early
Middle Ages
Florin Curta

The Edinburgh History of the Greeks, 1786 to 1913: The Long
Nineteenth Century
Thomas W. Gallant

Forthcoming titles
The Edinburgh History of the Greeks, 323 to 30 BC: The Hellenistic
World
Joseph G. Manning

The Edinburgh History of the Greeks, 1453 to 1785: The Ottoman
Empire
Molly Greene

The Edinburgh History of the Greeks, 1768 to 1913

The Long Nineteenth Century

Thomas W. Gallant

EDINBURGH
University Press

To Dad

© Thomas W. Gallant, 2015

Edinburgh University Press Ltd
The Tun – Holyrood Road,
12(2f) Jackson's Entry,
Edinburgh EH8 8PJ

www.euppublishing.com

Typeset in 11/13pt Sabon
by Norman Tilley Graphics Ltd, Northampton
and printed and bound in Great Britain by
CPI Group (UK) Ltd, Croydon CR0 4YY

A CIP record for this book is available from
the British Library

ISBN 978 0 7486 3605 1 (hardback)
ISBN 978 0 7486 3199 5 (webready PDF)
ISBN 978 0 7486 3606 8 (paperback)
ISBN 978 0 7486 3607 5 (epub)

Contents

Illustrations and Maps

Illustrations

Maps

Tables

Acknowledgements

This volume in the Edinburgh History of the Greeks covers the crucial period when they went from being a stateless nation embedded in a pre-Modern, multinational empire to a people divided among their own nation-state, Greece, the Ottoman Empire and a rapidly globalising diaspora. This is a big story that must be told on a grand scale. Because of the scope of the book and the multiple historiographies that it engages, it has been a long time in preparation.

Over years that I have been working on it, I have accumulated many intellectual and practical debts. First, I want to express my deepest thanks to Carol MacDonald and her colleagues at Edinburgh University Press. They have been extraordinarily generous in helping me at every turn. The book has benefited from the many discussions that I have had over the years with my fellow Greek historians, among whom I want to single out Antonis Liakos, Doxis Doxiades, Sakis Gekas and Emilia Salvanou. While working on the book, my thinking about Greek history and the need to contextualise it in multiple historiographies has been shaped by collaborating with some of the brightest young minds in the field today. I have learned as much from working with the doctoral students in UC San Diego's doctoral program in Modern Greek History as they have learned from me. In terms of the hard work of writing, Sadie, Sabrina and Marley were my constant sources of inspiration and most of the book was written in their company. The one person without whom this book could never have been written is my wife, partner and lifelong friend, Mary P. Gallant. Her contributions are so many that they defy enumeration. Words cannot convey my deepest appreciation for all that she does. Lastly, this book is dedicated to my father, Robert A. Gallant. He has always been an inspiration to me and I owe him an eternal debt of gratitude for being the best father that a son could ever have.

Series Editor's Preface

The Edinburgh History of the Greeks is a multi-volume, chronological series covering the history of the Greek people from Antiquity to the present. Each volume combines political history with social and cultural history in order to tell the story of the Greek people over the course of recorded history in an exciting, novel and innovatory way. Drawing on resources from anthropology, archaeology and history, as well as political science, philology, art, literature and law, the books will be rich in diverse in their coverage.

The Greeks suffer from too much history, some have said. Indeed, library bookshelves sag under the weight of the massive number of tomes devoted to the history of Greece during ancient, medieval and modern periods. This series differs from them by focusing on the history of a people, the Greeks, and not a place, Greece. The story will reflect the fluctuating dynamics of change while primary sources and accounts of the lives of individuals and communities will give life to the text.

The history of the Greeks over the long durée must be told on a vast and at times even global scale, and so the Greek world is not just taken to include the area traditionally associated with ancient Greece or the territory of the modern Greek state, but encompasses all areas where Greeks have settled, including the diaspora of modern times.

Thomas W. Gallant

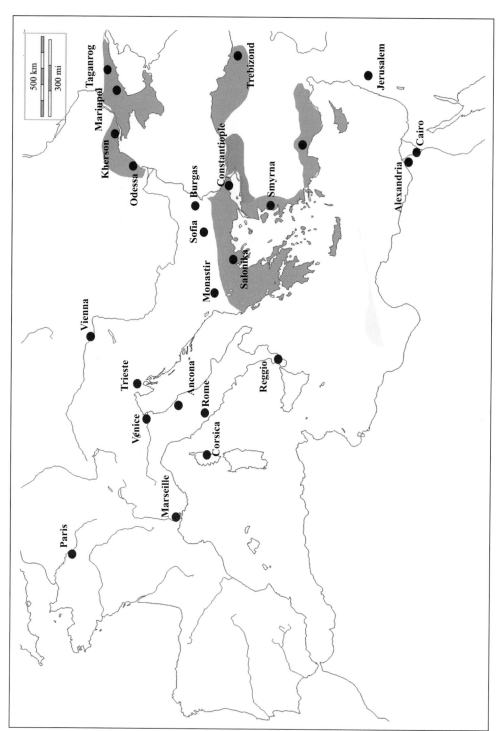

The Greek World during the late Ottoman period.

CHAPTER 1

The winds of change

The early morning night sky lit up in a stunning burst of bright orange as the main mast of the 'Real Mustafa', the Ottoman flagship and the empire's largest ship-of-the line, exploded, raining fiery embers onto its sails (Fig. 1.1). Soon the ship was engulfed in flames. Over the next few hours almost the entire Ottoman fleet would be destroyed in the narrows of Çesme under a constant barrage of cannon fire from the Russian fleet. Of the seventy-three Ottoman ships that had entered Çesme Bay, located in the straits between the island of Chios and the coast of Anatolia, fewer than a dozen made it out intact. While the fleet was smouldering in Çesme Bay, elsewhere in the empire another disaster was unfolding. A joint Ottoman-Tatar army confronted a Russian force on the banks of the Larga River, a tributary of the Prut River. At a place called Varlea the Ottoman commander Abdi Paşa and the Crimean Khan Kaplan Giray arrayed their massive army. Outnumbering the Russian forces led by General Peter Rumiantsev by almost three to one and with a seven-to-one superiority in cavalry, victory seemed assured. Instead the battle turned into a rout. The deployment of the Russian forces in regimental squares nullified the Ottoman-Tatar cavalry and repeated bayonet charges broke the Ottoman infantry lines. While not the worst defeat on land that the Ottomans would suffer in the 1768–74 Russo-Ottoman War, it set the pattern for the remainder of the conflict. With the destruction of its fleet and the defeat of its army on the Danubian frontier, 7 July 1770 has to go down as one of the worst days in the long history of the Ottoman Empire.

The 1768–74 Russo-Ottoman War marks a critical turning point in world history. For many historians, it inaugurated an issue that would impact European Great Power relations for the next 120 years: the Eastern Question. Of more practical and immediate importance were the numerous and significant developments that occurred as result of the war and the treaty that ended it. And so, because it was the event that started the long nineteenth century in

Figure 1.1 *The Battle of Çesme (1848) © I. K. Aivazovsky Museum, Theodosia, Crimea.*

Southeastern Europe and the Eastern Mediterranean, we need to begin with an examination of this fateful conflict.

The Russo-Ottoman Wars 1768–92

By 1768 the Ottoman Empire had experienced the longest continuous period of peace in its history. Not since the 1739 signing of the Treaty of Belgrade that ended the three-year-long Ottoman-Hapsburg War had the empire been at war with any of its European rivals. The breathing space was much needed. Ever since the disastrous invasion of the Hapsburg Empire and the siege of Vienna in 1683, the empire had been pretty much at war with someone. After the debacle of the Holy League War and the loss of significant territories, such as the Morea (the Peloponnesos), the empire had made a comeback of sorts, reclaiming that region in 1717 and regaining control of Belgrade in 1739. After almost half a century of war, the empire was finally at peace and that gave it an opportunity to deal with the economic and political fallout from the wars and to rebuild its social and administrative foundations. So, while the rest of Europe was engaged in costly and brutal conflicts, such as the Seven Years' War (1756–63), following the advice of a number of competent Grand Viziers, the Ottoman Empire remained outside the fray – until 1768.

On 23 October the Ottoman Empire declared war on Russia, with disastrous consequences. The reasons why Mustafa III made this decision were many. Though she had only been on the throne for a short time, Catherine II of Russia was making it clear that she would pursue a very aggressive, expansionist foreign policy. This set her on a collision course with her southern neighbour. One contributing factor to the outbreak of war was Russia's continued interference in the affairs of the Crimean Tatars, who were Muslims and vassals of the Ottoman sultan. The other more important issue related to the ongoing power struggle in the Polish-Lithuanian Commonwealth. Catherine's installation of a handpicked candidate, who was widely opposed, threatened to spark a civil war that could destabilise the region. One group of disaffected Polish nobles settled near the Ottoman border and petitioned the Porte for assistance. When Russian troops, who had been sent to capture the rebels, repeatedly violated the border and finally sacked the city of Balta, the Porte faced a critical decision: acquiescence, humiliation and peace, or retaliation, honour and war. As tensions between Istanbul and St Petersburg escalated over these and other issues, Britain, Prussia and some Ottoman officials, like Muhsinzade Mehmed Paşa and Resim Efendi, counselled against war, while France and other Ottoman politicians, such as Grand Vizier Hamza Paşa and his successor Mohammed Emin Paşa, pushed for war. Seduced by the idea of obtaining the prestigious title of Ghazi, or warrior of the Faithful, and confronted with an egregious violation of his empire's borders, Mustafa opted for war.

Though in a state of war in 1768, with the exception of some Tatar raids into Russia, little happened until the spring of 1770 as both sides prepared for a prolonged campaigning season. Early in 1770, the Russian war plan started to take shape. The conflict would be contested on three fronts, two military and one diplomatic. The first military front was the northern coast of the Black Sea and Crimea. By the summer of 1770, Russia had mobilised an army of over 100,000 men, including regular army troops, Cossack irregulars and some militiamen. Many of the soldiers were veterans whose mettle had been battle-tested during the Seven Years' War (1756–63).

Arrayed against them was a much larger but inferior Ottoman force. The once mighty and feared Ottoman military machine was but a pale comparison of its former self. There were still the Janissary corps and a sizable contingent of timar cavalry, but neither of them was the formidable force that it had once been. In the case of the Janissaries, the abolition of the devşirme system earlier in the century, the Halil Petrona revolt of 1730, and the long period of quiescence between wars (1739–68) transformed the corps from a full-time military organisation into part-time militia manned by cooks, petty craftsmen and pimps (Tuck 2008: 471; Aksan 1993; 1998: 26; Grant 2005; for an assessment of the Russian military and its war strategy, see Davies 2013).

Even more dramatic was the precipitous decline in the competency of the cavalry. Though timar-holders were still expected to take to the field as sipahis, heavily armoured mounted warriors, their numbers were greatly reduced and few of them were trained and combat ready. For the first time, the majority of the Ottoman military would consist of armed irregulars of the levend. Like other states in Europe, the Ottoman Empire recruited men to form armed militias; these men were mobilised and served in the region they were from and their main function was to assist the local government in maintaining law and order, and during times of war they would be mustered to supplement the Janissaries and the sipahis. During the eighteenth century as more power was devolved to the local level, regional officials had to rely increasingly on the levend. When the empire embarked on war with Russia, the orders went out to ayan and kadis at the kaza level (this being a district within an administrative province) to enrol militia troops. According to the best estimate we have, between 100,000 and 150,000 troops were recruited through the levend. Poorly trained and lacking in discipline, these irregulars constituted the core of the Ottoman army that faced Russia in the northern campaign (Aksan 1998; 2007; Menning 1984).

The second military front was at sea. In what one historian calls 'one of the most spectacular events of the eighteenth century' (Anderson 1954: 44), Russia assembled a war fleet and deployed it in the Mediterranean, catching the Ottomans off-guard and posing a threat to Istanbul. Under the overall leadership of Count Aleksey Orlov, the fleet was deployed in two contingents. The first departed from Russia in August 1769 and arrived in the Aegean in December, and the second set sail in October and arrived in May 1770. Both squadrons put in at British ports for resupplying and outfitting, without which the naval invasion would not have been possible. In addition to this material assistance, the Russian fleet also benefited from the addition of British naval personnel. Experienced captains, like Samuel Greig and John Elphinston, joined the fleet and took command of Russian warships. They and other British officers would play critical roles in the war at sea (Anderson 1954; Stone 2006: 81).

The third military front was supposed to encompass numerous areas in the Balkans and was to involve the Ottoman Empire's non-Muslim populations. Russian agents in Bosnia, Herzegovina, Montenegro, Albania, Crete and the Morea tried to incite the local populations to rise up in rebellion, holding out the promise of Russian financial and logistical support, and even the possibility of their liberation from the Ottoman Empire. Of these areas, the most important for the Russians was the Morea because the peninsula's ports could provide safe haven and resupply depots for the fleet. So important was the Morea that a high-ranking officer, Fyodor Orlov, Aleksy's younger brother, was sent to coordinate the rebellion with the Greek leadership. Because of his involvement this uprising is referred to in Greek historiography as the Orlov Rebellion. None of these attempts to mount a third column inside of the Ottoman Empire came to much, though the Orlov rebellion had important consequences for Greece and the Greeks.

This was a curious war, with two years of intense military activity, 1770 and 1774, interspersed with lengthy periods of inactivity during which negotiations took place. Because the main theatres of war were so distant from each empire's centre, it took considerable time for each side to mobilise and deploy its force. Thus, there was the long hiatus between the declaration and the actual commencement of the war. By the spring of 1769, each side had its military in place, and it was Russia that was the aggressor. During the first campaigning season, the Russian forces were under the command of General Aleksandr Mikhailovich Golitsyn and he detrained to attack the Ottoman fortress at Khotin (Hotin); located on the banks of the Dniester River, Khotin was the most important fortification on the Ottoman-Polish border, and should it fall, the Russians would obtain easy access to Moldavia. The fortress capitulated in September by which time it was too late for Golitsyn to press the advantage and invade Moldavia. For this failure, he was relieved of his command in the autumn of 1769. His replacement, General Peter Rumiantsev, would not make the same mistake.

Rumiantsev devised a much more audacious campaign strategy for

1770. As Golitsyn had done, he marched his army in an arc along the northern border of the Khanate, crossing the Bug, the Dnester, and the Prut rivers. With Khotin, located further upstream on the Prut, in Russian hands, he did not have worry about this flank. He divided his forces in two; one contingent, under his command, marched south along the Prut and confronted the main body of the Ottoman army; at the same time, the second army commanded by Peter Panin swung eastward to isolate and then besiege the major Ottoman fortresses of Bender and Akkerman, both on the Dnester, and then Ochakov (Özü in Turkish) at the mouth of the Dnieper River estuary. The plan worked brilliantly.

In a series of battles along the banks of the Prut, Rumiantsev dealt the Ottoman army devastating defeats first at Riabaia Mogilla on 17 June, next on 7 July at the River Larga, and finally the most crushing blow of all at Kagul (also known as Kartal) on 1 August. At that battle, his 42,000 men confronted the main body of the Ottoman forces: 25,000 Janissary infantry, 35,000 levend troops, and 80,000 cavalry. Once again deploying his forces in regimental squares including field artillery, he was able to nullify his opponents' numerical superiority in cavalry and with a coordinated bayonet charge, he smashed through the Ottoman lines. The Janissaries put up fierce resistance but the same cannot be said for the levend irregulars, who fled in the face of Russian steel. The battle turned into a rout, and then a massacre, with thousands of Ottoman soldiers perishing in the swollen waters of the Danube. Following this crushing defeat, Rumiantsev marched south and attacked the Ottoman fortress at Ismail; its defenders quickly capitulated, as did the garrisons at Bender and Akkerman. By the end of 1770, then, the Russian army was poised on the northern bank of the Danube and possessed most of the Ottoman fortresses along the northern Black Sea coast.

Matters fared no better for the Ottomans at sea. In May, the second Russian fleet arrived in the Aegean and rendezvoused with the one that had arrived the previous December. After putting in at various ports in the Morea, the fleet sailed across the Aegean toward Asia Minor seeking a confrontation with the Ottoman flotilla. As was the case on land, at sea as well the Ottomans had a decided numerical advantage; in this case the fleet under the command of the Kapudan Paşa, Mandalzade Hüsameddin Paşa, numbered 73 ships with over 1,300 guns while the Russian fleet consisted of only 21 ships and 712 guns. But what the Russian fleet lacked in numbers, it compensated for with superior seamanship and better armaments.

The two forces met in the open sea early in July. After an initial skirmish, the Ottoman fleet retreated into the straits of Çesme. There it took up a position in the bay, its own formidable numbers now augmented by the artillery in the fortress on the edge of the bay. On 5 July, the Russian fleet deployed across the mouth of the bay, and the battle commenced, culminating in the devastation of the Ottoman ships in the early hours of 7 July. Indeed, if not for the actions of Cezayirli Hasan Paşa, who managed to break through the Russian line with three other ships of the line, the entire fleet would have been lost. For his valiant efforts he was promoted to Kapudan Paşa and his actions later in the war prevented the Russians from blockading the Dardanelles. Nonetheless, with the disaster at Çesme, the Russian fleet now controlled the Aegean.

Also in 1770 the Orlov rebellion erupted (for an assessment of how the Orlov revolt has been treated in Greek historiography, see Rotzokos 2011b). Even before Fyodor Orlov arrived in the Morea with a handful of men and a boatful of supplies, machinations were afoot regarding a possible insurrection by the Greeks. Another officer, this time a Greek member of the imperial artillery corps, named Georgios Papasoğlu, (Nagata 1995: 108) had been active in the region, meeting and plotting with wealthy Christian notables called kocabaşis. The call to arms resonated especially strongly with one of the most powerful of them, Panagiotis Benakis. According to one source, he was the wealthiest man, either zimmi (Christian) or Muslim, in the Morea; in addition to owning as private property six çiftliks, or agrarian estates, near the city of Kalamata and another four near Patras, he also controlled much of the southern Morea's external trade and the collection of its taxes. As befitted a man of his wealth and power, Benakis controlled a patronage network that included both Muslim ayan and Christian kocabaşis, as well a very large number of armed men. It was Benakis whom the Russians chose to lead the rebellion, and according to one rumour, he had even been commissioned into the Russian army with the rank of general. Working with Fyodor Orlov, Benakis mobilised men and materials for an uprising in February 1770 so that the Morea would be under their control when the second contingent of the Russian fleet arrived.

'The Orlov rebellion … was absurd in conception, devoid of genuine libertarian teleology and brutal and chaotic in execution' (Alexander 1985: 49). This assessment is as accurate as it is harsh. The uprising was never anything more than a power struggle between

Benakis and the other factions that opposed him, more specifically those led by the most powerful Muslim ayan in the Morea, Halil Abdi Bey of Corinth, and by the Zaimes (Zaimoğlu), a powerful Christian family from Kalavryta. All of these factions had as members Christian kocabaşis and Muslim ayan, and each had at their disposal cadres of warriors. For some months, men from across the region had been telling the mütesellim (acting governor), Hassan Effendi, that Russian agents were actively inciting some of the kocabaşis and even some ayan to rise in rebellion, but except for apprising the Porte of these rumours, he did nothing.

In mid-February, Fyodor Orlov, along with his Greek collaborator, Antonios Psaros from the island of Mykonos, and about 500 soldiers landed at Kalamata. Orlov and some of his men joined with Benakis and his 4,000 fighters, and together they attacked the garrisons at Koroni and Modoni in Messenia. Psaros and the rest of the Russians marched eastward and rendezvoused with two large warrior bands, one under the leadership of Yiorgakis Mavromichalis and the other led by the brothers Koumoundouros, and together they attacked the city of Mistra. Coalitions of forces also rose up and attacked the fort at Patras, the garrison at Leondari, and the town of Kalavryta. With the exception of the battle at Mistra, which resulted in the city being captured and most of the Muslim population massacred, the uprising was a dismal failure.

There were many reasons for this lack of success. First, the vast majority of the population, that being the reayas (commoners), failed to respond; instead they remained loyal to their lords, be they ayan or kocabaşis. Second, many kocabaşis decided not to join the rebellion, while others, like the powerful Zaimes family from Kalavryta, actively opposed it, mainly because it was being led by their political enemies. Androusakis Zaimes even wrote to one ayan, Süleyman Penah from Gastouni, that they had nothing 'to fear from our reayas, [so] please be at ease. If any of them participate in the rebellion, I will kill them myself' (cited in Nagata 1995: 109).

What the Russians did not realise was that they were about to become entangled in a fierce, long-standing power struggle between competing factions. So, the minute they picked one side as their ally, they alienated the other factions. The Russians unsuspectingly stepped into a hornets' nest and it would cost them (Alexander 1974; 1985; Tzakis 2011, especially pp. 26–7; Fotopoulos 2005: 231–52).

Third, the rebels had neither the manpower nor the resources to storm the Ottoman fortresses, or the luxury of time to besiege them.

Because, fourth, unfortunately for the Russians and the Greek rebels, one of the Ottoman Empire's most competent military men was resident in the Morea when the rebellion broke out, and he took the lead in crushing it. Muhsinzade Mehmed Paşa, whom we met earlier, had been Grand Vizier up until the start of the war with Russia. Because he opposed it, he was dismissed from his post. After a brief retirement to the island of Lesbos, he was commissioned in July 1769 as commander of the garrison at Nafplion.

Upon arrival in the Morea, Muhsinzade Mehmed Paşa went on an inspection of the eyalet's military installations and was appalled at the state they were in. At his own garrison, he found on duty only a fraction of the men listed on the muster rolls. Most of them, he learned, were in the employ of the Ayan of Corinth, Halil Abdi Bey, collecting a salary from him as well as from the state. He also found that the equipment was in ill repair, that supplies were low, and that discipline among the troops was non-existent. Compounding these problems was the fact that over 5,000 (100 companies) of the best Muslim warriors had been mobilised through the levend and were now fighting with the army on the Danube. As rumours of the impending rebellion spread, he accelerated his preparations. He made pacts of friendship with many of the most powerful ayan and sipahis, like Halil Abdi Bey and Ahmet Ağa Hotoman, and with military captains, such as the Tzanis brothers. Using his political connections in Istanbul, he made sure that the Porte was informed about developments in the region, and this soured relations between him and Hassan Efendi, the acting governor, who saw him as a political threat.[1]

Shortly after the rebellion broke out, the Porte appointed Muhsinzade Mehmed Paşa as Muhafısı (Protector) and Serasker (commander-in-chief) of the Morea. Recognising that the forces at his disposal were insufficient, he requested and received permission to contact ayan in Macedonia and Thessaly who were mustering troops through the levend for service on the Russian front and to ask them to send their men to the Morea. Ayan from Salonika, Florina, Kastoria, Argos Orestikon, Farsala, Trikala and Larissa answered the call and dispatched 10,000 (200 companies) battle-ready militiamen, many of them Albanians, to suppress the rebellion. As was customary, militia forces were very poorly paid and supplied and so they were compensated for their service with loot and booty that they took from the local population. Thus, at the same time that they were fighting the rebels, the levend troops were also terrorising the local population in the manner of an eighteenth-century Mafia (Vlachopoulou 2007).

The insurrection was quelled on 9 April. Muhsinzade Mehmed Paşa had assembled most of his forces at the capital of Tripolis, while at the same time ensuring that his allies had taken up their positions at various points around the region. Psaros and a force of approximately 15,000 marched on the city. Though numerically superior, most of the Greek force consisted of untested and untrained peasants. Early in the morning of the ninth, Psaros launched an assault on the walls of Tripolis. It took only a few withering volleys from the troops within to shatter the Greek lines. Muhsinzade Mehmed Paşa then ordered a counter-attack by the sipahi and the levend cavalry. The battle was over quickly and definitively, with Greek casualties totalling between one third and one half of their men. Ottoman forces all across the region then went on the offensive. The insurrectionists were routed and the fortresses relieved. Those rebels who could, like Psaros and Benakis, left with their Russian allies, while those who could not, sought the best terms of surrender they could. As we shall see, the Orlov Revolt had manifold and serious consequences for the Greeks of the Morea and beyond.[2]

After the eventful year of 1770, the war went into a lull. During 1771, the Russians consolidated their position along the Danube and invaded Crimea in support of their diplomatic initiative, discussed earlier; and it worked: Sahib Giray Khan accepted the Russian offer of independence (Fisher 1970; Finkel 2005: 376). Fresh off his successful suppression of the rebellion in the Morea, Muhsinzade Mehmed Paşa was reinstated as Grand Vizier and placed in command of the army of Danube. Both armies faced formidable challenges in supplying their forces, and in the Russian case, an outbreak of plague wreaked havoc with its numbers. While the Ottomans were spared that problem, they faced their own difficulties. Consequently both Rumiantsev and Muhsinzade Mehmed Paşa looked to negotiate an end to the conflict; and under a truce that lasted from April 1772 to March 1773 (with the exception of some minor skirmishes in June 1772), the contours of a settlement began to emerge.

In spite of its military success, Russia was willing to grant numerous concessions to the Ottomans. Partly this was due to the continuing problems with the army, especially the plague. There was the massive expense of the war that was putting a strain on imperial finances. Lastly an insurrection called the Purachev Revolt had broken out and the empire had to mobilise resources to deal with it. One element of the draft agreement, however, caused the peace talks to collapse and for fighting to recommence in 1774: this was the stipulation that the Crimean Khanate would become an independent state under Russian protection. Under heavy pressure from the Sheikulislam and other high-ranking members of the Ulema, the new sultan, Abdülhamid I, recognised that his reign would be a short one if he was to become the latest Ottoman emperor to cede Muslim land to infidels. The final round of fighting was brief. After initially holding their defensive position along the southern bank of the Danube, the Ottoman forces were driven back and trounced first at Kozludja (in what is now Bulgaria) on 25 June and then even further south at Shumla, where their headquarters were, on 1 July. Now the Porte had no choice but to accept whatever terms Russia choice to impose.

The Treaty of Küçük Kaynarca, signed on 21 July 1774, is one of the most important documents of the modern age. This agreement had 'disastrous consequences for both the Ottomans and the Tatars. After 60 years of economic growth and reputable international standing, the long war and difficult peace with Russia now left the Ottoman Empire politically unstable, with an exhausted economy, an uncontrolled movement of decentralization in the provinces, and a devastating loss of face in the international arena' (Şakul 2009: 493).

Here are the main conditions laid down in the treaty. Some of them were substantive, while others were more symbolic in nature. Substantively, the most important was the one that forced the Porte to recognise the independence of the Crimean Tatar Khanate and that henceforth the Crimea was to be under Russian protection; this was a grievous blow to the empire internally and externally. Russia also gained new territories: to the east, they obtained the steppe lands of Greater and Lesser Karbada, north of the Caucasus, while along the Black Sea coast to the south and west, they obtained control of the fortresses of Kerch and Yenikale on the Sea of Azov and Kilburnu on the Dnieper estuary.

Other articles gave Russia additional rights and prerogatives in the Ottoman Empire. For example, Russian merchants were given unrestricted access to the Black Sea and the Mediterranean via both sea and overland routes; they were also given special dispensations in regard to import duties and tariffs. Moreover, Russian consuls obtained the right to dispense 'berats' or protege status to Ottoman subjects, thus affording them all of the legal rights and economic privileges, including those just mentioned. And, since the treaty also gave Russia the right to establish consular offices anywhere in the empire, this practice quickly became widespread, especially, as we shall see shortly, among the empire's Greek subjects (Sonyel 1991). Lastly, the Porte had to pay a massive war indemnity, and this, on top of the colossal financial burden already caused by the war, exacerbated the empire's economic woes.

Some elements of the treaty were primarily symbolic, but that does not mean that they were any less important. Indeed, in the long term, a couple of them (Articles 7 and 14) proved to be far more significant than most of the substantive clauses discussed previously. Article 7 stipulated that 'the Sublime Porte promises a firm protection to the Christian religion and to its Churches' (cited in Davison 1976: 469). Forcing the sultan to make this promise was a grave insult because it was a foreign infidel ruler who was in essence commanding him to do something he was already committed to doing, that being to protect his Christian subjects, in accordance with the pact which bound him to the zimmis (non-Muslims as discussed in volume 8 of this series; see Balta 2008). Moreover, by compelling the sultan to make this promise, Article 7 implied that Russia had the right to set the conditions for the treatment of his Orthodox Christian subjects. Article 14, likewise, was susceptible to a similar interpretation. This clause stated that Russia had the right to construct a 'Russo-Greek' Orthodox church in the Istanbul neighbourhood of Beyoğlu and to make representation to the Porte on its behalf. On the face of it, this would appear to give Russia the same right that had been given to other European countries, France, Britain and Prussia for example, to construct places of worship for their people resident in the Ottoman capital. But later Russian leaders, and many historians, took Article 14 to mean that Russia could interfere in Ottoman affairs on behalf of the Orthodox Church (Davison 1979). Lastly, the treaty also compelled the Porte to recognise officially the title of 'Empress or Emperor of all the Russians', thus according the Russian ruler a status equal to the sultan's.

As bad as the treaty was from the Ottoman perspective, it could have been worse. As it was, the treaty made Russia relinquish a great deal of territory that its army occupied. Catherine could have claimed these lands as Russia's by right of conquest. Given how poorly the Ottoman army and navy had performed, even with all of its problems, Russia could have pressed the issue militarily to the point of threatening Istanbul and thus giving itself an even stronger negotiating position. But for Muhsinzade Mehmed Paşas negotiating skills and Russia's other pressing needs, the peace settlement might have been much more onerous. Nonetheless, the Treaty of Küçük Kaynarca was a very serious blow to the empire and it set in train a series of confrontations between the empire and its neighbours that would make the situation even worse.

The years between 1774 and 1787 witnessed an unquiet peace and it was a period marked by two persistent developments. The first of these was the continuation of Russian aggression towards the Ottoman Empire. And the second was an ongoing power struggle within the Ottoman government between the hawks, who wanted to meet Russian aggression head on and avenge the defeat of 1774, and the doves, who wanted to avoid war in order to push through a series of reforms of the empire's finances. Caught in between these factions was Sultan Abdülhamid I (1774–89). Never a man of strong character, the inexperienced monarch vacillated, favouring first one and then the other faction. In 1787 these two trends, Russian aggression and misplaced Ottoman bellicosity, would intersect and war would erupt again. And the cause of the war would be Crimea.

The Russians moved quickly to take advantage of the new powers given to them over the Tatar Khanate. They installed Şahin Giray as khan and supported him in subduing his rivals. This move strengthened the war party's hand in Istanbul and in 1778 they initiated hostilities in the Crimea in the name of restoring peace and stability to the region. When this threatened another war with Russia, the peace party was able to persuade the sultan to support them. And in an act of appeasement the following year, the Ottoman Empire officially recognised the khanate of Crimea as an independent state. This move did not forestall further Russian intervention in the region but in fact emboldened it. The result was that in 1784 Russia formally annexed the Crimea. The political pendulum now swung back to the war party, leading to a declaration of war in 1787.

The war was an unmitigated disaster for the Ottoman Empire. Its armies along the Danube were routed; key fortresses fell to Russian assaults; Bucharest and Belgrade were captured by Russia's ally, Austria; and crushing naval defeats gave Russia control of the Black Sea. Nonetheless, the new sultan, Selim III, determined to carry on his uncle's war by enacting reforms to raise funds and by making alliances with his enemies' enemies, such as Sweden, which launched an attack against Russia, and Prussia, which mobilised forces for an invasion of Austria. Finally, England, disturbed at Russia's successes, put great diplomatic pressure on St Petersburg to bring hostilities to a close. The resulting pact, the Treaty of Jassy (9 January 1792), consolidated Russian gains and perpetuated the crisis within the Ottoman Empire.

All told, then, the events between 1768 and 1792 had a tremendous impact on all of the peoples of the Ottoman Empire, and none more so than the Greeks. The situation of Orthodox Greeks within the empire changed dramatically. And Russian policies toward its new territories, called 'New Russia', ushered in a new relationship between it and the Hellenic world.

Catherine's Greek project

Greeks had lived in Russia for centuries; indeed, the northern shores of the Black Sea had been home to Greek colonists since ancient times. Because of the excellent work by archaeologists and ancient historians, that story is well known. What is not as widely appreciated is that the Greek presence in Russia continued after antiquity, and though the size of the Greek population waxed and waned over time, it remained sizable and significant. From the sixteenth century onward, Greek merchants established trading houses and émigré communities in all of the major cities in Russia and Ukraine (Kiev, Nezin, Lvov and Kharkov, for example). While none of these communities on its own was all that large, taken together they represented a fairly significant Greek presence. So the settlement of Greeks in the New Russia after the Russo-Ottoman War of 1768–74 must be seen in the context of a much longer-term engagement between Greeks and Russia. Nonetheless the migration of over 250,000 Greeks from the Ottoman Empire to 'New Russia' represented a new and very important development for the Greeks and anchored even more firmly southern Russia as part of the Greek world (Kardasis 1998; 2006 Katsiardi-Hering et al. 2011).

Tzarina Catherine had a dream. She would recreate the Eastern Orthodox Roman (Byzantine) Empire with a member of the royal family on its throne, and its capital in the great city of Constantinople. This was not a vision that came to her overnight. Instead it was an idea that developed incrementally as Russia became more and more involved in Ottoman affairs, particularly as they pertained to the Greeks. By the late 1770s the project was taking shape, as evidenced by her having minted a commemorative medallion to mark the birth of her grandson, not coincidentally named Constantine, on which was embossed the image of Hagia Sophia. It took on its full form during the 1780s as shown by the tour of New Russia that she undertook with the Austrian Emperor Joseph II. During this sojourn she unveiled at Kherson a ceremonial arch on which was inscribed in Greek 'The Way to Byzantium' (Finkel 2005: 382). This none too subtle message made manifest her intentions. By re-creating the Byzantine Empire under Russian protection, she would not only unite the two most important Orthodox nations – Russians and Greeks – but she would also liberate from the 'yoke' of Islam the venerated heartland of the Classical Greek world so dear to the heart of supporters, like herself, of the Enlightenment.

Even before her project had achieved its final form, she had already solidified links between Russia and the Greeks through her policy of settling Greeks in the territories of New Russia. It should be noted that it was not only Greeks whom Russia sought to settle its new frontier but other Orthodox peoples such as Serbs, Albanians, Moldavians, Wallachians and Armenians. But without a doubt, she had a special place in her heart for the Greeks.

Sea of Azov

The initial settlement of Greeks occurred while the 1768–74 war was still in progress and the immigrant population consisted mostly of refugees from the Peloponnesos and the Aegean islands who had taken refuge with Russian forces. Some of these people were transported and settled in the Crimea, while others were taken to the city of Taganrog on the northern shore of the Sea of Azov. It had been captured in 1769 and the settlement of Greek refugees there began the following year. They were soon joined by people fleeing their homeland out of fear of reprisals for their actions during the Orlov Rebellion. This group consisted mostly of men who had fought on the losing side. In 1775 alone, for example, over 2,000 families were settled in Sevastapol. In exchange for grants of land and financial support, the heads of these households were enrolled into militia battalions; there were two in the Crimea, called, respectively, the Spartan Brigade and the Balaclava Brigade. Soon this unplanned settlement policy was replaced by an official, systematic and well-financed one.

The Russian government issued manifestos in 1784, 1785 and 1792, aimed at recruiting Christian immigrants from the Ottoman Empire, mostly Greeks, to repopulate New Russia. These immigrants settled mostly in the towns around the coast of the Sea of Azov. In one decree, for example, the Russians made clear that the settlement of Greeks was seen as a reward 'for those who served us with excellent zeal in the last war with the Turks' (Bartlett 1979: 135). As one of these rewards, the Russians provided them with mortgages to buy land and grants to build houses, and mandated that repayment of the loan began only after a period of ten years. In addition immigrants were exempt from property taxes for ten to thirty years and as an inducement to merchants, they were exempted from many tariffs and duties. Greek men who agreed to serve in a militia received additional benefits. Not surprisingly, Greeks mostly from the Peloponnesos and the Aegean Islands left the Ottoman Empire in droves and migrated to New Russia, settling mainly in three cities and their hinterlands: Taganrog and Mariupol on the northern shore of the Sea of Azov, and Odessa in the northwestern corner of the Black Sea.

Taganrog had been for a long time an important Ottoman economic outpost and fort on its northeastern frontier. The city fell to the Russians in 1769 and the following year they began to settle Greek refugees there. Over the next two decades close to 30,000 Greeks from various parts of the Ottoman Empire would follow them. Unlike the first group, these later immigrants were drawn to the city mostly for economic reasons. Artisans and merchants from Smyrna, for example, established shops and businesses in Taganrog, inaugurating a long period of close economic relations between the two cities. Of particular importance was the silk industry. By 1805, over 45,000 Greeks called Taganrog home, dominating the economic and political life of the city. Numerous Greeks rose to prominent positions and became exceptionally wealthy.

Ioannis Varvakis from the Aegean island of Psara, for example, became one of the richest Greeks in the world after Catherine the Great granted him special economic privileges relating to the caviar industry as a reward for his services during the 1768–74 war. Some of the most prominent merchant families of the Greek diaspora, such as the Rallis, Rodokanachis, Marazlis and numerous others, had a base of operation in Taganrog. By 1783, Greeks dominated foreign trade, controlling almost two-thirds of the export market. Throughout the nineteenth century this vibrant city remained an exceptionally important economic gateway, connecting the economic systems of Asia and Europe through the Sea of Azov and the Black Sea, and Greeks continued to dominate the city's economic life.

In 1778, a few thousand Greeks who had been settled in the Crimea asked for and received permission to migrate to the Sea of

Azov region. Led by their spiritual leader Bishop Ignatios, they settled near a small fort that had formerly been held by Cossacks. They called their new settlement Mariupol. Over the next ten years, they would be joined by almost 15,000 more Greek immigrants. These newcomers founded twenty-three villages in the hinterland of the city, settling on land provided by the Russian state. The population in this area was much more dispersed than it was in Taganrog or in some of the other Greek communities in New Russia. They were also more intimately involved in agriculture than Greeks elsewhere, and they had greater interaction with the indigenous population. Inter-marriage soon led to a form of assimilation – so much so that they actually developed a very distinctive form of Greek that was barely intelligible to Greek speakers elsewhere. The greater emphasis on agriculture in Taganrog did not mean that Greeks played a less important role in the mercantile and commercial life of the city than elsewhere. It is just that in Mariupol there were more Greek peasants. Together with Taganrog, Mariupol gave the Greeks almost a monopoly over commerce on the Sea of Azov. As important at these two cities were they were soon eclipsed by an even more vibrant and prosperous port–city: Odessa.

Odessa

The Treaty of Jassy that ended the 1787–92 Russo-Ottoman War gave Russia the coastal territory along the Black Sea between the rivers Bug and Dneister, including a cliff-top fortress overlooking the excellent harbor of Hadji-Bey. Soon, a city on the bay blossomed. Rechristened Odessa, it quickly become the most important city in New Russia and Greeks played a prominent role in its success. About 100 families who had been displaced by the 1768–74 war settled in Odessa. They were the first of many more to come. 'The advantage to be gained from these settlers [Greeks], with their ability in maritime service, their special loyalty to Russia, which is shown by the sacrifice of the fatherland and the very justice of reward for their service, convince us that the Commissioner should turn his attention to them' (General A. Zubov in a dispatch to Catherine, 1792. Cited in Kardasis 2001: 20). And so he and his successors did.

By imperial decree settlers were given land free of charge, financial aid to establish households and a ten-year exemption from debts and taxes. Men who volunteered in the Greek militia were given additional plots of land based upon their rank. By the turn of the century, over 40,000 acres of land on the outskirts of the city had been given to Greek settlers. From this modest start, the influx of Greek immigrants rose steadily over the next two decades, punctuated by periodic larger numbers of immigrants whenever conflicts within the Ottoman Empire compelled them to flee. By 1816, the Russian government estimated that almost 12,000 Greeks lived in Odessa, accounting for approximately one-third of the population. More important than its size, however, was the Greeks' role in the economy.

By the 1820s, Greek merchant houses had assumed a commanding position in the commercial life of the city. Over a dozen family-controlled Greek companies had amassed fortunes greater than one million rubles; among them were Theodore Serafino, Alexander Mavros, Dimitrios Inglesi, Alexander Kumbaris, Vasilii Iannopulo, Gregory Marazli, Kir'iakos Papakhadzhis, Il'ia Manesis, Iohannis Ambrosiu, and Dimitrios Paleologos (Herlihy 1979: 401). And within a few years, four of them were listed as among the ten richest men in the entire Russian Empire. By the middle of the next decade two families, the Rallis and the Rodokanachis, would eclipse even them. In 1832, these two merchant houses alone accounted for almost 10 per cent of the Odessan import-export trade. These family businesses created commercial networks that connected Odessa to major markets of the Ottoman Empire, Western Europe, the Middle East and even across the Atlantic to the United States. They exerted at times a near monopoly over the trade in grain, cattle, leather, tallow, iron and a host of other commodities. In addition to controlling foreign trade from the Russian Empire, Greeks also played a critical role in the financial sector, founding banks and maritime insurance companies. Southern Russia, then, became home to the wealthiest Greeks in the world.

While it is easy for us to focus our attention on the rich and famous, we should not lose sight of the fact that they accounted for only a small percentage of the Greek population in Russia. Greeks also played a critical role in controlling domestic commerce in the region. According to one estimate, Greeks exerted a near monopoly over trade in the Sea of Azov and up the Don River. Greeks also featured prominently in Odessa and Taganrog as small businessmen, shopkeepers, vendors and the like, and as artisans. As we noted earlier, many Greeks received grants of land as a condition of their immigration. With the exception of Mariupol, it appears that very few remained agriculturalists. Most of them leased their land to others while they resided in the city and made money from commercial activities. This was especially the case in Odessa.

The majority of Greek immigrants made their adopted country their new homeland, becoming Russian subjects of Greek descent. Zannis Rallis, for example, in a letter to the US State Department, on whose behalf he was acting as counsel in Odessa, referred to himself as 'a Russian subject, born on the island of Scio (Chios) in the archipelago, and by birth of Greek origin' (Herlihy 1979: 407). Over the course of the century Greeks would become ever more widely assimilated into Russian society. But even among first- and second-generation Greek immigrants, the group we are most interested in, participating in Russian society and politics was important. Greeks established schools and charitable institutions that served the needs of the broader community as well as their own. They participated actively in the civic life of the new Russian cities. Dimitri Inglesi, originally from Kefalonia, for example, was mayor of Odessa from 1818 to 1821.

In sum, one of the most important developments for Greeks between 1774 and the outbreak of the great insurrection of 1821 was the establishment and development of Greek Russia. Tens of thousands of Greeks, along with very large numbers of other Ottoman Orthodox subjects – Serbs, Bulgarians, and so on – left the great Muslim empire to find a brighter future in a new land. And many of them did. The consequences of Greek migration to Russia are many and important. As we have seen, some of them became exceptionally wealthy, while others managed to create a life for themselves and their families that would have been impossible had they remained in the Ottoman Empire. Artisans and small entrepreneurs achieved success outside the confines of the Ottoman guild system. Greek peasants obtained land and prospered in ways that would have been almost impossible if they had stayed in their natal villages. The great migration to Russia expanded the Greek diaspora and connected East and West. Ideas as well as goods flowed between and through the diaspora, and it was not a coincidence, as we shall see, that Greek Russians played critical roles in the movement to create an independent Greek state and in the actual struggle itself.

Greeks in Russian service

One of the other important consequences of the establishment of Greek Russia and the development of a prosperous Greek merchant elite was the involvement of Greeks in service to the Russian state. Many of the men who were to play critical roles in the 1821 rebellion had experience as soldiers and politicians in Russia or as servants of the empire abroad. I begin with some examples of those who rose to prominence in service inside of the empire. Skalartos D. Sturdza was a member of a prestigious Phanariot family that over the years had performed many valuable services to the Ottoman Empire. Most recently, Skarlatos had been Hospodar of Moldavia before he and his family was forced to quit the Ottoman Empire for their anti-Ottoman role during the Ottoman-Russian War of 1787–92. Welcomed by Russia, the state granted the Sturdzas landed estates and Skarlatos was given a very comfortable pension as well. Members of the Sturdza family soon obtained high-ranking and important positions in government. His son, Aleksandr, for example, served in the Ministry of Public Education before moving on to the Ministry of Foreign Affairs where he served in the Asiatic division as the expert on Danubian issues. In that capacity he was a member of the Russian delegation at the Congress of Vienna (1814–15).

Another good example would be Spyridon Destunis. He was a member of an extended family that had immigrated from Kefalonia, one of the Ionian islands, to Odessa, where under the leadership of his uncle Ivan, the family became extremely wealthy and well connected politically. In addition to being a prominent writer, scholar and translator, particularly of ancient Greek works into Russian, Destunis also served as a high-ranking officer in the Ministry of Foreign Affairs.

The most famous of the Greeks in Russian government service was without a doubt Ioannis Kapodistrias. He was a member of an aristocratic family from another of the Ionian islands, Corfu (Kerkira). His political career began when he served in the government of the Russian sponsored Ionian Republic. In 1807, when the islands were given back to the French, Kapodistrias relocated to Russia and entered the Russian diplomatic corps. He rose quickly up the career ladder and from 1815 to 1822 he served as joint foreign secretary of the Russian Empire. These three statesmen were clearly exceptional, but they represent a much broader group of men of Greek descent, or Greek immigrants, who assimilated into Russian society and who served the empire faithfully. Aleksandr Sturdza spoke for many of them when he described himself as 'an Orthodox Christian, Greek by descent, and a loyal and dedicated servant of the Emperor' (Prousis 1992: 309).

Greeks also joined the Russian military, and some of them rose to the highest ranks. Many of these soldiers would play important roles in the 1821 insurrection. Most noteworthy amongst this group was the Ipsilantis family. Like his predecessors, Konstantinos Ipsilantis had served the Porte in a number of capacities, including holding the post of governor, or hospodar, of Wallachia during the 1806–12 Russo-Ottoman War. Because of his actions during that conflict, he was deposed and rather than face charges in Istanbul, he fled to Russia, along with his family. All four of his sons obtained an elite education, paid for directly by Tsar Alexander I himself, and then enrolled in the elite Imperial Guards regiment of the Household Cavalry, where they all served with distinction. His eldest son, Alexandros, had an especially noteworthy career. For his conduct in the defence of Moscow, he was promoted to the rank of captain. In 1813 he was promoted to lieutenant colonel of a Hussar regiment and lost his right arm in the Battle of Dresden. After being promoted to colonel he was a member of the Russian contingent at the Congress of Vienna, after which the Tsar appointed him as his aide-de-camp. In 1817 at the age of twenty-five he was promoted to the rank of major general. While not as impressive, his brothers also rose to high ranks in the Russian officer corps (Arsh 1985: 75–6; Prousis 1994: 8–9; Stites 2014: 197–9).

While exceptional, the Ipsilantis brothers are nonetheless representatives of a larger group. Between the 1780s and the 1810s, numerous Greeks, many of them products of academies like the Cadet Corps of Foreign Co-religionists (originally founded to educate Greek immigrant children), entered Russian military service. This had important consequences for the future of the Greek world. First, these men learned well the craft of war, and not surprisingly, many of them would flock to the banner of rebellion in 1821. Second, while in the military they formed bonds of friendship with Russian officers, including many who belonged to radical organisations like the Decembrists. This development would also become important during the 1821 war, both in terms of personal relationships and for the spread of revolutionary ideas. Third, the presence of so many Greeks in the upper echelons of the Russian military helped to foster the belief amongst Greeks both inside and outside of the Ottoman Empire that Russia would be their saviour.

Thousands of Greeks who resided outside of Russia, mostly in the Ottoman Empire, also entered into service on behalf of the Tsar. We need to focus on the two most important areas, and these who served as (1) members of irregular military units and (2) as consular officers in the major eastern Mediterranean cities. It became routine when Russia went to war with the Ottoman Empire for it to mobilise and organise into irregular units Christian subjects of the Porte. We saw this policy taken to the extreme during the Orlov Rebellion. But the practice really reached its high point during the Napoleonic Wars (1797–1816).

Ottoman Christians were recruited and deployed by all of the French Empire's enemies but the Russians were especially active in two regions – the Danubian Principalities and the Ionian Islands. Greeks, in particular, dominated the latter. From 1799 until 1807, the islands were an independent state, the Septinsular Republic, under Russian protection. Russian troops and officers stationed in the republic helped to train thousands of regular and irregular troops drawn from the islands and from the mainland (Pappas 1991). This militarisation of Ottoman and Ionian Greeks had important ramifications. First, it established personal bonds between Greek and Russian soldiers that would prove consequential later on. Second, it created even more Greeks proficient in the art of war. Third, it made available ever increasing quantities of firearms, as well as the building of armouries and gunpowder mills. To say that by 1821 the Balkans were awash in guns would be going too far, but not by much.

One of the stipulations that the Ottoman Empire had agreed to in the Treaty of Küçük Kaynarca was to allow Russia to establish consular offices in all of its major cities. From 1774 onward, Russia appointed Ottoman Christians, mostly Greeks and a few Armenians, to be its consuls. In doing so they were building on a centuries-long practice whereby European diplomatic missions were awarded a number of berats by the Porte to employ Ottoman subjects to perform a variety of duties for them. A great incentive for local men to become protégés of a foreign mission was that this status accorded them special legal rights and privileges denied to other zimmis. Enjoying a form of diplomatic immunity from Ottoman laws gave these men a special place in society. Over the years, the system began to be abused with Western diplomats actually selling berats to Ottoman subjects. This practice helped to reinforce the idea that the various European powers had the right to extend protection to co-religionists inside the Ottoman Empire. France, for example, began to assert that it could act as protector of Catholics; Britain did the same for Protestants. And, of course, this opened the way for

Russia to claim that it had the right to protect its co-religionists, followers of the Orthodox faith.

From 1774 onward this increasingly meant using Ottoman Orthodox, especially Greeks, to act as the empire's consular officers. This development had serious and important consequences. First, it meant that St Petersburg received intelligence about what was happening in the Ottoman Empire as perceived through Greek eyes. Second, it enabled increasing numbers of Greeks to obtain special privileges as protégés because the Russians issued them with berats. Third, the practice obviously helped to reinforce the idea that Greeks had a special bond with Russia.

All of these developments helped to link Russia tightly to the Greeks. There developed, then, what we might justly call a 'special relationship' between Greeks and Russia, one aspect of which has been called by one eminent Greek historian, Paschalis Kitromildes, the 'Russian expectation' (Kitromilides 1992: 354–5). The expectation was that one day Mother Russia would deliver Greeks from the grip of Ottoman control. As important as the Russian dimension was for Greeks after 1774, there were other developments that shaped the social, political and economic life of Greeks in the Ottoman Empire, and it is to some of these that we turn now.

Notes

1. There was considerable tension between the two men. At the same time that Muhsinzade was informing Istanbul of impending trouble in the Morea, Hassan Efendi was telling the Porte that all was well and that he had the situation under control.
2. There was some uprising elsewhere in the empire. But with the exception of the one on Crete, they amounted to little. The rebellion on Crete fared slightly better because the Russians had landed more men and material on the island, but it also was quickly snuffed out. The only uprising of any consequence was the one in the Morea.

CHAPTER 2

New Greek realities

Figure 2.1 captures one of the 'new Greek realities' that emerged during the last quarter of the eighteenth century and the first few years of the nineteenth century and that was the rapid and widespread development of Greek diaspora merchant communities around the world, but especially in Europe. Greeks established commercial trading houses in every major European city, and in numerous minor ones. In some cases, pre-existing communities were enlarged and in others, new settlements were founded. The expansion of the Greek commercial trading networks not only fostered the creation of a wealthy and prosperous new sector of society, but it also exposed many Greeks to the latest intellectual and political developments in Europe.

The scene opposite aptly captures the interplay between traditional Ottoman Greek society and the West. Two of the central figures in this scene remained garbed in traditional clothing. The figure on the lower right wears the traditional clothing of an Aegean islander. The figure in the centre of the scene wears the turban and robes of a traditional kocabaşi as he smokes his hookah. Seated in between them is another Greek merchant, but he is attired in Frankish (European) costume making him almost indistinguishable from any French or German bourgeois. The scene vividly captures the mixing and the cultural interplay between East and West. The merchants of the diaspora connected Europe and the Near East and formed a conduit for the spread of wealth and ideas from the West to the East. This period, however, also saw dramatic changes to the treatment of Greeks within the Ottoman Empire as well as abroad. Some of these developments were positive, while others were negative. Combined, they helped spur on the movement for Greek independence and exerted a marked influence on how the Islamic state treated its zimmi or dhimmi (non-Muslim) population. Let's look first at most important positive ones.

Figure 2.1 *East meets west in the 'Greek' cafe in Vienna (1824) © Stadthistorisches Museum, Vienna.*

The mercantile economy

By the end of the eighteenth century Greeks dominated merchant shipping between the Black Sea, the Mediterranean and beyond to Europe and America. We have already discussed the situation in southern Russia and on the Black Sea. As we saw, Greeks flying under the Russian flag came to dominate maritime commerce and especially the extremely lucrative grain trade between Russia and the West (Kremmydas 2006). What needs emphasis here is that Greeks also came to dominate Ottoman flagged shipping as well.

> By the 1780s, the Ottoman fleet was comparable to or even bigger than those of the once omnipotent sea powers of Genoa and Venice. The Ottoman fleet was involved in the long routes of the Mediterranean and the Greeks were the traditional local seafarers of the Ottoman Empire who worked as merchant captains and seamen in Istanbul, the Black Sea and the Aegean ports, as shipwrights in the Ottoman shipyards, as crews in the Imperial Ottoman fleet, or as crews and captains in the fleets of the Barbary corsairs. They owned small craft for the coastal trade between the islands and the main coasts of Greece and Asia Minor. In the late eighteenth century they

emerged as the most dynamic merchant fleet in the Mediterranean and took advantage of European rivalry for the economic and political control of the Levant. (Harlaftis and Laiou 2008: 5)

In addition, Greek captains and crews also plied the waters flying the flags of Austria, Venice, Great Britain and Ragusa. So ubiquitous were Greeks in Mediterranean shipping that Greek, and in particular Ionian Greek, became the lingua franca, as it were, of the Eastern Mediterranean and Greek became almost as important as Italian in the Western Mediterranean as well (Gallant 2009: 18; Burrows 1986: 111).

Greeks were not only heavily involved in Mediterranean trade but they also participated in Ottoman trade in other parts of the world, like India, though they were not the dominant group there. That role was filled by Armenians and Muslims of various nationalities. Taken together, however, we can fully agree with the following assessment of the importance of international commerce after the 1770s:

> Due to the activities of the Greek merchant marine, various sectors of Greek society came to be directly and indirectly involved in sea trade. As some of their members accumulated appreciable amounts of capital local elites became more powerful by investing in merchant vessels. In addition maritime trade fostered the incipient commercialization of agriculture in the Morea and international conjunctures largely determined these developments; they formed part of the broader 'incorporation process' which after 1800 made the Ottoman economy into a part of the European-dominated world system. (Pissis 2008: 164)

We should not, however, overlook the importance of internal maritime trade to the commercial life of the empire. As Daniel Panzac has noted, 'domestic was more important than international trade throughout the eighteenth century' (Panzac 1992: 202). And Greeks played a major role in the internal economic life of the empire. They did so, however, at different levels. At the macro-level, the same large, family-owned trading houses, traders' coalitions and joint stock companies that dominated international trade also participated in domestic shipping. At the lowest level, there were the small operations, often consisting of a family which owned a single boat that they used to move goods short distance. This so-called tramp shipping may have been small in scale but in aggregate petty traders contributed significantly to the economic life of the empire. And in the Aegean and along the coasts of the southern Balkans, Greeks played a critical role in this trade. So, as the flow of goods through port cities like Patras, Smyrna, Salonilka, Messolonghi and Alexandria accelerated and as island communities such as those on Chios and Psarra became ever more central to Ottoman commerce, Greek merchants, traders, brokers and middlemen, captains and sailors, and dockworkers prospered (Frangakis-Syrett 1998; 2006; Frangakis-Syrett and Wagstaff 2004; Küçükkalay 2008; Katsiardi-Hering 2011; Papakonstantinou 2011a, 2011b; even women came to play prominent roles in Greek commerce: Minoglou 2007).

While it is certainly the case that Greek merchants and traders played a disproportionately important role in Ottoman maritime trade it would be a mistake to discount their important role in over-land trade as well. To be sure other ethnic or religious groups, such as Jews, Armenians and Muslim Arabs, were far more important than Greeks in the commercial life of some regions of the empire, especially to the east and the south; they dominated overland trade within the empire's European provinces and between them and central Europe. Greek trading houses and merchant communities were established in almost all of the major cities of central Europe from as far back as the sixteenth century. But the pace and the flow of commercial transactions that they undertook accelerated during the latter part of the eighteenth century and into the nineteenth century. Caravans traversed between all of the major cities of the Balkans, like Salonika, Yanya (now Ioannina in Epiros), Moscho-poulos, Sofia and Belgrade. Well-travelled routes linked them to the major cities of central Europe. No place was more important than Vienna and by 1800 the city was home to hundreds of Greek trading houses. Consumable commodities such as tobacco, coffee and rice, raw materials like furs, leather and hides, and fabrics such as wool, silk, and in particular cotton, all flowed largely through Greek hands into the major market-cities of central Europe. Men such as Spiros Ioannou and families such as the Pondikes from Salonika typify this development (Inglesi 2004; Papakonstantinou 2008). Some Greek communities, such as the village of Ambelakia in Thessaly, grew wealthy through the production of specialised products, in this case, cotton yarn (Petmezas 1990; Katsiardi-Hering 2008; 2011).

There was also a very large and lucrative domestic overland trading network that Greeks tapped into, at the centre of which was Istanbul. Each year massive quantities of materials flowed into this consumer giant. Especially important, of course, was food and in particular the staff of life – bread. Ensuring that the city had a steady and affordable supply of food was one of the royal government's perpetual concerns. So much so that it was not uncommon for sultans to visit markets in order to inspect conditions and prices. Selim III (1789–1807) once visited the bread market at Divan Yolu and witnessed a riot when people were unable to procure bread; he immediately ordered his grand vizier to deal with the situation because nothing could galvanise public unrest faster than a bread shortage. So important was the grain supply that he created in 1792 an Imperial Grain Administration (Boyar and Fleet 2010: 168; for the grain trade of Istanbul during this period generally, see Sasmazer 2000). To be sure, foodstuffs flowed into the city from all parts of the empire and traders from all groups participated in it, but Greeks played a vital role in trade from the central and southern Balkans, and especially in the very lucrative grain trade between Thessaly and Istanbul (Sakalides 2002). Huge flocks of sheep and goats and herds of cattle were needed to provide the city with dairy products and hundreds of thousands of animals were slaughtered each year to give the people meat. Greeks played an important role in the Ottoman European meat trade both as shepherds and as middlemen and brokers (Kasaba 2009: 32; Lyberatos 2010). As important as the capital city was to Ottoman domestic trade, we should not lose sight of the fact that all of the Balkans were interconnected by a network of travelling market fairs and caravans that served all of its towns and cities. So prominent were Greeks in this commerce that it became almost axiomatic that if someone was a merchant, he was a Greek.

From the 1770s to 1821, the economy of the Ottoman Balkans and the Eastern Mediterranean became ever more tightly bound with the emerging Eurocentric world economy. The empire's vast trading network literally spanned the globe from Southeast Asia to North America. Much of this trade and commerce internationally was in the hands of Greek trading houses. Domestically as well Greek merchants and traders, artisans and craftsmen were of vital importance. The economic development of the empire during this period has three important consequences for Greeks. First, there emerged a large and wealthy Greek merchant elite both inside and outside of the empire; and these were not separate and distinct groups but, in fact, were tightly connected. The expansion of maritime trade was of particular importance in this regard. Second, the prosperity of the times was not restricted to just the upper class, and so a new group emerged on the scene: the Greek bourgeoisie, consisting of petty merchants, middling commercial brokers and artisans. Third, the Greek diaspora grew in size and expanded in distribution, not only contributing to the material betterment of their lives but also exposing them to the ideas, ideologies and contemporary trends that were sweeping Europe and the West in the age of revolution.

Ottoman governance

While the economic developments of the time led to the formation of a transnational, cosmopolitan Greek commercial class, internal political crises caused by the empire's disastrous foreign wars resulted in some Greeks obtaining greater power and influence in the imperial government. Right from the start of Ottoman imperial expansion, there was scope for non-Muslims to obtain power and influence in the government. The easiest way, of course, was to convert to Islam. Once incorporated into the Dar ul-Islam, or the House of Islam, converts could rise to positions of power, and many of them did. Members of the Christian aristocracy, for example, converted and kept their lands and titles.

From the early days of the empire, however, there were also opportunities for non-Muslims to keep their faith, yet obtain positions in the empire's ruling structures. That the empire organised its subjects on the basis of religion, the so-called millet system, and gave religious leaders a great deal of autonomy in governing their co-religionists meant that Greeks could achieve considerable power and influence through the institution of the Orthodox Church. This was especially the case with the leader of the church, the Ecumenical Patriarch; in addition to serving as the head of the church, he was also the leader of the Orthodox community in secular matters – a function that is best captured by his other title: the Millet-başi. Over time there developed administration needs that could best be filled by non-Muslims, and one group of Orthodox Christians above all others came to dominate them. This group was called Phanariots.

'Phanariots were an Ottoman Christian elite which, despite structural impediments, imperial ideology, and religious doctrine that would preclude their participation in Ottoman governance, ascended to power in multiple political arenas between the 1660s and 1821' (Philliou 2009: 151; see also her book from 2011). Their name derived from the tradition that they resided in the Phanar district in Istanbul, an old and venerated neighbourhood that was also home to the Patriarchate. Tradition had it as well that Phanariots were descendants of the old Byzantine aristocracy, but this was more of an invented tradition than a real one. The reality was that the boundaries of the group were fluid and, since they did not practise endogamy, that is, only marrying one another, the ancestral background of members was constantly changing. Wealth and status were inherited and along with them came rank, privileges and higher education.

Throughout the eighteenth century the number and variety of positions in the Ottoman government that Phanariots filled increased, and none were more important than the position of Hospodar of the Danubian Principalities of Moldavia and Wallachia. Attaining the position of hospodar cost its holder and his family massive sums, but the expense was worth it. More than one Phanariot family amassed a fortune through their control of the principality's finances. They needed to as well because they had to expend a small fortune to get the appointment in the first place. The position of hospodar became even more lucrative and powerful after 1774 as each treaty that ended the various Russo-Ottoman wars increased the autonomy of the principalities and thus the power of its governor. Phanariots served the Ottoman state in other capacities as well. Next in importance was through the position of dragoman of the Porte, acting as translators and diplomats for it. Dragomans and hospodars, like other Ottoman officials, served at will of the sultan and, just as for their Muslim counterparts, the rewards could be great. But so too were the risks. Failure to fulfil one's duties to the state had dire, indeed often fatal consequences. Nonetheless, by the early 1800s the Phanariots constituted the most powerful and influential group of zimmis in the Ottoman Empire (in addition to the work by Philliou, on the Phanariots, see also: De Groot 2010; Cazanisteanu 1982; Patrinelis 2001; Rothman 2009).

Troubled times

As we saw in the previous sections, there were many positive new 'Greek realities' that emerged after 1774 but there were a number of negative ones as well. Some of these were more general in nature, affecting large numbers of people including Greeks, while others were more restricted and localised in their impact. A couple of general ones that had an impact on the Ottoman territories of Europe (especially Rumelia and the Morea) and Asia Minor related to the empire's constant war fighting.

The first of these was economic. Islamic holy law prohibited non-Muslims from fighting in the Ottoman military; there were some exceptions but for the non-Muslim reaya this was the case. Instead, their contribution was to provide food and logistical support. The state collected grain, fruit, vegetables and animals through the implementation of a requisition tax. The more and the longer that the empire was at war, the greater the level of exaction from the non-Muslim reaya population. Other taxes were also raised to fund the empire's wars. In addition, primary producers were compelled to sell goods and animals to the state at prices set by government officials and often these were artificially low. Moreover, since local officials did the actual purchasing, there was ample opportunity for abuses and corruption. Lastly, the quantities of goods and materials that the military required were prodigious. Over the course of the 1768–74 war, for example, the army of the Danube consumed millions of pounds of grain and hundreds of thousands of animals. This burden fell heavily on the rural population, but what made it even worse was that simultaneously the men who owned much of the land, both Christian kocabaşis and Muslim ayan, began to impress harsher terms on them. The result was increasing rural impoverishment (Aksan 1993; Shusharova 2011; Tuck 2008).

If increasing levels of poverty were not enough, the rural population also had to deal with an increasingly insecure countryside. As we discussed earlier, each time the empire went to war, tens of thousands of Muslim men were mobilised through the levend system to serve as irregular troops; at the same time, non-Muslims, particularly Greek and Christian Albanian warriors, were hired and deployed as armatoles and derebends to guard the empire's roads and mountain passes. At war's end, the levend troops were demobilised and many armatoles went out of government service (Fig. 2.2). This produced a huge number of unemployed or underemployed armed men. Some were hired by local lords to fill their private gangs, while others were retained for garrison duty. Many, however, took to the mountains and became outlaws.

At times the fighting between the armatoles and brigands was fierce. So, in some ways, when the empire's external wars ended, a form of civil war took its place. Caught in between the bandits and the agents of the state were the common people. Their plight did vary from place to place and from time to time. We know, for example, that they suffered from the depredations of the demobilised Albanian levend troops who went rogue in the Morea after the end of the 1768–74 war. So terrible were their activities that one historian even

Figure 2.2 *A Greek armatole (1829) © Pierre Peytier.*

compares them to the Mafia (Vlachopoulou 2007; on bandits, banditry and rural unrest in the eighteenth-century Balkans, see Anscombe 2006). So powerful and dangerous had they become that it took the combined might of the local Ottoman officials and Muslim ayan, and the Greek kocabaşi to eventually suppress them. With order restored, the ayan and the kocabaşis consolidated their position as the region's elites.

The ayan and kocabaşis

While it would be, in my view, too early to call for a 'requiem' for the Ottoman Empire by the end of the eighteenth century, as one historian has done, it is the case that the internal organisation of the empire's governing structures and institutions underwent critical changes during the course of the century (Kechriotis 2008). One of the most important responses to the various foreign wars, coups and forced regime changes, and the ongoing fiscal problems that the empire experienced was decentralisation. It is commonly argued that decentralisation equalled decline, and the 'decline paradigm' has been a persistent feature of Ottoman historiography. But this is not necessarily so. Devolving some power and allocating some administrative functions to the provincial level can also strengthen an empire, so long as the state can control and hold accountable local-level functionaries.

The ability of the imperial government in Istanbul to effectively control such a huge territory with pre-modern communication technology was always a formidable challenge, but because of the numerous and severe crises of the eighteenth century its capacity to do so was lessened even more. The result was that many of the core aspects of governance had to be delegated into local hands. The most important of these of functions for our purposes was: (1) tax collection and other fiscal matters, (2) dispute resolution, (3) military mobilisation, (4) the maintenance of law and order. The first of these enabled local men to gain great wealth through life-lease tax farming, while the other three opened up new spaces for them to get power. As a consequence there developed across the empire, though we shall focus just on the Balkans and especially on those in the Peloponnesos called Mora ayanlari, new groups of power brokers and an elite that were both Christian and Muslims. Moreover, because of the ongoing crises, the Porte had lost much of its capacity to control and hold accountable these provincial notables. Let us begin with the Muslims (Adanir 2006; Adiyeke 2008; Finkel, 2005: 387–432; Khoury 2006; Kyrkini-Koutoula 1996; Özdeğer 2011; Sadat 1972; Stamatopoulos 2007; Tuluveli 2005; Zens 2011).

A class of men called ayan and the corresponding institution to which they belonged, the ayanlik, had been around for centuries. They were notables who constituted a local level elite. Sometimes ayan held positions in the government as appointees of the Porte, but government service was not a prerequisite for being considered an ayan. Some were members of the Ottoman military order, known as the askeri, and received grants of land in exchange for their service in the imperial cavalry but others were not. In sum, this was a very mixed bag of individuals. Their role in local society was more clear-cut: they acted as both a buffer and a bridge between the reaya, both Muslim and Christian, and the organs of the state. Many were landholders and played vital roles in the local economy as well. During times of war they were expected to mobilise manpower, coordinate the collection of materials and supplies either through the requisition tax or by purchase, and to go to battle themselves, depending upon their status and position. During the eighteenth century, and especially after 1774, the position of the ayan in society changed dramatically, especially in the Balkans. Decentralisation was certainly important, but it was more the form that this devolution of power took that matters most. Changes to the fiscal and military organisation of the empire contributed most to the rise of ayan to power, transforming them from local big men into into state officials – even governors – notables, warlords, landlords, plantation owners, fiscal agents and business entrepreneurs.

The lifeblood of the empire, like any state, was tax revenue. There were three critically important changes to the Ottoman tax system. The first was the switch from the payment of taxes in kind to payment in cash; this introduced an intermediate step whereby commodities had to be transferred into money. The second was the switch from temporary contract-based tax farming to life-term, inheritable leases (in Turkish, it is called mukataa). This shifted the balance of power away from the central treasury to tax farmers called mültezims. The third important change was the introduction of corporate tax responsibility (called maktu) (Darling 2006; Salzman 1993). This meant that rather than taxes being levied on individual heads of households, tax liabilities were assessed on larger units, an entire village or a neighbourhood in a town, and the collectivity was responsible for collecting and paying these levies. As local men of means ayans were perfectly poised to exploit this new system. Some were able to become rich as tax farmers themselves. Others filled the role of middlemen and brokers, collecting revenues from the tax units assigned to them, keeping a portion for themselves and then channelling the remainder upward to the holder of the lease.

This was a system susceptible to abuse. As one historian has noted, 'another side-effect [of mukataa] was the unmistakable inclination of tax farmers to over exploit their units' (Adanir 2006: 166). Usury and widespread peasant indebtedness resulted from abuses of the system. Ayan, and their Christian counterparts, purchased land as private property and so grew even more powerful. A cycle of economic growth and prosperity for the local notables began, with a concomitant downward cycle of debt and impoverishment for many peasants (Anscombe 2006: 95 provides a vivid description of just how easily this happened in many places). Land and taxes became inextricably bound. 'The first, and arguably the most important trait of any ayan was his attachment to the land tenure and revenue raising system of the state' (Zens 2011: 437).

The second springboard to power and prominence for ayan was the military crisis of the empire in the second half of the eighteenth century. As I noted earlier, the 1768–74 war with Russia was the first time that the Ottoman military had to rely primarily on irregular militias, the levend. Much of the responsibility of mobilising the irregular units fell to local notables in two ways. First, as local men of power and authority the notables worked with state authorities to enforce the conscription of local men into the state-funded militia. Second, many ayan hired armed men as their personal gangs to protect their estates, assist in tax collecting, and combat brigandage; when called upon to, they would place them at the service of the state, sometimes even leading them on the campaign (Anscombe 2006: 89–91 and 96–9; Anastasopoulos 2010). Ayan became indispensable to the Ottoman war machine: 'The ayan's new military responsibility gave them greater legitimacy in the eyes of the central government and more power within the provinces, since loyalties created on the battlefield usually did not wane with the ceasefire' (Zens 2011: 343; see also Shusharova 2011 and Levy 1982).

Reform of the Ottoman tax system and military organisation had profound and unforeseen consequences.

> Decentralization was no longer merely a matter of optimizing the collection of taxes and allocating the tax load within a community or of setting up a militia to fend off rural bandits. Increasingly this question also involved issues of sovereignty, in other words, decentralization implied a direct threat to the political regime, which had already suffered a loss of legitimacy. (Adanir 2006: 178)

And this direct threat came from this newly empowered group, the ayan, especially when some of them were able to translate their success at the local level into official political and economic power regionally. Two such men in particular stand out: Osman Paşvanoglu of Vidin and Tepedelenli Ali Paşa of Yanya (modern Ioannina in Epiros) (Fig. 2.3) (Zens 2002; 2004; 2011; Gradeva 2005, 2007). They played crucial roles in the move towards rebellion in Greece and the Balkans and we shall return to them shortly, but first we need to

Figure 2.3 *Tepedelenli Ali Paşa of Epiros (1825) © Louis Depre, Wikimedia Commons.*

examine the other group that came to prominence in the latter part of the eighteenth century, the Greek equivalent of the ayan: the kocabaşis.

Since the conquest of Greece and the Balkans and their incorporation into the Ottoman Empire, non-Muslims played a vital role in government. The organisation of the peoples of the empire into groups based on religion by the millet system thus gave considerable autonomy to clerics as the leaders of their co-religionists. There were also groups like the Phanariots, who, as we have seen, were able to find a niche in the Ottoman administration. In addition, from its inception the empire granted special statuses and greater self-rule to people from certain regions and places who offered specific services or resources vital to the state. For example, the Aegean islands were given a very high level of autonomy and exemptions from certain

Figure 2.4 *Early nineteenth-century Greek kocabaşi (1825) © Otto Magnus von Stackelberg.*

taxes because of the contribution they made to the fleet and maritime commerce (Balta 2006; 2008; Kolovos 2006; 2007). On the mainland, certain villages which occupied strategic locations like mountain passes were likewise rewarded. Places that had particularly important resources, like iron ore or other metal deposits, or commercial products, such as mastic from the island of Chios, received special dispensations. But the development in the late eighteenth century of a Greek, secular and landowning elite called kocabaşis (*proestoi* or *prokrites* in Greek) represented a new and exceptionally important event in the history of Greeks in the pre-national period (Fotopoulos 2005; Kostantaras 2013; Masters 2009; Papastamatiou 2011; Stamatopoulos 2007). As a Greek historian has noted, 'it would not be hyperbole to characterize the period from 1715–70 as a "good time" [for the Morean kocabaşis]' (Fotopoulos 2005: 231). And they only got better after the 1770s.

The rise of the kocabaşis in the Morea and Rumelia was caused by, and was connected to, the same fiscal and military reforms that led to the ayan flourishing (Fig. 2.4). In the Morea and in much of Rumelia as well, especially in the countryside, Muslims were in the minority and so it is not surprising that Christian-dominated villages and communities produced their own leaders. Prominent local men were selected or elected to councils that regulated communal affairs, adjudicated local disputes, and organised the collection of communal taxes (see Doxiadis (2011; 2012) and Ursinus (2004) on their legal roles). Just as the Muslim ayan filled the space between the local communities and the state, so too did the kocabaşis. Occasionally, they became mültezim, purchasing at auction the rights to collect certain specified taxes, such as the cizye or poll tax levied on all non-Muslims, the tithe that everyone owed to the state, or the *ad valorem* taxes on commodities such as silk, salt, grain and olive oil. More often, however, they subcontracted the right to collect these taxes from a mültezim.

The career of Panagiotis Benakis shows well how the system worked (Papastamatiou 2011, see especially tables 1–2). By subleasing tax collecting, Benakis and his family were able to amass a considerable fortune. Though most of his activities took place before 1774, his actions are typical of his peers, except that the scope, capacity and extent of their involvement in tax collection only became even greater after the end of that fateful war. Like ayan, kocabaşis also preyed upon the reaya by inflating the amount of taxes due and by ensnaring them in debt; kocabaşis would lend villagers the money that they needed to pay their taxes. Of course, the loans came with a very high interest rate. Christian notables invested heavily in land, creating their own estates, which increased the wealth that they could then deploy to obtain more tax farms. Through their land holdings and the mechanism of debt, they also came to control the lion's share of the surplus production from the countryside. Just like ayan they also employed retinues of armed men, consisting of a captain and his followers, to guard them and their property and to ensure that those who owed them money pay up.

The kocabaşis also enjoyed considerable political power. In exchange for their help in driving out the Venetians earlier in the century, Sultan Ahmed III issued a royal edict stating that the Peloponnesos would be ruled by them with regard to almost all internal affairs. In addition they had representation at the provincial level. The Mora valisi, or governor of the Morea, was required to meet on a regular basis with an executive council that consisted of both ayan and kocabaşis and there was even an official governmental post, filled by the Porte, called the Morayiannis. This Christian dragoman advised the valisi in all matters relating to the Orthodox community. Finally, the kocabaşis also retained representation in Istanbul itself. Each of the major kocabaşis families employed representatives, often family members, called velikides, who lobbied on their faction's behalf with the imperial divan (Kostantaras 2013: 4–6; Stamatopoulos 2007; Pylia 2007; Fotopoulos 2005: 253–344; Kyrkini-Koutoula 1996: 139–81). They were in fact often quite successful in their efforts. On occasion they even orchestrated the removal of high-ranking Muslim Ottoman officials from the province, as was the case with Hadji Ali Haseki, the on-again, off-again voyvoda (Ottoman governor) of Athens during the late eighteenth century. Kocabaşis families such as the Deliyiannis, the Londos and the Zaimes, then, grew richer and more powerful as the eighteenth century wore on, and they became powers to be reckoned with.

Later traditions and nationalist historiography paints a stark picture of a society in the Morea and Rumelia riven by divisions based upon religion. And certainly there was systemic, legal discrimination against non-Muslims. Moreover, this was also a wealth-stratified society, with groups like the ayan and kocabaşis at the top and the labouring classes below them. But the reality was that there was a good deal of cooperation between the dominant groups. Factions formed and power struggles erupted, often ending in lethal violence. But these factions quite frequently included both Christians and Muslims working together (Stamatopoulos 2005). In other words, it was not uncommon for an alliance of some ayan and kocabaşis families to form and then to engage in power struggles with their opponents. Ioannis Deliyiannis recounts in his memoirs how at one point during the 1810s, ayan and kocabaşis leaders 'made a frightful oath, the one on the Koran, the other on the Gospels ... that from this point forward they would consider themselves as brothers' (cited in Kostantaras 2013: 638). This moment of fraternal unity would not last long as developments at home and abroad would soon tear this society apart.

Structural changes in the administration of the Ottoman Empire, especially in Greece and the Balkans, led to the emergence of new Christian and Muslim power brokers and warlords who represented a potentially lethal threat to imperial rule. That threat became even more acute and imminent when the empire became embroiled in the wars being fought in the West to decide the fate of Europe. When Napoleon Bonaparte came east, the game changed dramatically, and ayan and kocabaşis would henceforth play extremely important roles in the power struggles that the French intervention unleashed. They were not, however, the only groups whose lives were changed by the arrival in the region of imports from the West. Enlightenment ideas found fertile ground among Greek-speaking intellectuals and their spread paved the way for the revolutionary movements of the early nineteenth century.

Enlightenment

Intellectuals in the Ottoman Empire were profoundly influenced by the Western European Enlightenment but rather than just slavishly adopting it, they engaged with the novel ideas of writers like Voltiare, Montesquieu and Rousseau, adapting them to their own Ottoman institutional situation. For that reason, scholars have given a variety of names to the movement in the East. Among the various appel-lations applied to it are: the Greek Enlightenment, the Modern Greek Enlightenment, the Neo-Hellenic Enlightenment, the Balkan Enlight-enment and the Enlightenment in Southeastern Europe. None of them are totally satisfactory. Those that feature 'Greek' in the title are misleading in that they convey the sense that the movement was restricted to ethnic Greeks, and this was not the case. There were, for example, prominent Serb, Romanian, Bulgarian and Vlach Enlight-enment writers. The last labels convey a sense of the geographical frame in which the Enlightenment took hold but they also suffer from being too restrictive: there were centres of Enlightenment thought in the East that do not fit into either frame. Neo-Hellenic, or those deploying Greek, are more acceptable but only if it is made clear that they refer to language, and not to nationality or ethnicity. Most, though by no means all, of the major Enlightenment texts in the East were written in Greek, which was, after all, the language of religion and education. Regardless of how we label it, what we are talking about is an intellectual movement that emerged in the Orthodox Christian academies during the eighteenth century. It drew its inspir-ation and core set of ideas from the Western Enlightenment but modified and transformed them to fit the situation in the Ottoman Empire.[1]

A useful way to trace the development of the Enlightenment is to discuss the most important scholars chronologically and to think of them as generations. The most important writer in the first genera-tion was Nicholas Mavrogordatos (1680–1730). In works published in the 1720s, he challenged the older system of learning that was based upon Orthodox religious texts and the writings of ancient authors, especially Aristotle, and of education that called on students to receive, not challenge, the ideas contained in them. Mavro-gordatos argued in favour of science and scientific inquiry and he called on his fellow intellectuals to challenge the received wisdom. His work triggered a debate between those called the Ancients, who supported the older knowledge regime, and those called the Moderns, who shared his perspective. The debate between the two took place exclusively within the confines of the Orthodox Christian academies, involved primarily a small group of intellectuals, who were also clerics, and had little impact outside of the confines of higher education. Indeed, even within the confines of the patriarchal schools, they gained little traction.

Exemplary of the next generation, which spans the period from the 1740s to the 1780s, were Evgenios Voulgaris (1716–1806) and Iossipos Moisiodax (1730–1800). The former championed the cause of Enlightenment philosophy and scientific inquiry; the latter did as well, but he added three new dimensions to the debate: the secular-isation of knowledge, rational humanism and liberal progress. The leaders of this second generation were truly transnational scholars, whose educational formation took place both in the traditional centres of Orthodox learning and also in the universities of Western Europe, and especially in Italy. Though still opposed by the church hierarchy, their work tipped the balance in favour of the Moderns and strongly influenced the next generation of scholars, who would take what had previously been a debate between intellectuals and turn it into a public discourse.

The third generation of intellectual scholars flourished from the 1790s onward. They were a transitional group, bearing some resemblances to the previous generations but also important differ-ences. The most important distinctions were that this cohort of writers had a greater familiarity and engagement with the West, and many important Greek thinkers resided in the diaspora. Second, far fewer of them were religious clerics and, third, as a consequence, more of them had no connection to the Orthodox academies. Lastly, and most importantly, their works were much more overtly secularist and political, particularly after the French Revolution of 1789. Predicated on Enlightenment ideas, the overthrow of the absolutist Bourbon dynasty and the establishment of a republic founded on the principle of popular, 'national' sovereignty had a profound impact on Christian intellectuals in the Balkans. It showed that regime change was possible; to use the language of the time, 'tyranny' could be toppled and the oppressive political systems of the Old Regime could be cast off and replaced by ones founded on the Enlightenment principles of liberty, equality and social justice. For people, like members of the Millet-i Rom, living in an absolutist state and subject to legal discrimination based on religion, these ideals were profoundly influential. Lastly, if the legitimacy of the new, post-revolutionary state rested on popular sovereignty, then this raised the critical question as to identity, belonging and national consciousness. In sum, it raised the issue as to what was the nation and what criteria determined inclusion in it.

The origin of a specifically 'Greek' national consciousness cannot be pinned down to a precise moment in the past, but instead must be seen as part of an ongoing process (Sotiropoulos 2009, 2011). Nonetheless, it is clear that the development of national consciousnesses among the subject populations of the Ottoman Empire took on a clearer coherence and developed at a more rapid pace among the third generation of Greek Enlightenment thinkers. As noted earlier, diasporic Greeks had grown in affluence and prominence during the last few decades of the eighteenth century, and because of the greater freedoms accorded them and their exposure to intellectual currents in Western Europe, it is not surprising that the intellectual basis of Greek nationalism was most coherently formed among this group. Two of the third-generation writers stand out from the rest for their vision and the impact of their ideas: Adamantios Korais (1748–1833) and Rigas Velestinlis (c. 1757–98).

Adamantios Korais was born in Smyrna to a Chiote father and a Smyrniote mother. As the son of a wealthy Rom family, he received an unconventional private education. While in his early twenties, Korais went to Amsterdam to oversee his father's silk trading interests there. He was to remain abroad thereafter. Finding little satisfaction in commerce, he switched careers and attended medical school at the University of Montpellier. But that life was not for him either. He soon found his true calling as a scholar of Classical Greece.

From his home in Paris, Korais played a leading role in formulating the intellectual foundation of Greek nationalism. Repulsed by the violence he witnessed during the French Revolution but steeped in hatred for the Ottoman Empire, he was thus torn by his firm belief that Greece must be freed from the 'yoke of tyranny', but not by violent, revolutionary means. Instead, he preached a middle way of emancipation through education. Through his work in Classical philology, Korais aimed at inculcating Greeks with a sense of their ancient heritage. His emphasis on the need to resurrect Greece's ancient glory stemmed in large part from his intense hatred of the Orthodox higher clergy – 'monkish barbarians' as he once called them – whom he blamed for the degraded state of the populace. For Korais, then, the model for a new Greece should be ancient Athens rather than medieval Byzantium. It was, thus, through his efforts as a linguist and in particular his development of *katharevousa* (a purely literary language that combined elements of ancient Greek with the popular spoken language called dimotic Greek) that he intended to give Greeks a means to invigorate that heritage. Though he had much to say about the 'moral' regeneration of the Greeks, he never explicitly described the type of polity he foresaw rising from the ashes of the Ottoman Empire. Though there are hints that for him three elements were key: (1) that the imagined national space of independent Greece conformed to the area dominated by the ancient Greek city-states, (2) that the key marker of Greek identity was language, and (3) that its cultural heritage derived from the ancient world and not from Orthodox Christianity. He lived to see the creation of an independent Greek state, though he played no major active role in its creation, and in fact, worried when hostilities broke out that that the rebellion was premature.

Rigas Velestinlis more than anyone else was the father of the revolution. His career track hews more closely to the older model. At a young age, because of his quick mind and evident intelligence, he came to the attention of the Orthodox priest in his natal village of Velestinlis in Thessaly An ethnic Vlach, Velestinlis was Hellenised through education and spent much of his earlier years studying at various Christian academies and monasteries. But he left the scholarly world to become a civil servant and a revolutionary. He held numerous notable administrative posts, such as secretary to Alexander Ipsilantis, the dragoman of the Porte in Istanbul, a cleric in the service of various Phanariote hospodars in Wallachia, and as advisor to Osman Paşvanoğlu in Vidin.

Highly educated and a gifted linguist, he was well suited to act as the conduit for the transmission of revolutionary ideas and ideals from the West to the East. Based in Vienna and imbued with the revolutionary fever emanating from France, he actively sought to spread the contagion of liberation to the Balkans.

In a series of works, Rigas both spread the gospel of violent revolution and sketched out a vision for the new Balkan republic that would emerge form the ashes of the Ottoman Empire. In his *The Rights of Man*, he transferred some of the key aspects of the French *Declaration of the Rights of Man and the Citizen* into a Balkan context. In Article Three on the equality of all men before the law, for example, he explicitly stated that this included both Christians and Muslims. Other articles as well emphasised that these fundamental natural rights appertained to all groups and all religious denominations. He also called for the abolition of slavery and for the use of Greek as the common tongue of the new Motherland. In the *New Political Constitution of the Inhabitants of Rumeli, Asia Minor, the Archipelago, Moldavia and Wallachia*, he provided a more detailed a blueprint for the new state's constitution. The new polity was to be a secular, democratic republic modelled on Jacobin France. He referred to it as a 'Greek Republic' but, as he clearly noted, Greek in this context meant citizen, not ethnicity: 'the Greek People [consists of all] those living in the Empire, without distinction of religion or language ...' (Article Two). He was even more explicit in Article Seven: 'The sovereign people consists of all inhabitants of this Empire, without distinction of religion and speech, Greeks, Bulgarians, Abanians, Vlachs, Armenians, Turks and every other kind of race.' In sum, Rigas wanted a secular, multi-ethnic, liberal democratic state that geographically resembled the Byzantine Empire. This was a noble vision that was not to be. Finally, he recognised that the common people needed more than political ideals to be roused to action, and so he penned a revolutionary anthem: the Thourios. This stirring poem became the Greek Marseilles, and it was widely disseminated and sung. It ends with the following call for action:

> Let us slay the wolves who impose the yoke,
> Who cruelly oppress both Christians and Turks;
> Let the Cross shine over land and sea;
> Let the foe kneel down in the face of justice;
> Let men be purged of all this sickness;
> And let us live on earth, as brothers, free! (lines 121–6)

Because of his activities, the Ottoman authorities considered him a traitor and a wanted man. While attempting to smuggle radical publications from Austrian-controlled Italy into the empire, Rigas was captured. He was transported to Vienna where he was imprisoned. After intense lobbying by the Porte, he and seven other Greek radicals were extradited to the empire. The verdict was never in doubt and on the night of 24 June 1798, in a Belgrade prison,

Rigas was executed by strangulation. With his dying breath, he supposedly uttered the following: 'This is how brave men die. I have sown; soon the hour will come when my nation will gather the ripe fruit.' And, indeed, it was to be his ideas that would have the most influence on the thinking of those who would lead the rebellion of 1821.

Rigas's was not the only vision of what a liberated Greek state should look like, nor was his the only voice calling for rebellion. The anonymous author of the *Greek Rule of Law*, or *A Word About Freedom (Elliniki Nomarhei, iti Logos peri Eleftherias)* published in 1806, for example, framed his call for revolution with a detailed catalogue of the horrors suffered by the subject Christian population of the empire. But unlike many others, he viciously attacked fellow Greeks for their roles in perpetuating the suffering of their people. He saved his most savage diatribe for the clergy. For this writer, the war of liberation meant not only throwing off the yoke of Ottoman rule, but also the tyranny of the Orthodox Church and the heavy-handed domination of the 'Turkified' Greeks of the ruling class.

Conversely, another widely held view was that it was the church that held the key to liberation. Proponents of this idea argued that Orthodoxy was the only force capable of mobilising the mass of people to rise up against the infidels. They looked back to the future for their new Greece. What they foresaw was a new Byzantine Empire: Greek, theocratic and monarchical. The idea of Byzantine Hellenism resonated most loudly with the Phanariots of Istanbul. That there was not a unitary revolution vision is not surprising. What is significant is that all shared in the belief that the time was ripe for some form of readjustment or even overthrow of Ottoman rule. A series of developments in Ottoman Europe during the first two decades of the nineteenth century proved them correct. A critical point of departure in the slide to revolution was the French invasion of the Ottoman Empire in 1798.

The French intervention

'Fortune, do you abandon me? Only 5 more days!' Napoleon Bonaparte is supposed to have uttered these words on the morning of 1 July 1798 as his great armada was approaching the Egyptian port city of Alexandria (cited in Cole 2007: 20; see also Black 2003; Bierman 2003). He was in a race to land his forces safely before the British fleet under Lord Horatio Nelson could catch up with him. On this occasion, fortune favoured the Frenchman, and Napoleon's great invasion of the Ottoman Empire began. So too did the next phase of the Eastern Question, and when the Napoleonic Wars were over, the Eastern Mediterranean and the Balkans would be dramatically changed.

After landing his army, Napoleon scored a string of stunning victories over the Egyptian Mamluk forces, culminating in their destruction at the Battle of the Pyramids. French success, however, was short-lived. On 1 August, Admiral Nelson and the British fleet engaged their French counterpart in Aboukir Bay. In the ensuing battle the French fleet was devastated. The superior battle plan and greater proficiency of the British gunners led to the almost complete destruction of the French navy. Napoleon would continue the war, and even score some notable victories, such as his defeat of the Ottoman expeditionary force in 1799, but in the absence of naval support, the long-term prognosis for his campaign was not favourable. Even after his return to France and the defeat of the French army in Egypt, the Mediterranean and the Balkans were now closely connected to the struggles for hegemony in Europe. Moreover, the wars would have a profound impact on the region's economy as well. We need now to examine in more detail these and the other consequences of Napoleon's Mediterranean adventure.

Ottoman leadership was shocked by the French invasion of Egypt (Finkel 2005: 410). They had not seen it coming because France had traditionally been the Ottoman's best friend in Western European. So France's violation of their territory caught them off-guard. And Napoleon's pronouncement, that he was doing this to assist the empire in bringing an unruly province back under its control, rang hollow. One result of the French adventure was to push the Ottomans into an unlikely alliance with their traditional enemy, the Russian Empire. The two old adversaries signed defensive treaties in 1799 and in 1805; in the intervening period, they even cooperated in military campaigns in the Balkans, culminating with the seizure of the Ionian Islands and their being placed under Ottoman protection and Russian control. But the era of rapprochement proved temporary. Napoleon's stunning victories over the Austrians in 1805 and the Russians the next year at Austerlitz changed the situation dramatically. These victories and French assurances of support, including even direct military intervention, led the Ottomans to renounce their Russian alliances and to once more align themselves with France.

The Porte's aims were twofold. First they hoped to get back some of the territories in the northern Balkans that the Austrians had taken from them and, second, they saw an opportunity to re-exert Ottoman control of the Danubian Principalities. Selim thus dismissed the pro-Russian hospodars, Konstantinos Ipsilantis and Alexandros Mourousis, and replaced them with men more loyal to the empire. France landed an expeditionary force in Dalamatia and this led the Russians to occupy militarily the Principalities. The result of these moves was renewed tensions and then war with the Ottoman's old enemy, the Russians.

Fighting between them began in 1805 and continued intermittently until 1812. The war was waged, by and large, along the Danube frontier, in the Caucasus, and on the Black Sea and the northern Aegean. The Ottomans fared poorly both on land and at sea. The war cost Selim III his throne and his life; his eventual successor, Mahmud II, faced formidable challenges domestically and abroad, and so the outcome of the war with Russia was never really in doubt. On 28 May 1812, twelve days before Napoleon launched his fateful invasion of Russia, the Porte signed the Treaty of Bucharest ending the war. The treaty granted further concessions to the Russians with regard to the Danubian Principalities, rendering them essentially a Russian possession.

The Napoleonic Wars had profound consequences on the Ottoman Empire. One casualty of war was Sultan Selim III. His attempt to modernise the Ottoman military in the context of an ongoing conflict proved difficult and alienated many powerful factions among the ruling and military classes. This culminated in his overthrow in 1807 and the ascendancy to the throne of Mahumd II. The old military institutions, the Janissaries and the levend corps, would remain in place – outdated and as ineffective as they were. Another important development during wartime was the Serbian revolt, about which much more will be said shortly. Related to both of these developments was the continued devolution of power from the centre to the provinces. Powerful local notables such as Osman Paşvanoğlu of Vidin and Tepedelenli Ali Paşa of Yanya were able to expand and strengthen their power (Anastasapoulos 2005, 2007 on the impact of decentralisation on Vidin). While nominally loyal to the state, these power-hungry warlords posed a deadly threat to the integrity of the empire.

In many ways the most powerful warlord of them all owed his ascendancy directly to the French adventure in Egypt. Mehmet Ali's origins are unclear. He was, of course, a Muslim but beyond that there is no unanimity. According to some accounts he was of Greek descent; in others, he is said to have been an Albanian, and in still others it is claimed that he was Kurdish. We know for sure that he was from the city of Kavala in northern Greece and that he was multilingual, preferring to use Greek in his dealings with foreigners even though he still had to go through a translator. He came from a family of tobacco merchants who had also played important roles as commanders of the local levend irregular corps. When, in 1801, Selim III mobilised for the invasion of Egypt, the order went out to call up the levend, including 300 men from Kavala. Mehmet Ali was appointed deputy commander and, when his superior decided to return to Kavala, he found himself in charge of his unit. Having distinguished himself in battle, he was rapidly promoted. The situation in Egypt was chaotic and when the Ottoman governor proved incapable of dealing with it, in 1805 the Ulema of Cairo appointed Mehmet Ali to take his place. Skilful, ruthless and determined, by 1811 he had bested his foes and consolidated his position. Though he came to power with the blessing of the Muslim clergy, he was much more flexible when it came to religion, and he appointed many Greeks and Armenians to his administration. From the time of the Napoleonic Wars onward, Mehmet Ali's power and influence would only increase, and he would play a critical role in the history of the region.

A very important economic development initiated by the Napoleonic Wars was the acceleration of a trend that we have already looked at, and that was the increasing dominance of Greeks over merchant shipping in the Mediterranean and the Black Sea. The war at sea undoubtedly disrupted maritime commerce, but it did not stop it. Markets had to be satisfied; raw materials needed for wartime production had to be transported to the places of manufacture; people had to be fed. The result was that the pace and flow of commodities through the Mediterranean continued during the war years, with one important difference. The British were largely removed from the commercial scene through a combination of the French embargo and the predatory activities of pirates at sea. The void left by the British withdrawal was filled by American traders and, most importantly, by Greeks (Galani 2011; Marzagalli 2005). As we have seen, from 1774 onward, Greeks, whether flying under the flag of the Ottoman Empire, the Russian Empire, the Venetian Empire, or even the Holy state of Jerusalem, came to exert a very powerful hold over maritime commerce in the Black Sea and the

Mediterranean and beyond. The absence of the British and the disruption to French maritime commerce in the Mediterranean created a space that Greek ship captains and shipowners readily filled, leading to what one historian has called a Greek 'economic boom' (Galani 2011: 184).

Another consequence of the wars was the militarisation of non-Muslim society, and particularly of Greeks, inside and outside of the empire. The ongoing conflicts stretched Ottoman resources thinly and, since so many Muslim levend troops were fighting on the Danubian front, the Porte and many local authorities had to rely on non-Muslim, mostly Orthodox Greek and Albanian armatoles, to act as the internal police force. In addition, there were other Orthodox Greeks and Albanians who were getting weapons and learning how to use them. The Great Powers, and especially the British, organised and trained local men into bands of irregulars.

The most famous of these groups were the Corsican Rangers, a highly decorated and battle-hardened corps that was made up of men of many different nationalities and not just Corsicans. As Britain and France became more deeply involved in the Balkans, they formed local irregular corps there. During the French period of occupation on the Ionian Islands, for example, General François-Xavier Donzelot recruited and trained a force of over 5,000 Greeks and Albanians, mostly from the mainland. After the British established a stronghold on the island of Zakynthos in 1809, many of these men joined the new Duke of York's Greek Light Infantry. Austria organised ethnic Serbs into irregular units called the Freicorps. The Russians always recruited irregular bands of Balkan Christians (Serbs, Greeks, Albanians, Romanians and others) in Moldavia and Wallachia to support their regular army. The bottom line was that at the end of the Napoleonic Wars there were many more Orthodox Christians who had guns and who knew how to use them (Stathis 2007: 174; Reid 1996).

It was not only inside the Ottoman Empire that Greeks were becoming increasingly proficient in the martial arts. Many Greek emigrants or men of Greek descent residing outside of the Ottoman Empire received military training and, indeed, some of them rose to high rank in one or more of the Great Power armies. This was especially the case in the Russian Empire. Many Greeks fought in the Russian army on the Danubian front and in the defence of Russia against Napoleon's invasion in 1812. Many of the military leaders of the Greek insurrectionary forces learned their craft in the Russian army. But there were also Greeks who fought in Napoleon's army and even in the British forces. Many of them would also play critical roles in what became the Greek war of Independence.

By the time Bonaparte met his Waterloo, the winds of change had blown through the Ottoman Empire. All across its vast territory, very important and fundamental structural changes altered some of its most basic features. The once-feared Ottoman military was but a sad reflection of its former self, and the attempts by the reformist Sultan Selim III failed. Decentralisation and the devolution of critically important government functions to the provincial level led to the formation of alternate and competing centres of power. New groups, in particular Muslim ayan and Christian kocabaşis, emerged as key players on the scene. The spread of Europe's wars to the empire now meant that the Eastern Question would loom large and that any outbreak of conflict in Europe would soon spread to the Eastern Mediterranean world and vice-versa. The emigration of huge numbers of Ottoman subjects, mostly Christians and many of them Greeks, to Russia and to all of the major cities of Europe, created diasporic, transnational communities over which the Porte could exert little control. So at the same time that Western Europe was closing a bloody chapter in its history, in the East the door to war was opening.

Notes

1. The literature on the Greek Enlightenment is vast. My discussion of the topic has been deeply influenced by the works of Paschalis M. Kitromilides. His voluminous works are the essential starting point for any discussion of the topic; many of his most influential essays have been compiled, revised and published in a volume (2013). To be recommended among his earlier works are his foundational biography of Iossipos Moisiodax (1992) and the collection of essays he edited on Adamantios Korais (2010). The works of Stratos Myrogiannis (2012), Dean Kostantaras (2006), Petros Pizanias (2009b; 2011b) and Dimitrios Stamatopoulos (2007) have also influenced heavily this discussion of the Enlightenment.

CHAPTER 3

The war that changed the Greek world

Sunday, 9 October 1831, was much like any other one for the inhabitants of Greece's capital city of Nafplion. But events that day would change the course of the nascent country's future irrevocably. Ioannis Kapodistrias, independent Greece's first president, rose early in the morning and decided to attend Mass at the of church of Agios Spiridonos, in spite of his servants' and bodyguards' admonition that he should remain home. After he passed the mosque across the street from the church and turned to enter Agios Spiridonos, he encountered a small group of people waiting to welcome him. Konstantinos and Yiorgios Mavromichalis, the brother and son of Petrobey Mavromichalis, one of the most prominent leaders of the Greek rebellion, stepped forward as if to greet him. Suddenly Konstantinos drew his pistol and fired; the bullet missed its mark and struck the church wall, where the hole it made is still visible today. Leaping forward, yataghan in hand, he stabbed the president in the stomach just as his nephew put a bullet into the president's head (Fig. 3.1). Seconds later one of Kapodistrias's bodyguards shot and wounded Konstantinos. The enraged mob fell upon him and beat him to death. His lifeless body was dragged to Sintagma Square where it was strung up and defiled, until some men took it down and threw it into the sea. Yiorgios Mavromichalis eluded capture and hid in the house of the French resident, Baron Rouen, who promptly turned him in. His trial by court martial was brief and the verdict never in doubt. On 22 October, unrepentant, he was executed for his crime.

Kapodistrias's assassination aptly captures many of the aspects of the seminal event discussed in this chapter, that being the Balkan-wide insurrection that began in 1821 and resulted in the creation of the first independent Greek state in 1828. First, like many of those who would play prominent roles in the rebellion, he came from the diaspora. A nobleman from the island of Corfu, he was an Ionian Greek who had spent most of his adult life either in Russia or

Figure 3.1 *The assassination of Ioannis Kapodistrias © Kerkyra Municipal Library.*

elsewhere in Western Europe. Indeed, when he arrived in the country as its first president, it was the first time he had ever been in continental Greece. Outsiders, like him, were critical to the revolution. His background captures another essential element of the War of Independence: it was a European, perhaps even a global event. Second, his death is representative of another prominent aspect of the Greek rebellion: that it was a conflict beset from the onset by internecine fighting amongst the Greek leadership. Kapodistrias was only another in the long list of victims of Greek civil discord, and he would not be the last. Finally, his Russian background captures another critical aspect of the rebellion, and that was that the war entangled the European Great Powers in the affairs of Southeastern Europe and the Ottoman Empire. By so doing, it continued and greatly deepened an engagement that would only end with World War I.

The road to revolution

The significance of the Greek War of Independence transcends the bounds of Greece and Greek history.[1] It not only changed the fundamental fabric of the Greek world, but its impact was felt from Russia to Latin America. First and foremost, of course, the war led to the creation for the first time in history of an independent Greek nation-state. Next, it was the first successful secessionist uprising by a subject population against an imperial power since the American Revolution of 1776. It provided a model for later nationalist struggles elsewhere in Europe and in the Americas. The conflict was the first real test of the conservative Concert of Europe that emerged out of the Great Power Congress of Vienna in 1816. Finally, the Greek War of Independence had a profound impact on the Ottoman Empire. Indeed, arguably it was the most important event in the history of the empire since the reign of Suleiman the Lawgiver. At first, because the struggle quickly took on a pointedly religious dimension – Christians versus Muslims – the war strengthened the position of the Islamic establishment. However, in dealing with the rebellion, Mahmud II and his supporters had to initiate radical reforms, such as the abolition of the Janissaries, which changed the fundamental fabric of the empire. The era of Ottoman reform really begins with the Greek War of Independence. Because of it, 'the Ottoman Empire was ready as it never had been to accept modernity together with its nation-state building tools' (Erdem 2005: 67). The Ottoman move towards modernity had a profound impact on its people, including the huge Greek population that remained in the empire even after the creation of the independent Greek state. The Greek War of Independence, then, was an event of transcendent importance.

The question we need to ask now is why did this secessionist insurrection begin in 1821 and why did it take on the eventual form that it did? Why was it successful? In order for a revolution to take place, three critical factors have to be in place. First, there have to be ideas that challenge the status quo and that provide an alternative vision to current realities. As we have seen, the Enlightenment had done just this. It provided a body of ideas about freedom, justice, equality before the law, and fundamental civil liberties that resonated amongst many subjects of the Ottoman Empire, both Christian and Muslim. Second, there has to be a leadership cadre that can disseminate these ideas to the wider population and that can mobilise mass support to initiate change. Third, there has to be mass discontent with the current situation. We can call these 'structural factors' and all of them have to be in place for a successful revolution to occur. As we will see in this chapter, all three of them developed in Ottoman Europe during the first two decades of the nineteenth century. But we still need to explain why the rebellion began in 1821.

And to do this we need to examine specific events that occurred during the 1810s that resulted in the outbreak of revolution in the spring of that year. The first step on the road to revolution took place, not in Greece, but in Serbia.

Serbian revolt – national or local?

One of the key developments in the move toward nationalist revolutions and the partitioning of the Ottoman Empire in Europe were the rebellions in Serbia between 1805 and 1815 (Malešević 2012). Serbs had served in an Austrian irregular unit called the Friecorps during the 1790s war. Since Serbia was now the frontier between the empire and Austria, and since Serbs were now subjects on both sides of the border, Selim III found it expedient to accede to the calls from Serbian leaders for certain reforms. Among the privileges accorded to the Serbs was the right to collect their own taxes and to bear arms and form militias. Also the Porte granted them certain land rights and protections from abusive officials. Lastly, the balance of power at the local level was shifted through the formation of local Christian councils that dealt with internal matters and that liaised with the Porte's officials. Thus Serbians obtained greater local autonomy and influence in government. The problem was that the central authorities in Istanbul could issue proclamations and make promises, but because of decentralisation they were frequently unable to enforce them fully. The key problem in the Paşalik of Serbia was the Janissaries. Here, as elsewhere, they had gone rogue. As in the Morea, they were operating like a Mafia-style organisation and racket, providing 'protection' at a price – usually of course it was protection from them. They held entire villages hostage and even took over entire estates. Both Christian knezes (the Serbian term for kocabaşis) and Ottoman officials saw them as a grave menace to peace and security.

The Janissaries had fled when the city fell to the Austrians in the previous war. When the city was reclaimed as part of the Treaty of Jassy, Selim ordered that the Janissaries not be allowed back. But they had a powerful ally closer to the scene whom they called on for support. Osman Paşvanoğlu, Ayan and Paşa of Vidin, saw an opportunity to increase his power and influence beyond the boundaries of his own province by supporting the Janissaries in their bid to return to Belgrade. Together early in 1797 they struck. The central government appointed Hadji Mustapha Paşa as Valisi of Belgrade because of his background as an Orthodox convert to Islam, and because of his willingness to work with the Serb knezes to implement the new reforms. As one of his reforms, Hadji Mustapha Paşa ordered all Serb men to arm themselves with a long musket, two pistols and a yataghan or to incur a fine and suffer a beating. He needed armed men, even if they were Christian (Zens 2004: 160). Together, this new Serb militia and the Ottoman garrison repulsed the Janissary attack on the city and indeed were driving them back to Vidin when outside factors intervened.

In 1798, as we discussed in the last chapter, Napoleon invaded the Ottoman Empire. Faced with the might of the French army, the empire had to mobilise a huge force. This had two important implications for Serbia. First, the Porte had to shift forces from the Danubian frontier, along which there was no threat because Austria was also at war with France, and this meant depleting the garrison of Belgrade. Second, Selim needed Paşvanoğlu's help. The master of Vidin controlled supplies and men that Selim needed for the war in Egypt. Part of the price of Osman's help was the restoration of the Janissaries. After Hadji Mustapha was assassinated, they took control of the city and by 1802 they were threatening the countryside as well. Serbian volunteers began to rally around a wealthy pig merchant from Shumadija, Karageorge Petrovich.

By 1804, Karageorge had created a militia of close to 30,000 armed men. Sensing that their position was becoming more precarious, the Janissary leadership decided on a pre-emptive strike. They would decapitate the Serbian forces by assassinating the leadership. In a coordinated attack numerous knezes were slaughtered, precipitating a crisis that demanded Istanbul's immediate attention. An imperial firman ordered the Ottoman governor to cooperate with Christian Serbs and a fatwa from Şeyhülislam made it acceptable for Ottoman forces to wage war and confiscate the property of the Janissaries, fellow Muslims.[2] All went well and within a relatively short span of time, they defeated the Janissaries.

With their common enemy vanquished, divisions developed between the Serbian leadership and Ottoman authorities. The Serbs presented the Porte with a proposal to grant them greater local autonomy. As the negotiations foundered, the Serbs looked north for an ally. Russia, however, was allied with the Ottomans and did not want to jeopardise that alliance over Serbia. Open conflict erupted between Ottoman forces and the Serb militia. While successful initially against the forces of numerous Rumelian ayan, the Serb rebellion was eventually suppressed. A number of developments accounted for this failure. First, the war between the two empires that started in 1806 meant that even though Russia supported the Serbs in spirit, they could do little more. Then, Paşvanoğlu died in 1807 and the Ottomans reasserted control of Vidin and its resources. Nonetheless, limited Serbia home rule was included in the Treaty of Bucharest in 1812. Serbs were to enjoy an autonomous status, much like the Aegean islanders; they could collect their own taxes and pay tribute to the Porte; and the empire was to deploy only a limited number of troops in Belgrade and elsewhere. Neither side had any intention of implementing this clause and when Napoleon invaded Russia, all bets were off. Russia's preoccupation with the French left the Ottomans with a free hand and they crushed the Serbian revolt. By 1813, then, the province had been restored to Ottoman control.

A new leader of the Serb cause emerged at this time: Miloš Obrenović. His rivalry with Karageorge made him an acceptable choice as leader of the Serbs. Ottoman re-occupation had not gone well. Many of the newly recruited levend troops from western Rumelia and Albania committed atrocities and looting. Ottoman authorities tried to mediate but the situation spun out of control. In April 1815 the insurrection began anew. Obrenović was very much the diplomat, assuring the Porte that this was not a revolution against the sultan but rather a protest against governmental abuses. He also went on a diplomatic mission to seek assistance from the Great Powers, high-level representatives of which were meeting in Vienna. He met frequently with Ioannis Kapdistrias, one of Russia's delegation and an Ionian Greek, and on two occasions he even had an audience with the Austrian emperor Francis. The affairs of the Ottoman Empire and the Serbian situation were discussed at Vienna but none of the powers, including Russia, was prepared to take action. Nonetheless, the message emanating from Vienna was clear: that the balance of power in Europe had to be maintained, that the French Revolution's legacy had to be suppressed, and that peace and stability were to be the order of the day. Serbs would get no help but the Ottomans had to tread lightly in dealing with them. In the autumn of 1815 they compromised. The Paşalik of Belgrade would become a semi-autonomous province of the Ottoman Empire and organised largely along the lines set out in Article 8 of the 1812 Treaty of Bucharest (Anti 2007).

The Serbian insurrection and its settlement had important ramifications for future developments in Ottoman Europe (Gounaris

2007). First, they led to the establishment of yet another semi-autonomous territory in the empire, in which Christians largely ruled themselves. It may not have been large in size but it was significant because it showed others that home rule was possible and that the partitioning of the empire was feasible. Second, the new Serbian principality was strategically located at the crossroads of the Balkans and Europe: at its centre was Belgrade, the gateway to Europe on the Danube; it bordered Austria and the Danubian Principalities, and it was relatively close to Russia. In short, Serbia further entangled the Great Powers in Ottoman Balkan affairs. Third, there was now a well-armed and battle-hardened Christian militia in the region that could potentially provide the vanguard for a larger insurrection. And lastly, it stood as an example. Other groups asked themselves, if the Serbs could gain self-rule, why not us? In regard to this last point, as important as Serbian semi-autonomy was as a beacon of hope, it paled in comparison to what happened at approximately the same time on a group of islands off of the coast of Greece. The creation of the independent United States of the Ionian Islands had far-reaching consequences for Greeks everywhere.

The Ionian factor

According to popular legend, when plotting his Mediterranean campaign Napoleon observed that capturing the Ionian Islands would make him a master of the Mediterranean.[3] After his whirlwind defeat of the Austrian forces in northern Italy, Napoleon's France obtained the islands with the Treaty of Leoben on 18 April 1797. Shortly thereafter, French forces under the leadership of General Antoine Gentili seized the islands, and the Treaty of Campo Formio, which signalled the demise of the Serenissma Republic of Venice, then formalised that occupation. The French Revolution came to the islands along with the Gallic army. Liberated Ionians planted trees of liberty and adopted other symbols of the French Revolution. The aristocracy was abolished and the Golden Book in which their names had been inscribed was burnt. The French installed a popular, liberal and democratic government based on the French revolutionary constitution of 1795. Factional squabbles between competing aristocratic parties jockeying for power resulted in intrigue and violence. Sectional fighting plagued the islanders for the next twenty years, as they were passed back and forth between the Great Powers. The French held the islands until 1799 when a joint Ottoman-Russian expeditionary force drove them out. The arrangement agreed to by Russia and the Porte was that the islands were to be an independent state paying tribute to the Ottoman Empire and under Russian military protection. Thus, an independent Greek state appeared for the first time in history: the Septinsular Republic.

The new state was a democracy dominated by the aristocracy. As an independent state, the republic conducted its own foreign policy, largely shaped by a brilliant young Ionian aristocrat named Ioannis Kapodistrias, raised an army that Russia trained, and developed a flourishing commercial economy. Though independent, it was also very much under Russian influence. When the short-lived alliance between the Ottomans and the Russians collapsed and war erupted (in 1806), the Septinsular Republic fell completely under Russian control until the Treaty of Tilsit ceded the islands back to Bonaparte in 1807. The islands' strategic importance led the British to launch a military expedition against the French forces on the islands in 1809. There had previously been fighting between pro-British Ionians and the French, but the landing of British forces elevated the conflict to a new and higher level. French resistance on all of the islands except for Kerkira proved limited. By October 1809, Zakynthos had fallen; within a matter of three months, the others followed suit. Only the garrison on Kerkira stood firm, and did so until shortly after Napoleon's abdication in 1814. At this point, Britain forces occupied all of the islands (Pagratis 2011; 2012).

The question of what to do with the islands was debated by the Great Powers at the Congress of Vienna. Because of their strategic location, each of the major powers was reticent about letting any one of the others annex them completely. The tempestuous events that had engulfed the islands after the French takeover showed that the rambunctious Greeks could not be accorded home rule. After much deliberation, on 5 November 1815 a solution was arrived at: the islands were to be granted independence within the framework of Great Power-guaranteed protection. The islands were, thus, united into a single independent state, called the United States of the Ionian Islands. Basing their argument primarily on the grounds that their forces had liberated the islands and that they still had troops on the ground, Great Britain sought and obtained an agreement that placed the islands under the protection of the British crown. How heavy or light Britain's protective hand would be was an issue left open. All that the treaty stipulated was that a lord high commissioner would be appointed by the king to coordinate Anglo-Greek affairs.

Soon after the establishment of the protectorate, a constitution was promulgated that set up the system of self-rule. Modelled on the charter of the Septinsular Republic, the islands had a limited democracy with enfranchisement based on age and wealth, as was access to political institutions such as the senate. Much power, however, was reserved for the British. The Lord High Commissioner commanded the British military forces that garrisoned the islands for their protection, had veto power over the Ionian Senate, appointed the members of Executive Council of State, and he and his representative wielded control over the islands' mercantile, commercial and foreign affairs. Ionians were citizens of the United States of the Ionian Islands, but as subjects of the British crown they also enjoyed a special status internationally. Most important, however, was the fact that for the second time in just over a decade, the Ionian Islands were an independent Greek state (Gallant 2001).

Ionian independence was a critically important event at the time. At the most basic level it showed that obtaining independence was possible. Greeks on the mainland looked across the narrow straits and saw a self-governing Hellenic state. Just as importantly perhaps, they now understood that the Great Powers were not averse to further partitioning of the Ottoman Empire and to establishing new countries out of its ruins. Ionian independence had practical as well as symbolic significance. By the late 1810s Ionian islanders had created a diaspora that stretched across Europe and the Mediterranean. Given that they had been part of Venice's empire for hundreds of years, not surprisingly there were close connections between them and Italy and the Western Mediterranean. During the last quarter of the eighteenth century, the Ionian diaspora expanded into Russia, both as immigrants and as temporary workers involved in maritime commerce. In short, Ionians were everywhere.

Just as impressive as the diaspora's areal extent was the depth to which Ionians had integrated into their adopted homelands. Ionians like Destunis and Kapodistrias walked the corridors of power in St Petersburg, for example, as diplomats and politicians. The government of the Septinsular Republic created a dense network of consular offices across the Mediterranean and especially in the Ottoman Empire; when the republic fell, most of those men stayed on in their posts but now as representatives of the Russian Empire. Ionian islanders, therefore, were in a key position to help shape developments in the area. In sum, the islands stood as a symbolic beacon of the possibility of Greek independence. Ionians, many of whom were ardent supporters of that cause, were in positions where they could help to make that happen, and when the rebellion broke out, Ionians like Vlad (Ioannis) Vlassopoulos, the Russian consul in Patras, were in the revolutionary vanguard. Lastly, the islands themselves acted as a conduit through which lawyers, guns and money could pass in support of the movements for Greek independence.

Secret societies

There could be no Greek insurrection without an organisation to lead it, and one emerged in the 1810s. The European 'age of revolution' was also the era of secret societies (Angelomatis-Tsougarakis 2010). Revolution is impossible without leadership and since revolt is treasonous, men dedicated to the cause had to operate in secret. All across Europe such organisations appeared. In Italy, there was the Carbonari and in Russia, the Decembrists, for example. Liberal movements to resist the conservative counter-revolution's attempt to restore the *ancien régime* in the aftermath of the French Revolution and Napoleon flourished everywhere. Diaspora Greeks were members of some of them, as well as forming their own national liberation groups. And there were many of these, though most never amounted to much. Two, however, did: the Philomouso Etaireia and the Philiki Etaireia.

The Philomouso Etaireia (Society of the Friends of the Muses) was a philanthropic and educational organisation established in Vienna in 1814. The organisation soon founded branches in almost every major European city, but especially important were those in Russia. The society gathered funds to build schools and other educational and cultural establishments in Ottoman Greece and to support Greek students studying at European universities. In this regard, it resembled similar societies in places like Odessa and Taganrog. What was special about the Friends of the Muses in Russia was that it enjoyed the support of many of the most powerful and wealthy Greeks in the empire. Kapodistrias, Strudza and Destunis, for example, all actively worked on the society's behalf. While not an explicitly political organisation, the Society had the goal of fostering Greek liberation through education. They believed that by elevating the moral character of the Greek population through the study of Classical texts and ecclesiastical writings, Greece would eventually be liberated with Russian assistance. Liberation for them was a long-term goal that would come gradually and without violent revolution

(Prousis 1994: 14–18; Panagiotopoulos 2003: 11–12; Panagiotopoulos 2011: 104–5).

The Philiki Etaireia, or 'Friendly Society', became the most important Greek revolutionary organisation and, while it shared the Society of the Muses' goal of Greek independence, it differed completely in regard to means and methods. Its goal was to foment a violent revolution against the Ottoman Empire. Emmanouil Xanthos, Nicholaos Skoufas and Athanasios Tsakalov, three merchants from different regions of the Ottoman Empire, founded the Philiki Etaireia in 1814 in Odessa. Xanthos was initially the driving force behind the organisation. Though based in Odessa, because of his olive oil business he travelled widely in the Balkans. One of his trips took him to the island of Lefkada, one of the Ionian islands. The ideas of the French Revolution had taken root there during the period of French rule. Not only did Xanthos become stirred by the notions of liberty and freedom while staying on the island, but he was also introduced to the murky world of secret societies when he was enrolled into the island's Free Masons' lodge. Like many members of the diaspora communities, Xanthos believed that liberation for the Greeks would be achieved through the actions of the major Western European powers. The Concert of Europe crafted by Klemens von Metternich at the Congress of Vienna dashed any such hopes. The conservative crowned heads of Europe combined to maintain the status quo, and that policy extended even to relations with the Ottoman Empire. The Philiki Etaireia was established when it became clear that if freedom was to be attained, the Greeks and the other Christians in the Balkans would have to do it themselves.

If the Friendly Society was to have any chance of success it would have to appeal to a wide spectrum of Balkan Christians (Greeks, Serbs, Romanians, Bulgarians and Albanians) and would have to recruit as members as many prominent men as possible, and it would have to do so in secret. Accordingly, it modelled itself on similar secret societies that some of its members were familiar with. There was a central committee of twelve men, the Apostles, and one of their most important tasks was to recruit in their assigned region as many wealthy and powerful men as possible. After this move, the organisation's membership expanded rapidly both in size and in geographical scope. Influential men both inside and outside of the Ottoman Empire joined.

Organisationally, the membership was divided hierarchically into four civil ranks and two military ranks. The ranks were based on wealth and responsibilities. In order to maintain secrecy, only members from the highest ranks knew the identities of members from outside of their immediate cell. This compartmentalisation meant that, unlike other such groups, the Philiki Etaireia was able both to attract a substantial membership and to elude detection and suppression. The organisation brought together men from many levels of society – merchants, professionals, kocabaşis, clergymen, armatole and bandit captains, and many prominent Phanariots, like the Greek-Russian military officer Alexander Ipsilantis, the society's supreme leader, and hospodar Michailis Soutzos, joined. Very large numbers of Greeks in the Russian consular service became ardent members. Ionian islanders were especially active and because of the Ionian diaspora, they were particularly successful in getting recruits. The society, however, never really became a mass movement in the truest sense of the term; according to the surviving membership lists very few peasants, shepherds or workers were members.

The Philiki Etaireia was, nonetheless, the largest secret society and it provided an organisational base for the dissemination of revolutionary ideas and for coordinated action. But there was a very significant downside to its large size. Along with size came diversity of aims, ambitions and viewpoints. Ideologically, except for the goal of liberation from Ottoman rule, little else connected the membership. Some prominent leaders envisioned a new Byzantine Empire, based on a Greek theocratic monarchy; others fervently wanted to create a multi-ethnic secular republic founded on the principles of the French Revolution and based on the visions that Rigas had delineated. These fissures would only emerge after the actual onset of hostilities. Initially at least, because of its size and the number of important leaders whom it counted as members, the Philiki Etaireia had emerged as a Balkan-wide revolutionary organisation. By 1820, all of the pieces were in place for a Christian uprising in the Balkans. Only a spark was required to set ablaze the conflagration of war.

Tepedelenli Ali Paşa

The precipitating factor in the Greek rebellion was the civil war between Tepedelenli Ali Paşa, Yanya Valisis, against his master, Sultan Mahmud II. In a cultural landscape littered with larger-than-life characters, Tepedelenli Ali Paşa stands out. An enormous man with enormous appetites, the so-called 'Lion' or 'Diamond' of

Ioannina, left a lasting imprint on the history of Greece and the Balkans. Finding the historical Ali is not easy. Westerners, travellers and historians alike, have projected onto him their darkest Orientalist fantasies, portraying him as the quintessential Oriental despot (Fleming 1999). In Greek historiography he is portrayed as a brutal and merciless ogre who exploited and debased his Christian subjects. He was the murderer of innocent Greek men and the defiler of their helpless women. Cruel, tyrannical and bloodthirsty, Ali was truly a monster. Or was he? Both the Greek and the Western images of Ali are fantastic and inaccurate. Placed in their proper historical context, an examination of the voluminous material that survives from his archives along with Ottoman and Russian sources shows that in most respects Ali was not especially different from any other Balkan ayan. What made him special was that he was more successful at Ottoman power politics than most of his contemporaries.

Two things contributed heavily to his success and his longevity. First was his flexibility and adaptability. While he himself, of course, was a Muslim, representing a Muslim state, Ali surrounded himself with qualified and competent men regardless of their faith. Most of his closest advisors were Greek-speaking Orthodox Christians and his preferred language, even in his private life, was Greek. His top military commanders were men like the Muslim Omar Vryonis from Berat and the Greek Odysseus Androutsos. He rewarded and promoted men based on their performance, not their religion, and he punished or crushed anyone in his way equally. Second, he never sought to translate his provincial power into a position at court and so he never got caught up in the political intrigues that swirled through the corridors of power in Istanbul. Ministerial careers at court tended to be brief and to end badly for the office holder. Instead, Ali was content to build his own central-western Balkan domain within the empire. He organised and ran his province well; under him Epiros and Ioannina flourished economically and culturally. His province had the best road network in the Balkans, in spite of it being one of the most mountainous. He monopolised the tax farm for the province, making sure to send Istanbul its cut while retaining a lion's share for himself. He thus amassed an enormous personal fortune, including over 1,000 çiftliks (private estates), 250,000 flocks, and a cash reserve that the Porte estimated at 500,000,000 piasters (US$ 23,450,000,000) at the time of his death.[4]

Militarily, he never failed to provide levend troops when the empire went to war or to impose the war requisition taxes. In exchange for this support and because of the fact that he could muster at least 40,000 well-trained men, Selim III and then Mahmud II largely turned a blind eye as he expanded his power base across the Balkans. Those ayan or kocabaşis who would not accept his terms of alliance (submission) were crushed; those that did were rewarded. He used his wealth and influence to get his sons appointed as beys and even as valisi of the Morea. His arrogance and his power grew apace. During the Napoleonic Wars, he conducted unilateral foreign policy that on more than one occasion clashed with Istanbul's wishes. By the mid-1810s, petitioners from all faiths were appealing to Ali and not to the sultan to resolve their grievances.[5] So powerful had he become that he threatened the role of the emperor as the ultimate dispenser of eydalet (justice), a role at the heart of Ottoman imperial legitimacy. By 1820, Mahmud II and his close advisor, Mehmet Sayyd Halet Efendi, had managed to curb the power or to eliminate Balkan ayan who resisted the centre's attempt to impose its will, that is, to reverse decentralisation. It was now Ali's turn.

Using as a pretext a personal feud that had developed between Ali and Ismail Paseo Paşa, bey of Serres, Mahmud ordered Ali to appear before the Divan in Istanbul to give an account of his actions. He had until 1 June 1820 to comply with this directive. Ali knew it was a meeting from which he would not return. He thus refused to obey a direct order from his sovereign and so was declared an outlaw. Ismail Paşa was given authority to muster an army, levy a war tax and then to subdue the Lion of Ioannina. He was the wrong man for the job, having had negligible experience leading men in battle and commanding little respect from the other Balkan ayan. So, he made scant progress against Ali.

In the winter of 1820–1, he was relieved of his command and Hurşid Paşa, the Valisis of the Morea, was promoted to the rank of Serasker (commander-in-chief) of Rumeli, given a war-chest of one million piasters (US$ 20,000,000), and the authority to levy levend troops from no less than thirteen paşas. Hurşid was a formidable opponent. He had commanded the army that ended the Serbian rebellion, and before that he had performed outstandingly during the 1806–12 war with Russia. Also, having previously been grand vizier (1812–15), he knew how things worked in Istanbul and had valuable allies (and opponents) at court. Ayan formerly attached to Ali switched sides; military commanders like Omar Vryonis and Androutsos, along with their men, were persuaded by Hurşid's largess to join his army. Hurşid Paşa's elevation to commander of the army sent to defeat Ali had three important consequences. First, it assured the outcome: Ali would fall within a year. Second, the imposition of the war requisition tax on an already destitute and desperate peasantry elevated the level of mass discontent in the region to a new high. Paying the war tax was for many farmers and shepherds a life or death issue. Third, the mobilisation of so many warriors depleted the garrison forces along the Danubian frontier and in the Morea. Ali's war had presented the Philiki Etaireia with an opportunity. The time for planning was over; now was the time for action.

Ali Paşa had known of the existence of the Philiki Etaireia for some time. Indeed, some of his key advisors were high-ranking members of it. Recognising the need to forge alliances against the coming storm, Ali negotiated pacts with warrior groups like the Souliotes and various Albanian bandit gangs, and he made overtures to the leadership of the Etaireia. Each side saw an opportunity to achieve its objectives by cooperating with the other. There was also deep mutual distrust. The winter of 1820–1 was a busy time. Hurşid Paşa was gathering arms and mobilising his forces. Ali was bracing for the onslaught, promising much to his erstwhile allies, hoping thereby to retain their loyalty. The leadership of the Etaireia was endeavouring as best it could to coordinate the activities of agents and Apostles scattered across all of Southeastern Europe in an attempt to initiate a Balkan-wide uprising. Everything came together in the spring of 1821 for the Millet-i Rom to rise as one and to topple the Osmanli dynasty that had 'oppressed' it for 400 years.

1821: So it begins

From the start, the insurrectionary civil war that became the Greek War of Independence was a complicated and often messy affair. Later nationalist historiographies portray it as a far more coherent and coordinated event than it really was. In the spring of 1820, Alexander Ipsilantis became the supreme commander of the Philiki Etaireia. His selection signified two things; first, as he was a prominent member of the Russian military establishment with connections to the monarchy, it suggested that Russia would support the cause. Second, as a battle-hardened commander, it indicated that a military initiative might be in the offing (for a good, recent synopsis of Ipsilantis's career, see Stites 2014: 186–239). By this time, the society had acquired a large and diverse membership, which had its advantages and disadvantages. Of course, having more members, and especially wealthy and powerful ones, was a plus; but on the other hand, more leaders meant a greater diversity of aims and aspirations. Though the various leaders were in contact with one another, coordination was difficult because of poor communication, fear of capture, mutual distrust and conflicting goals. Nonetheless, over the course of 1820, a plan was taking shape.

Tepedelenli Ali Paşa's revolt changed everything. An Ottoman civil war would now be raging in the heart of the Balkans. The empire had to mobilise resources from officials and ayan throughout the Balkans in order to confront the renegade paşa, and this had to be done at time when Mahmud II and his grand vizier Halet Efendi had to worry about the loyalty of the Janissaries in Istanbul and the growing threat of war with the Shi'ite Qajar dynasty of Persia. By the end of summer, Ali had repulsed the initial attacks against him and he would, therefore, live to fight another day. Soon winter arrived and closed the Pindus mountain passes, thus giving him time to prepare his next year's campaign. This development along with the elevation of Hurşid Paşa to the position of commander-in-chief presented the Etaireia with a golden opportunity. At a meeting in the Bessarabian town of Ismail in November they formed their plan. Since Hurşid Paşa would undoubtedly bring the best of his troops from the Morea to fight Ali Paşa, it would be the ideal place to launch the insurrection. So, they decided that Ipsilantis and a small group of advisors would make their way to Trieste and from there to the Peloponnesos, where they would take up leadership of the revolt. But their plans soon changed.

In December, Alexander Soutzos, Hospodar of Wallachia, became deathly ill. Scion of a very prominent Phanariot family, he had occupied key positions in the Ottoman government for over twenty years. For many of those he was Hospodar of either Moldavia or Wallachia. He knew of the Etaireia and was not a supporter. His colleague across the border in Moldavia, Michalis Soutzos, was, and he had pledged his personal forces to the Etaireists. With Moldavia, the Ottoman province bordering Russia, secure and with a power vacuum forming in Wallachia, the Danubian Principalities now seemed a better choice of where to raise the banner of revolt. Their decision was made easier due to the fact that there was already present in the Principalities armed units ready to fight.

One force, under the command of Tudor (Theodore) Vladimirescu, was especially important. He was a military captain who had commanded a Romanian irregular force on behalf of the Russians during the 1806–12 war. Not only was he a battle-hardened commander, but he was also a Russian subject and a member of the Etaireia. A Greek warlord operating in southern Moldavia, Yiorgakis Olimbios, also had a substantial force under his command and he committed it to the cause. Finally, the Etaireist leadership remained firmly convinced that Milos Oberenoviç would bring Serbia and its massive militia into the fray. So, they decided to jump on the coat-tails of Ali's war. Assuming that the bulk of the Ottoman forces would be arrayed against Ioannina in the next campaigning season, they would foment rebellions by Christians in three regions – first, in the Danubian Principalities of Moldavia and Wallachia, then in the Peloponnesos and finally in Istanbul.

An uprising in the Peloponnesos was crucial. Its remoteness from the centre of the empire, the very high ratio of Christian to Muslims inhabitants, the number of powerful Greek kocabaşis resident there, and the considerable number of armed bands elevated the chances of the rebellion there being successful. It could then provide the rump of a Greek-Christian state. Riots in the streets of Constantinople would bring the rebellion right to the sultan's doorstep and this could perhaps trigger his overthrow – similar unrest had certainly led to the demise of more than one of his ancestors. In any case, the streets of the city would run red with blood, forcing the Orthodox patriarch to support the movement and, perhaps most importantly of all, compelling Russia to enter the fray on their behalf. The northern front, then, was the key.

The war in the north

On 31 January 1821, Alexander Soutzos died and his death triggered insurrection. Vladimirescu immediately issued a proclamation calling on the people of Wallachia to take up arms and join his rebellion. But against whom? Not the sultan. Tudor made it crystal clear in his proclamation, and he reinforced it in a letter that he sent to the Porte, that his revolt was not against the Osmanli dynasty or Islam. Instead he was calling on Wallachians to overthrow the oppressive regimes of the Greek Phanariots and the Romanian Boyars. The avaricious hospodars and their dependents had grown rich fleecing the province, while the land-owning boyars were bleeding the peasants dry. There has been much debate over what exactly Tudor's real intentions were. As a member of the Philiki Etaireia, he should have been calling for insurrection in the name of independence and freedom from the Ottoman *ancien régime* and not for the overthrow of the Phanariots, many of whom were fellow Etaireists. Was he cynically using the Etaireia as a springboard to catapult himself into power as prince of Romania after driving out the Romanian and Greek ruling class? Or was his proclamation a pretext, a way to get Romanian peasants, who would not otherwise do so, to join the fight for Greek-led independence (Tappe 1973: 139–40; Ilicak 2009: 327–90)? What is clear is that with his declaration open hostilities in Wallachia commenced. Rebellion in Moldavia would soon follow.

The early morning fog on the Pruth River was pierced by a ferry-boat crossing from the Russian to the Ottoman side. It was 6 March1821 and Alexander Ipsilantis, along with twenty of his closest advisors, was invading the Ottoman Empire. Resplendent in his general's uniform, the one-armed leader of the Philiki Etaireia disembarked from the ferry and set off for the Moldavian capital of Jassy. Upon arrival he met with hospodar Michailis Soutzos, who agreed to give him his support, placing his household guard under the general's command. Ipsilantis made it known that 70,000 Russians would soon be crossing the border. He issued his own proclamation, calling on everyone to join him and that with the assistance of a 'tremendous power', they would soon be free (Tappe 1973: 141; Ilicak 2009: 324).

Greek, Serbian, Albanian, Bulgarian and even some Romanian militiamen answered the call. Nicholas Ipsilantis, Alexander's younger brother, arrived from Russia with 800 infantrymen and engineers dressed in their black Russian uniforms (Ilicak 2009: 323). A few days later 1,200 members of the recently disbanded Greek militia of Odessa joined them. Then, Colonel Yiorgos Kantakouzinas appeared at the head of the Sacred Band, a special force made up of Greek students from the military academies in Odessa, Taganrog and Mariupol. A sizable force was taking shape, but everyone knew that it was not enough to take on the mighty Islamic Empire. And so all eyes turned to the city of Leibach (modern Llubljana in Serbia) where the leaders of Europe, including Tsar Alexander I, were meeting to discuss how they would deal with the rebellion that had broken out in Italy. What would Russia do and how would the Ottomans respond?

The answer came on 17 March and it was unequivocal. In dispatches to Russian diplomatic missions across the region, Alexander I made it crystal clear that he denounced the insurrection in the strongest terms. Vladimirescu was acting without Russian support and contrary to Russia's interests. He declared him a bandit, whom he stripped of his status as a Russian subject. At this juncture, Alexander had not yet learned of Ipsilantis's activities. When he did, however, he immediately issued a similar dispatch in which he denounced the violation of Ottoman space by Ipsilantis and his men and disavowed the insurrection. Underscoring that no Russian military aid would be forthcoming, three battalions of the Army of New Russia left for Italy, where they were to join with Austria in putting down the Italian uprising, and two others were sent to seal the border with the Ottoman Empire.

Yet, according to Lord Strangford, British ambassador to the Ottoman Empire, the Porte was willing to give Russia the benefit of the doubt, but they were still suspicious (Prousis 2010: 52). Their conviction that Russia was behind the uprising would only become firmer. The other development that shaped Ottoman perception of the insurrection was the massacre of the Muslim populations of Jassy and Galati, suggesting that this was not merely a protest against Ottoman misrule but was in fact a war of religion. And, if this was a war of Orthodoxy versus Islam, then how could Russia not become involved in its capacity as protector of Orthodox Christendom? To allay this fear, Gregory V, the Ecumenical Patriarch and Millet-başi of the Millet-i Rom, excommunicated anyone who joined or supported the insurrection. Russia and the church had, thus, forsaken the rebels in the north.

After the Russian denunciation, things went from bad to worse for the rebellion in the Principalities. Milos Obrenoviç announced that Serbia repudiated the uprising and would have nothing to do with it. Without the prospect of Russian assistance, rifts developed among the leadership of the rebellion, especially between Vladimirescu and Ipsilantis. By mid-April, the situation was becoming tenuous and perilous. Michalis Soutzos abandoned the cause and fled to Russia, and he was not the only one who was looking to get out. Because right around that time Russia agreed to allow the Ottoman army to invade Moldavia and Wallachia.

On 13 May, three divisions crossed the Danube, two entered Moldavia and one marched on Wallachia. Within a matter of weeks the Ottoman army had recaptured all of the major cities, including Bucharest. Faced now with impossible odds, various insurrectionary leaders looked to escape. Vladimirescu opened negations with the Porte and when this was discovered, Ipsilantis had him executed. The reason given was that he had violated his oath of membership to the Philiki Etaireia. The Etaireist army was isolated and trapped. The end came on 19 June when the Ottomans crushed it at the Battle of Dragatsani Bridge. Ipsilantis fled into Austria, where he was captured, imprisoned and died. His forces scattered. Some managed to escape back into Russia. Others remained in Moldavia, but by the end of summer they too were wiped out. The fighting in the north was at an end. The insurrection, however, was not.

The Morea in flames

Probably the most iconic image of the War of Independence is the scene of Bishop Germanos, the Metropolitan of Patras, raising the banner of revolution at the Monastery of Agia Lavra near Kalavryta. He is surrounded by many of the heroes of the movement as they swear an oath to achieve liberty or death. The day was supposedly 25 March (5 April on the Julian calendar) and so that date is still celebrated as Independence Day. The only problem is that the event never happened, and indeed, very little of note occurred on the twenty-fifth. It was the case, however, that a number of crucial, short- and long-term developments came together in late March and early April that led to uprisings first in the Morea and then all across Ottoman Europe, the Aegean Islands, Asia Minor and the Levant. The Morea and central Greece were, for a number of reasons, always the most propitious areas for a successful insurrection.

First, Christians outnumbered Muslims by a ratio of six to one. Moreover, the vast majority of the Muslim population was geographically concentrated in the towns. If the Christian population, or even a substantial portion of it, revolted, then the Muslim population would find itself outnumbered and isolated. Also, the Muslim population was split between those who were descendants of Greek converts and more recent immigrants, mostly from Albania. And there was no love lost between the two, with many Greek Muslims quite willing to acquiesce to the removal of the Albanians. Second, there was in place a leadership cadre (the Mora ayanlari consisting of kocabaşis and Muslim ayan) and an organisational structure (the councils of kocabaşis) that could lead a rebellion. Third, over the previous forty to fifty years, landholdings had become concentrated among a relatively small group of Christian and Muslim landowners and this meant that the preponderance of Greek Christian peasants had to eke out a living as best they could, combining sharecropping and other activities. The result was wide-spread and endemic poverty. Fourth, there were large numbers of men-at-arms who belonged to gangs, many of whom had experience fighting in militias during the Napoleonic Wars.

In the years just before 1821, a number of specific events or devel-opments in the Morea made the time ripe for rebellion. 1816 and 1820 were lean years for farmers; three consecutive bad crops compounded by the global depression that Europe experienced after the end of the Napoleonic Wars drove the already destitute peasantry to the brink. The imposition of the war requisition tax of 1820 pushed many over the edge. Not surprising given that, according to one estimate, the total tax burden on Christian peasants in the Morea increased by 261.5 per cent between 1820 and 1821 (Stathis 2007: 178, note 4).[6]

At a time when many were hungry and some even starving, they were also being asked to pay more to the state. Their anger was palpable and their rage made many ready to rebel. So too were the wealthy. The latter part of the 1810s saw power politics in the Peloponnesos become much more deadly. The jockeying for ascendency among Mora ayanlari and between them and the Ottoman establishment became more intense. Three kocabaşis factions in particular were in the eye of the storm. The Deliyiannis family and its supporters had achieved a paramount position by the early 1810s, only to find themselves locked in a struggle with their rivals, the Londos faction and the Perroukas faction. During the course of the decade, prominent members of each group were executed by order of a Mora valisis who backed one or the other factions. A compromise agreed to between the leading kocabaşis families in 1816 abated the internecine fighting somewhat, but this was a fragile peace (Stamatopoulos 2007; Pylia 2007; Fotopoulos 2005: 253–344; Pizanias 2003: 42–6).[7] Into this maelstrom, a new and potentially destabilising element was introduced: the Philiki Etaireia.

During 1819 and 1820, the society had been very active recruiting members in the Morea, and though notables never constituted more than a fraction of its membership, their participation was vital (Pizanias 2009b: 35). Gregoris 'Papaflessas' Dikaios was especially active in helping to organise and coordinate the society's activities in the region. The Mora ayanlari found themselves in a difficult situation. Joining the society, let alone participating in an insurrec-tion, carried with it potentially great rewards but also entailed lethal risks. Matters came to a head at a meeting convened by Papaflessas in Vostitsa in February 1821. It was the moment when the leaders of the great families had to make their intentions known. As one of the Perroukas brothers wrote: 'The kocabaşis from Kalavryta [Zaiamis], [Andreas] Londos from Vostitsa and Kanellos [Deliyiannis] from Karytaina, uncritically agreed with the orders of Papaflessa, and thoughtlessly began the recruitment of fighters, which brought the situation to this point [i.e., rebellion]' (cited in Stamtopoulos 2007: 160–1). By the spring of 1821 all of the factors necessary for successful insurrection were in place. One last development would lead to open rebellion.

In February as Hurşid Paşa was preparing to lead his troops north against Tepedelenli Ali Paşa and having heard rumours about possible riots or other forms of unrest, he issued an ultimatum to the heads of all of the major Christian Mora ayanlari that either they or one of their sons were to present themselves to Mehmed Salih, the kaimmakam (acting governor), to be held as hostages to vouchsafe their good conduct. The deadline was the Orthodox Feast of the Annunciation (25 March). Anyone who failed to do so would be proclaimed an outlaw, forfeiting his life and his property. Coupled with this demand was an imperial edict that all non-Muslims were to surrender their firearms to the nearest Ottoman garrison. Any Christian found in possession of a gun would be considered a criminal and would be executed. Now was the critical moment and men faced a fateful decision: compliance or insurrection. Most chose the latter.

Three days after the ultimatum lapsed, Petrobey Mavromihalis and the Messenian Senate issued a proclamation written by Alexandros Mavrogordatos that served as the Greek declaration of independence:

> The insupportable yoke of Ottoman tyranny has weighed down for over a century the unhappy Greeks of the Peloponnesos. So excessive had its rigours become, that its fainting victims had scarcely strength enough to utter groans. In this state, deprived of all our rights, we have unanimously resolved to take up arms against our tyrants ... Our mouths are opened; heretofore silent, or employed only in addressing useless supplications to our tormentors, they now celebrate a deliverance which we have sworn to accomplish, or else to perish. We invoke therefore the aid of all civilised nations of Europe, that we may the more promptly attain to the goal of a just and sacred enterprise, reconquer our rights, and regenerate our unfortunate

people. Greece, our mother, was the lamp that illuminated you; on this ground she reckons on your philanthropy. Arms, money, and counsel, are what she expects from you. We promise you her lively gratitude, which she will prove by deeds in more prosperous times. (Gordon 1832, vol. 1: 183)

Copies translated into all of the major European languages were delivered to the consular officers of the Great Powers in Patras for immediate transmittal to their respective governments. This declaration of insurrection only formalised an existing state of affairs. Over the previous weeks there had been sporadic episodes of violence. In Messenia, for example, a group of peasants attacked an Ottoman tax collector and his entourage. Formalisation, however, was important because it established a clear and unambiguous line between those who affirmed their loyalty to the Ottoman state and those who did not.

Rebellion spread like wildfire across the Peloponnesos. In the countryside, gangs of armed peasants attacked the estates of wealthy ayan, many of whom evacuated their properties and, along with other Muslims, they endeavored to make their way to an Ottoman-controlled fort. In some cases, Greeks whom they employed as their guards deserted, while in others, they actually assaulted their former bosses. The main focus of the rebels, however, was the fortresses and the Ottoman garrisons. Petrobey Mavromichalis and his men, for example, took the city of Kalamata and attacked the garrisons at Modoni and Koroni. Bishop Germanos at the head of a large contingent of Achaian peasants marched on Patras. Theodoros Kolokotronis led a sizable force of veteran fighters against the capital city of Tripolis (Alexander 2010). Within weeks, the Morean countryside had been cleansed of Muslims and Jews who either fled or were slaughtered and every Ottoman garrison (Nafplion, Monemavasia, Acrocorinth and Mistras) was under siege. Only Yussuf Bey, Ayan of Corinth, and his force of about 1,000 men remained at large, engaging Greek insurgents in Achaia and the Corinthia. By the middle of April, the Greek rebels had secured most of the Morea.

Why was the insurrection in the Morea so much more successful than the one in the Danubian Principalities, for example? Some factors, like the skewed ratio of Christians to Muslims, have already been mentioned. The one that I think was most important, however, was the greater preponderance of people who joined the insurrection. Why was this? First we have to appreciate that different people participated or not for different reasons. Some, especially amongst the business, merchant and educated classes, were motivated by nationalism and liberal ideals. Others saw a chance to advance themselves materially and politically. But the key question is why did so many peasants take up arms and slaughter their former landlords and neighbours? Few of them even knew of, let alone espoused, the ideas of the Enlightenment. A clue can be found in the peasant language of rebellion. When they marched on Patras, Achaian peasants chanted as their war cry 'Freedom, freedom in the name of Christ' (Ελευθερία, ελευθερία διά πίσι Χριστού) (Stefanini 1829: 50). Freedom to them, I suspect, was not some abstract ideal relating to civil liberties and rights but rather freedom from oppression and exploitation by landlords and tax collectors. Equally important was the second part of their chant: in the name of Christ. To them this was a religious struggle. As Marios Hatzopoulos (2009; 2011) has shown, peasant understandings of the pre-war developments were grounded in folktales, omens and prophecies. What motivated the peasants to rebel were bread, land and religion (Theotokas and Kotaridis 2006: 29–40). And so in the Morea it was a mass revolt and not just the rising of a few notables and their gangs.

Soon the rebellion spread across the Balkans and the Eastern Mediterranean as community after community decided to join the cause. By mid-April most of the Greek and Albanian Christian villages of Boiotia and Attica had risen, soon followed by those in western Greece (Aitolia and Akarnania). In June, Greek Athenians rose up and besieged the Ottoman garrison on the Acropolis. The Aegean islands, beginning with Hydra, Poros and Spetses were not far behind. Greeks on Cyprus and Crete attacked Ottoman forces and Muslim civilians (Andriotis 2003). To the north, the banner of rebellion was unfurled in Thessaly and Macedonia. To be sure, there were Greek communities that decided not to rebel. On the rich and prosperous island of Chios, the Orthodox leadership denounced the rebellion and pledged their loyalty to the Ottoman government. The collective leadership on the Catholic islands of the Cyclades, such as Tinos, Syros, Thera and others, did so as well. Nonetheless, by the summer of 1821 the Ottoman government was confronted with insurrections from the Danubian region in the north to Crete in the south, and from the Adriatic Sea in the west to the shores of the Levant in the east. As well as having to deal with the civil war against Tepedelenli Ali Paşa and an invasion by Persia along its eastern frontier, the empire faced widespread insurrection in its heartland.

The empire responded vigorously, and in many areas effectively, to these challenges. The Greek uprisings in areas such as Thessaly and Macedonia, where the Ottomans had sizable military forces, were easily put down. As we have already seen, by the end of summer the insurrection in the north had been completely crushed. While fighting persisted slightly longer, the rebellions on Crete and Cyprus were also largely extinguished. The same could have happened in the Morea and central Greece but for the actions of Odysseus Androutsos and a few other Rumelian armatole captains. Soon after intelligence about the uprising in the Peloponnesos reached him, Hurşid Paşa dispatched Omar Vryonis, an Albanian ayan and former military captain to Tepedelenli Ali Paşa, with 6,000 infantry and 300 cavalry to relieve the besieged garrisons and to suppress the uprisings. Leaving his base in the city of Lamia on 23 April, Vryonis drove a Greek rebel force from the Alamana Bridge on the River Sprechios, thus opening the road down the east coast of central Greece to Boiotia and then Attica. However, he did not want to proceed southward through the famous pass of Thermopylae without first securing his right flank from ambushes, and so he marched his army to the upland basin on the west side of Mount Kallidromo. There at a khan (or inn) near the village of Gravia he encountered Androutsos. Though badly outnumbered, the Rumelian captain inflicted enough damage on the Ottoman force to compel Vryonis to retreat to Lamia and to regroup. Later that summer (25 August), he marched south once more and yet again he was repulsed. Greek forces laid a carefully designed ambush in the narrow pass of Vassilika and scored a stunning victory. Vryonis had no choice but to retreat, and with the end of the campaigning season coming soon, another assault on the rebels would have to wait. By the end of 1821, the Greek insurrection that erupted all across the Ottoman Empire had been largely suppressed. The Danubian Principalities had been secured. The rebels in Rumelia were routed. Tepedelenli Ali Paşa was hanging on for dear life. Due to the heroic efforts of a few warlords and their men, however, central Greece and the Peloponnesos remained in rebel hands. The leadership of the rebellion there now had time to consolidate its gains, establish a functioning government and prepare for the assault that would surely come in 1822.

Ottoman response

How did the Ottomans perceive the events of 1821 and how did they act on their perceptions?[8] Based on Ottoman archival materials it is clear that their initial responses to the news that Ipsilantis had invaded the empire and then to the news that members of the Millet-i Rom all across the empire were rising up in rebellion were: (1) shock and surprise and (2) a firm belief that Russia was behind the whole thing. It appears that the central government in Istanbul knew very little about the incipient rebellion, and it had learned about it only at the last minute. Two weeks before Ipsilantis invaded the Danubian Principalities, the Ottoman authorities captured a man named Aristides Papas. He was a messenger bringing Milos Obrenoviç of Serbia dispatches from Ipsilantis. Under torture, he revealed even more about the planned uprising. Based on information extracted from Papas, the Porte learned about 'a very secret plot ... that had been in the making for many years to rise the Greeks up in order to trample upon the Muslims' (Ilicak 2009: 322; the quote is taken from a report to the government based on Papas's interrogation). But it appears that they knew little else beyond this.

So, if the uprisings were the surprise, then who was revolting was the shock. That it was the Greeks, and specifically the Phanariots, who were leading the rebellions especially infuriated the Ottoman leadership. That Phanariots were in charge seemed obvious. The Ipsilantis brothers and other Greek members of the Russian military were Phanariots. As was Michalis Soutsos, Hospodar of Moldavia. The Phanariot conspiracy, in their view, reached into the very heart of the Ottoman government. Theodoris Negris, for example, a dragoman in the Porte, was on a ship bound for Paris where he was to take up the position of Ottoman ambassador when the rebellion broke out. That Negris broke off his journey and declared for the uprising was positive proof of just how high the Phanariot conspiracy went. This led Mahmud II and his advisors to believe that the insurrectionists aimed at seizing Istanbul itself.

The Ottomans viewed the Greeks in general and the Phanariots in particular as the chosen people amongst infidels. Phanariots and kocabaşis had, in their view, flourished through their participation in shared governance. Greeks occupied key and powerful positions in government, a policy that in the past had raised the ire of many Muslims. So the Ottoman perception of the rebellion in April 1821 was that it was a Phanariot-led uprising and that 'the aim of the infidels was to inflame the peaceful reaya and, God forbid, to annihilate all Muslims' (Ilicak 2009: 328; the passage comes from an imperial firman to the governors of all of the Ottoman provinces). The Ottomans, then, viewed the events of spring 1821 as both an attempted coup d'état and a religious war.

The Ottoman state's initial responses were shaped by this perception. First, the government issued an imperial firman commanding all Muslims to arm themselves and ordering all members of the Millet-i Rom to disarm. Guided by Shariat law, the Şeyhülislam promulgated a Fatwa stating that any Christians who joined the rebellion violated that Dimmi pact and so could be killed with impunity, their property confiscated and their families enslaved. Since it was nearly impossible to know who did or did not support the revolution, any Greek became fair game. And the violence against Greeks, especially in Istanbul and Smyrna, only increased as news of the slaughter of Muslims in the Principalities and in the Morea became known. Examples, such as this one recorded by an eye-witness in Istanbul, became commonplace:

> An unfortunate Greek had ventured out to a baccul, or huckster's shop, for some article, and was hastily returning, when he met a Turk who was walking just before me. The Greek pressed himself up to the wall as close as possible to let him pass, when the Turk, deliberately drawing his yataghan, pinned him to the place where he stood. The poor man fell dead on his face, and his assassin walked over his body, and, wiping his bloody yataghan, entered a coffeehouse, where I afterwards saw him quietly smoking his chibouk. (Walsh 1836: 306; for an account of the violence in Smyrna, see Prousis 1992)

Not knowing which Greeks it could trust, the government trusted none. This was especially true for Phanariots and the leadership of the Orthodox Church. The Ecumenical Patriarch and Millet-başi of the Rom, Gregory V, was brutally executed on Easter Sunday, 22 April 1821, even though he excommunicated the rebels (Fig. 3.2). The reasons were, first, as leader of the Orthodox Church and head of the Orthodox community, he was responsible for ensuring that his flock remained subservient to the state, and in this he failed. That he was detected helping prominent Phanariots escape to Russia and that he was from Karytainia, one of the centres of the rebellion in the Morea, only elevated suspicions about his loyalty. So, like other high-ranking Ottoman officials, including the Grand Vizier Benderli Ali Paşa and Mahmud's closest advisor Halet Efendi, who failed in their jobs, he paid for his failure with his life.[9]

Figure 3.2 The execution of Patriarch Gregorios V in 1821 © Von Hess 1836, Wikimedia Commons.

April and May witnessed a pogrom against Greeks in Istanbul. In some cases, the people executed were implicated in the rebellion, but in most, they were not. The Greeks were caught in a no-win situation: if they stayed in the city, they were open to attack. If they tried to escape and were captured, then this proved that they supported the insurrection, and so faced execution or exile. Hundreds of prominent Greek politicians and clergymen were killed and thousands more were exiled to towns in central and southern Anatolia. By the end of summer, however, Ottoman policy changed. Only Greeks who were openly in revolt were targeted; any others who averred their loyalty to the state had their rights restored, including their right to life, own property, and to be free from enslavement. Partly this change in policy was due to the collapse of the Danubian rebellion and the suppression of the insurrections everywhere except the Morea and the islands, and partly it was due to pressure exerted by European powers, especially Russia.

In no uncertain terms, Alexander I denounced Ipsilantis's invasion and the Greek rebellion. Yet, Mahmud and his advisors still harboured deep suspicions that Russia was the hidden hand behind both. There was just too much circumstantial evidence of Russian involvement for them to think otherwise. The Russian army, for example, clearly seemed to be actively supporting the rebels. Most of the officers in Ipsilantis's army had served or were still serving in it and maintained close relations with their comrades. Indeed, Ipsilantis himself, and presumably others as well, did not resign his commission but instead sought and was granted a two years' leave of absence (Bitis 2006: 99). The rebel army in the Principalities was dressed in Russian uniforms and fought with Russian arms. According to one source, Papas, the captured courier discussed above, the general staff of the Russian Second Army in Bessarabia were advising Ipsilantis and were present when he gave him the dispatches (Bitis 2006: 22–4). That he was able to muster men and arms in Odessa and then to march freely across New Russia indicated to the Ottomans that Russian civilian officials, at best, turned a blind eye to these activities and, at worst, condoned them. In other parts of the empire where revolts took place, Greeks in the Russian consular service played leading roles. Surely, Ottoman leaders surmised, St Petersburg must know of these activities and yet did nothing to stop them. Then, lastly, there was the fact the authorities in New Russia continued to allow refugees, including known rebel supporters like Michalis Soutsos, to enter Russia and refused to extradite them when asked.

The Ottomans were correct in believing that key Russian institutions, like the church and the military, and the Russian people supported the Greeks. It was the court of St Petersburg that was out of touch. But that soon changed. The official Russian policy as determined by the Tsar and the Foreign Ministry moved closer to the view held by its people. Two developments led to this policy shift. The first was the executions of hundreds of members of the Orthodox Church hierarchy. These killings, as well as the other evidence that this was becoming a religious conflict, compelled the leadership of the Russian Orthodox Church to lobby the Tsar to intervene in support of their co-religionists. The other was the heightening tensions over the issue of whether or not the Ottomans could seize and search Russian vessels in Ottoman waters to determine if they were conveying rebels seeking to escape or carrying contraband supplies destined for the rebel forces. In the summer of 1821 these two issues almost led to another Ottoman-Russian war, which, of course, was what the Philiki Etaireia wanted all long. But that did not happen. The two sides reached a testy compromise, something that was made easier when Mahmud altered his policy regarding who could be persecuted. This uneasy Ottoman-Russian accommodation meant that the Greek rebels were on their own to face the empire's wrath in 1822.

The critical years

The fateful year of 1821 ended with the Greek rebellion against the Osmali dynasty hanging on by a thread and 1822 did not start well. In February Hurşid Paşa captured and beheaded Tepedelenli Ali Paşa. With that war over, Hurşid could turn his attention to affairs in the south. But political opponents in Istanbul accused him of stealing part of Ali's fortune and so he was ousted, and in fact committed suicide, and a new man was put in charge: Mehemd Dramali Paşa. He was from a prominent Thracian ayan family and he was one of Hurşid's commanders in the war against Tepedelenli Ali Paşa. From his base in Yanya he planned the summer campaign that would end the Greek rebellion. He would command one army that would march down the east coast of Greece through Boiotia and Attica, relieving the Ottoman garrisons along the way. Then, he would cross the Isthmus and rescue the men trapped in the impregnable fortress of Acrocorinth. From there he could launch an assault on Nafplion, where the Ottoman forces were still trapped in the fortress of Pelamydes, and where the leadership of the Greek rebel state was located. While he was doing this, Omar Vryonis, his second in command, was to lead a force down the west side of Greece and then, after capturing the fort at Messolonghi, he was to cross the channel and retake Patras. The two armies would then converge on Tripolis. Dramali was confident that the rebellion would be over by the autumn, and in this, he was completely wrong (Map 3.1).

At the head of a force of 12,000 infantry, 600 regular cavalry and 200 deli cavalry (light armed skirmishers), Dramli left Larissa in early July. Initially the plan worked perfectly. He was able to seize control of the coastal and inland roads by either driving off the Greek forces

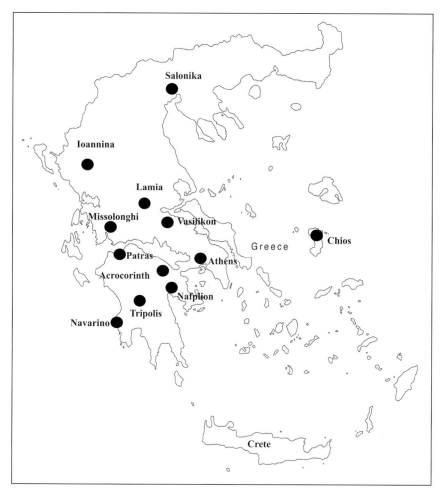

Map 3.1 Key sites during the War of Independence.

or negotiating a peaceful settlement. His forces swept across the plains of Boiotia and he bypassed Athens in the belief that others would soon relieve it. Quickly marching southward, he took the Isthmus and marched on Corinth, driving off the Greek rebel forces. By 17 July, he secured Acrocorinth as his base of operations. In addition, he was now joined by local ayan like Yusuf Hali Bey of Corinth and their men who had been fighting in Patras. Giving his troops only a brief rest, one week later Dramali crossed the mountains that separate the Corinthia and the Argolid and marched on Nafplion. Believing that the Greeks would surrender, flee or fight and lose, he planned on a very quick campaign. Consequently, he did not outfit his army adequately with supplies. This he did over the objections of Yusuf Hali Bey and other locals who warned him that once he crossed the mountains he would be dangerously exposed and could be easily cut off from his base of operations. They cautioned him to wait until the Ottoman fleet arrived in the Corinthian Gulf, because it could support his efforts from the sea and could keep his forces supplied. Their advice fell on deaf ears.

Marching through the narrow defiles, his forces entered the Argolid. While doing so he made his most serious mistake: he failed to post guards to protect the mountain passes. Contrary to his expectation, the Greeks would not face him in battle on the plain. Instead, they divided their forces into three groups. One, under Dimitrios Ipsilantis marched south and encamped at the Mills on the coast road. Kolokotronis mobilised a sizable force in the mountains on the western side of the plain, and Papaflessa and Nikitas Stamatelopoulos concentrated their men in the mountains to the east of the plain. A deadly trap was forming. Greek peasants burnt their crops and spoiled their wells before taking refugee in the city. Dramali could neither compel the Greek troops to give battle nor could he take the city by force. As his supplies dwindled, he had no choice but to retreat.

On 8 August he walked into the trap. The Greeks had blocked the Dervanaki pass and arrayed their men on the heights above the narrow road through the mountains. It was a slaughter. Dramali and about 800 men made it out alive. Dramali committed suicide rather than face disgrace and what was left of his army fled north, harassed by rebel forces along the way. Eastern Greece and the Morea were now secure.

So too was the west. Alexander Mavrogordatos at the head of a force consisting of Greek bands and Western mercenaries confronted Vryonis and his army at place called Peta, near the city of Arta. Vryonis won a Pyrrhic victory. Though he won the battle and slaughtered most of the Western mercenaries, he lost both men and time. The former was less important than the latter because it gave him too little time to compel the fortress at Messolonghi to surrender before winter set in and threaten his supply line. Consequently, he had to lift the siege and return to Ioannina.

1822 witnessed two other major developments that had a profound impact on the revolution. The first of these was a series of naval victories. Before the rebellion, Greeks were an essential element of the Ottoman fleet. Most of the ship captains and many of the sailors were Greek islanders. When the rebellion broke out, large numbers of them deserted and a few captains even commandeered their ships. Wealthy Greek merchants placed their vessels at the service of the rebel navy. In 1822, the Greeks scored a number of notable victories. The most important of these took place near the island of Tenedos, where Captain Konstantinos Kanaris sank the flagship of the Ottoman fleet. With their successes at sea, the Greeks ensured that supplies and war materials could reach the rebel army on land, while at the same time impairing the empire's ability to relieve its besieged troops in the Morea. In response, Mahmud invited Barbary corsairs to enter the war with the promise of riches from plunder and slave trading. The war at sea, of course, disrupted commerce in the Eastern Mediterranean and, as we shall see, this became a concern for European powers, especially Great Britain. Another event in 1822 captured Europe's attention: the massacre of the Greeks of Chios.

Chios was one of the wealthiest and most prosperous Greek islands. It owed its prosperity to its monopoly on the production of mastic, to being home to numerous successful commercial firms, and to its strategic location. The island was one of those places that was so important that the Ottoman state granted it special concessions, and in this case, one of those was home rule. When the rebellion erupted, the Greek leadership, both secular and sacred, declared against it and affirmed the islanders' continued loyalty to the state. Mahmud demanded and received approximately 100 hostages, most of them from the island's most prominent families. The Chian leadership may have spoken for the community collectively but not for all of its members. Many Chians supported the rebellion; some, like Adamantios Korais, did so from afar with their pens, while others closer to home took up arms. There was still unrest in the Eastern Aegean and it centred on the nearby island of Samos. A rebel contingent plundered a number of villages on the coast of Asia Minor and even attacked the Muslim quarter in the town of Chios, looting and burning houses there. So a force was dispatched to deal with it. As an eyewitness recalled, he

> saw a colossal Armada advancing, with its bloody standard [the red Ottoman flag] beckoning to us in the breeze. Seven ships of the line stood before us like monsters of the deep. Twenty-six frigates and corvettes accompanied by smaller craft and innumerable boats, rolled towards us like a gilded tide of devastation. (Castanis 2002 [1851]: 26)

Thirsting for revenge for the mass killings of Muslims, Kara Ali's troops stormed the island. By the time they were finished as many as perhaps 100,000 people lay dead or in the hands of slave traders. News of the massacre quickly spread far and wide, prompting cries of outrage from the governments of Europe. The fact that the Grand Vizier and the Şeyhülislam vehemently denounced the killings and even executed Kara Ali mattered little (Aksan 2007: 292). Some members of the British parliament called for military intervention and the position of the war party in St Petersburg became even stronger. The massacre on Chios did more to generate popular support for the Greek rebellion than anything else. Nonetheless, the official policy of the Great Powers remained non-intervention throughout 1822 and 1823 (Rodogno 2012: 66–72 on the British and French responses and Prousis 1994: 61–2). Their view continued to be that the war was a conflict between a sovereign state and a group of disgruntled subjects. If the insurrection was to result in independence, then the Greeks needed to establish a state of their own.

Impaired governance

As we have seen, Greeks had been actively participating in local governance for a long time; the important point here is 'local'. At the time of the revolution, there did not exist any institutional structures that bound together the elites from each locality or region. This intense localism, combined with the fact that many of the kocabaşis participating in the rebellion had been political rivals, made forging a united revolutionary leadership extremely difficult. Cleavages regarding the political goals of the war existed among the Greek rebel leadership from the start, and the rifts only became deeper and more diverse as Greeks from the diaspora, from the disbanded court of Tepedelenli Ali Paşa, and from the Phanariot community of Istanbul arrived in the Peloponnesos. As Douglas Dakin has noted:

> The [indigenous] Greek upper classes wanted Ottoman society without the Turks, the military classes [kapoi and armatoli] wanted to carve out for themselves so many independent satrapies and become miniature Ali Paşas [sic], while the lower orders simply desired to improve their lot, escape taxation, to own and increase the size of their plots and to move up the social scale. (Dakin 1973: 78)

In addition, there were the Greeks of the diaspora who flocked to the 'motherland' with heads filled with republican ideologies and dreams of a resurrected democratic past. Keeping these competing and disparate interests together proved one of the greatest challenges of the war.

All parties agreed on a few issues. That political victory, in the form of independence, required Great Power intervention was one. Another was that they had yet to face the full might of the Ottoman Empire, and that they had to take advantage of the Porte's indecisiveness. A third was that they needed desperately and quickly money and arms. As we have seen, a cold wind blew from St Petersburg, and in the context of the ongoing political unrest in Portugal, Spain, Piedmont, Naples, and Belgium, the governments of London, Paris, and Vienna were equally unsympathetic to the Greek cause. The maintenance of the status quo and the concert of Europe were paramount. In order to garner the support of the Western powers, the Greek leadership had to declare unilaterally their independence and promulgate a constitution creating a government, which could then open negotiations with the Great Powers. All the while they had to cast their cause not as a national struggle based on liberal principles, which would have won them few supporters in post-Napoleonic Europe, but as a religious conflict between an oppressed Christian population and their Islamic oppressors.

Shortly after the insurrection began, the Maniate chieftain Petrobey Mavromichalis convened a congress in Kalamata to draft a constitution and establish a government. Representing almost exclusively the Peloponnesian kocabaşis, the congress created a senate, called the Messenian Senate (Μεσσηνιακή Σύγκλητος) and elected Petrobey as president. Neither enjoyed much legitimacy anywhere else in Greece. The kapetanoi and men doing the fighting felt that they had been cheated out of power. Dimitris Ipsilantis, brother of Alexander, claimed that he spoke for the Philiki Etaireia and refused to accept the writ of the new government. Finally, as other areas of Greece became liberated the leadership there formed their own ruling councils. In the northern Peloponnesos there was the Achaian Directorate (Αχαϊκόν Διευθυντήριον), while in Greece north of the Isthmus there were the Organisation of Western Greece (Οργανισμός της Δυτικής Χέρσου Ελλάδος) and the Legal Command of Eastern Greece (Νομική Δίαταξεις της Ανατολικής Χέρσου Ελλάδος) (Papageorgiou 2003: 67–8). Each of these adopted their own constitution and organisation. If the revolution was to have any chance of success, this fragmentation of political leadership had to be remedied.

To deal with this unacceptable situation a National Congress at which all parties would be represented was convened in Epidavros in December 1821. After weeks of intense debate, Alexandros Mavrokordatos, Theordoros Negris, and an Italian lawyer, Vincenzo Gallina, presented the assembly with a provisional constitution, roughly modelled on the French constitution of 1795, which the delegates passed. The new Greek state was to be a democratic republic founded on the principles of civil liberties and equality for all. Moreover, it was explicitly an Orthodox Christian nation-state. As the preamble states, it is 'the Hellenic (Greek) nation' [το Ελληνικόν Έθνος] that has risen against 'the terrible Ottoman dynasty' and that now declared the existence of its own independent state. But who belonged to the nation and the state?

Religion was certainly a critical element. The very first article of the constitution specified that 'the official religion in the Greek state is the Eastern Orthodox Church of Christ' but that other religions would be tolerated. The fact that almost the entire Muslim and Jewish populations had already been expunged from the territory of the new state made this a moot point, meaning that this clause was only really applicable to the Catholic islanders. Article Two defined who belonged to the body politic. According to Section 1 of Article Two: 'All indigenous inhabitants of the state of Greece who believe in Christ are Greeks, and they enjoy all political rights without distinction.' In this formulation, then, Greekness was defined by residence and religion.

A second clause provided for the inclusion of those who had come to territory of Greece and now resided there. This definition of citizenship proved problematic as the territories under the control of the provisional administration continued to change, meaning that one moment a person could be 'indigenous' but not at the next. Moreover, Christians of various 'ethnicities' – such as Albanian, Vlach and Serbian – resided in the 'liberated' territories and were participating in the rebellion, and so by this definition they were Greeks. The criteria for Greek citizenship remained problematic for decades to come.

The provisional charter also specified the organisational structure of the government. The former Ottoman kazas were reframed as eparchies (counties) and each eparchy was to elect a senator. The senate had legislative powers and the authority to elect five of its members to constitute the executive branch. The term of the senate was one year. The executive appointed the heads of the eight ministries, none of whom could be senators. Mavrokordatos was elected as the first president. The new government's main goals were to mobilise the peasantry and prosecute the war, press the Greeks' appeal for assistance from the West, and end the factional squabbling. It succeeded somewhat with the first but failed utterly with the others.

A Second National Congress was called in April 1823 to modify the constitution and elect a new government. The Peloponnesians, and especially the military captains, dominated this session. The new charter revised the structural organisation of the government and modified the power and procedures of some of it branches. It also changed the citizenship criteria, introducing language. The new formula gave Greek nationality and citizenship rights to non-native Christians residing in areas that had joined the insurrection so long as their mother tongue was Greek and so long as they expressed their desire to become a Greek citizen in front of a revolutionary govern-ment authority. But this formula was also problematic. There were people in groups in the liberated territories, some of whom played prominent roles, for whom Greek was not their mother tongue. This definition also raised serious problems with respect to people who continued to reside in the Ottoman Empire but who considered them-selves to be ethnically Greek. And so the problem of defining who belonged to the Greek nation and who was entitled to citizenship rights in the new state remained problematic.

As to the political consequences of the second National Congress, Morean kocabaşis and military captains dominated the new govern-ment with Petrobey as president and Kolokotronis as his vice-president. The virtual exclusion of leaders from western and central Greece and of Western-orientated diaspora Greeks doomed this national government as well. Unity was absent even within the provisional national government. Frustrated by the actions of members of the executive council, who were not military men, Kolokotronis seized and imprisoned them. Open conflict between factions in the government erupted soon thereafter. This lack of political unity was to prove very costly.[10]

1824 marked a pivotal point in the war. Financially, the situation was becoming dire and so, in order to sustain the war effort, the provisional government contracted hefty loans from the London financial market (Chatziioannou 2013: 33–55, see especially 44–5; a second loan was contracted in 1825, and this marked the beginning of the Greek indebtedness). Militarily, the gains of the previous three years soon began to slip away and were finally lost as various factions turned on one another in what became ironically a civil war within a civil war. What were the causes of these divisions and who constituted the various factions? The first and largest group, of course, was the common people. The peasants who had initially joined in the fighting lost their enthusiasm as the war dragged on. They had not signed on to serve garrison duty besieging walled towns, especially not while land was lying free for the taking back home. Many returned to their farms and villages to reap the immediate benefits of the departure of Ottoman landlords. The first of these was land. Muslim proprietors or the Ottoman state owned the majority of the land and with the forced departure of the former and political separation from the latter, plentiful land was available for the taking. Families occupied evacuated land as squatters. But this set them on a collision course with the Provisional Administration, which claimed that deserted Ottoman land belonged to the state as national land. These properties were, after all, one of the few material resources that the revolutionary government had at its disposal.

Another source of tension between the peasantry and the state was taxes. One of the major sources of discontent amongst the rural population had been the high level of Ottoman taxes. Even though now taxes were an expression of the social contract between equal citizens and their state and not exactions forced on them as oppressed subjects, and even though the overall tax burden was substantially lower than it had been under the Ottoman Empire, many peasants still resented the new levies and contested paying them. Compounding the tax issue was the fact that the peasantry bore the burden of feeding the revolutionary military, whether they wanted to or not. The sources report numerous episodes where armed gangs of Greek fighters descended on a village and 'requisitioned', that is, seized, food and animals. The result of these developments was that the peasantry deeply distrusted the revolutionary state and many withdrew from hostilities (Bozikis 2011).

This left the fighting to be done by the bands of irregulars, former bandits and armatoles. While they could be an effective guerrilla fighting force, they were ill suited for sustained, disciplined military campaigns; they owed their allegiance to their captain; and they were largely interested in pay and booty. After the Jewish and Muslim populations had been driven out of the war zones and their properties plundered, there was no one else left to loot and get booty from – except fellow Greeks or ships at sea. This meant that the men who constituted the rebel military expected to be paid by the revolutionary state. Pay for the fighters placed an enormous fiscal burden on the Provisional Administration, and one that it often could not bear. Warriors looked to their captains to get them their pay and this obviously created great tensions between the military leadership and the government. When monies were not forthcoming, some captains gladly accepted Ottoman piastres and switched sides. This meant that one day's allies became the next day's enemies.

Politically, the tensions between the Peloponnesian faction and the one made up of islanders, diaspora Greeks, and men from central Greece increased to the point where the revolutionary government fractured. The faction that was technically the lawful government based on the Second National Assembly and led by Mavromichalis and Kolokotronis relocated the capital to Tripolis. This led to Koundouriotis and Mavrokordatos and their group declaring that they constituted the only legal government of liberated Greece. Civil war erupted, further jeopardising the future of the revolution. Captains loyal to one faction fought against those attached to others, refraining a pattern of behaviour that had plagued the region from the 1770s onwards. This internecine conflict cost Greece some of its best military leaders, like Odysseus Androutsos who was betrayed by his closest friend. The civil war put in jeopardy all of the gains of the previous three years. Internationally, however, for a variety of reasons, in 1824 the Greek cause became far more visible and took on a new importance in the diplomatic deliberations of the Great Powers. One of the great ironies of the war was that success was achieved at a time when the Greeks were in fact losing on almost all fronts because of self-inflicted wounds.

Philhellenism

On 5 January 1824, Lord Byron arrived in liberated Greece. He had been on the scene for some time, residing on the British-protected Ionian Islands. But his actual arrival on Greek soil was rife with both practical and symbolic importance. The Greek War of Independence touched a chord in Western Europe and North America in ways that none of the other post-Napoleonic liberal revolutions did. Imbued with a feeling of Romanticism, Christian humanitarianism and a burgeoning sense of neoclassicism, men such as Lord Byron found a 'noble cause' in the Greek struggle against the Ottoman Empire (Beaton 2013 is the best account of Byron's activities in Greece). Philhellenes, as these men and women came to be called, were a very mixed lot but all together they played a critical role in the war (Droulia 2003; Klein 2000; Komis 2003).

One of the earliest and most important groups of Philhellenes was made up of military men. Almost all of these were soldiers who had fought in national armies during the conflicts that had raged from the mid-1790s and who were left without a war since the demise of Napoleon (Rodriguez 2009). Some came out of an admiration for the Greeks and others for more complicated reasons. The case of Nikolai Raiko captures the sentiments that motivated many. He was a Russian military officer who went to Greece to fight in 1822. After having distinguished himself many times in battle, he stayed in Greece after independence and was rewarded by President Kapodistrias, who made him military governor of Patras. After returning to Russia later in life, he explained that he joined the rebellion because of the 'the news of the feats [of my] coreligionists' and by 'a sense of national honor to aid the Greeks' (Prousis 1994: 52). His sentiments of religion and honour were widely shared by many. Another group of fighters who flocked to the Greek cause were revolutionaries whose own movements had been suppressed in their own country, such as the many men who belonged to the Italian Carbonari movement (Pecout 2004). Foreign freemasons supported the cause through groups such as Les Enfants Adoptifs de Sparte et d'Athénes which brought together French, Italian, Swiss and German freemasons (Rizopoulos and Rizopoulos 2008: 211). Then, of course, there were mercenaries who joined the Greek side for money. Foreign Philhellene soldiers played an important part in the war, especially after 1825.

Romanticism and Christian humanitarianism motivated many idealistic European and American young men either to go to Greece and to join the conflict or to remain at home supporting the Greeks by raising money and by lobbying with their respective governments. Romanticism's glorification of ancient Greek culture easily elided into eager support for the oppressed, 'enslaved' and debased contemporary Greeks. Leading Romantic artists and writers, such as Lord Byron in England and Alexander Pushkin in Russia, lent their names, gave money, and, in some cases, their lives, in support of the Greek cause (Güthenke 2008; Beaton 2013; Prousis 1994: 84–157). Their vision was shared by countless university students who had been reared on the Classics and who had embraced liberalism. Disillusioned by the stifling intellectual environment of conservative counter-revolutionary Europe, they saw in the Greek uprising a great and noble cause: to repay the debt that the West owed to the Greeks. As Rufus Anderson, an American evangelical Philhellene put it:

> The names of the learned Greeks are embalmed in history who … brought the philosophy and literature of their forefathers into Italy [the West]. A like renown awaits the benevolent pious men, who shall take the lead in carrying back to Greece the improvements of Western Europe and America. (Anderson 1832: 23; for more examples of American views on the revolution, see Hatzidimitriou 1999)

Anderson epitomises the other dimension of Philhellenism: religion and Christian humanitarianism. The Greek rebellion was to these people both a religious war, pitting enlightened Christianity against 'barbaric' Islam, as well as an epochal clash of civilisations. Philhellenic organisations such as the British London Committee (founded in 1823), the French Comité Grec (1825), and the American Board of Commissioners for Foreign Missions were responsible for raising monies to support the insurgents, bringing the conflict to the attention of the wider world, and for keeping it there until the Great Powers could be cajoled into intervening. But would that intervention come in time to save the revolution?

The empire strikes back

By the end of 1824, it was clear to Mahmud II and his inner circle that a new approach was needed to crush the Greek insurrection. The sultan remained as wedded as ever to the plan to destroy the Greek rebellion by 'fire and sword', but it had become painfully obvious that the old-style military, based on Janissaries, deli cavalry, and irregulars, was obsolete and ineffective (Aksan 2009). A complete overall of the war machine was required but this would take time and money, and he was running short of both. Moreover, he knew from hard experience and from the example of what happened to his predecessor, Selim III, that reforming the military, especially the Janissaries, was a venture fraught with danger. He had for a long time harboured a desire to modernise the Ottoman army by introducing Western military organisation, weapons and tactics. But the persistence of conflicts in various regions of the empire, the Danubian Principalities, Greece and Persia for example, and the ongoing possibility of war with Russia rendered this almost impossible until 1824. Consequently, before he could reform his military, he needed help confronting the Greeks and so Mahmud II had to strike a bargain with the only ruler who possessed a Western-style army that could help do this, and that was Mehmet Ali of Egypt.

Though nominally his vassal, Mehmet Ali was for all intents and purposes a ruler in his own right. As discussed previously, Mehmet Ali was an Albanian from Kavala who capitalised on the opportunity created by Napoleon's invasion of Egypt to obtain the position of Viceroy of Egypt and by 1811 he had consolidated his grip on this exceptionally important province. He instituted numerous reforms that bolstered Egypt's rural economy and, based on its export trade in sugar, wheat and cotton, the province flourished. Mehmet Ali deployed state revenues to build up his military. He established the first Western-style conscript army in the Near East: the Fellahin Army. Equipped with Western arms, including bayonet-mounted muskets, and trained by French advisors to fight in closed ranks, Ali's army became a formidable force (Aksan 2007: 306–13). At the same time, he also upgraded the Egyptian fleet. Mehmet Ali had already assisted his master by suppressing the insurrections on Crete and Cyprus and at this crisis moment Mahmud needed his assistance once again (Andriotis 2003).

The Egyptian viceroy's participation in crushing the rebellion was not based on any major objection to the Greek cause. Many Greeks in Alexandria and elsewhere in Egypt belonged to the Philiki Etaireia, and indeed some were even members of his government. Moreover, almost all of his economic advisors were Greek merchants and he knew that most of them supported the rebellion. Some even pleaded with him to stay neutral, but to no avail. Mehmet Ali's opportunism got the better of him. So, he listened to Mahmud's offer and they struck a bargain. In exchange for the formal cessation of Crete and Cyprus to his control and the appointment of his son, Ibrahim Paşa, as governor of the Peloponnesos, Mehmet Ali would unleash his army and navy against the Greeks. Rumour had it that the Morea was to be cleansed of Christian Greeks and colonised by Muslim Egyptians. As Mehmet Ali himself put it, with the addition of these territories, he would become 'the most important man in the Ottoman Empire' (Fahmy 1997: 38). Shortly after the agreement had been reached, Mahmud introduced measures to reform the Janissary army and to create a new one manned by troops trained in the European manner. Janissaries, especially those in Istanbul, resisted and threatened to topple the monarchy. But Mahmud struck first. In an event known as the 'Auspicious Incident', on 16 June 1826, the

Janissary Corps was abolished and thousands of Janissaries were executed (Aksan 2007: 313–42; 2009; Levy 1971). The creation of a new Western-style army called 'The Trained Triumphant Soldiers of Muhammad' commenced. While the reform of the Ottoman military was taking place, the war to crush the Greek rebellion continued with Ibrahim and his Egyptians playing the leading role.[11]

In 1825, the empire struck back. Having secured the sea-lanes between Egypt and Crete and using the great island as his base, Ibrahim Paşa launched his assault on the Morea. He headed a formidable force, consisting of 10,000 regular infantry, 1,000 cavalry, 3,000 irregulars, 180 field artillery pieces, 25 warships, and 100 supply ships. On 24 February, his armada landed at Methoni in Messenia. Within a week, his men had secured a beachhead and captured the fortress of Neokastro. If they could take the Greek stronghold of Old Navarino, then they would have a base of operations from which they could threaten the entire Peloponnesos.

The Greeks paid heavily at this point for the disastrous civil war. The power struggle ended with Koundouriotis's faction victorious and so it mobilised a strike force to confront Ibrahim. Some of Greece's best commanders, like Giogrios Karaiskakis, Kitsos Tzavellas and Konstantinos Botsaris, confronted the Egyptians. Missing were other leading captains, like Theodoros Kolokotronis who was in prison facing a charge of treason, and their men, whose participation might have swung the contest Greece's way. The revolutionary army gallantly defended Old Navarino but to no avail, and it fell on 23 May. Ibrahim quickly dispatched a force to seize the major roadways into the interior of the peninsula. At a place called Maniaki, Papaflessa and 3,000 men tried to stop them, and failed (1 June 1825). Without a pause, the Egyptian forces cut a swathe through the Morea, destroying villages and enslaving thousands of people as they went along, and in a matter of weeks, they had retaken Tripolis.

Kolokotronis and other leaders were released from custody, as everyone was desperately needed if the revolution was to survive. Ibrahim struck out in two directions. First, he marched on the capital of the Provisional Administration in Nafplion. A vastly outnumbered contingent of Greek and Philhellene troops led by Ioannis Makriyannis inflicted on him a stinging defeat at the Battle of the Mills. Nafplion was saved, but the same cannot be said for the city of Argos, which Ibrahim completely destroyed. The Egyptian army then marched into the mountainous interior of Arkadia where

Figure 3.3 *Greek Herakles and the dragons, artist unknown. The baby Herakles killing the two 'dragons' sent to murder him. This lithography is an allegory on the Greek situation after the Egyptian invasion.*

Kolokotronis has amassed a force of about 10,000 men, but more importantly, Ibrahim wanted to destroy the water-powered gun-powder mills at Dimitsana. After this highly successful campaign, Ibrahim retired to his base at Methoni to resupply his army in preparation for a new campaign in the spring of 1826. The war was going no better in central Greece.

The new Ottoman Serasker of Rumeli was a battle-hardened veteran, Reşid Mehmed Paşa, and he reprised the same strategy that had been adopted in 1821 and 1822, namely a two-pronged invasion. As the cartoon (Fig. 3.3) aptly shows, like the baby Herakles, the infant Greek revolution faced two dragons, an Ottoman one from the north and an Egyptian one from the south. The mythical hero slew his foes: would the Greeks do the same?

Forces totalling almost 35,000 men were divided into two contingents; the larger branch, led by Reşid Mehmed Paşa, marched down
the Ioannina-Arta corridor in the west, the other made its way
through Boiotia to Attica and then to the Isthmus. Having seized the
initiative, he marched his army through the mountain passes of
Epiros and descended into Aitolia and then Akarnania, leaving a path
of destruction in his wake. His target was the fortress at Missolonghi.
Whoever occupied this strategic location controlled the mouth of the
Gulf of Corinth and the gateway into the Peloponnesos. By late April,
his forces had laid siege to the city, whose population had burgeoned
with troops sent to reinforce the garrison and with refugees. Through
the summer of 1825, the contest continued with the Greek defenders
repulsing Ottoman attacks and even launching some successful
sorties. What saved the city, however, was Greek control of the sea,
allowing Admiral Miaoulis to keep it supplied with food and war
materials. In the autumn, Karaiskakis, probably the Greeks' best
commander, arrived with reinforcements and was able to harass
Reşid's forces from the rear.

Fortunes changed in December. First, Miaoulis and the fleet
departed, meaning that Missolonghi would not be resupplied.
Second, Ibrahim captured Patras and then crossed the gulf and joined
Reşid. The city was now blockaded by land and sea, and repeated
attempts by Karaiskakis and other Greek commanders failed to
break through the Ottoman lines. By April conditions inside the fort
were grim. The food supplies were exhausted, and that included all
of the city's cats and dogs. Starvation was imminent. A desperate plan
was hatched. On the night of 22/23 April, Karaiskakis would attack
the Ottoman camp from the rear. This would be the signal for every
able-bodied person in the fort who could carry a weapon to rush
out and try to break through the Ottoman lines. Few made it.
The old, the young and the infirm remained in the city to face the
consequences. Thousands took refuge in the central armoury and
committed mass suicide by igniting the gunpowder stores. Thousands
more were captured and the lucky ones were sold into bondage; the
heads of over 2,000 others were staked on the fort's walls.

The fall of Missolonghi was a catastrophe militarily but a victory
symbolically. Much like the Alamo in American history, the self-
sacrifice of the people of Missolonghi breathed new fire into the
hearts of many. The defeat became a rallying cry for renewed resistance. Just as importantly the event resonated widely and loudly
outside of Greece. News of the slaughter and the heroism of the

Figure 3.4 *Combat devant Missolonghi 1826 © Bibliotheque Nationale, Paris, France. Popular lithograph published in Western Europe by Philhellenes in order to raise awareness of the plight of the Greeks fighting in the revolution.*

Greeks spread across Europe and to the US. Artists such as Eugene Delacroix painted evocative and moving depictions of the events. More importantly a torrent of lithographs and drawings appeared in mass circulation periodicals (Fig. 3.4). Songs and even operas were composed, extolling the sacrifices of the Greeks and denouncing the barbarism of the 'Turk'. People in Europe sang songs about Missolonghi and even ate their meals on plates and dishes illustrated with scenes from the siege. Missolonghi did more to mobilise mass support for the Greek cause than any other event in the war. But would that be enough to sway the governments of Europe to intervene before it was too late?

After Missolonghi, matters went from bad to worse. Reşid re-supplied his army and marched eastward. He took the cities of Boiotia and in summer laid siege to the Greek forces on the Acropolis of Athens. In a last chance gamble to keep the revolution alive, a National Assembly was convened to try and restore unified leadership. A new provisional government was formed that appealed for aid from Europe. It also deployed whatever monies were left in the coffers to purchase supplies and to hire experienced fighters like Sir Richard Church and Lord Thomas Cochrane. The new leadership rallied the remaining rebel forces to try and save Athens. On this last point, they were unsuccessful. Led by Makriyannis, the besieged put up a valiant defence but numerous attempts to break through the Ottoman lines failed. In one of these attempts, Karaiskakis was slain, depriving the revolution of its best general.

Political unity proved to be short-lived, and civil discord hampered the war effort once again. After almost a year's siege, Athens fell in 1827 and with its capture, Reşid restored Ottoman control over all of central Greece. Out-gunned, out-manned, and running desperately short of money and supplies because of the horrendous devastation wreaked in the countryside by Ibrahim's army of occupation, the situation was becoming grim for the Greeks and especially for one group of people – women.

The burden of the war increasingly fell most heavily on Greek women. In contemporary Greek popular culture, the women best remembered from the war are heroic figures like Laskarina Bouboulina and Manto Mavrogenous, who actually took part in the fighting (Angelomatis-Tsougarakis 2008). But far more prevalent were the thousands of nameless women who had to deal with the myriad challenges that the war presented. Women, no less than men, bear the burdens of war but this is especially the case in civil wars, like the Greek War of Independence, where the battlefront and the homefront occupy the same space. Women whose husbands, brothers and sons were off fighting had to take over the job of running the farm, undertaking all of the jobs usually done by men. And as war needs consumed ever more resources from the country-side, it was women as household managers who had to devise ways to keep their families fed. Increasingly, this was becoming harder to do. Poverty and destitution spread across the region and affected thousands.

Women also had to confront the physical ravages of war. Thou-sands of women were brutalised and raped by Ottoman troops, and sad to say, occasionally by Greek fighters as well. When villages were captured, the men were often executed and it was the women and children who were left to face the horror of slavery. Tens of thousands were sold in the slave markets of Istanbul, Smyrna and Alexandria; some were ransomed back by relatives but institution-ally, because of the poor financial state of the Greek revolutionary government, outsiders had to step in, like the Austrian emissary at Messenia who ransomed thousands of women and children (Frank 2012: 427, note 63) or the American missionary Jonathan Miller who helped to redeem scores of people (Miller 1828: 73–4; 1974

[1829]).[12] These were the fortunate few; the majority of women remained enslaved for the rest of their lives. In sum, the war was wreaking terrible havoc on Greeks in the war zone, and by the end of 1827, the fate of the uprising itself hung in the balance. What had started as a Balkan-wide conflagration was quickly being reduced to a series of brushfires. If not for the intervention of the Great Powers, the rebellion would have been extinguished that year.

Great Power reaction

Great Power interest in the Greek rebellion can only be understood in the context of the conservative counter-revolution exemplified by Metternich's concert of Europe. Stability and maintenance of the status quo were the order of the day, but eventually the disruption to each of the powers' economic interests, as well as their mutual distrust, led them to intervene in the Eastern Mediterranean. The Greek revolution caused serious damage to the economic interests of all of the Great Powers and the US. This disruption in trade and commerce, alongside the growing tide of Philhellenism, increased the pressure on the Western governments to do something about the war. The persistent tensions and clashes between the Porte and Russia, however, meant that any Russian-led initiative to settle the Greek Question had little chance of success. Consequently, over time Great Britain came to play the leading role in the search for a solution.

Even though the British government had been unsupportive of the rebellion at the start, many prominent political figures personally were sympathetic to the cause. Also, the widespread philhellenic sentiment of the British people created a climate supportive of British intervention. In the summer of 1825, the Greek government passed an 'Act of Submission.' In this petition, the Greeks agreed to place themselves under the protection of His Majesty's government and they accorded Britain the right to select a ruler for the Greek state. Even though Prime Minister George Canning rejected the petition, many Members of Parliament, including some in his own party, pushed for acceptance. The Provisional Administration sent a similar petition to Russia and so the door was cracked for more direct Great Power involvement. It swung open wide with the death of Tsar Alexander I in December and his replacement by the much more ambitious Nicholas I early in 1826.

The new Tsar's more aggressive stance toward the Ottoman Empire and his more open sympathy to the Greeks increased the risk of a Russo-Ottoman war that could lead to greater Russian influence in the region. To forestall this happening, Canning sent the Duke of Wellington to Russia to open negotiations (Cowles 1990). The result of these talks was the Anglo-Russian Protocol of 4 April 1826, in which they proposed that Greece become an autonomous state within the empire, that it pay a tribute to the Porte, and that its ruler be designated by the sultan. In short, it would resemble the Serb Principality. In return, Mahmud II was to withdraw his troops.

A number of developments protracted the negotiations some-what. First, the war was going so well militarily that Mahmud II hoped to make the negotiations moot by reconquering Greece before he faced an ultimatum. Second, Canning died and his successor, the Duke of Wellington, had the Greek Question much lower on his foreign policy agenda. On the plus side for the Greeks, however, the Third National Assembly on 11 April 1827 elected Ioannis Kapo-distrias as the new president of Greece. Because he enjoyed much greater credibility with the Western powers and in fact resided in Geneva, he was a more effective advocate for the Greek position. In addition, Nicholas I was becoming ever more impatient with the lack of action and the reactionary Charles X began to push for greater French involvement in the region. The result of these developments was the Treaty of London signed by Great Britain, the Russian Empire and France. This agreement reiterated many of the key aspects of the April Protocol, but it also called for an immediate armistice, set a time limit for compliance, promised Great Power protection during the armistice and authorised the dispatching of a joint fleet to guarantee the peace.

A combined French, Russian and British armada under the command of British Admiral Edward Codrington assembled in the Eastern Mediterranean. He was a distinguished naval officer and an ardent supporter of the Greek cause and a member of the London Philhellenic Committee. Consequently, in dealing with the two sides he was anything but even-handed. When it became clear that Ibrahim was refusing to adhere to the terms of the armistice, on 20 October 1827 the allied fleet sailed into Navarino Bay trapping the Ottoman-Egyptian fleet. When the captain of HMS Dartmouth tacked too close to an Ottoman ship, its commander, believing that he was about to be attacked, ordered his men to prepare fireships. Seeing this, the British officer thought that he was about to be attacked and so pre-emptively opened fire.

The battle that decided the war thus commenced. The allied fleet consisted of twenty-seven ships armed with 1,324 guns and they faced eighty-nine ships with 2,240 guns. In spite of being badly outnumbered, as verbal accounts state and as underwater archaeology confirms, it was no conquest. Sixty Ottoman or Egyptian vessels were sunk at no cost to the allies (Papatheodorou, Geraga and Ferentinos 2005).

The defeat at Navarino severed the lifeline to Egypt that sustained Ibrahim's expedition. He now paid the price for his scorched earth policy. He determined to fight on, but a devastated Morea could not sustain his army.

> Ibrahim's ... troops were sick and starving; consequently some regiments had revolted, some had deserted and tried to make their way to Rumelia by land, killing and stealing on their way. The rest were reduced to eating animals which had died, and even eating pigs. (Marsot 1984: 217)

He held out for almost a year, making periodic forays into the interior. Under an agreement negotiated between Mehmet Ali and Codrington, in October 1829 Ibrahim evacuated to Egypt what was left of his once mighty force. The Great Powers were now deeply entangled in the Greek Question, and though they had not intended it, it was on the side of the revolution, and this was especially the case with Russia.

The Russo-Ottoman War

In Istanbul, Mahmud II was both infuriated and humiliated. Outraged, he demanded that the allied fleet be withdrawn after its unprovoked act of war and that the empire be compensated for the loss of its ships. He directed his ire primarily at Russia. Ever since Ipsilantis's invasion, tensions ran high between the two empires, threatening war on a number of occasions. The autumn of 1826 was one of those moments. War was averted through negotiations that led to the signing of the Akkerman Convention. Because of turmoil inside the empire, and especially the destruction of the Janissaries earlier that year, the Porte was in a weak bargaining position and so had to accept unfavourable terms regarding the disposition of Serbia and the Danubian Principalities. Russian participation in the Battle of Navarino was the last straw.

On 20 December 1827 Mahmud II declared Jihad against the Russian Empire. The Russian 'infidels', the declaration of war proclaimed, sought nothing less than the destruction of the 'Sublime State of Muhammad' (the Ottoman Empire) and the 'eradication of the Muslim millet from the face of the earth' (cited in Aksan 2007: 343–4). As protector of the realm and defender of the faith, Mahmud II had no choice but to fight.

The Russo-Ottoman War lasted until September 1829 and it was fought on two fronts: the Caucasus and the Danube frontier. Reşid Paşa was promoted to serasker of the army of the Danube, which contained the majority of the new Western-style army called the Asakir-i Mansure.[13] He faced the brunt of the Russian forces and, through 1828 and into 1829, his forces held the line. Both sides suffered heavy casualties, more from disease and dysentery than from wounds suffered in combat. In the east, the Ottomans fought a mostly defensive campaign in the mountainous regions of the central Caucasus. Fortunes changed in the summer of 1829. Russian forces broke through the Danube defence line, marched through Bulgaria and in mid-August captured the city of Edirne. The vanguard of the Russian army was now only sixty miles from Istanbul. With his capital in a state of panic, Mahmud II had to acquiesce to Russia's demands.

On 14 September 1829, Russia and the Ottoman Empire signed the Treaty of Adrianople/Edirne. The terms of the treaty were harsh. The Ottomans: (1) Ceded territory along the Danube and in Georgia, (2) Opened the Dardanelles to all commercial vessels, (3) Guaranteed Serbia autonomy, (4) Gave greater autonomy to Moldavia and Wallachia, (5) Agreed to pay a massive war indemnity, (6) Accepted Greek autonomy. This last clause merely ratified a situation that already existed. From early 1828 onwards, there was an autonomous Greek state and it was under new leadership.

The Kapodistrian regime

In the summer of 1827, the Third National Assembly elected Ioannis Kapodistrias president of the fledgling state. When he disembarked at Nafplion on 8 January 1828, it was the first time he had ever set foot in revolutionary Greece. As we have seen, Kapodistrias had enjoyed a long and fruitful career in the foreign service of the Russian Empire, at one point holding the rank of Privy Councilor to Tsar Alexander I. Greek nationalists, including the Philliki Etaireia, had long wooed Kapodistrias but he did not join them, though both of his brothers did. When Ipsilantis launched his invasion and started the rebellion,

Kapodistrias spoke out against it, expressing his belief that the time for action was not right. As the horrors of the war became evident, he used his position to encourage Russian intervention for humanitarian reasons. This led to his departure from the Russian Foreign Service. He relocated to Geneva and devoted himself to keeping the Greek Question alive in European political circles.

For a variety of reasons, then, he seemed an ideal choice for president at that crucial moment in 1827 when the Powers were still equivocating on what action to take and still deliberating on the fate of Greece. First, he was not associated with any of the existing factions and so was not caught up in the highly charged political vendettas that the civil war had created and which continued to hamstring every effort at creating a united government. Second, he was an accomplished diplomat and so had credibility with the foreign offices of the Great Powers. This did not mean that he was baggage-free. The French and British feared that he would tilt toward St Petersburg and make Greece a Russian satellite. And there were those in Greece who harboured reservations about him. But all told, he was the best man for the job. Nonetheless, in the end, his tenure proved to be as short as it was turbulent (Loukos 2003; Papageorgiou 2011).

Kapodistrias faced numerous formidable challenges. First, the Ottoman Empire had not given up hopes of still carrying the day. Indeed, even after the war with Russia began, Mahmud II continued to press the hard line even though some of his advisors were now telling him that the best course of action would be to seek 'peace at any price in the name of saving the remaining part of the Empire' (Sheremet 1992: 46). He remained committed to suppressing what the Porte continued to call the 'bandit revolution'. Though greatly reduced in number and in quality, Ottoman forces nonetheless still occupied much of central Greece, including the towns of Boiotia, Athens and Missolonghi. In addition, for the first nine months of his tenure, Ibrahim and the remnants of the Egyptian army were still on the loose in the Peloponnesos. Greece under Kapodistrias, then, remained a country at war, and it was a struggle that had to be fought under very unfavourable conditions.

Much of Greece lay in ruins and the rural economy had ground to a halt. A humanitarian catastrophe was also underway. Tens of thousands of people were homeless and penurious, many facing starvation (Komis 2003). Lastly, the state was deeply in debt and its coffers empty. But, because the Great Powers were deliberating what the boundaries of autonomous Greece would be, it was imperative

Figure 3.5 *The new Greek army (1829) © Pierre Peytier. By the late 1820s, the Greek government had created a small army modelled on Western European forces. This painting by the French artist, Pierre Peytier, depicts an officer and some enlisted men in the new army.*

that Greek forces liberate as much territory as possible so as to have a stronger claim on them at the negotiating table. To continue the war, Greece needed a Western-style army and so he took steps to create one (Fig. 3.5). In this task they were assisted by a French expeditionary force that arrived in August. Its task was to execute the removal of Ibrahim and his army from the Peloponnesos, and not to fight against Ottoman forces. Nonetheless, its arrival freed up Greek troops that could be deployed elsewhere (Saitas 2003).

In the spring of 1829, they launched attacks all across central Greece. Agostino Kapodistrias, the president's brother, and Richard Church led the forces in the west; Kitsos Tzavellas those in central Greece, and Ipsilantis those in the east. They were successful everywhere. In a moment fraught with symbolism, on 8 May 1829, the Greek army retook the fortress at Missolonghi. Then, in what turned into the last battle of the war, in late September, Greeks defeated an Ottoman force at Peta. Appropriately enough, Ipsilantis commanded them and so finished what his brother had started.

Besides the war, Kapodistrias faced other challenges at home and abroad. He proved once again to be a fine diplomat, ably representing Greek interests at the Great Power conference on Poros in August 1828, which drafted the broad outlines of a settlement. The recommendations of the Poros group provided the framework for the London Protocol of 3 February that declared Greece to be an independent state that would be ruled by an absolute, hereditary monarch. To fulfil this role, the Powers approached Prince Leopold of Saxe-Coburg. Though he was the widowed son-in-law of King George IV of Great Britain, he was acceptable to Russia and France. In April 1830, he agreed to become king of Greece, only one month later to change his mind. While the issue of the monarchy remained open, Kapodistrias continued to preside over independent Greece.

Domestically, he introduced many reforms aimed at solving some of Greece's most pressing problems. He promulgated legislation for land distribution, awarding grants of land to some, providing loans for the purchase of state lands, and awarding legal recognition to lands usurped during the first days of the war. New taxes were imposed. He created a new system of education, founding schools based on the British Lancastrian model. He built hospitals and orphanages to care for the casualties of war. Local administration was radically reformed, shifting the balance of power from the local community to the central state. In short, within the space of a relatively span of short time and during an ongoing war, Kapodistrias tried to mould revolutionary Greece into a 'modern' Western polity.

By temperament, Kapodistrias was ill-suited to play the role of mediator and conciliator; tired of having to barter with indigenous Greek power brokers, he opted instead to rule through a council of his appointees, most of whom were Greeks from the diaspora. His decision to suspend the constitution, disband the legislature and to rule by executive degree cost Kapodistrias a great deal of support, and split Greece's political class into two factions, one that continued to support him and another that wanted the restoration of constitutional rule (Papageorgiou 2011). This schism between Kapodistrians and Constitutionalists would have a lasting impact on Greek politics. In addition, his policies and his personality made him enemies.

In some regions of the country, the leadership even refused to recognise his authority. Petrobey Mavromichalis was one of them, opposing the president's policies and leading a boycott of paying taxes. Finally, in January 1831, Kapodistrias had him arrested and imprisoned on the charge of treason. Once again, civil war was in the offing. The merchants and captains from the islands, who had borne the war at sea and in doing so incurred heavy financial losses, sought financial compensation. When Kapodistrias denied their demands, they threatened to secede from Greece. In August 1831, Greece witnessed the terrible sight of the revolution's two finest admirals, Kanaris and Miaoulis, fighting one another. Internal discord was threatening to tear the new country apart and, in the end, led to the president's brutal slaying.

'Brother, put your flocks in safety. The President, our father, has been murdered' (cited in Woodhouse 1973: 502). This unnamed shepherd was spot-on with his warning to his friend to hide his sheep and goats. Kapodistrias's assassination plunged the country once again into civil war, and this time the fratricidal fighting was even more horrendous and destructive than before. One could aptly refer to the years between the president's death and the arrival of King Otho as the period of anarchy.

After ten years of fierce fighting against their Ottoman masters and amongst themselves, the Greeks of central and southern Greece had achieved independence. But the new state's future was uncertain. Beset by deep internal divisions and, after the president's assassination, without a viable government, its fate hung in the balance. Kapodistrias perhaps captured the situation best when he concluded that 'Greece is now in the hands of God, and the Great Powers'. Great Britain, France and Russia would decide on the new state's borders and they had already selected its new king: Otho of Bavaria.

Notes

1. A wave of new scholarship is fundamentally revising our understanding of the Greek rebellion and its wider significance. Here are some examples of the type of revisionist work that has appeared over the last few years: Erdem 2005; 2007; Lekas 2008: Loukos 2008; Michailidis 2010; Rodriguez 2009; Theotokas and Kotaridis 2006; 2009; Veremis and Koliopoulos 2010; Vogli 2011. Of special importance are the two collections of essays edited by Pizanias (2009a; 2011a).
2. His ruling, however, did not go unchallenged. Numerous muftis spoke out against it as a violation of Sharia law, and a cleric under Paşvanoglou in Vidin even issued his own fatwa countermanding the one from Istanbul.

3. The Ionian Islands are Kerkira (Corfu), Paxos, Lefkas, Ithaka, Kefalonia, Zakynthos and Kythera.

4. Anscombe 2006: 95 discusses Ali's landed possessions. The monetary figure seems outrageously high and was probably inflated by Hurşid Paşa's enemies, who accused him of keeping part of Ali's fortune after the Lion of Ioannina was defeated. In 1837 one piaster equalled US$ 4.69 in today's currency.

5. People from the nearby sanjak of Karafeyre (modern Greek Veroia) appealed to Ali to adjudicate a dispute. In his ruling, he employed the style and formulas of imperial, sultanic decrees (Anastasopoulos 2006: 28, note 8). Any of the sultan's subjects could present him with a petition of grievance and it was the ruler's duty to address it; this practice was critical to the relationship between the monarchy and its subjects.

6. This figure seems exceptionally high, but even if it is an exaggeration, the conclusion that taxes went up substantially seems obviously correct.

7. The agreement reached between the Deliyiannis, Londos and Perroukas factions was called the *Synyposchetikon*, in English the 'Compromissum', on 1 April 1 1816, and it constituted a truce of sorts: Stamatopoulos 2007: 152.

8. Only recently have scholars begun to explore the rich materials in the Ottoman archives in Istanbul in order to study the Ottoman response to the Greek rebellion. The results of their work are already providing us with new insights, see Erdem 2005; 2011; Ilicak 2009; Kitromilides and Ilicak 2010; Laiou 2009; 2011; Loukos 2007; 2008; Theotokas and Kotiaridis 2011.

9. For the rest of the decade, the divan only appointed ethnic Bulgarian clerics to the position of Patriarch, an indication of how completely they distrusted the Greeks.

10. On the constitutions and citizenship: Alivisatos 2003; 2011: 40–52; Anastassiades 1982; Michailidis 2010; Papageorgiou 2003; Rotzokos 2011a; Theodoridis 2003; Vogli 2007; 2009; 2011.

11. The best accounts of Ibrahim's expedition are Yiannopoulos 2003 and Sakellariou 2012.

12. On Ottoman slavery generally, see Toledano (1982; 1998); Erdem (1996: 126–7 and 2005: 70) discusses the issue of slavery ransoming during the war and Zilfi (2012: 123) notes that some Greek women enslaved in Egypt refused repatriation to independent Greece, presumably out of shame.

13. For detailed discussion of the war, see Aksan 2007: 343–61; Bitis 2006: 274–348.

CHAPTER 4

Contested state formation (1832–63)

> It is impossible to tell you what the excitement and enthusiasm was like ... As soon as I arrived in the throne room, I shook hands with the Regents and expressed to them my happiness at their election and my trust in them. Then I went out on the balcony twice where I was greeted with cheers from the people ... In the evening I returned to the town which had been illuminated for several evenings ... The people soon recognized us and surrounded us to such an extent that the Bavarian officers had to keep the crowds back ... When I returned to the palace I went out onto the balcony three times. Enormous candelabras were brought out onto the balcony to illuminate the scene. This wonderful reception fills me with great hopes for the future. (Letter from King Otho to his father, King Ludwig of Bavaria, 8 February 1833, cited in Bower and Bolitho 1939: 40–1)

The text above and Figure 4.1 capture the sense of jubilation that marked the beginning of King Otho's reign in Greece. Both ruler and realm were in their youth and the period of his rule from 1833 to 1862 was characterised by the attempt to create a centralised modern state along Western lines in the Eastern Mediterranean. The endeavour was fraught with difficulties, and at best we can say that Greek state formation during these formative decades was impaired. It started so well. On that late winter's morning in 1833 when the Bavarian prince disembarked from the British warship Madagascar, it seemed like a new day had dawned. The sectarian fighting ceased; the last of the Ottoman forces were gone; freedom had come at last; and Greece's future as a Western state and society seemed assured. As Otho's letter to his father illustrates, both ruler and ruled embraced each other with an air of optimism and in the hope for a better future.

The moment of joy and unbridled optimism, however, did not last long and Otho's tenure on the throne ended badly. Twenty-nine years after his arrival in Greece, Otho was expelled by his people. After a holiday at sea, the Greek fleet would not let him return, not even to collect his personal belongings. Just as a British ship brought him to

Figure 4.1 Arrival of King Otho in Greece, Peter von Hess (1835)
© bpk | Bayerische Staatsgemäldesammlungen.

his new homeland, so too would one of Her Majesty's vessels take him away. Devastated by what he saw as a cruel betrayal by scheming politicians, he died a few years later still dressed in traditional Greek costume and still mistakenly convinced that his people loved him. The vagaries of Otho's reign track closely with the ups and downs of the first few decades in the life of the new Greek state, but before we can analyse those issues, we need to examine a very important and controversial issue, and that is: what exactly was the nature of the independent Greek state?

The nature of the new Greek state

There is a debate amongst historians about the nature of the new Greek state. Some argue that it was one of the first 'modern' states in Europe, while others consider it to be a hold-over of the *ancien regime* (Alivisatos 2011: 74–85; Hering 1992; Kostis 2005; Lekas 2008; 2009; Lyrintzis 2008; Vogli 2011). Modern and modernisation are two terms that will come up frequently in this debate and the terms will recur throughout this study. What is meant by them is contested by scholars. Politically, modern connotes a system of government in which sovereignty is vested in the people, or even better the nation. Thus, the term nation-state is used to describe a modern polity. This form of political association stands in distinction to earlier forms of governance that were characterised by absolute monarchy or some other form of royalist rule. The elision of nation and state indicates that the boundary of the state and the territorial extent of the nation should be coterminous. Ideally this would mean that each nation should have its own state. Political modernisation refers to the process of transformation from pre-modern to modern systems of governance. For some scholars, then, the war of independence was a moment of modernisation. So, was the new Greek state a 'modern' one? The answer has to be a qualified 'No'.

The treaty that established the new Greek kingdom created a fundamentally pre-modern system of government. Even though there had been a discussion amongst the Great Powers about introducing a democratic element, the state they created was essentially an absolute monarchy. Sovereignty and power were vested in the person of the king, in this case Otho of Bavaria, and in his hereditary successors. So, certainly during the first ten years of independent Greece's existence it was a pre-modern state. To what extent was it a national state? While the documents and agreements all refer to 'Greeks' in a national sense, was there really a Greek nation in 1832? The answer to this question is complicated. To the extent that there was an identity that bound together the majority of the population in Greece it was based upon religion. During the war, the majority of the Jewish population was driven out of the war zone and the vast majority of Muslims were killed, fled or converted to Orthodoxy. Consequently the majority population in Greece was Orthodox.

Ethnically, however, the population was very mixed. There were Bulgarians, Serbs, Montenegrins and Albanians who had fought in the war and then remained, thus becoming Greek subjects (Roudometof 1998: 31). Even amongst those who possessed a consciousness of being ethnically Greek, there was great diversity. There were groups such as the Tsakones from Lakonia and the Arvanites of Attica and Boiotia who thought of themselves as Greek but who otherwise had very little in common. They spoke distinctive dialects that were almost mutually unintelligible. Dimitris Hatziaslanis, aka Dimitrios Vyzantios, in his 1836 play *Babel*/Βαβυλωνία captures wonderfully this cultural disconnect in a scene where two men have such a wildly different understanding of the meaning of the same word that one kills the other over a perceived insult (Vyzantios 2006: 138–42). Included in the body politic were also people who considered themselves Greeks by language and national consciousness but who were not Orthodox. There were, for example, Catholics residing primarily on some of the Cycladic islands who had in fact not even participated in the rebellion. In sum, in the 1830s we cannot really speak about a single unitary Greek nation nor of a modern state.

A better way to approach this problem, and the one adopted here, is to see both nation-building, that is, the creation of a Greek national body, and state formation as processes that unfolded across the nineteenth century and that eventually created the Greek nation-state. Complicating matters further is the fact that only a tiny fraction of the Greek nation was included in the boundaries of the new state (Map 4.1 and Table 4.1). Another part of our story, then, is to understand what impact the War of Independence and the creation of the new state had on those who remained in the Ottoman Empire and on the Greeks of the diaspora. As in so many other areas, when we shift our focus from the study of Greece to the study of Greeks we have to broaden our geographical frame of analysis and examine these developments transnationally. Our discussion of nation-building and state formation begins by looking at the formative years of independent Greece and on the fate of those who remained outside of it.

Governance and politics

The second son of King Ludwig I of Bavaria and Therese of Saxe-Hildburghausen, Otho had been born on 1 June.[1] Already quite disinterested in child rearing, because Otho was not destined to rule, his father largely left his son's care and education to Catholic priests. Early on there was even talk about his entering a career in the church, but that plan fell through and the young prince was left to follow his favourite pastimes – swimming and horseback riding. In his youth, Otho was vainglorious, stubborn and frivolous, but also good-natured and kind. Throughout his life, Ludwig chided Otho for his 'incurable irresoluteness', urging him in effect to grow a backbone (Bower and Bolitho 1939: 72; Dümler and Jung 2002). By disposition and upbringing the young prince was ill-suited and ill-equipped to deal with the fractious Greek political leadership, or that matter the strong-willed and contentious Bavarians who accompanied him to Greece.

Otho had been discussed as a possible ruler of Greece early on in the Great Power negotiations. There were advantages to his candidacy: his father was not firmly aligned to any of the major

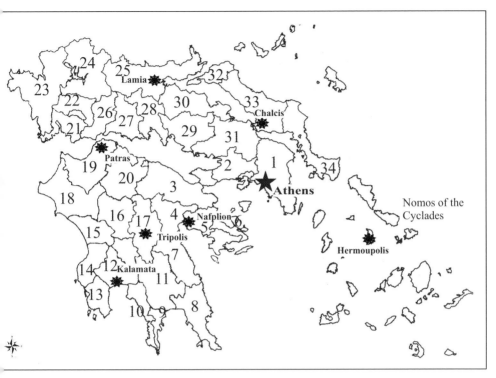

Map 4.1 The kingdom of Greece, 1832: boundaries and provinces.

Table 4.1 *Provinces of the kingdom of Greece, 1836.*

1. Attika	13. Pylias	25. Phthiotidas
2. Megarid	14. Trifylias	26. Navpaktos
3. Corinth	15. Olympias	27. Doridos
4. Argos	16. Gortynos	28. Parnassos
5. Nafplion	17. Mantineias	29. Livadias
6. Ermonidas	18. Ilidas	30. Lokridos
7. Kynourias	19. Patron	31. Thebon
8. Epidavros Limiras	20. Kalavryton	32. Istiaias
9. Gytheio	21. Missolonghi	33. Halkis
10. Oitilou	22. Trichonidos	34. Karystos
11. Lakedaimonos	23. Xeromeri	35. Cyclades
12. Kalamon	24. Evrytania	

Based on: Petmezas 2003: 17

powers, the youthful prince was an ardent Philhellene, his political views were moderately conservative, and he was young and malleable. But his youthfulness, ardent Catholicism, and inexperience counted against him, and so the Powers initially passed him by in favour of Leopold, Duke of Saxe-Coburg. When Leopold removed himself from consideration and other possible candidates demurred, the Powers turned once again to the Bavarian monarch to inquire about his son. After a series of lengthy negotiations, in 1832 Ludwig signed the London Convention with Russia, France and Great Britain (notably absent of course were the Greeks) that installed Otho as the first king of Greece.

The most important terms of his selection were these: Otho became absolute monarch and his crown was to be passed on through hereditary primogeniture. In order to secure public order during a time of uncertainty, the treaty stipulated that the Powers guaranteed Otho's personal safety; consequently, a force of 3,500 Bavarian troops accompanied the new king and Bavarian officers were appointed to supervise and train the regular Greek army. Lastly, the Powers guaranteed the sovereignty of the new state and pledged loans totalling 60,000,000 francs; the money was to be distributed in three payments, only the first of which was actually scheduled in the treaty. Thus secure in its borders, protected by the shield of the West, and bankrolled by western loans, liberated Greece greeted its youthful ruler.

Since Otho was a minor, the treaty gave Ludwig the authority to appoint a three-man regency to rule until his son came of age on 1 June 1835. Otho was of two minds as to what he should do until he came of age. On the one hand, he recognised that he needed to take his place in Greece as soon as possible; but, on the other, he was extremely worried about what his role would be and what he would do while others carried out the practical tasks of creating a new country. He fretted that he would wander about with nothing to do and that he would become a figure of fun. In the end, he chose to go to Greece, trusting that his father would select competent and loyal men to be his regents. To carry out the challenging task of ruling Greece, Ludwig appointed Count Joseph von Armansperg, Professor Ludwig von Maurer and General Karl Wilhelm von Heideck. This troika exercised almost complete control of the Greek government. Armansperg's background was in finance and diplomacy, and he had served King Ludwig as his Finance Minister and as Minister of Foreign Affairs. He was a supporter of individual liberties but was also a staunch monarchist. Because of his efforts to strengthen economic connections within the German-speaking world, he fell out of favour with Ludwig, who saw an opportunity to remove his ambitious underling from Munich by sending him to Athens to advise his son. Even though Armansperg spoke no Greek and had scant familiarity with the country, he was invested with executive control over the government. He was charming and socially adroit, but also ambitious, scheming and unscrupulous. His detractors saw him as a wily careerist who was using his time in Greece in order to rehabilitate his standing in Munich. If this was so, then his plan failed because when he was fired from his position in Athens, his public career came to an end. Nonetheless, throughout his tenure as leader of the Greek government, padding his own résumé took precedence over helping build the new Greece.

Von Maurer came from a completely different background. He had studied law at Paris and Heidelberg and was considered one of the leading jurists in Europe. He was tasked with devising the system of local and central government, promulgating codes of law and designing a system of civil and criminal justice, as well as overseeing the daily operation of the government. Through his energetic efforts, he laid the foundation of a modern, Western legal and administrative system. Unlike his colleagues, Von Mauer did know Greek – unfortunately, it was the ancient kind. While personally a man of great integrity, he was also hard-headed, unbending and arrogant, and these traits made him many enemies.

Von Heideck was the only one of the regents who had prior experience in Greece. He joined the revolution in 1826 and distinguished himself particularly at the Battle of Athens. Kapodistrias promoted him as commander of the garrison of Nafplion and then military governor of Argos. He seemed like an excellent choice to undertake the daunting task of administering the military affairs of the new state: he knew the country and the leading Greek politicians and military leaders, and he spoke vernacular Greek. But this turned out not to be the case. He was far more interested in pursuing his painting and in building up his seashell collection than he was in reforming the armed forces. These, then, were the three men who would guide the young king in creating a new country. In the early years, Armansperg dominated the scene and Otho was almost an irrelevancy in his own realm.

A very telling episode from the early days of Otho's residence in Nafplion captures just how isolated and disengaged the young monarch was. Armansperg decided to hold a soirée one evening at his spacious home in the city. Otho was, of course, invited but with no greater pomp or attention than any other guest. When the royal carriage arrived, neither the count nor even his wife were there to greet him. Nor was this the only snub he would endure that evening. Upon entering the ballroom, he was courteously received by various guests but not by his host, who recognised the royal presence with a mere nod of his head. It was Armensparg's daughters who came to the young king's rescue by whisking him off to socialise with them. This made some sense because they were the only people in the room even close to Otho in age. As this, and numerous other episodes show, his early years in Greece were very difficult and, on more than one occasion, he expressed to his father and his brother his fervent desire to return home. Nonsense, they told him. Stay the course and work with the regents was their advice. But it was evident to all concerned that for much of the 1830s Armensparg was in charge.

Greek leaders, then, played only subsidiary roles in the governance of their own country. Westerners were appointed to almost every major position. This 'Bavarianism' became a source of much friction among Greek politicians. Compounding the Greek dependency on the Bavarian protectorate was the considerable influence exerted by the representatives of the Great Powers. The factionalism that had developed during the war, and especially during the Kapodistrian period, continued but in modified forms. The old wartime factions now formed 'parties', each of which looked to one of the representatives of the Great Powers for support. To be sure, these were not political parties in the modern sense. Rather, they were loose coalitions of men who shared certain beliefs, ideologies and a vision for the future of the country. There were four parties: the Russian, the French, the English and the Constitutionalist.

In political terms, the Russian party was the most conservative and the English party, not surprisingly, was the most liberal. The Russian party was the descendent of the old Kapodistrian faction. It remained conservative and pro-absolutist. Its adherents' worldview was one that looked backwards and that privileged religion as the primary mechanism of social order. In this case, of course, that was Orthodoxy. The party, then, sought to solidify relations within the Orthodox world and was committed to an irredentist ideology that espoused the 'emancipation' of their co-religionists still in the Ottoman Empire and the creation of a greater Greek Orthodox state with Constantinople as its capital. The party drew its support from

Table 4.2   *Party membership by class, 1833–43.*

	Kocabaşi		Political class		Military	
	Number	%	Number	%	Number	%
Russian	14	22	19	32	20	41
French	20	32	19	32	14	29
English	15	24	15	25	7	14
Constitutionalist	14	22	7	12	8	16
	63	100	60	100	49	100

Papageorgiou 2005: 401–8

Table 4.3   *Party membership by place of origin, 1833–43.*

Party	Autochthons			Heterochthons			Total	% of total
	Number	% of total	% of party	Number	% of total	% of party		
Russian	35	23	65	19	31	35	54	25
French	42	28	75	15	24	26	57	27
English	44	29	68	21	34	32	65	31
Constitutionalist	29	19	80	7	11	20	36	17
	150	100	100	62	100	100	212	100

Papageorgiou 2005: 401–8

the old military class, in particular the captains like Kolokotronis, from the pre-eminent kocabaşis families from the Morea, the old political elite, like the Phanariots who had settled in the kingdom, Ionian islanders, and emigrants from Russia. The majority of their members (65 per cent) were autochthonous, that is, native to the territory of the Greek state, rather than heterochthonous – though it did have the largest percentage of heterochthonous members of any of the parties (Tables 4.2 and 4.3; Papageorgiou 2005: 401–8).

Though the Constitutionalist party that had developed during the presidency of Kapodistrias still existed, it was much reduced in size and was in fact the smallest of the parties. The majority of its members split off into two groups and formed, respectively, the French and English parties. Ioannis Kolletis led the French party. It favoured a constitutional monarchy with limited democracy based upon wealth. Not surprisingly, its model state was France's July Monarchy, a regime that combined a relatively weak monarchy with a plutocratic parliament. Three-quarters of their members were natives, equally divided between kocabaşis, former administrators and military men. It was the most aggressive in its opposition to Otho and the Bavarian regime. The last major faction was the English Party, led by Alexandros Mavrogordatos. The party was easily the most liberal and the most committed to establishing a pluralistic democratic system. Among autochthons, its support came from merchants who had strong commercial links with England. It also attracted heterochthons from the diaspora in the West. Of the three parties, it was the one that had the least support from the military class. What all of them shared was a desire for participation by Greeks in the governance of their new country.

In real terms, however, the war for 'liberation from a foreign yoke' had resulted merely in a change of masters. Whether it was under Armansperg or Otho, the government of Greece was autocratic and its administration dominated by Germans and other foreigners. To be sure, there was some participation by Greeks as members of a cabinet that advised the crown. But, when important action was needed, the key decisions were made without even a nod in their direction, rendering the Greeks' role in practical governance largely irrelevant. In addition, government positions were filled on the basis of personal connections or patronage. In exchange for a political appointment, an appointee owed allegiance to his patron and was thus obligated to do favours on his behalf. Patronage and the lack of transparency in governance persisted for decades, as they did in most nineteenth-century states.

The turbulent political scene in post-war Greece revolved around a convoluted triangle of factions and power groupings that made for some very strange bedfellows. Factions developed within the Bavarian administration and each of them forged alliances of convenience with one of the Greek parties and with one of the foreign delegations. The Greek factions likewise sought the support of one of the big three: France, Britain or Russia, which were themselves intensely active in promoting their country's vested interests in the Eastern Mediterranean (for a discussion of the Russian perspective, for example, see Rendall 2002). Any endeavours to reconstruct war-ravaged Greece, then, had to negotiate these difficult and daunting political waters.

The state of the country

On top of the complicated political situation, there were numerous other problems that Otho and his advisors had to confront. Economically, the country was in ruins. Simply put, bread and butter issues topped the Bavarian agenda. During the course of the insurrection and the subsequent civil war of 1832, over 662 villages had been devastated. In spite of the significant strides made during the presidency of Kapodistrias, there were still thousands of refugees who needed food and shelter. In towns such as Patras, Kalamata, Tripolis and Athens, few houses stood above their foundations. Visitors to these ruined settlements paint stark pictures of the devastation, describing Greeks living like beasts in makeshift hovels and shacks. 'Homeless men roamed the land looking for work, while orphans and widows sought some kind of protection and sustenance' (McGrew 1985: 19). Thus, destitute and displaced, the rural populace looked to their new king for relief.

The agricultural infrastructure, on which their economy was based, lay in ruins. Over two-thirds of the olive trees and three-quarters of the vineyards had been destroyed. Three-quarters of the olive and flour mills had been reduced to rubble. Of the estimated pre-war flocks of over 100,000 goats and sheep only approximately 10,000 remained. Vast sums of money were needed to rebuild the infrastructure of the agrarian economy. But above all, economic reconstruction depended completely on the redistribution of land. The peasants, then, looked to the young king for bread, land and peace. Other groups as well felt that they were owed much because of their roles during the war. The kocabaşis who had led and paid for the war wanted land, power and pay for their men. The shipowners who had been the backbone of the fleet and who had spent a great deal of cash on the war wanted indemnity payments. The men-at-arms who had fought the war wanted regular pay as soldiers or land, or both. Satisfying all of these claimants, even with the monies available through the foreign loans, was impossible.

Throughout his reign Otho faced fiscal crises. Dwelling within Greece's bounds were only 750,000 Greeks compared to over two million who were still under Ottoman rule. Most importantly in respect to the economic future of the kingdom, the fertile plains of Thessaly and lacustrine basins of Macedonia lay outside the kingdom. Major cities and entrepôts that Greece claimed as part of its national space, like Salonika and Smyrna, and the island of Crete, remained in the Ottoman Empire. In spite of the expertise and connections that the Greeks of the diaspora brought with them when they settled in the new kingdom, manufacturing and trade remained underdeveloped. The economic conditions in Greece presented the government with a major challenge: how to stimulate growth, satisfy the immediate needs of the population, and pay the war indemnity owed to the Porte. The only feasible internal source of revenue entailed taxing the very thing that needed to expand: agriculture. Even before that could become an issue the government had to deal with the complicated but crucial issue of land ownership.

The land situation in Greece was chaotic and complicated. As we have seen, during the period of Ottoman rule, 65 to 75 per cent of the cultivated land in Greece was in Muslim hands, either through private ownership or in one of the conditional tenures bestowed by the monarchy. By war's end, the vast majority of the Muslim population had either fled or been killed. The land of the deceased was up for grabs, and while some of those who fled the carnage managed to dispose of their land, many others had not. The same was true for the pre-war Jewish population. The revolutionary governments nationalised all such property and used the newly confiscated lands as collateral on international loans. In 1832, some Greeks still possessed land that they had legally acquired before the war. Others held legal title to estates that they had purchased from Muslims during the conflict. And still others were in possession of land that they had usurped as war booty or that had been given to them by Greek warlords in lieu of payment for their services. When Kapodistrias came to power one of his top priorities was to commission a survey to determine who legally owned which lands. By so doing he hoped to determine the location and extent of the national lands, and, then based on that survey, to calculate the amount of compensation owed to the previous owners. Kapodistrias's program met with stiff resistance and had not progressed very far at the time of his assassination. The land issue was so important, however, that it quickly became a priority for the new Bavarian regime. One step they took to increase the amount of national land was to confiscate church property. Of the existing 525 monasteries in the kingdom's territory, the state closed and seized the land of 394 of them (Makrides 2009: 56).

On 7 June 1835, less than one week after he had become sole ruler, Otho issued the 'Law for the Dotation of Greek Families'. The culmination of many years of labour, this legislation was to be the capstone of the Bavarian economic and social policy of reconstruction. While thoughtfully crafted in theory, the law paid scant attention to the realities on the ground in the Greek countryside, and so it produced results very different from those intended by the lawmakers. The law stipulated that all native-born and foreign-born Greeks, and all non-Greeks who had fought in the war and continued to reside in Greece were eligible to receive a 2,000 drachma government note with which to purchase national land. Each head of a household, and this included war widows, bid on parcels of land varying in size and quality up to the limit of their note. No one could obtain more than four hectares of national land. Once purchased the land became private property to be held in perpetuity. In return the owner incurred a mortgage that mandated a payment of 6 per cent of the purchase price annually for thirty-six years. Missing two successive mortgage payments put the owner in default on his note and the land was returned to the state for reallocation. The crown claimed an additional 3 per cent of the purchase price in an annual property tax that was to be paid in cash, not kind. This then was the scheme that the government hoped would create a stable landholding peasantry and that would set the state on the road to fiscal responsibility.

The scheme, however, was fraught with difficulties. First, the four-hectare maximum was too low. Even under the best of conditions, this amount of land would barely provide basic subsistence to the average family, let alone cover the mortgage and taxes. Moreover, the 2,000 drachma allocation was predicated on the normative price for a hectare of cultivable land being 500 drachmas. This proved to be unrealistic. Prices at the land auctions varied from 1,350 drachmas per hectare for basic arable land, to 2,600 for vineyards, to over 5,000 drachmas per hectare for irrigated gardens (McGrew 1985: 165). As a result those peasants who had to rely solely on the government note were able to acquire farms of only between one and three hectares, and usually the land they purchased was of the lowest quality. Even in the best of years, such minifundia would not have fed the average family. But Greece possessed a very high-risk agricultural environment in which even a six-hectare farm would have failed to provide subsistence one-sixth of the time (Gallant 1991: 101–12). Peasants either had to somehow acquire non-national lands – usually by renting parcels from wealthier landholders – or they had to find other sources of income, of which there were precious few in postwar Greece.

The family farms created by the dotation scheme were born into dependency and debt, and that soon translated into poverty. At the same time, the auction system was very susceptible to manipulation and corruption. A few wealthy men were able to exploit the loopholes in the system to acquire sizable estates with the best land. In short, the rich got richer and the poor poorer. The novelist Pavlos Kalligas aptly captured the peasants' verdict on the dotation law:

> What else are the laws and the state today but an exit-less labyrinth of rules deliberately multiplied to satisfy a swarm of insatiable intriguers who are nourished by the sweat of the people whom they render each day more impoverished and drive to brigandage? (Kalligas 2000 [1865]: 17)

Land, debt and poverty remained persistent features of the Greek countryside throughout the nineteenth century and beyond.

Otho's government, then, found itself in a difficult situation. On the one hand, it passed land reform laws, distributed land to the peasants and provided them with low-interest loans to help them cultivate that land; while on the other, it had to then claim back from them valuable resources in the form of taxes. In addition to the taxes on the national lands, discussed above, a tithe of 10 per cent was levied on privately held land as well. As one jaundiced observer of the Greek scene noted: 'The connexion [sic] between the Greek government and the people of Greece is wonderfully simple. The Greeks pay taxes and the government spends them' (A Correspondent, *The Spectator*, vol. 14 (1841): 949). The tax-collection system, moreover, only made matters worse. It combined the older mechanism of tax farming with a new system operated by government civil servants. Both were open to manipulation and corruption. Evasion by taxpayers became rampant and peculation by tax collectors rife. The result was a very insecure income to the state. Since internal sources of revenue were inadequate, borrowing from Greeks abroad, foreign banks and financiers was repeatedly resorted to. Indebtedness was the result in both cases. Debt, as we shall see, remained a serious problem for Greece throughout the modern epoch.

In spite of the obstacles, the reconstruction of Greece from the devastation after eleven years of war did occur. The merchant marine recovered from the wartime loses and once again much of the sea-borne freight of the Mediterranean was in Greek hands. According to one estimate, the value of mercantile trade handled by Greek ships rose by 194 per cent between 1833 and 1840, and by 1840 the value of that trade was in the order of 80 million drachmas. Not surprisingly given the low level of agricultural production and very modest industrial output of the kingdom of Greece, most of the trade handled by Greek ships was transit trade between the Ottoman and Russian Empires and Western Europe (Harlaftis and Kostelenos

2012; Harlaftis 1996; 2003). Because of the development of mercantile trade, islands such as Syros and ports cities like Patras began to flourish once again. Syros in the Aegean literally became the crossroads of the Mediterranean. By 1837 the majority of trade between east and west passed through the island. Its capital city of Hermopoulos grew in size, from a population of 150 in 1821 to over 12,000 in 1840 and in wealth (Kardasis 1987: 23–63; Loukos 2004). Patras, on the northwestern tip of the Peloponnesos, also witnessed a remarkable recovery during the age of Otho. The first decade of independent rule, then, witnessed an economic recovery of sorts, but the nature of that recovery, based on mercantile trade rather than a solid productive base, was to have a lasting impact on the Greek economy.

After the economy, the paramount issue facing the royal government was security. The war of liberation had been fought by a combination of a very small army made up of Western-trained, regular troops and much larger bands of irregulars made up of former bandits, ex-militiamen and armed peasants. Military warlords, as we have seen, held sway over their band as their own personal property. The Bavarians, as had Kapodistrias before them, recognised that no national government was secure so long as warlords commanded their own private armies. They faced roughly the same options as the ill-fated first president: incorporate or eradicate the rootless gangs of irregulars. If anything, the situation facing them was even more acute than it had been for Kapodistrias. The civil war of 1832 had elevated the level of militarisation of the countryside and its outcome left stranded large numbers of disgruntled tough men who wanted their back pay, land and a livelihood. They looked to the boy king to give these things to them.

Otho and his regents had other ideas. They believed that a modern army, trained in the Western style and loyal only to the monarchy, could ensure the government's security. The 3,500 Bavarian troops that accompanied the king were soon augmented by 5,000 additional troops, all German volunteers. They were to form the core of the new regular army.

On 2 March 1833, the regency issued a decree disbanding the irregulars; another law that banned the possession of firearms without a government licence quickly followed it. Enforcement of these laws, however, could easily have plunged the nation into civil war yet again. So, the regents offered some inducements to get compliance. Older warriors would be enrolled into an honorary battalion and be provided with retirement benefits. Veterans could also send their sons to the newly established national military academy on Aegina free of charge. Finally, younger, able-bodied veterans could enlist in the new force on favourable terms. The idea was that Greek troops, trained and commanded by German officers, would compliment the Bavarian mercenaries in the new modern army. Still others were offered the opportunity of enlisting in the new gendarmerie that had been established to police the countryside.

Few Greeks responded favourably to these measures. Warlords were loath to lose the stick that gave them leverage in their attempts to gain political power locally. Uniforms, strict discipline, hard training and low pay were anathema to the proud and independent mountain warrior/brigands who made up the rank and file of the irregular bands. Thus, few answered the government's appeals favourably. Only a handful of able-bodied men enlisted in the regular army. More became gendarmes because this gave them complete discretion to exploit the local peasants in ways that they already had been doing. One old warhorse, at least, saw as a sham the government's schemes to disarm him and his comrades by offering them medals and honours, characterising these things as 'a bone [for us] to lick until [our] teeth finally fall out' (Koliopoulos 1987: 85). Most irregulars reverted to their old ways and became brigands or gunmen for hire. Some bandit gangs crossed over into Ottoman-controlled northern Greece and plied their craft there, using the border as means to play the Porte and government in Athens off against one another. Others formed bandit gangs that roamed the countryside of Attica and the Peloponnesos. Armed conflicts between them and the forces of the state were inevitable.

Between 1834 and 1840 numerous armed uprisings occurred. Some, like those in the Mani in 1834 and in Akarnania two years later, involved hundreds of men and required a sustained campaign by government forces to restore peace (Fig. 4.2). Equally important was the endemic banditry that flourished throughout the peninsula. Otho made a number of concessions, like dismissing the Bavarian troops and replacing them with Greeks, which helped to alleviate the situation somewhat. But brigandage and unrest would continue to plague his government and insecurity was a perennial problem, especially in the border zone. The situation was no better at sea than it was on land. Just as disgruntled, demobilised members of the revolutionary army proved a powerful destabilising factor on land, so too did pirates at sea. During the war, the Greek fleet had

Figure 4.2 *Greek police and Bavarian troops fighting Greek rebels (1830s), artist unknown © Thomas W. Gallant Photographic Collection.*

systematically preyed on Western-flagged ships that were sailing to Ottoman ports, arguing that they were preventing supplies from reaching the enemy. Though reasonable, this line of argument carried little weight in Western capitals. After independence, Greek piracy was indefensible and a source of contention between Athens and the Great Powers. Moreover, as Aegean pirates increasingly became less discriminating about whom they attacked, piracy proved detrimental to the Greek economy as well as providing a flashpoint for conflict with the Ottoman Empire. Issues over law and order, then, proved critical in the formative years of the new Greek state (Aroni-Tsihli 1989).

Political stability more broadly also proved elusive in the first decade after independence, and the monarchy's state-building initiatives only made matters worse. Otho and his advisors showed little sensitivity to indigenous traditions in social organisation, local governance, law and education as they attempted to impose Western models of governance. Take the situation with law and justice. Under Ottoman rule, people had options as to which legal system and which competent authority they would present their grievances. Depending on the nature of their case, a man or a woman could go before an Orthodox cleric and have their dispute settled by Orthodox canon law called the *Hexabiblos*. But, if they wanted to, they could go before a Muslim judge called a kadi to seek justice. Not only were people under the jurisdiction of more than one formal legal code (Orthodox Church law, Sharia, and imperial edicts and orders), they were also subject to an informal code based on local traditions. All across the Greek world, village councils of elderly men adjudicated conflicts and provided a communally based system of dispute resolution. Legal pluralism gave people choices and allowed them to go forum shopping in regard to the law.

Bavarian centralisation threatened the old order. The state drafted and then imposed a unified code of criminal justice and established a centralised court system. State courts and statutory criminal law replaced the old ways and deprived people, especially women, of the flexibility and autonomy of action that they enjoyed previously (Doxiades 2011; Gallant 2012). This development, not surprisingly, generated dissent and opposition to the regime. Among local elites, moreover, old cleavages from the war years remained and new ones connected to the struggle for power in local elections and for influence with the royal court developed. The political system established in 1834 made such developments inevitable. The kingdom was divided administratively into ten nomarchies (prefectures), fifty-nine eparchies (sub-prefectures), and 468 demes (counties) (Map 4.1). Nomarchs and eparchs were nominated directly by the king; demarchs were appointed by him from a list of three elected by a small number of the wealthiest men in each deme. This level of state centralisation violated social norms that vested power in the hands of local men, that privileged local customs over state law, and that had flourished for centuries under the Ottomans. The state's centralising policies rankled with the men who had for centuries wielded local power. The extreme centralism at the heart of the new administration trampled on the long and storied tradition of local rule. And it challenged, in theory at least, the power of the local elites (Mavromoustakou 2003: 29–35).

Adding further fuel to the political fire was the religious question. On 4 August 1833, a royal decree drafted by von Maurer, Spyridon Trikoupis, a prominent politician, and Theoklitos Farmakides, a leading Orthodox cleric, established an autocephalous Orthodox Church of the kingdom of Greece with Otho as its titular head. This was to be an explicitly 'national' church, that is, a church of the Greek nation. It would be governed by a synod headed by the Archbishop of Athens, but as an institute the church was a branch of the

Greek state. This step was in keeping with actions taken by each of the revolutionary governments, beginning with the very first, which stated in its constitution that the Orthodox Church was inseparable from the Greek state.

The establishment of the autocephalous church had manifold consequences. First, it set a precedent for linking nationalism and religion institutionally that every one of the secessionist movements in the Ottoman Balkans would follow. Second, it raised the vexing question regarding what would be the relationship between the new Greek national church and the Ecumenical Patriarchate in Istanbul. After all, the Patriarchate had vehemently opposed the Greek uprising and, moreover, it remained a multinational religious organisation under the control of the Ottoman state. The question, then, was what would be the relationship between the two Orthodox Churches? For one prominent Greek intellectual, Adamantios Korais, the answer was that there should be none:

> From this hour the clergy of the liberated parts of Greece no longer owe recognition to the ecclesiastical authority of the Patriarch of Constantinople who remains contaminated under the throne of a lawless tyrant ... A clergy of free and independent Greeks is most unfitting as long as it obeys the commands of a Patriarch chosen by a despot and forced to bow down before a tyrant. (Korais cited in Frazee 1969: 102)

In fact, the Holy Synod of Greece voted in 1836 to sever all relations with the Patriarchate and the two churches remained estranged until 1850.

There were, however, powerful voices in the kingdom that from the moment of independence pressed for unity with the Great Church. After 1834, this faction was led by the powerful cleric Konstantinos Oikonomos. He was born in a village in Thessaly in 1780. His father had been a cleric and he followed in his footsteps. He earned a reputation as being a powerful preacher and news of his charismatic following reached Constantinople. In 1808 Patriarch Gregory V invited him to the capital. He was in Constantinople when the rebellion erupted. In the face of the prosecutions against Christian leaders, he fled to Russia, taking up residence in Odessa. His stay there was brief. In 1822 he relocated to St Petersburg, where, within a short time, he became a leading advisor to Tsar Alexander I on Greek affairs. He moved to the kingdom of Greece in 1834, but not before receiving a royal blessing and a generous stipend. On his way to Greece, he undertook a diplomatic mission that saw him meet with the Prussian Emperor, Wilhelm I, in Berlin and the pope in Rome. When he arrived in Greece there was widespread suspicion that he was acting as an agent of the Russians. He led the conservative faction that wanted to embed the new kingdom in the greater Orthodox community (Frazee 1969; Makrides 2009; Tzanaki 2009: 31).

In addition to this split, there was another faction, led by Theophilos Kairis, which argued that the new state should have its own religion. Kairis was born on 19 October 1784 to one of the most prominent families on the island of Andros. At the age of eight, he was sent to the Virgin Mary of the Orphans School, also known as the Oikonomou's School located at Kydonies/Aivali in Asia Minor. He continued his studies, working with some of the leading Orthodox intellectuals of the time. He particularly excelled in the sciences. In 1803, he emigrated to Italy where he studied theology, philosophy, mathematics and physics at the University of Pisa. Having completed his studies there, he relocated to Paris where he became a close confidant of Adamantios Korais. Kairis, unlike Korais, viewed the French Revolution positively and during his time in France he developed a deep love of liberalism. In sum, he was a true child of the Enlightenment. In 1810, he returned to the Ottoman Empire and he held a number of teaching positions between then and the outbreak of the war in 1821. He returned to his native island where he drafted its declaration of independence. He fought heroically during the conflict and received numerous wounds that impaired his health for the rest of his life. As a liberal dedicated to the idea of republicanism, he was profoundly disappointed by the presidency of Kapodistrias. Not surprisingly, he was an ardent foe of Bavarian absolutism, and on one occasion even refused to accept a medal from the king.

During the 1830s, he was active as a teacher and as a religious agitator. He believed that the new country needed a new religion. He developed a doctrine of belief that he labelled 'theosebism'. Based upon deism, this new faith espoused a belief in God as the creator of the universe but rejected the idea that God interfered in human affairs, much less that the Bible was the received word of God or that Jesus Christ was his son. Theosebism promoted the idea that the Bible was just one of many texts that could guide human morality. Kairis opposed all organised religions and saw the Orthodox Church as an oppressive force. Not surprisingly, he ran afoul of the church hierarchy, and the Holy Synod banished him. During his exile, he travelled widely in the Ottoman Empire and in Western Europe before returning to Greece in 1844. Though he was allowed back, nonetheless, his relationship with the Holy Synod remained strained until finally on 21 December 1852 he was placed on trial for proselytism. He was found guilty and sentenced to a prison term, though he served less than a year of it before dying (Theodossiou et al. 2004).

In addition to these disputes among Orthodox clerics, there were other issues involving religion that caused dissent. One had to do with the Catholics. There was a sizable Catholic population in the new kingdom and this raised the issue of their spiritual needs and their relationship to the papacy. Implicated in this matter, of course, was the fact the royal family was Catholic and had no intention of converting to Orthodoxy. Finally, the activities of Protestant missionaries aroused opposition because of the widespread suspicion that they were proselytising the youth through their supposedly educational endeavours (Repousis 2009). On numerous occasions, the religious question led to eruptions of violent unrest: the most important of these was the Papoulakos affair.

Christoforos Panayiotopoulos, also known as Papoulakos, was a butcher and a pig merchant from central Greece. While suffering from a typhus-induced hallucination, he received a vision from God, in which he was told that he was to lead to a mass movement to restore traditional Orthodoxy. When he recovered, he became a messianic preacher, travelling around the Greek countryside extolling against the king, whom he accused of being an atheist and of sharing with the French and the British the goal of destroying Orthodoxy. He also assailed the institutions of the new state, like the University of Athens, which he referred to as 'the devil's tool', and Jews, whom he accused of being 'crypto-Muslims' and defilers of Christ. His zealous message resonated with religiously conservative peasants, and at the height of his movement he had over 6,000 followers. In addition, he came to the attention of the Philorthodox Society, which supported his opposition to Otho's regime. On 26 May 1852 he actually mobilised his followers into a rebel army and marched on the city of Kalamata, where he was defeated by the Greek army. He was arrested, convicted and sentenced to prison, but because of his ongoing popularity, the government opted to release him rather than make him into a martyr. Episodes like this show that the persistent and heated contestation over the religious question bedevilled the Bavarian monarchy throughout its duration (Makrides 2009: 56; Zelpos 2011: 69).

The Philorthodox Society was perhaps the most prominent example of this development. It had been around since the revolution and its members were dedicated to fostering closer relations among and between the greater Orthodox community, that being Russia, Orthodox Christians in the Ottoman Empire, and of course in Greece. The society drew most of its membership from adherents to the Russian party, and many of them held high positions in the government. By early 1839, as it became increasingly clear that Otho had no intention of converting to Orthodoxy or of producing an heir who would be raised in the Orthodox faith, the society decided to force his hand. It endeavoured to coerce Otho to convert or to abdicate in favour of an Orthodox candidate. There were even rumours that they intended to physically kidnap the royal couple and to hold them captive until they choose one of those options. The king was in a quandary. On the one hand, he and his closest advisors knew that the society's membership came from the Russian party, but they did not know who they were exactly. On the other hand, Otho needed the Russian party to staff his government, because the alternative was to appoint men from the other parties who were committed to curtailing his powers through the promulgation of a constitution. In the end, the conspiracy came to nothing and it was revealed that only a small number of men were involved. Nonetheless, this episode was significant because it showed the depth of feeling that the religious issue generated and it indicated that men of the Greek political class were willing to take direct action to achieve political change, which they eventually did in 1843 (Petropoulos 1968: 329–43; Marangou-Drygiannaki 2000; Dialla 2009; Theodorou 1992).[2]

The international context

Any assessment of the Greek world after the creation of the new kingdom has to include a discussion of what this development meant for Greeks outside of its boundaries and what impact it had internationally. One issue that arose as a consequence of independence that needed to be addressed then and that we, as historians today, have to deal with now regards identity and terminology. As we saw earlier, before independence, identities in the Ottoman Empire were varied and fluid, but the official terminology for referring to groups was not. Greeks who were Orthodox were members of the Millet-i Rom, and were referred to, and called themselves, Romioi (Romans). The term

'Hellenes' (Έλληνες) was employed, but not widely. Modern scholars use the terms 'Greeks' or 'Ottoman Greeks' to refer to them. After independence, however, there were now two formal yet distinct Greek statuses: subjects (and after 1844, citizens) of the independent Greek state and Greek subjects of the Ottoman Empire. The Ottomans referred to the former as Yunaniler (Hellenes) and their state as Yunan, while the latter continued to be described by the older terminology. Scholars, however, have not been as consistent, with many deploying the term 'Greek' interchangeably to refer to citizens of the kingdom and subjects of the empire. Others have used various terms to refer to the latter. Some opt for 'Ottoman Greek', while others prefer 'Greek Orthodox Christians' or 'Greek Orthodox Community' (Doumanis 2013: 8–11) or even just 'Orthodox Christians' (Ozil 2013: 9–10). Each of these terms has strengths and weaknesses. Those that deploy Orthodox as the key descriptor leave out non-Orthodox Greeks, like the many Catholic Greek islanders. Those that denote the entire Orthodox community also include many non-Greeks, such as Bulgarians and non-Greek Orthodox Christians. From this point on, we shall use 'Greek' to refer to citizens of the kingdom of Greece; to designate Greece in the Ottoman Empire we shall deploy 'Rom' and its cognates or Ottoman Greeks interchangeably. For Greeks of the diaspora, I use hyphenated terms such as Greek-American and Greek-Russian to refer to their communities. None of these terms are perfect, but they do capture the complexity of the identity issue that arose when one part of the Greek world was cleaved off as a separate entity from the political domain where the vast majority of Greeks still lived.

A key element of foreign relations between Greece and the Ottoman Empire was the border. The new land boundary between the kingdom and the empire made little sense in terms of either physical or human geography. As a consequence, the borderland remained a flashpoint of tension between the two. The border stretched from a line beginning in the Ambracian Gulf in the west, extended through the rugged mountains of the interior and ended up on the east side of the peninsula at the Pelasgic Gulf (Map 4.1). It became known as the Arta-Lamia line, even though one of those cities, Arta, remained in the Ottoman Empire. A team of British surveyors drew the boundary, trying as best they could to follow the natural topography of peaks and ravines. They paid scant attention to the human dimension. As one scholar has noted: 'The boundary cut across migratory paths of nomads, and residents of certain villages suddenly found their crops and water sources on opposite sides of the boundary' (Gavrilis 2008a: 37). Indeed, in one case, the border actually ran through the middle of a village and the villagers had to decide which side they wished to be on and then they moved their houses accordingly.

The result of all this was the creation of a border that was utterly indefensible. What I mean by this was that neither the Greek nor the Ottoman side could effectively prevent cross-border movements. Indeed what developed was a frontier zone that both sides recognised as a zone of interaction. Policing the border became less a matter of preventing illegal border crossings than of managing them. While the fluidity of the borderland allowed social life and economic activity to continue much as it had before, it also allowed banditry to flourish. Brigands and outlaws manipulated the frontier, committing crimes on one side of the border and then easily slipping over to the other side. In fact, bandit activity fostered cooperation between the border patrols on each side: something that was made easier by the fact that on occasion members of the same family were hired as border guards by both sides. Even though out of necessity the Greek–Ottoman border became a frontier zone rather than a rigid linear boundary, it remained a flashpoint that at any moment could trigger war between the two states (Gavrilis 2008a; 2008b; 2010; for a critical assessment by one of the men who helped define the border, see Baker 1837; for a general discussion of bandits and borders, see Gallant 1999).

In spite of the treaties that created the secessionist state of Greece and that made France, England and Russia the guarantors of that independence, there was still uncertainty as to whether or not Mahmud II might try to recoup his losses as he tried to reform his empire (Anscombe 2010). A conflict within the Ottoman Empire ensured that this did not happen. Tensions were building between the Porte and Mehmet Ali of Egypt over a number of issues. Mehmet Ali felt that the sultan had failed to live up to his promises. After all, the Egyptian had expended a great deal in the expedition to the Morea and, even though it had met with defeat, he still expected to receive his promised rewards, in particular the governorship of Syria. Mahmud reneged on that promise. Another source of tension between the two was Mehmet Ali's suspicion that Mahmud planned to depose him as part of his centralising reforms of the empire. So, in 1831 Mehmet Ali ordered his son, Ibrahim Paşa, to invade Syria. The Egyptian army quickly took the province and then marched on Istanbul itself. After scoring a number of brilliant victories, the

Egyptian army was poised to seize the capital and install Mehmet Ali as sultan. At this juncture the Great Powers intervened and brokered a settlement that included making Ibrahim governor of Syria. A second round of fighting began later in the decade, and once again external brokerage led to a settlement (Abu-Manneh 2010; Aksan 2007: chapters 8–9; Fahmy 1997; Marsot 1984). The Ottoman Civil War had important consequences. First, it inhibited direct interference in the affairs of the new kingdom by the Porte. Second, it entangled the Great Powers, especially Great Britain and Russia, even more in the affairs of the Eastern Mediterranean, taking the Eastern Question to a new level. Third, it gave greater impetus to the Ottoman government to carry out reforms within the empire. These reforms would have far-reaching consequences and it is to them that we turn next.

In exchange for their support in settling the dispute with Egypt, France and Great Britain put pressure on the new sultan, Abdülmecid, to continue the social and political reformation of the empire begun by his predecessor. And this he did on November 1839, when he issued an imperial edict called the Gulhane Imperial Rescript (or the Rose Garden Decree). It continued the process of Ottoman Reformation and is referred to as the Tanzimat. These reforms had an impact on all subjects of the Ottoman Empire, including, of course, Ottoman Greeks. The reorganisation of the empire took place in two phases; the first, in 1839, that we will discuss here and a second round that took place in 1856, which we will examine shortly.

The overall aim of the Tanzimat was to create a European-style governing structure and to modify the social contract between ruler and ruled that would abolish the religiously-based discriminatory laws. According to the imperial decree, henceforth all of the sultan's subjects were equal in the eyes of the law. At a stroke, this did away with the centuries-old system of legal inferiority for non-Muslims. Among the basic rights bestowed on all subjects were the rights to due process and *habeus corpus*. It guaranteed the property rights of all individuals and protected their honour from assail. In addition to protecting personal rights, the reforms also reorganised the judiciary and the tax system. The organisational structure of the central and the provincial administrations were revamped and modernised. While some Ottoman Greeks opposed the Tanzimat because it displaced them from their position as the most privileged of the non-Muslim groups, on balance it was more beneficial. Ottoman Greeks were better able than most to exploit the new openings created by the reforms, and many of them would achieve considerable political power, while others would benefit economically. Indeed, so impactful were the reforms that many Greeks from the kingdom migrated to the Ottoman Empire. The new opportunities being opened by the reforms contrasted sharply with the ongoing troubles that beset Otho's Greece.

Constitutional monarchy

Opposition to Othian absolutism ran deep, but there were times when it manifested itself more openly. The winter of 1836–7 was one such moment. In late November Otho wed, taking as his bride Amalia of Oldenberg. Though quite young, she embraced her new country and its people warmly. She was a proud Philhellene who quickly learned Greek, adopted Greek traditional dress and actively engaged in social work. On the negative side, she was a staunch Catholic, had a quick temper and a very strong personality that she imposed on her more malleable husband. Within a short time, she was a power to be reckoned with in her own right, especially after von Armensparg's dismissal in February 1837. With a new wife and a different set of advisors, Otho endeavoured to rule as a paternalistic autocrat. It did not go well. The religious question remained prominent, and if anything became worse. There was also a series of other events that elevated opposition to him.

One had to do with his military reforms. As part of the process of 'Hellenising' the armed forces, the new law mandated selective conscription, and this did not go over very well. On the island of Hydra in 1838, for example, seamen who were to be pressed into service as naval marines rioted, chanting that they preferred death to conscription. Similar scenes were played out elsewhere in the country.

Otho's handling of relations with the Ottoman Empire also generated discontent. Many people believed that Otho had missed a golden opportunity to advance Greece's cause during the decade-long conflict between Mehmet I and Mehmet Ali. Even more disturbing were the steps he was taking towards rapprochement with the Porte. In 1839, his foreign minister, Konstantinos Zografos, negotiated a commercial treaty that restored diplomatic relations between the two countries. Even though this agreement would have brought Greece numerous economic benefits, it was widely denounced and, in fact,

Otho's own council of state refused to recognise it. All of the tensions that had been building for more than a decade came to a head in 1843.

On the night of 14 September 1843, Colonel Dimitrios Kallergis led a bloodless coup that toppled the absolute monarchy. Kallergis was a descendant of one of Crete's most important families and he was the nephew of Count Karl Nesselrode, Foreign Minister of Russia. When he became an orphan, the count took him in and saw to his education, first in St Petersburg and then in Vienna. When the War of Independence broke out, Kallergis rushed to join and he led a cohort of revolutionaries from Crete. When the regular Greek army was formed, he joined and became an assistant to Colonel Fabier. During the Kapodistrian presidency, he rose through the ranks. His ascendancy in the Greek political world was certainly helped by his having married into the Rentis family, one of the most prominent clans in Corinth. In 1842, he was appointed commander of the Royal Guard based at the garrison of Goudi. Plots against Otho had been hatching for some time and their existence was well known. When Otho's attempt to arrest the ringleaders failed, Kallergis called out the Royal Guard and marched on the palace. The square in front of it soon filled with people. Shouts of 'long live the constitution' and 'death to the Bavarians' rang out from the crowd. After consultations with Kallergis and other military leaders, meetings with heads of the major parties and audiences with Great Power delegations, Otho saw that his position was untenable. Without a drop of blood being shed, the Bavarian absolute monarchy came to an end.

In the wake of the military coup, Otho reluctantly agreed to far-reaching and fundamental changes to the kingdom's government. Elections were held and 243 deputies were elected to a constituent assembly, which convened on 20 November 1843. From this body, a committee of twenty-one was given the task of writing the first Greek constitution. When they finished their work, the full assembly over-whelmingly passed the document and then, on 7 March 1844, it was presented to the king. After some initial wrangling, he agreed to accept it. A new system of government was thus established. Otho would rule as a constitutional monarch. There would be a bicameral legislature (consisting of the Vouli or Lower House of Parliament, and the Gerousia, an Upper House or Senate) elected on the basis of mass enfranchisement (any male with property over twenty-five years of age could vote). Greece became in theory one of the most democratic states in Europe (Louvi 2003).

Otho, however, retained the power to appoint or dismiss unilaterally government ministers, to dissolve parliament, and to veto legislation. With the counter-signature of a minister, he could issue executive decrees as law, and with the agreement of the prime minister, he could appoint for life members of the Gerousia. Otho agreed in turn that his successor to the throne would be Greek Orthodox (Alivisatos 2011: 94).

During the deliberations on the constitution, a contentious issue arose that threatened to disrupt the proceedings and that created deep divisions in Greek society. The matter had to do with who had the right to hold political appointments and to participate in government. In other words, they focused on the issue of (1) who was a Greek citizen and (2) whether all Greek citizens were equal. The issue of defining who belonged to the nation had long been problematic. No single marker, be it religion or language, was sufficient in determining who belonged to the Greek nation. There had, of course, been attempts to define the criteria for citizenship; all of the charters drafted by governments during the revolution, for example, had done so. Moreover, in 1835, the Bavarian regime implemented a law that specifically defined Greek citizenship. This status was granted to anyone whose parents were Greek naturals, to all Philhellenes who had fought for at least two years during the national struggle, and any Christians who had migrated to the kingdom after the protocol of 16 June 1830. Moreover, a person born in Greece of foreign parents could acquire citizenship after coming of age and anyone born abroad to a Greek father had the right to claim Greek citizenship. Under Othonian absolutism, this was not a paramount issue since whatever rights citizens had derived from the monarchy.

With the introduction of democracy, however, who was entitled to full citizen rights became of paramount importance. The idea that a state could have citizens with differential citizenship rights was, at the time, quite common; France under the July Monarchy, for example, distinguished between active and passive citizens. In Greece, at issue was whether or not those who were native born (autochthons in Greek) and those who were non-natives (heterochthons) should have equal right to participate in the political process. The dispute stemmed from the resentment that had been simmering among the native population since the presidency of Kapodistrias, during which Greeks from abroad occupied most of the key positions in government while growing rich buying up newly nationalised lands. After ferocious debates that threatened to erupt into violence, the National

Assembly voted 'Resolution B'. This law created three categories of citizens, the first two of which were eligible for government service while the third would be only after a period of residence in the kingdom. This prejudicial law would be modified in 1856 and abolished by the Constitution of 1864, which treated all citizens, regardless of their place of birth, as equal (on the citizenship debate, see Alivisatos 2011: 91; Vogli 2007; 2009; Michailidis 2006; Mavromoustakou 2003: 37–46).

Political parties did not arise in the wake of parliamentary democracy. Instead factionalism took a new form. Hierarchical pyramids of power centring on a single prominent man developed and were held together by patronage networks. No one played the new power politics better than Ioannis Kolettis and he left his imprimatur on mid-century Greek politics. He was able to form working alliances with both the Western modernisers and the traditional power brokers while becoming closely tied to neither. Politics by personalities as exemplified in the career of Kolettis set the pattern for the political culture of Greece until the 1870s.

This crafty veteran of political intrigue was appointed Prime Minister of Greece under the new system in 1844 because he enjoyed the support of the king. His faction occupied only 22 of the 127 seats in the Lower House. Through lavish use of gifts and bribes, cajoling and intimidation, Kolettis managed the new parliament. His faction grew in size and he personally monopolised power, holding the portfolios, at one point or another during his three-year term, of Foreign Affairs, Justice, Interior, Culture and Public Instruction, and Finance as well as being prime minister. Coupled with his autocratic inclinations were his populist tendencies: he knew the value of popular support in a democratic system. As a contemporary, George Finlay noted about Kolettis: 'He could hear the first whispers of public opinion, and he knew to avail himself of its support as soon as it made its voice heard' (Finlay 1971: vol. 2, 197).

Kolettis is best remembered as the man who first articulated a vision that became called the 'Megali Idea', or Great Idea (Stouraiti and Kazamias 2010). What he meant by this was that the Greek War of Independence that had resulted in the creation of the kingdom of Greece was incomplete. The war of liberation would not be complete until the territorial boundaries of the Greek state had been expanded to encompass all of those regions in which Greeks were the majority. To be sure, Kolettis was not the first to espouse this view. It was an idea that was in circulation throughout the 1830s. What he did was to give it clarity and coherence, and since he articulated this vision in a speech he gave as foreign minister, it gave the appearance that it was official policy. Moreover, it was meant to be a pointed rejoinder to the infamous Resolution B that carved out preferential rights for Greeks resident in the kingdom over those who remained in the Ottoman Empire. The Megali Idea became the driving force of Greek foreign policy for the next seventy years and it was Otho's inability as constitutional monarch to fulfil the Megali Idea that contributed to his eventual downfall. There were, however, numerous other developments during the critical decade of the 1850s that had a major impact on the Greek world and that led to a regime change in 1863 (Gekas 2013).

The transitional moment

1848 was the year of revolutions in Europe. Beginning in Paris and then spreading all across the continent, with a few notable exceptions, social revolutions erupted and challenged the conservative order of post-Napoleonic Europe. Fuelled by a combination of middle-class discontent at their continued lack of access to power and debarment from the political process and the deeply felt grievances amongst the newly emergent working class, people took to the streets and in remarkably short order either overthrew or forced their governments to make major changes. In the end, however, it was the middle class that emerged from 1848 as the winner. Neither Greece nor the Ottoman Empire experienced social revolutions directly. Nonetheless, the 1848 revolutions had an impact on them.

The uprisings that began in Paris in February of that momentous year were driven by a number of factors. One of them was a reaction against the stultifying conservative order that had reigned in Europe since the demise of Napoleon. Especially among Europe's emerging middle class, the old order's insistence on denying them political rights motivated liberals everywhere to revolt. Another important factor related to the newly formed industrial working class. Workers' grievances revolved around workplace conditions and bread-and-butter issues. This Liberal-working class alliance proved a heady combination and, when confronted with their uprisings, almost all of the governments of Europe had to make major concessions, particularly to the bourgeoisie. In some regions of Europe, however, most particularly in the Habsburg Empire, another dimension of the uprisings and insurrections was nationalism. Newly emergent national groups rose up and sought to create their own nation-state.

Nationalist revolts directly impacted the Ottoman Empire, destabilising its frontier zone with the Habsburgs. When Romanian nationalists rose in revolt and declared the unification and independence of the Danubian Principalities, the empire's territorial integrity became threatened. This led to a short-term alliance between the Russian and Ottoman Empires, whose combined military forces easily suppressed the insurrections. But tensions between the two remained high, as Russian troops occupied Transylvania and remained in Romania. In addition, the Ottomans had to confront internal insurrections in Serbia, Montenegro and Bulgaria (Aksan 2007: 426–7). Though successful in suppressing these, the forces of nationalism that 1848 unleashed would have long-term consequences for the empire, and to a lesser extent for Greece as well. Though not directly impacted by the 1848 revolutions, they, along with other developments specific to Greece, inaugurated a decade of crises that altered the kingdom's developmental trajectory in fundamental ways.

Don Pacifico was a British Jew from Gibraltar living in Athens. On Easter Sunday 1847, a mob gathered in front of his house. Some began to throw stones, smashing windows, and then two burly men launched themselves against the doors and broke into the house. The place was ransacked, his possessions pillaged and much of his house destroyed: sixteen windows were smashed, with their grills and shutters torn down. Moreover, when the Greek police arrived, they did nothing to stop the mob. Don Pacifico complained bitterly to the Greek government and demanded compensation. When that was not forthcoming, the British government became directly involved. The dispute between Pacifico and the Greek government eventually made its way to the floor of the British parliament. The episode played a critical role in alienating Britain and, in particular, its foreign minister Lord Palmerston from Greece. So deep did the division between him and Otho's government become that he ordered a military embargo of Athens until such time as Don Pacifico received compensation. But this was not the only case of Greece's bad behaviour alienating one of its guarantor powers (Fleming 2008: 23–9; Hannell 1989; Hicks 2004; Makrides 2009: 87–8).

Another episode, involving a British subject, occurred at the same time as the Don Pacifico affair and it exacerbated the increasing tension between Greece and Britain. Captain John Parker was a former British soldier who retired to the Ionian island of Kefalonia, where he married Kiara Assani, the daughter of a Greek aristocratic family and took up employment as the forest ranger on the island's Black Mountain. At this time, the Ionian Islands were a self-governing state under the protection of the British Crown. Criminal justice fell under the jurisdiction of the Ionian government and so Parker was an employee of the Ionian police department. On 8 May 1849, Parker and his pet dog were brutally murdered while patrolling the mountain. There was at this time a radical movement on the island that sought unification with the kingdom of Greece. The year before Parker's murder there had been an outbreak of anti-British violence, and there was every indication that another rebellion was in the offing. The police investigation uncovered evidence that suggested that officials in the Greek government were complicit in Parker's killing. That Greek officials impeded the murder investigation seemed to confirm British suspicions, thus escalating further tensions between London and Athens. Having already alienated both France and Russia, Greece was on the verge of losing the support of the third of its protecting powers. Moreover, it was fast gaining a reputation as the 'bad child' of the Mediterranean (Gallant 2015, forthcoming).

The one mid-century event that more than any other had the greatest impact on the Ottoman Empire and Greece, however, was the Crimean War (Badem 2010; Figes 2010). In the case of the former, the conflict once more plunged it into war against its traditional enemy, Russia, but in this case it was joined by Great Britain and France. The war put the Greek kingdom in a delicate position, because it pitted two of its three guarantor powers against the other. Moreover, it saw the alliance of Greece's nemesis, the Ottoman Empire, with the two European states that have been most directly responsible for its independence. In the case of the greater Greek world, the situation was even more complicated because the war placed Greek-Russians on one side and Ottoman Greeks on the other.

The war marked the end of the era of Great Power cooperation that had kept the peace in post-Napoleonic Europe, and it was the growing tension between them over the Eastern Question that triggered the conflict. Under the aggressive leadership of Napoleon III, France sought to reclaim its status as a global power, including reasserting French influence in the Eastern Mediterranean. Much as Russia claimed that it had the moral, if not the legal, right to protect the Orthodox population of the Ottoman Empire, France now demanded similar recognition with respect to the Ottoman Catholic population. It demanded that the Porte recognise it as the sovereign authority over the Holy Land and, to symbolise this new-found prophylactic right, to transfer control over the Church of the Nativity in Bethlehem from the Ecumenical Patriarchate to the Catholic Church, threatening to take more dramatic action should Istanbul decline. In response, the patriarch pleaded with Russia to intervene on behalf of the Orthodox Church. The Ottoman government was now caught in the middle of a power struggle between Paris and St Petersburg. It chose the former over the latter and this led to the declaration of war in October 1853.

The Ottoman Empire went to war against the Russian Empire yet again. For our purposes, we do not need to go into the details of the war except to note that the major theatres of conflict were in Crimea, along the Danube and on the Black Sea. It is how the war impacted the Greek world that concerns us, and its ramifications were many.

Four hundred years after the fall of Constantinople (1453–1853), Otho and his government saw an opportunity in the Crimean War to advance the Megali Idea. Urged on by vague Russian and Austrian assurances that it would support the Orthodox populations of the Balkans who rose up against the Ottomans, Greece dispatched military forces to the border and ordered armed bands to infiltrate the frontier regions of Thessaly and Epiros with the intent of fomenting insurrections. These areas were vulnerable because the Ottomans had moved armed forces from them to the war front. Moreover, they were confident that the local Orthodox population would rise up and join with their co-nationals to proclaim unification. War fever spread throughout the kingdom, and there was even a rumour that Otho himself would lead the invasion.

This did not happen, but by January 1854 Greek bands had made significant inroads and were even besieging the city of Arta. Everything changed quickly. Even before France and Britain entered the war in March, they were putting pressure on Greece to pull back the rebel bands. When Otho demurred, asserting that as the only Christian king in the Near East he would never abandon the sacred struggle for liberation, a joint Franco-British force landed at Piraeus and occupied Athens. Otho had no choice but to declare Greece's neutrality. Figure 4.3 aptly captures this degrading moment, showing Great Britain giving Greece a kick in the pants while France looks on. This humiliation was soon joined by the ignominious defeat of the Greek rebel bands by Ottoman forces. Except for some military

Figure 4.3 *France and Britain humiliating Greece, 1854, artist unknown © Sarivari.*

officers who resigned their commissions, formed a unit called the Greek Legion and went to Crimea to join the Russian army, Greece's role in the war was at an end. But the war's impact on other areas of the Greek world continued.

For Greek-Russians, the war was a disaster. First, the main theatres of the conflict were areas where there were significant Greek-Russian populations, such as Taganrog, a majority Greek city that was severely damaged by British bombardments. Second, the conflict greatly disrupted international commerce, in particular the lucrative grain trade, much of which Greek trading houses controlled. Even the profits gained by supplying the Russian armed forces did not make up for these losses. For Ottoman Greeks, there was more of an upside. Many Greek, Armenian and Jewish merchant houses reaped war profits by outfitting and supplying the Ottoman army. The events leading up to, rather than the war itself, did much to solidify the position of Phanariots in the Ottoman administration. In the decade after the beginning of the Tanzimat, Phanariots were able to regain positions of prominence in the imperial government that they had lost during the 1820s. Whether it be as governors of Samos or as intermediaries between the government and the Ecumenical Patriarchate, they played vital roles in administering parts of the empire. In the run up to the war, Stephanos Vogorides, for example, was a major player in the negotiations over the Holy Sites (Philliou 2011: 152–69). The situation of Orthodox Christians would change even more dramatically after the war's end.

The Crimean War had far-reaching consequences for the Greek and Ottoman worlds. The Treaty of Paris, signed in March 1856, fundamentally altered power relations in the region and the Eastern Question entered a new and more dangerous phase. First, the signatories to the treaty agreed to guarantee the territorial integrity of the Ottoman Empire as one of the conditions of its inclusion in the Concert of Europe (Adanir 2005). This alone struck a blow to the Greek Megali Idea and the movements for independence amongst other Balkan Christian groups; it also blunted Russia's ambitions to act as protector of those movements. The neutrality of the Black Sea was assured and it was declared a demilitarised zone. The treaty also affirmed Ottoman sovereignty over Moldavia, Wallachia and Serbia but now under the protection of the Great Powers rather than Russia alone. Sultan Abdülmecid had to agree to grant the Danubian Principalities their own system of government as defined in a body of law called the Organic Statutes, and, perhaps most importantly, to accede to another round of internal reformations. This second phase of the Tanzimat had far-reaching consequences for Ottoman Greeks, as we shall see in the next chapter. The treaty generated much hostility in Russia, which saw it as a significant blow to its prestige. For the Greeks of Russia, it also marked a fundamental turning point. From this point on, for the vast majority of them, their future lay in Russia and their engagement with the kingdom of Greece and the greater Greek world would be largely economic and not much more.

In Greece, Otho's fortunes never really rebounded from the humiliation suffered in 1854. A series of lacklustre administrations did little to rehabilitate Greece in the eyes of Western Europe nor, to a large extent, even amongst its own people. The religious issue still loomed large. Otho and Amalia were growing older and had still not produced an heir, and they remained steadfast in their adherence to Catholicism. The Risorgimento in Italy (1861) put into stark contrast Otho's singular inability to advance the Greek national cause. This was partly a reflection of his government's political and financial

Figure 4.4 The last known photograph of King Otho after he returned to Bavaria (1865) © Wikimedia Commons. He died shortly after this photograph was taken.

weakness and of the disfavour in which the Greek monarchy was held by France and Britain. The forces of opposition to the Bavarian regime continued to grow in strength. Radical nationalist university students tried to assassinate Queen Amalia in 1861and barely failed, and a military revolt centred in Nafplion in early 1862 was only marginally suppressed. Matters came to a head later that year.

In mid-October, Otho and Amalia left Athens to tour the Peloponnesos; they wanted a respite from the political hothouse in Athens and they wanted to hear first-hand the opinions of 'real' Greeks. While they were away, revolts broke out at numerous garrisons around the country, and when they tried to enter the port of Piraeus, the Royal Navy blocked them. In their absence, a blood-less coup had taken place. A provisional government had seized power, declaring the abolition of the Bavarian monarchy. Amalia, the stronger of the two to the end, urged her husband to fight, but he would not; his will to resist had evaporated when he was informed that none of the guarantor powers would come to his rescue. Otho left Greece a broken man. He spent the rest of his life, which turned out to be only a few years (he died on 26 July 1867), in Munich, often seen still wearing the traditional Greek fustanella (Fig. 4.4). He had come to love his adopted country but its people never loved him back. There would, then, be a new administration in the kingdom of Greece and this momentous political change would come at a time when the entire Greek and Ottoman worlds were in a state of flux.

Notes

1. His given name was of course Otto, but that name was not easily rendered into Greek and so throughout his reign Greeks referred to him as Otho.
2. The society did not cease to exist because its plot failed this time. It continued to be a vibrant source of opposition to Otho, a denouncer of modernity – one leading member, for example, referred to the steamship as the work of the devil – and a proponent of closer cooperation between Greece and Russia. It was not until Russia began to espouse a policy of Pan-Slavism rather than Pan-Orthodoxy that the society dissolved (Zelpos 2011: 69).

CHAPTER 5

Liberal modernisation: successes and failures (1863–93)

The three decades after Otho's departure were a time of transition and change in the Greek world. In the kingdom, after a period of instability, two parties, led by two profoundly different men, emerged and dominated the political scene. Harilaos Trikoupis and Theodoros Deliyiannis, pictured opposite (Figs 5.1a and 5.1b), each in their own way undertook initiatives that aimed to modernise Greece. Their efforts achieved some notable successes but many failures as well, culminating in the country's financial collapse in the mid-1890s.

The two drawings opposite capture the intensity of their rivalry. The drawing on the right is from an anti-Trikoupis piece of political propaganda, in which the devil exhorts the viewer to literally 'blackball' Trikoupis by casting a black ball into the ballot boxes of candidates representing his Modernist Party. The poster on the left tries to persuade the voter to support him based upon rational self-interest. The price tags surrounding each of their portraits show the viewers that, economically, they did better under Trikoupis. One price tag, for example, lists the price of bread under him at 40 drachmas as opposed to the 60 drachmas that it cost when Deliyiannis was in power. Others depict staples, like rice, coffee and meat, as being likewise cheaper under him. On the right side of each portrait are listed their major accomplishments; for Trikoupis, these include railways, roads and public order, whereas for Deliyiannis the list includes anarchy and fiscal ruin. For most of the period covered in this chapter one or the other of these men would be at the head of the Greek government, trying to fulfil their agenda, but they did not do so in a vacuum. The last three decades of the nineteenth century were a time of intense political, social and economic transition the world over, and so we have to situate what happened in Greece into broader regional and international frameworks. We begin, however, with the political transition from Otho to the new 'crowned democracy' under King George I.

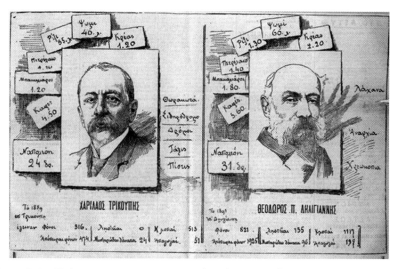

Figure 5.1a *Trikoupis campaign poster, The Election, February 6, 1894* © Astir.
The two most important politicians of their era: Harilaos Trikoupis and Theodoros Deliyiannis.

ΜΑΥΡΟ ΟΠΟΥ ΤΡΙΚΟΥΠΗΣ

Figure 5.1b *Anti-Trikoupis propaganda, 7 April 1885* © Asmoadios.

Political change

The overthrow of the Bavarian regime and Otho's departure created
both constitutional and successional crises. The former focused on
the relative balance of power between sovereign and parliament; the
latter touched directly on the question of sovereignty and autonomy.

A constituent assembly was called in 1863 to address both issues, but it soon became evident that the Protecting Powers had no intention of relinquishing their prerogative to appoint the new king. Therefore, the assembly spent its energies debating the constitutional question.

While in theory the Constitution of 1844 shared power between the monarchy and parliament, in reality it had given the king sufficient powers to exert control over the elected branch. A National Assembly was convened on 22 December 1862 to draft a new constitution and to deliberate on the choice of the dynasty. A new charter was eventually promulgated in 1864 and it was far more democratic than its predecessor. For a start, sovereignty was invested in the Greek people, not the monarchy. Whereas Otho had been crowned 'King of Greece', the new monarch was to be 'King of the Greeks'. The difference between the two titles is extremely important. In the former formulation, the ruler is bequeathed dominion over a geographical space, the land that constituted the country of Greece and all that lay in it. The latter privileged the nation and connoted that the ruler reigned through the consent of the people. Numerous articles in the new constitution clearly vested sovereignty in the people. This was to be a constitutional monarchy, or a 'crowned democracy', a Βασιλευομένη δημοκρατία (*vasilevoméni dimokratía*) in Greek. Second, reflecting this shift in the locus of power from the throne to the people, the old appointed senate was abolished and instead there was to be a single-chambered parliament vested with full legislative powers and elected by direct, secret ballot of all Greek men over the age of twenty-one who owned some property or who followed a trade or occupation. Third, rather than being open-ended, as they were in the 1844 charter, in the new constitution, the monarch's powers were restricted to those specifically adumbrated in the document. As the debates in the constituent assembly made clear, the king's powers, however, were still going to be considerable. He would have the power to appoint and dismiss ministers, dissolve parliament, disburse funds, declare war and contract treaties. Because the new king would thus wield considerable power, who sat on the throne of Greece was an extremely important question (Maroniti 2008; Alivisatos 2011: 107–53; Gardika 2008; Lyrintzis 2008).

The decision as to who would be the new king of the Greeks was in the hands of Greece's guarantor powers – France, Great Britain and Russia, and not the Greek people, though when given the opportunity, they made their choice clear. In a plebiscite in December 1862,

241,202 votes were cast and 95 per cent of them were for Prince Alfred, Queen Victoria's second son. But having a member of the British royal family on the throne of Greece was completely unacceptable to the other protecting powers, as well as being opposed by Queen Victoria herself, and so the search for a suitable king continued. It had to be someone from a prominent, yet not too partisan royal house. Chosen eventually was Prince Christian William Ferdinand Adolphus George of Holstein-Sonderberg-Glücksbrug, the son of the future King of Denmark. He would reign as George I, King of the Hellenes until his death at the hands of an assassin in 1913. At the time of his passing, he was the longest serving monarch in Europe.

George was eighteen years old when he ascended to the throne. Determined to learn from the mistakes of his predecessor, he did not bring with him a large entourage of foreign administrators, he did not fall prey to the factionalism that so beset Greek politics, and he made explicitly clear from the start that though he intended to adhere to the Lutheran faith, his children would be Orthodox. Finally, he was a firm believer in constitutionalism, and so he readily accepted in principle the idea that while he reigned as monarch, he did not rule the state. At times his impatience with Greek politicians gave him pause, but he never really challenged the separation of powers. He enhanced his position with the Greek people further by taking an Orthodox, albeit Russian, bride and then solidified it by siring an Orthodox son and heir, and by auspiciously naming him after the last emperor of Byzantium – Konstantine. Over the course of their long marriage, George and his queen, Olga, produced eight children; five sons and three daughters, one of whom died as an infant. All of the boys received a thoroughly European education that included a stint at the German Imperial War Academy. Through marriage, George utilised his royal progeny to create connections to all of the major ruling houses of Europe, including all three of Greece's protecting powers. Greece's royal family, then, took its place among the aristocracy of Europe. The question was, whether or not the country as whole could become as 'European' as its monarchy.

In spite of the new dynasty's arrival under a revised constitution, little seemed to have changed in the rough and tumble practice of Greek politics. Powerful personalities continued to hold sway through their clientelistic networks. There is a tendency in Greek historiography to single out the widespread use of patronage as a, if not the, root cause of Greece's political instability and supposedly impaired modernity. The problem with this argument is that it assumes that patronage was an exceptional practice during the nineteenth century when, in fact, it was not. Patronage was at the core of every democratic polity at the time. The web of clientelism spun by Boss Tweed in New York City's Tammany Hall, for example, was far more extensive and infinitely more corrupt than anything that developed in Greece. Patron-client bonds made politics work just about everywhere, and Greece was no exception. New cleavages did appear, however, based on broad differences regarding economic development and liberalism. One faction tended to be more liberal supporting economic growth through industrialisation and urging greater government intervention in both the social and economic spheres; this group drew its support primarily from younger, educated men who had a more Western outlook, and the growing urban middle class and entrepreneurs. The other group was conservative in orientation, preferring security through stagnation rather than progress through friction; its base of support tended to be among the old *tzakia* families and large landowners. These two broad political divisions would lead eventually to the formation of rival political parties after 1882.

More important in defining Greek political culture until the 1880s were localised political clubs, which sprang up in increasing numbers. Social clubs, societies of various sorts, and associations sprang up all across the Greek world; some focused mainly on charitable works, while others dealt with matters secular as well as sacred, but all of them had a political dimension to them as well. Clubs like the 'Korais', the 'Athanasios Diakos', and the 'Rigas' united like-thinking men and enabled more coherent political discourse to develop; they also linked Members of Parliament with the local power brokers in their constituencies. A good example is the club 'Athanasios Diakos' based in Lamia, Phthiotis. In 1875, this club had fifty-nine members: twenty-five lawyers, thirty large landowners, and four physicians. The group was 'plaine' in orientation and so their leader Konstantinos Diovouniotis, whom they got elected in three successive elections, was a follower of Dimitrios Voulgaris. Diovouniotis was client to Voulgaris, seeking from him perks and privileges; Diovouniotis in turn answered to the members of his club by looking out for their interests; the members of the club shared their leader's ideology and promised their support by mobilising votes.

Nikolaos Papaleksis, for example, in 1885 guaranteed at least 350 votes for his patron; how he could make such a boast was simple: that was the number of agricultural labourers employed on his large currant plantation near Olympia. The implication was clear. Those of his workers who did not vote as he instructed them would soon be looking for other employment. Intimidation, extortion and other strong-arm tactics made up what was referred to as 'the system' through which powerful men created their factions. In urban areas, artisans' associations and merchants' guilds, like the Athens-based Guild of Green Grocers, also provided vehicles for political acculturation and acted as vehicles for mobilising electoral support. Out of this patchwork of clubs and guilds, political factions were formed and parliamentary democracy practised under the 1864 Constitution.

In spite of the changes, the political system was deeply flawed. An examination of the period 1865–75 shows these defects clearly. During that decade there were seven general elections, and more importantly, eighteen different administrations: the longest lasted twenty months and the shortest a mere fourteen days! The difficulty was that King George had the power to appoint or dismiss ministers without cause, and so he could create or collapse administrations at will. If a key piece of legislation became blocked or if the budget failed to pass, the monarch dissolved the government. Since there were no set voting blocs, the government had to cobble together a majority vote every time it wanted to pass a law. This meant that there was constant horse-trading in order to obtain votes, and this not only made governing a delicate balance act but it also fuelled the perception that the entire system was corrupt. Political leaders, then, had to constantly juggle a variety of demands in order to keep their fragile ruling coalitions together. Lastly, and most importantly, since the king could appoint as prime minister whomsoever he desired, even men with only a handful of MPs supporting them were asked to form governments, and conversely, the leader of the largest group of members might find himself denied the leadership of the chamber. This was a recipe for political gridlock as well as a mockery of the democratic process.

Internal transitions, regional reframings

There were two extremely important internal transitions during the formative years of the new constitutional democracy that helped to shape Greece's development over the last few decades of the nineteenth century. One, the suppression of brigandage, brought to a resolution a problem that had plagued the country for decades, and the other, the emergence of romantic nationalism, profoundly influenced its internal politics and foreign relations. We begin with the latter.

The last few decades of the nineteenth century witnessed a transformation in the idea of nationalism. It began to take on a new and more virulent form, sometimes referred to by historians as hyper-nationalism, and it postulated that the nation was the greatest social good and that all aspects of life, both public and private, were sublimated to the greater national good. A concomitant development was the racialisation of nationality, whereby it was believed that different nations were in fact also different races. By essentialising nationality as biological, hyper-nationalism reified group boundaries and rendered cultural assimilation impossible. The fluidity of identities that was prevalent earlier no longer pertained. There was a cultural dimension to this process as well, one that romanticised the nation. For this reason, some scholars speak of Romantic Nationalism, the term that I prefer to use. Romantic Nationalism emerged from the confluence of nationalism, constitutionalism and the idealisation of popular society, especially the peasantry, as the glorified repository of national culture. National belonging was based upon blood descent, as well as shared religion, culture, language and history. The political expression of Romantic Nationalism was made manifest in constitutions such as the 1864 Greek Constitution that enshrined the principle of popular sovereignty. The people, that is, the nation, were now the font of legitimate authority, and so, while it was the laws as enshrined in the constitution that made the state, it was the people who organically constituted it. The nation was now the paramount political body.

Greek Romantic Nationalism was based upon three essentialised unities: the first of these we can call the Greek Unity. This was the cultural dimension of the Greek nation. It was culture as preserved in popular society, called in Greek the λάος, that connected the Greeks of today with their glorious ancient ancestors. The second element we can call the Christian or the Orthodox Unity. The shared bond of religion gave the nation a unique spiritual core that was the expression of divine providence. The third element was the Roman Unity. This referred to the political inheritance of the medieval Byzantine Empire that framed Greece's imagined national space (Konortas 1998). Finally, Romantic Nationalism emphasised that the nation-state was the highest form of social organisation, that it was divinely inspired, quintessentially modern, and a manifestation of a distinct set of unities that made each nation unique (Tassopoulos 2007; Petmezas 2009a; Gazi 2009; Kokosalakis 1987). Lastly, it postulated that the greater national good superseded everything else, including the truth.

> The [historian's] duty is both scientific and national. It is only the historian's pen that can compete with weapons. Therefore, those nations which have not yet accomplished their high mission and achieved national unification should tie their potential national grandeur to two anchors: military organization and the development of historical studies; these are both necessary for claiming national rights ... Indeed, there is no greater companionship than the one between the historian's desk and the military camp. On both, one and the same flag waves, the country's. (Spyridon P. Lambros, 1905: in his inaugural lecture as Rector of the National and Kapodistrian University of Athens. Cited in Gazi 2000: 84)

History, and indeed all of the social sciences, were sublimated to one single and unitary goal and that was not the furtherance of scientific truth, but instead of the National Truth. Romantic Nationalism was a powerful force that shaped world history, culminating with the First World War.

Another problem that had been besetting Greece since its formation came to head during the early days of the second constitutional period, and that was banditry. During the early years after independence, the state faced a considerable problem with demobilised veterans who were unable to find meaningful employment and turned to outlawry. Even as aged veterans passed away, brigandage remained problematic. The inability of the state to exert monopoly over legitimate violence, because of the small size of its military and the underdeveloped state of the police, created a space in which outlaws could flourish. The disposition of the Greek-Ottoman border also facilitated the activities of outlaws who could play off the border, preying on caravans and villages on one side and then escaping to the other. If anything, brigandage in Greece became even more widespread and more violent during the 1850s and 1860s. There were numerous instances of wealthy Greeks being kidnapped by bandit gangs and held for ransom. So prevalent did the practice become, that there even developed an unwritten set of rules, which both kidnappers and victims and their families understood and adhered to.

Sotiris Sotiropoulos, a wealthy politician and future prime minister of the country, left a detailed and scathing account of the thirty-five days that he spent as the 'guest' of a bandit gang. But, it was not only the rich who fell prey to brigands. They terrorised villages, and there are numerous accounts of women, for example, being tortured and forced to give up the location of their jewellery and their dowry cash. Banditry flourished both because the state was unable to suppress it and because it actually needed such men of violence. As we saw earlier, these men of violence could be deployed as border guards and occasionally they were even hired to keep the peace. In the period after the introduction of democracy, men of violence like these were often employed by politicans to coerce votes and to intimidate their opponents. Unable to suppress banditry by force, the state often resorted to granting amnesty to get them to cease their activities. So prevalent had this practice become, that the new constitution of 1864 actually contained an amendment that forbade it.

The issue came to a head in 1871. A bandit gang kidnapped a group of Western tourists, including aristocratic members related to the British royal family. The British government placed great pressure on the Greeks to resolve the matter and to get the hostages released. The negotiations went awry, and the hostages were killed in an episode that became known as the 'Marathon Murders'. The brutal slaying of British blue-bloods reinforced the image of Greece in Western eyes as being a land of barbarism. It threatened the country with retribution from the Great Powers and it also hit deeply at home. It made manifest the close connection between the government and violence, and even corruption. Moreover, it challenged and tainted the Greeks' self image. Over the next few years banditry would be largely eradicated in Greece. This was achieved partly through forcible suppression; by deploying military forces to destroy bandit gangs. But also contributing was the fact that the international situation in the Balkans had changed, and those who might have taken up the ways of the bandit now could be directed towards another enemy that would be north of the border into Macedonia. Crimes in the countryside would, of course, continue but never again would widespread banditry beset the country (Jenkins 1999; Koliopoulos 1987; Tzanelli 2009).

These two developments were consequential primarily for the kingdom during the 1860s and 1870s. There were, however, con-currently happening a series of events that reframed international and transnational relations across the Greek world. The first of these was the accession of the Ionian Islands. During the 1850s, the numerical strength of the movement in opposition to British rule and in favour of enosis, unification with Greece, grew enormously. To be sure, there were still many members of the Ionian aristocracy and middle class who believed that the islands would be better off staying under the rule of the British rather than becoming provinces of the kingdom of Greece, but their voices were in the minority. Through the power now vested in the Ionian-controlled legislative branch, radical unionists endeavoured to make the islands ungovernable. Repeatedly through the decade of the 1850s, they disrupted the working of the government, voted for unrealistic budgets, and submitted petitions designed to humiliate Her Majesty's government. Administrative gridlock resulted. Not even a special mission by the noted Philhellene and liberal, William Gladstone, could salvage the situation. As the islands became more ungovernable and as their strategic importance to the British diminished, a discussion began in Colonial and Foreign Office circles about ceding the islands to the Greek Kingdom (Gallant 2001).

Three options were seriously discussed. Option one called for an expansion of the British military forces on the islands and the restoration of a more restrictive constitution. This course of action was rejected; the price in men and material would be too high when balanced against the strategic value of the islands. Option two envisaged the British keeping control of Kerkira while giving the other six islands to the kingdom of Greece. But many officials familiar with the islands suggested that this plan was unworkable: the Kerkirans would rise up in open opposition, if not revolt. The only remaining option was to cede the islands to the kingdom of Greece. But, the Colonial and the Foreign Offices recognised that they needed a pretext for doing so that would not make it appear that were giving in to the radical national unionists. The perfect occasion arose for such a gesture when King George I ascended to the throne. Led by an ambitious young diplomat, named Harilaos Trikoupis, Greece negotiated for the transferal of the islands to the kingdom. The protectorate had come to an end. Henceforth, the fate of the Seven Islands would be linked to that of Greece, and after some initial difficulties due to the islands' comparatively unique history, full political integration occurred. The accession of the islands was the first realisation of the Megali Idea. Moreover, since their acquisition was tied to George's enthronement, it boosted his popularity enormously.

While this was happening in Greece, important changes were taking place in the Ottoman Empire that were reframing the place of non-Muslims in Ottoman politics, the economy and society, as well as redefining interdenominational relations. After the Crimean War, the need to continue the Tanzimat (the internal reformation of the empire) was evident. Partly it was the price that the empire had to pay for Western European support and partly it was internally driven by internal reformers who recognised that the empire's continued existence was tied to its modernisation. The second phase of the Tanzimat began in 1856 and would continue for the next two decades.

The Hatt-ı Hümayn incorporated the previous reforms, but went even further in ensuring equality, civil rights and liberty. One consequence of the rescript was that many Greeks who had converted to Islam recanted and 'announce[d] that in their hearts they had never been Muslims and had secretly adhered to their former (Christian) faith' (Deringil 2012: 111). The reforms also opened up to non-Muslims economic and political spaces that had not existed before, and Greeks disproportionately exploited them. At the same time, the edict also redefined the relationship between the leadership of the non-Muslim religious communities and the state, and between those communities' leadership and their congregations. The denominational communities were granted much control of their own affairs at the same time that their leaders were being incorporated into the structure of Ottoman administration. The reforms enshrined the principle of equality between all imperial citizens, regardless of religion, while simultaneously endowing the denominational communities, the Millets, with greater coherence. It also gave them corporate rights that they did not possess before (Augustinos 1992).

Many Rom took advantage of the new opportunities that these two elements of the Tanzimat presented. Ottoman Greeks had for some time played important roles in banking but they grew even wealthier and more powerful between the 1860s and the 1880s. Capitalising on the empire's dire fiscal situation, men such as Andreas Syngrou, Theodoros Baltazzis, George Zarifis and Christakis Zographos, to name but a few, literally became the empire's bankers (Minoglou 2002; Birdal 2010: 23–5; Clay 2000; Exertozglou 2010; Frangakis-Syrett 2009; for their connection to banking in Greece, see Stassinopoulos 2011).

Their wealth gave them the ability to exert influence on the

Ottoman government and to attain stature and power in the Millet-i Rom. As the Ottoman economy became more closely integrated into the world economy, Rom merchants in Constantinople, Smyrna, Salonika and the other major port-cities expanded considerably their commercial networks and became fabulously wealthy, as their monumental townhouses in those cities attest (Özdemir 2003; Zandi-Sayek 2012; Pamuk 1987). As Chatziionnaou and Kamouzis have recently noted: 'From the mid-nineteenth century onwards the Greeks of Istanbul, as well as the other non-Muslim communities, managed to gradually improve their social position, promote their own economic interests and dominate the industrial and commercial sector of the city' (2013: 136). Many converted their new-found wealth into landed interests, carving out large estates. In addition, the reframing of the relationship between the Millets and the state bestowed more autonomy on communal organisations, and this opened up new political spaces that wealthy Rom exploited (Exertozoglou 2010; Kechriotis 2009, 2013; Tansuğ 2011). Other Ottoman Greeks also participated in Ottoman governance, as civil servants and government officials, with some of them occupying high positions in the central and provincial governments. In sum, the second half of the nineteenth century witnessed the emergence of a wealthy and powerful Ottoman Greek elite.

The impact of the reforms on ordinary Ottoman Greeks varied greatly depending on their station in life and where they lived in the empire. A recent case study of the Aegean Islands can give us some sense of what happened in those areas where Greeks were the majority (Strohmeier 2010). Economically, they prospered. On islands like Lesbos and Chios, they came to dominate both the cultivation and marketing of commercial crops, like olives, and the food industry. By the 1860s, the vilayet (province) of the Aegean enjoyed the highest level of per capita income of any Ottoman province. In addition, the islanders' role in commercial shipping rose to new heights. Because of their economic importance, the Ottoman government tried to ensure that the political reforms were enforced effectively, and this actually generated some resentment among the Rom population. Centralisation eroded much of the local autonomy that they had enjoyed for centuries, and the institution of equality in civic institutions, like the municipal councils, actually took power away from them. The law mandated equal representation on local governing bodies, with Christians and Muslims having equal representation, but since the population ratio was 90 per cent Christians to 10 per cent Muslims, this was anything but equal. Lastly, the islanders were able to play Greece and the empire off against one another, movingly seamlessly between the two polities in order to take advantage of educational and economic opportunities that each offered. While some Ottoman Greeks, like the Aegean islanders, on balance gained more than they lost with the Tanzimat reforms, others did not. In those places, resentment against the empire grew, and one place more than any other stands out in this regard: Crete.

The story of the struggle for the liberation and incorporation of Crete into the Greek nation-state began during the 1821 rebellion. Cretan Christians had joined their fellow members of the Millet-i Rom across the sea in the uprising and had been largely successful in the fighting against the Ottoman forces on the island. The tide turned, however, when Ibrahim Paşa invaded the island as part of his plan for the invasion of the Peloponnesos. The Porte was adamant that Crete not should be included in the new Greek kingdom, and the Great Powers agreed. The sultan then granted the island to Mehmet Ali of Egypt as a reward for his efforts during the war.

Egypt ruled the Cretan Christian population harshly and relations between the Christian leadership and the Egyptian government on the island remained very tense. Moreover, relations were tense between Cretan Muslims and Egyptian and Black African Muslims, who immigrated to the island. Some Christians chose to convert but most did not (Adiyeke 2008). The island was restored to the Ottoman Empire in 1840, a move that was initially very popular on the island. That soon changed. A series of governors, beginning with Mustafa Paşa (an unpopular hold-over from the days of Egyptian rule), failed to implement the Tanzimat reforms, at the same time that the economic situation on the island deteriorated during the 1840s. Cretans demanded administrative reforms and lower taxes, but they received neither. Mustafa, who governed the island until 1851, alienated both Christians and Muslims with his policies. Matters only got worse after the promulgation of the 1856 reforms because they also were not enforced.

In 1858, a group of Christian and Muslim Cretans petitioned the Porte, calling for full implantation of the new edicts. When this failed to happen Cretans split into three factions and began to mobilise for action. One group wanted to remain in the empire but only if the reforms were fully enforced. Another wished to see the island remain in the empire but on very different terms; they sought local autonomy and home rule, much like that enjoyed by Serbia and the Danubian

Principalities. Still a third group developed, and it sought nothing less than the unification of Crete with the kingdom. All of them shared a desire for the island's situation to change but they had radically different visions as to what that change should be (Şenışık 2011: 75; 2010; Kallivretakis 2006: 12–18; 2003).

On 3 August 1866, a general assembly of Cretan leaders met at the village of Apokorona to debate how to deal with the failure of the reforms. A force of 14,000 Ottoman troops confronted them and demanded the assembly disperse. Shots were fired from the Ottoman ranks. Seeing no other choice, the Cretans returned fire. In this manner, the first of three Cretan insurrections began. The rebellion quickly took on the contours of a guerrilla war. From their mountain redoubts, the Christian Cretan rebels and their Greek supporters pledged 'to fatten the eagles of the White Mountains [of central Crete] on the bodies of Turkish Pashas and Beys …' Unchecked, the Cretan Christian bands roamed the wilder regions of the island with impunity, while Ottoman forces focused their attentions on the towns and villages.

In many ways, this conflict resembled the one in Thessaly we discussed earlier. Volunteer brigades formed in Greece and street demonstrations drew thousands of Athenians from their homes. Men, material and money were collected and sent to Crete with the active encouragement of the government. Initially, the rebels were extremely successful, inflicting approximately 20,000 casualties in the first year of fighting. Since the Ottoman forces could not engage the insurgents in open battle, they took out their ire on the civilian population. The reports of atrocities, and in particular the self-immolation of over 400 men, women and children in the besieged monastery of Arkadi on 21 October 1866 (Fig. 5.2) aroused great sympathy in Europe and the United States. But once again the hard realities of Great Power politics were to prove cold comfort to the cause of Greek irredentism (Kallivretakis 2006: 18–21; 2003).

Other groups in the Balkans, in particular the Serbs under Prince Michael Obrenoviç, sought to gain advantage and so made demands on the Porte for concessions. This led to extensive bilateral negotiations between Greece and Serbia that resulted in the signing on 26 August 1867 of a treaty with seventeen clauses. The most important of these dealt with the size of the military contingents each side would provide in the event of war with the Ottoman Empire, the territories each side would acquire if the war was won, and the formation of confederated states in some areas if necessary. Russia,

Figure 5.2 *Ottoman troops attacking the monastery of Arkadi during the 1866 Cretan rebellion* © Illustrated London News.

as well, was using the pretext of the Cretan rebellion to extend its influence in the Balkans. This served to heighten Franco-British sensitivities and pushed them towards adopting measures to maintain the status quo.

By early 1869, the military tide was turning as the Ottoman fleet, through its blockade of the island, was depriving the insurgents of much needed supplies. Simultaneously, the diplomatic currents had also turned against the irredentist cause. With the assassination of Prince Michael and the continued opposition of King George, the Serbian alliance fell apart; France, Great Britain and Austria were pressuring Athens to compromise; the sultan was threatening to declare war on Greece; and the Russian Empire was adopting an ever more conciliatory tone. Finally, the volatility of the issue domestically had brought down three governments in three years. Compromise was the only solution. In the Paris peace talks of 1869 it was agreed that Crete would remain part of the Ottoman Empire but that there would be significant changes in how the islanders were to be governed and their legal status within the sultan's domain. The reform package was referred to as the 'Organic Laws' and it was the last, best hope for peace on the island; but, like the previous round of reforms, it proved to be largely a failure. The Cretan Question, there-fore, remained a key issue for the next forty years.

Not long after the cessation of the violence on Crete, another development occurred in the Ottoman Empire that altered the situation in the region dramatically, and that was the creation of a Bulgarian national church called the Exarchate. Going back to the writings of Saint Paisius of Hillendar in the late eighteenth century, there had been movement among some Orthodox Bulgarians to have Church Slavonic supplant Greek as the language used in church and in education. The creation of the Greek national church, the Autocephalus Church of Greece, after independence, not only caused a rift with the Patriarchate, but it also gave added impetus for the creation of other Balkan Orthodox national churches. This move-ment gained traction and wider support beginning in the 1850s and then really took off during the 1860s. The emergence of Romantic Nationalism as a major ideological force contributed to this move-ment because of the way in which it explicitly sublimated religion and the church to the greater national good. Bulgarian nationalists' aspirations for their own church played perfectly into Russia's ambitions to restore their hegemonic influence on the region. To support their Slavic brethren's desire for their own church, Russia, through its minister to the Ottoman Empire Count Nikolai Ignatiev, put diplomatic pressure on the imperial government to recognise an autonomous Slavonic church.

Bowing to this pressure, Sultan Abdülaziz issued a decree on 12 March 1870 that did precisely that. The Exarchate would remain under the ecclesiastical authority of the Patriarchate but it would have broad ranging and independent powers in those dioceses that, through the vote of a two-thirds majority, opted to join it. In response to the Patriarchate's foot-dragging over the implementation of the imperial decree, the Holy Synod unilaterally elected their own leader, Antim I. In response, Patriarch Anthimos VI ordered the Bulgarian church in Istanbul to be closed and a few months later, in September 1872, he convened a Patriarchal Synod to address the issue. After heated debate, it declared the Exarchate schismatic and excommuni-cated its adherents. This move escalated tensions between Russia and the Ottoman Empire, and inaugurated a heated struggle between the two churches for the allegiance of Orthodox Christians in Rumelia. The stakes, however, were much higher than just church attendance. Because of Romantic Nationalism, choosing to attend either the Grecophone or the Slavophone church made a statement about one's national consciousness. The Exarchate became the *de facto* Bulgarian national church and the dioceses that opted to join it became Bulgaria's national space. Greece's Megali Idea and Bulgaria's nationalist aspirations were now on a collision course (Gounaris 2007).

The new Europe

While these developments were taking place in the Greek world, events were transpiring elsewhere in Europe that would also have a profound effect upon it. The first of these was Italian unification (the Risorgimento). In 1861, after years of struggle the Italian peninsula was at last incorporated into a single political entity: the Kingdom of Italy. We saw in the last chapter how the creation of an Italian nation-state helped to generate further opposition to King Otho by under-scoring his singular inability to advance the Greek Megali Idea and in the following decade this event continued to resonate in the Greek world. First, at a practical level, there had been long-standing connections between Greek and Italian nationalist organisations. Greeks had fought in Italy in its struggle for unification, and Italians had fought in Greece during its war of liberation. This connection reinforced the nationalist forces in both places (Pécout 2004; Liakos 1985). Second, since Italian unification had been realised through Great Power intervention, Greeks continued to believe that, given the right circumstances and political leadership, the powers would support Greece's territorial aggrandisement. Third, on a more nega-tive note, the new Italy would soon adopt a more aggressive foreign policy stance in the Mediterranean and this would lead to repeated moments of contention between it and Greece. For good and for ill, the Italian Risorgimento stoked the fuels of Greek nationalism.

Another extremely important development for the region was German unification and the establishment of the German Empire in 1871. Through the 1860s, Otto von Bismarck skilfully charted a course that resulted in Prussia obtaining a hegemonic position in the German world and then after waging successful wars against Austria (1866) and France (1870), he orchestrated the political unification of the various German states into a single, united empire ruled over by Kaiser Wilhelm I. German unification ushered onto the world historical scene a new economic, political and military power that would soon surpass Russia in power and prestige, having already bested France. Previously Prussia had taken little interest in

Southeastern Europe, but now at the head of a new empire that would soon change. Meanwhile, the European power that had traditionally played the greatest role in the region, Russia, was also undergoing important changes.

Following Russia's defeat in the Crimean War, Tsar Alexander II embarked upon an ambitious modernisation programme that included the emancipation of the serfs, reformation of the legal system, reorganisation of the empire's finances, economic development and industrialisation, and a total overhaul of the empire's armed forces. These reforms had the potential to revitalise the empire and to re-establish it as the premier power of continental Europe, as well as putting it in a position to advance the causes of the Slavic peoples, and especially those who still laboured under the 'Ottoman yoke'.

Another conflict between two old foes had a profound impact on the Greek world and shaped how the region developed over the decades before the First World War. Russian honour had been deeply offended by its loss in the Crimean War, and the resulting Treaty of Paris only made matters worse. Russian popular sentiment was that that stain of dishonour had to be cleansed. So, during the 1860s, it endeavoured to reassert its influence in the Ottoman Balkans, except its policies were dictated by sentiments of Pan-Slavism rather than Pan-Orthodoxy. Russian pressure had been instrumental in the Porte's decision to establish the Bulgarian Exarchate Church and it was only looking for a pretext to justify more direct action in the Balkans, and that came in the late 1870s. France was prostrate after its devastating military defeat at the hands of Prussia (1871) and the internal chaos caused by the Commune in Paris. Its replacement by the new German Empire as a continental Great Power, created conditions in which Russia felt free to re-exert its influence in Ottoman Europe.

The event that directly led to war happened in Bosnia and Herzegovina. A series of bad harvests hit hard the Christian peasantry, most of whom worked land owned by Muslims. Already upset over their treatment by the local Ottoman officials, they rose in rebellion. Eager to reassert their dominance, Bosnian Muslims tried to crush them. A guerrilla conflict ensued. Chaos in Istanbul made matters worse. In the span of a few months, two sultans were assassinated. Royal disorder and the Bosnian insurrection provided others with an opportunity to take up arms.

In April 1876, Bulgarian revolutionary organisations launched mass uprisings all across the heartland of Ottoman Europe that threatened to tear it apart. The empire had to strike back immediately, but its military forces in the region were already stretched thin, and so it had to call on Muslim irregular forces called bashi-bazouks to deal with the Bulgarian rebels. Many bashi-bazouks were Circassian refugees from the Caucasus who had only recently been settled in the area and who had suffered greatly at the hands of the Christian population. Well into the summer of 1876, a brutal guerrilla war raged across Bulgaria. The civilian population on both sides suffered tremendously, and there were numerous massacres committed by both sides. One of the worst of these took place at the town of Batak, where thousands of Bulgarian Christians were slaughtered (Reid 2000).

Reports of what became known as the 'Bulgarian Horrors' circulated widely in the West and in Russia. In Great Britain, the public outcry over the violence, led by William Gladstone, the leader of the opposition Labour Party, put great pressure on Conservative Prime Minister Benjamin Disraeli's pro-Ottoman foreign policy. In Russia, even more dramatically, the brutal violence against people who were not only fellow Orthodox Christians but also Slavs fuelled cries for direct Russian intervention. The matter only became more serious when first the Principality of Serbia and then Montenegro both declared war on the Ottoman Empire. Through the autumn of 1876, the small Serbian Army, augmented by volunteers from all over Europe, including Greece, put up stiff resistance, but it was fighting an uphill battle.

Having first negotiated an agreement with Austria, Russia intervened to stop the bloodshed. Under its leadership, a conference of the Great Powers was convened in Constantinople on 11 December 1876. The terms that were taking shape in the negotiations would have resulted in the *de facto* partitioning of Ottoman Europe. And this was unacceptable. On 23 December, the sultan proclaimed the promulgation of a constitution that introduced democracy and equal rights for all citizens regardless of religion. Their hopes that this move would strengthen their position at the bargaining table were soon dashed, and the Porte had no choice but to reject the Great Power's terms. The failure of the Constantinople Conference resulted in Russia declaring war on the empire on 24 April 1877.

When the massive Russian army entered its territory, the Principality of Romania declared its independence from the Ottomans and so entered into the conflict. This meant that all of the Christian-ruled territories in the Balkans were now in a state of war with the empire, save one: Greece. The kingdom was caught in a dilemma. First, at the interstate level, its relationship with the Porte was at its most cordial. Powerful Ottoman Greeks, seeing an opportunity to increase their political status in the new democratic empire, put pressure on Athens to stay out of the war. An editorial in *Byzantis*, the most important Greek newspaper in Constantinople, for example, acknowledged that Greek irregulars had infiltrated the Ottoman Empire and were causing chaos. It then went on to assure its readership, however, that the government in Athens would not be so rash or reckless as to condone these activities, and 'that no Greek, or friend of Greece, could approve hazardous and ill-timed acts of aggression' that jeopardised the Rom population (cited in Ollier 1878, vol. 1: 441). Second, Athens eyed the activities of its northern co-religionists with suspicion. The establishment of the Bulgarian Exarchate, as we saw earlier, accelerated the development of Bulgarian nationalism and irredentism. It also created tensions and competing interests between Serbia and Greece. Athens was also compelled to reassess its relationship with Russia because Pan-Orthodoxy, the idea which had previously been the rationale for Russian intervention in the region, came to be replaced by Pan-Slavism: the former included Greece, the latter did not. Greece, then, was not overly enthusiastic about joining with Serbs and Montenegrins in the summer of 1876 when they declared war on the Porte. Russian intervention in the face of Serbian defeat led to a change in Greek policy. Fearful of being left out of the settlement if the Russians were victorious, Athens had to adopt a more aggressive policy. But it was also extremely reluctant to go to war, with all of the risks that that entailed. Greek popular opinion, however, was overwhelmingly in favour of direct action. The government, in the end, opted for indirect action that gave it plausible deniability.

Radical nationalist organisations, funded by domestic and diasporic merchants, artisans and labourers, channelled money and materials to the frontier. Irregular bands of volunteers under the command of recently decommissioned regular army officers streamed into Thessaly, Epiros and Macedonia (Fig. 5.3). There their guerrilla tactics proved remarkably successful in tying down considerable numbers of Ottoman troops and they effectively laid siege to the larger garrison towns by completely dominating the countryside (Fig. 5.4). Moreover, unlike during earlier incursions, the many Greek and other Christian peasants rose up and joined in the fray.

Figure 5.3 *Greek fighters in Thessaly during the 1877–8 Ottoman-Russian War*
© *Edmund Ollier, 'Cassels' History of the Russo-Turkish War', vol. 2, p. 85.*

Wherever the Greek forces drove out the Ottoman troops, they immediately set up free local governments. The uprisings further north in Macedonia, however, were not faring as well. Not only were the irregular Greek forces up against better-trained Ottoman troops, but the complexity of the situation among the local Christian population complicated matters significantly. Still Greece's proxy war was proving a success.

One of the reasons Greece irregulars were able to operate so effectively was that Ottoman forces along the frontier had been severely depleted in order to mobilise men to fight the Russians. Combined, the empires mobilised over one million men who were deployed along two war fronts – along the Danube in the west and the Caucasus in the east. Both sides sustained horrendous losses in this brief war, though less from battlefield casualties than from the ravages of disease. Having successfully forced its way into Ottoman Europe, the Russian army worked its way south through Bulgaria, confronting the Ottoman forces that mannned the major fortresses

Figure 5.4 *Greek insurrectionists attacking an Ottoman garrison in Thessaly and Epiros (1878),* © *Edmund Ollier, 'Cassels' History of the Russo-Turkish War', vol. 1, p. 423.*

across the region. This war was marked by few major battles and instead by difficult sieges and long slogs over difficult terrain. By the end of 1877, the Russians had broken through the last set of Ottoman defences and were now threatening Constantinople itself.

In January 1878, following in the wake of the successes of the irregulars in Thessaly, the uncertainty of the situation in Macedonia and the imminent Russian threat to the Ottoman capital, Prime Minister Alexandros Koumoundouros, with the support of King George, sought to bring Greece into the war. Unfortunately, the pace of events had overtaken them. Only three hours after the Greek parliament voted for the mobilisation of the army, an armistice was declared between Russia and the Ottoman Empire. If official Greek troops had occupied the liberated territories, then Greece would have been in a stronger negotiating position. As it was, Greece nearly came away from the war with nothing.

With the invading army only a short distance from the capital, the Porte had no alternative but to accept pretty much whatever terms the Russians wished to impose. The subsequent Treaty of San Stefano dealt the Ottomans a devastating blow. They had to cede additional territories to Serbia and Montenegro and recognise them as fully independent states, as it did with Romania as well. Russia received war reparations as well as territories, most importantly Georgia and Armenia along with some other places in the Caucasus. The big winners, however, were the Bulgarians. A new autonomous Bulgarian principality would be carved out of the empire's European heartland. It was to encompass the Bulgarian homeland, plus all of eastern Macedonia and Thrace to a point less than ten miles from Istanbul. With coastlines along both the Aegean and the Black Seas, this new Greater Bulgaria could control vital sea-lanes as well.

The Treaty of San Stefano posed an existential threat to the Empire and created a new Christian state whose territorial ambitions clashed with almost all of its neighbours. In short, it created a peace that could not stand – particularly when its full implications became known in the other capitals of Europe. Fearful that Bulgaria would be nothing more than a Russian satellite, giving it a base from which to threaten Constantinople and control of the Bosporus Straits, Britain raised strenuous objections and threatened to take stronger measures if necessary to prevent this from happening. To maintain the peace in Europe, Otto von Bismarck, the German Foreign Minister, convened a Congress in Berlin in the summer of 1878. The resultant Treaty of Berlin substantially revised the terms of San Stefano. Most importantly, it redrew thoroughly the boundaries of Bulgaria. Macedonia and Thrace were restored to the Ottomans, and Bulgaria was reconstituted and divided into two units within the empire: the northern territory became an independent principality, while the southern region was reformed as the province of East Rumelia (this awkward arrangement was short-lived and within a few years the two would be united into a single Bulgarian state in 1886).

Few were satisfied with the treaty. And its consequences cast a dark shadow over the region for the next twenty-three years. Rather than resolving great power differences over the region, it escalated them. The creation of new independent Balkan states did not end the movement to partition the Ottoman Empire in Europe, but in fact exacerbated it by adding another axis of competition and conflict. The new states each sought to fulfil their own irredentist dreams, except now their territorial expansion would not only entail conflict with the Ottoman Empire but with each other as well.

Though the kingdom had not officially entered the war as a combatant party, it scored an important irredentist victory as a result of the war. Even after the Treaty of Berlin had been signed, Greek irregulars pursued their guerrilla campaign. The Ottomans, who no longer had to deal with Russian forces, dispatched contingents by land and sea to confront the insurgency. The thin veil masking the fact that Athens had instigated and was still supporting the rebels was becoming increasingly transparent. War between Greece and the empire loomed. At this critical moment, Greece found an ally: Great Britain. Though relations between this powerful patron and its often unruly client remained fraught, they found a common interest in dealing with the Ottoman Empire. The resulting collaboration brought major changes to the Greek world. First, Great Britain obtained Cyprus (Varnava 2009; Holland and Markides 2006: 162–70) and second, Greece expanded northward. After years of protracted negotiations, in 1881, a bilateral agreement between the sultan and Greece was brokered.

The territories where the Greek forces had been most successful and where they had liberated territories, Thessaly and southern Epiros (the area around the city Arta), were ceded to the kingdom. A major step toward realisation of the Megali Idea had been taken with the addition of approximately 13,000 square kilometres of territory and 294,000 people. Incorporating the new territories proved difficult, as we will see. Moreover, the diplomatic victory was marred in the public's view by the fact that the part of Epiros which Greece received did not include the capital city of Ioannina, nor was any land in Macedonia included, and finally it left Crete outside of the national fold. For the remainder of the century the Greek irredentist struggle focused on these 'unredeemed' regions, but now, with the creation of the new, independent secessionist states, there were new claimants to those same territories. The partitioning of most of Ottoman Europe after Berlin did not, therefore, bring peace and stability to the region but instead engendered new competition and conflicts.

While the Treaty of Berlin may have ended the war between the Ottoman and Russian Empires, it also ushered in a new era of Great Power rivalries that would eventually end in 1914 with a world at war. Between the 1870s and the early twentieth century, the major countries of Europe went on a binge of imperial expansion, the scale and pace of which were unprecedented in world history. This phase of empire building was so distinctive that historians refer to it by a specific term: neoimperialism. Within the span of a few decades all of

Africa, much of Asia and numerous other parts of the globe became incorporated into one of the burgeoning European empires. To be a great nation, a country had to have imperial holdings. In what was conceived of as a zero-sum game, Great Britain, Germany, France and the rest engaged in a fierce competition over control of far off and distant lands.

Two new developments shaped the context of late nineteenth-century empire building. The first of these was the racialisation of nationalism, and the second was the wedding of this notion onto the Darwinian concept of survival of the fittest. Combined, the result was that Europeans came to see themselves as belonging to different races and that these races were competing for global hegemony. This was a struggle, they believed, that would eventually produce a single victor and that winner would be the superior race. The Balkans and Ottoman Europe occupied an especially important place in this imperial struggle because they were the one area in the world more so than any other where all of the Great Powers' vested imperial interests collided. What this meant was that any conflict in Ottoman Europe had the potential to trigger a pan-European war, and from 1882 onwards there was one place in the Balkans that was the locus of contestation between the empire and the Balkan secessionist states: Macedonia.

The Macedonia question

After the territorial adjustments made by the Treaty of Berlin and the subsequent unification of Bulgaria in 1886, the Ottoman Empire in Europe was reduced to just Epiros, Albania, Thrace and Macedonia, with the last of those being the most contested terrain. Over the centuries what Macedonia exactly meant changed. It had been an ancient Greek kingdom, a Roman province, and a component of numerous post-antique empires and kingdoms. By the late nineteenth century it was most widely recognised as a geographical territory, parts of which were included in three different Ottoman vilayets.

Macedonia was unique at the time in being part of the imagined national space of no less than four different states and the home of its own nation. Serbia claimed a large portion of northwestern Mace-donia because of national bonds – the majority of the population, it argued, were fellow Serbs – and by historical right – the region had once been part of the medieval Serbian kingdom of Stefan Duşan. In like vein, Bulgaria asserted its right to the region on much the same grounds, except their historical claim was based on the fourteenth-century empire of Tsar Boris. For Greece, Macedonia's 'Hellenic' character was a given. It was, after all the homeland of Philip II and Alexander the Great. In Greek nationalist historiography of the time, the medieval Eastern Roman Empire became reconstructed as Greek, and since Macedonia was a core part of it, it also was enshrined as one of Greece's 'ancestral' homelands. It should not be forgotten that Macedonia held a special place for the Ottomans as well. In addition to occupying a critically important space in numerous national imaginaries, Macedonia was also one of the most nationally and culturally diverse places in the empire. As well as Greeks, Bulgars and Serbs, there were huge numbers of Jews, mostly resident in Salonika, a very large and diverse Muslim population, and a sizable Orthodox Christian population that remained resistant to the siren's call of Balkan nationalism (Akhund 2009).

Macedonia held such importance not only for its symbolic value, but for practical reasons. It was incredibly important economically. The region itself was one the richest agricultural areas in the Balkans. Moreover, it was home to the second most important city in the Ottoman Empire: Salonika. The city was both a major site of industry and a commercial emporium of the first order. It was the economic gateway of the Balkans, connecting via railroad the main commercial overland routes from the Mediterranean to the Danube Basin and thence into central Europe (Gounaris 1985; 1993). Perhaps even more so than the region itself, it was a veritable *salade Macédoine*, with a population consisting of Jews (the majority group), Christians and Muslims, and a large number of Dömnes – Jews who had converted to Islam in the eighteenth century but who retained a distinctive identity and communal presence (Baer 2010). Greeks, Bulgarians, Sephardic Jews, Albanians, Circassians and many other ethnic groups inhabited the city's neighbourhoods. Geo-strategically important, economically wealthy and symbolically significant, Macedonia became the great prize and whichever state could get it would become the paramount power in the Balkans.

Four countries (Greece, Serbia, Bulgaria and the Ottoman Empire) and three churches (the Patriarchate, the Exarchate and the Serbian National Church) struggled for control over Macedonia. Beginning in the 1880s, all of them launched educational initiatives to try and persuade Orthodox Christians in Macedonia to declare a national identity and to choose a church. Education became a key battleground (Blumi 2001; Fortna 2002; Lory 2011; Papadakis 2006).

Priests and teachers were mobilised to proselytise on behalf of their faith. Grecophones tended to remain loyal to the Patriarchate, whereas Slavophones opted for the Exarchate. But for many the choice was neither simple nor straightforward. We know, for example, of families that split over the issue. A joke at the time was that only in Macedonia could the same mother give birth to a Greek and a Bulgar. Moreover, many remained resistant to these nationalist overtures, preferring the status quo and continuing to self-identify as 'Christians' and nothing more. As one historian has recently noted: 'Despite the efforts of agents serving Greek and Bulgarian nationalism in Ottoman Thrace, many Orthodox villagers considered themselves as belonging not to a nation but to a religious community' (Konortas 2010: 97).[1] Peaceful persuasion was simply not working.

By the early 1890s, each side adopted a more confrontational approach. To protect their co-nationals and to convince the undecided to make a choice, each side began to deploy armed bands. Organisations formed to coordinate their activities in Macedonia. On the Greek side there was the National Defence, which cooperated closely with the Greek consulates in three vilayets, and the Macedonian Brotherhood. The Slavic Brotherhood for Defence and Freedom mobilised men and resources in the name of Serbia. From the Bulgarian side there was the Supreme Committee of the Macedonian Revolutionary Organisation of the Interior (IMRO), which eventually split into two factions over whether or not Macedonia should become part of Bulgaria or an independent Macedonian nation-state. The insertion of armed insurgent bands into the region led to brutal sectarian violence that escalated interstate tensions (Perry 1988).

As it became increasingly clear that Macedonia was the flashpoint that could lead to a Balkan war, the Great Powers of Europe became more concerned about the ongoing struggle. It was obvious to all that the disposition of Macedonia was an issue to be decided in the European corridors of power. This made it even more imperative for each side to muster the strongest and most persuasive arguments possible as to why the region was theirs. And having the majority population was certainly at the top of the list. Thus getting people to declare their national allegiance took on an even greater importance. Each side, then, produced maps and conducted censuses that bolstered their arguments. Table 5.1 shows a compilation of the census results. To our eyes, these figures appear ludicrous but that should not detract from their importance. The numbers mattered, no matter how they

Table 5.1   *Macedonia population census data by country.*

Population	Bulgarian statistics	Greek statistics	Serbian statistics
'Turks' [Muslims]	449,200	634,000	231,000
Bulgarians	1,181,000	332,000	57,000
Greeks	228,700	652,700	201,000
Serbs	700	0	2,048,000

were arrived at. The Macedonia Question, then, cast a long shadow over the Greek world at the end of the nineteenth century.

The age of Trikoupis

At the same time that the Macedonia Question was emerging as the dominant national issue in Greece, an ambitious reformist politician rose to prominence who promised to modernise the country and by so doing to make it the paramount regional power. For him, the national issue would be resolved when Greece asserted its place in Europe as a modern and Western nation-state. His name was Harilaos Trikoupis (Aroni-Tsihli and Triha 2000; Triha 2009; Tzokas 1999). In 1874, as a 37-year-old politician he publicly addressed the problem of the causes of Greece's political gridlock and thus set himself on the path to becoming one of the most important leaders in the history of modern Greece. Trikoupis was born in the same year that the nation was formed, 1832. He was, then, a 'new man', born into the first generation after the War of Independence.

Trikoupis came from a prominent family. His father, Spyridon Trikoupis, had been a leading politician during the War of Independence and was a leading member of the English party afterwards. On three occasions he was Greece's representative to the United Kingdom including a posting from 1850 to 1861. Further solidifying his connection to the liberal wing of Greek politics was his relationship with his maternal uncle, Alexandros Mavrogordatos. Harilaos spent the first thirteen years of his life in England and that experience helped shape his world view. Fluent in English (throughout his life his Greek was heavily accented) and transnationally educated (in Paris and Athens), he firmly believed that, in order to modernise, Greece had to emulate the countries of Western Europe.

His career began as an attaché to his father in London. By 1863, he had replaced his father as head of the Greek mission and, in that capacity, he led the Greek negotiation team that hammered out the accession of the Ionian Islands. His ambition was not to remain a diplomat but to make a name for himself in domestic politics. He successfully competed for his home district of Missolonghi in the 1865 election and he subsequently rose politically as a follower of Alexander Koumoundouros, the leader of the liberal 'montaigne', who appointed him as his foreign minister in 1866. His tutelage under Koumoundouros did not last long. In 1872 he founded his own party called the Fifth Party. Few political pundits paid any attention, but not for long.

Trikoupis entered the political fray as a major player on his own with the publication in 1874 of his anonymous article 'Who Is To Blame?' in the newspaper *Kairoi*, in which he laid bare the causes of Greece's political turmoil. The response to his rhetorical question was manifestly evident to him: it was the king who was to blame by not appointing only majority governments. In the firestorm that followed the article's publication and Trikoupis's subsequent arrest for treason when his identity as the author became known, King George eventually relented and recognised the principle of *dedilomeni*. By so doing the king agreed that in future he would ask only the leader of the declared majority of Members of Parliament to form a government. If no one could obtain the pledged support of a plurality, then the king would dissolve parliament and call for a general election.

The ramifications of the new policy were far-reaching. Previously, each member of Parliament was effectively a free agent whose vote on any given issue had to be obtained by the prime minister in order to pass any legislation. As we saw, this often entailed horse-trading that bordered on corruption. The new system effectively forced politicians to come together in parties because now a faction had to have 50 per cent of the seats plus one in order to form a government. In the last twenty-five years of the nineteenth century, there were only seven general elections and much greater stability of administrations. Greater continuity of governance was the result. Two figures and their parties dominated Greek political life over the last few decades of the nineteenth century.

Trikoupis founded his New (or Modernist Νεωτεριστικό Κόμμα in Greek) Party in 1875, and between then and his departure from Greek politics in 1895 he would be prime minster on seven occasions (see Table 5.2). Throughout this period his primary political rival was Theodoros Deliyiannis, whose Nationalist Party was the standard

Table 5.2   The administrations of Harilaos Trikoupis.

Month took office	Years in office	Duration of administration
May	1875	6 months
November	1878	1 month
March	1880	7 months
March	1882–1885	37 months
May	1886–1890	52 months
June	1892–1893	11 months
November	1893–1895	14 months

Table 5.3   The administrations of Theodoros Deliyiannis.

Month took office	Years in office	Duration of administration
April	1885–1886	12 months
October	1890–1892	17 months
May	1895–1897	23 month
November	1902–1903	7 months
December	1904–1905	5 months

bearer of Greek conservatism. When Trikoupis was not in power, Deliyiannis was (Table 5.3). Trikoupis was utterly convinced that in order for Greece to become a 'modern' state it needed to develop economically and to become more liberal socially; in short, that it must westernise and industrialise. He was a nationalist and a firm believer in Greek irredentism, but he also believed that Greece's national ambitions could only be achieved after modernisation. While this transformation was in progress, he wanted a small but modern army capable of mounting a vigorous national self-defence.

As to what his opponent believed in, when asked that question Deliyiannis famously replied that he was against everything that Trikoupis stood for. That said, his National Party did have a platform and an ideology. Theirs was the one most directly connected to romantic nationalism. Their overarching goal was the achievement of the Megali Idea, but until that dream could be realised, they wanted a Greece that, though small, was proud and independent. Conservatives saw westernisation and modernisation as grave threats to traditional Greek society. They feared that westernisation would erode the essential fabric of Greek culture and morality. Industrialisation, they feared, would produce a working class whose existence would threaten the existing social order (Hadziiossif 1997).

Almost as different as the two parties' political philosophies were their leaders. Where Trikoupis was an awkward and uninspiring public speaker, Deliyiannis was a gifted orator whose public speeches were as rousing as his opponent's were diffident. Deliyiannis was a man of the people who truly enjoyed working the masses, making him Greece's first populist politician. Indeed, he was the first, and for some time, the only politician who actually travelled extensively around the Greek countryside. Trikoupis, on the other hand, rarely left Athens, and when he did it was to sojourn to Western capitals. He was also a workaholic and a micromanager who had little time for socialising. His arch-enemy, on the other hand, was a garrulous larger-than-life figure whose social circle was large and whose social life included not infrequent visits to local gambling establishments. These two dichotomous and domineering men led Greece through the tumultuous decades after the Treaty of Berlin.

During his nearly continuous term of office in the 1880s, Trikoupis set about the task of reforming and modernising Greece. His reforms can be divided into two groups, economic and social. The foundation of the Greek economy was agriculture, and so any development programme had to begin with it. Through the nineteenth century Greece remained a nation of agriculturalists. Roughly 75 per cent of the adult male population was involved in agriculture, fishing or forestry in 1870; the figure fell slowly but steadily through to the end of the century to the figure of 62 per cent in 1907. Economically, he wanted to modernise and make more profitable Greek agriculture. At the same, he also wanted to industrialise Greek manufacturing. The two processes were linked. A more productive countryside would be more profitable, thus giving peasants more disposable income with which to buy Greek-made goods, and higher levels of per-capita productivity which would create a surplus of cheap labour that would be available for work in the newly built factories. His goal was to create a cycle of economic growth, linking field and factory and lessening Greece's dependence on foreign imports. Massive amounts of capital investment would be needed to achieve this goal. Late nineteenth-century social modernisation meant expanding education and using the organs of the state to promote social justice. Both of these entailed massive amounts of government expenditure. Trikoupis and the New Party, then, articulated an innovative and ambitious programme aimed at nothing less than the reformation of almost all aspects of Greek society, economy and politics, while at the same time providing the country with a military capable of achieving the national goals. In sum, he believed that the country's modernisation could be achieved as his first priority without sacrificing completely its irredentist dream.

Providing both guns and butter, as it were, was a formidable challenge, and one that would require a great deal of money. In 1860, Athens found itself unable to comply with the terms it had renegotiated with France and Britain in the 1850s for the repayment of the 'independence debt' (the 2.8 million pounds still outstanding from 1824) and so the country was forced to declare bankruptcy for the second time in its brief history. As a stop-gap measure and a sign of good faith, Greece had to agree to pay one-third of the proceeds from the customs duties collected at Syros to help pay off the debt, while a more permanent solution to the debt crisis could be hammered out. The post-revolutionary 1862 governments, on top of all of the issues pressing on them, had also to deal with this financial crisis. In 1867 another round of negotiations over repayment of the debt was conducted and a tentative deal was reached that included a haircut reducing the debt to one million pounds, which was to be paid in new bonds. All parties refused to accept this arrangement and so Greece remained mired in debt and frozen out of Europe's financial markets. Eleven years later (1878) a deal, that Trikoupis helped broker, was finally reached and it included an exchange of securities with a denomination of 1.2 million pounds and guaranteed annual repayments amounting to approximately 75,000 pounds derived from the customs duties collected on Greek exports. Greece was now deemed creditworthy.

It was a perfect match at the right time. Beset by the doldrums of the ongoing global depression, European financial houses were looking for investment opportunities, and in Greece they found a ready and willing borrower. In order to undertake his ambitious modernisation programme, Trikoupis needed masses of capital, and now with the blessing of Europe's financial markets, he had a ready source. In 1879, French bankers lent 60 million francs at 6 per cent. Two years later, another loan worth 120 million francs was brokered again in Paris. In 1884, over 100 million francs of sovereign debt was issued, and a syndicate of French and Greek banks held the debt. In 1887, Le Comptoir d'Escompte of Paris lent Greece over 135 million francs, at 4 per cent interest. Guarantees for previous loans were pledged by the collection of customs duties, especially on the export of Greece's primary commercial crop – the currant grape. Foreign loans were also secured by revenues from the government

Table 5.4   Greek loans, 1880–92.

Year	Nominal	Real
1880	129,000,000	83,000,000
1884	100,000,000	63,353,759
1885	123,615,000	96,324,168
1887	130,000,000	90,990,000
1888	15,000,000	9,990,000
1889	155,000,000	111,506,327
1890	45,000,000	40,050,000
1891	15,000,000	13,000,000
1892	36,500,000	17,934,167
Total	754,215,000	539,448,421

Total by year in French francs

monopolies on petroleum, matches, gambling, cigarette paper and emery.

In 1889, the Greek Treasury issued more than 6.2 million pounds in debt to be held by banks in London, Berlin and Constantinople. In addition to that, he contracted a loan in 1890 for railway construction and several loans in 1892 totalling 37.6 million francs. Table 5.4 shows the loans that Greece received under Trikoupis. Trikoupis was embarking on a deadly race. His modernisation programme, if successful, would expand the Greek economy substantially and lead to much higher levels of revenue. In the long run, economic growth would produce governmental income streams that would more than offset the foreign debt. The pressing question was which would come first, economic growth or debt repayment. It was not long before the answer arrived (Lazaretou 1993; 2005).

Since independence there had been a constant clamour among the peasantry for land redistribution. At issue was the disposition of the formerly Ottoman-held land and monastic properties. Otho had attempted a variety of land reform schemes over the years. Between 1835 and 1857, under the Land Dotation programme of 1835, heads of individual households had purchased nearly 20,000 hectares. But so impaired were the earlier reforms that two additional laws, both enacted in 1871, were needed to rectify their deficiencies by accelerating the pace of the distribution of national lands on more favourable terms.

The aim of this new legislation was to secure firm legal ownership of the land for as many families as possible and to enable families to purchase the still unoccupied national lands. It was estimated that over 50,000 families occupied and cultivated land to which they did not have verifiable legal title. This placed them in a very vulnerable position vis-a-vis creditors; it made them less likely to make long-term investment in the productivity of the land; it meant that they had to pay the state a burdensome *usufruct* tax in addition to the other mandated exactions. Giving them legal title to the land, it was hoped, would solve all of these problems. But the main emphasis of the 1871 laws was to provide land to the landless and to allow those who owned only a small amount of land to expand their holdings. Learning from the mistake of the earlier scheme, the land parcels were not purchased through auctions, in which the prices could rise outside of the range that peasants could pay, but instead government assessors set the prices. Heads of households could obtain mortgages to purchase national land with a fixed term of twenty-six years, amortised at 3 per cent and with a 2 per cent annual interest payment. Though the laws had been enacted before he came to power, it was under Trikoupis that they were most vigorously applied. Between 1878 and 1911, the government financed 357,217 sales of land amounting to 265,000 hectares. All told, the 1871 land distribution scheme increased by over one-third the area of arable land under cultivation (Franghiadis 1990: 86–7; 2011: 115).

In addition to getting more families settled on national lands, Trikoupis also sought to expand the area of arable land available in the country. In the middle of the fertile basin of Boiotia, covering over 200 square kilometres, lay Lake Kopais. In addition to creating a malarial health hazard, this shallow body of water covered some of the richest soil in the Balkans. The idea of draining had been around for millennia with the first attempt having been made during the Late Bronze Age. In 1881 Trikoupis concluded negations with a consortium of Ottoman Greek entrepreneurs, led by Andreas Syngros, to drain the lake. They formed a company in Paris called the Compagnie Française pour le Dessèchement et l'Exploitation du Lac Copaïs and raised the necessary funding on the French stock market. Soon thereafter, they began the arduous work of dredging the canals and digging the tunnels that would eventually lead to the drainage water being deposited in the narrow straits between Greece and Euboea.

The project proved to be more expensive than they had thought and by 1887 the company was bankrupt. A joint English-Scottish company, the Lake Copais Company Ltd, took over and completed the job. Over 12,000 hectares of prime arable land now became available. The company held a concession over the land for a period of ninety-nine years (in the end, the company relinquished control of its holdings to Greece in 1954), and rented approximately 10,000 hectares to Greek farming families under fairly reasonable terms; tenants paid a rent equivalent to 20 per cent of the value of the crops produced on company land. On the remaining 2,000 hectares, the company built a model farm that it owned and operated. The project was a great success. In addition to providing support to numerous families, the area now produced two critically important commodities: cereal grains and cotton.

Economic modernisation was contingent on making agriculture more profitable and on connecting more closely the various sectors of the economy. Market integration and international competitiveness could be enhanced by the development of a comprehensive, national transportation network. Quite simply the reason for this was that the rugged terrain of Greece made transporting bulk goods overland very time-consuming and expensive. By lowering transportation costs, agriculture would become more profitable giving small farming families more disposable income and large landowners more capital that they could invest in the nascent industrial sector. Trikoupis, therefore, focused a major part of his economic reforms on facilitating the growth of the export sector by modernising the country's transportation network.

New roads, railways, and harbour works were to allow for the more rapid movement of goods from the countryside to the cities and the ports, and they would intimately connect Thessaly to the kingdom. Map 5.1 shows the extent of the road and rail networks from independence to 1911 and it shows the scope and scale of his building projects. Building the railways was especially important. Before Trikoupis, Greece had a single, nine-kilometre long railway, which ran from Athens to Piraeus. It was begun in 1858, around the same time that the Athens gasworks (*Gazi*) were built: the gasworks' need for massive amounts of coal was a major impetus for building it. Integrating the country's economy and making it more profitable mandated the construction of a nationwide rail network. This was accomplished by granting concessions to different companies from around Europe, along with one Greek company called SPAP (the Railways of Piraeus-Athens-Peloponnesos Company), and over the span of a dozen years, almost 1,500 kilometers of new track was laid. Built out of imported steel and used by imported steam engine-pulled

Map 5.1 The Greek railway network, 1892.

carriages, the railway provided a major boost to Greece's overall economy. Like almost all of Trikoupis's major infrastructure projects, it was costly and relied almost exclusively on foreign companies and imported materials (Anastasiadou 2005; Triha 2001; Dertilis 2009: 747–52; Sinarelli 1989; 2003).

One of the most important and expensive infrastructure pro-grammes was the dredging of the Corinth Canal. As with draining Lake Kopais, the idea of cutting a channel across the narrow isthmus that separates central Greece from the Peloponnesos had been discussed since ancient times, and such a project was actually started under the Roman Emperor Nero. But it was really only after the successful construction of the Suez Canal (1869) that the idea cutting

Figure 5.5 *The Corinth Canal in 1905 © Library of Congress Prints and Photography Division.*

of cutting Greece in half became a serious possibility. Indeed, it was two Hungarians, Colonel István Türr and Béla Gerster, two veterans from the Suez Canal project, who spearheaded the Corinth initiative. After having reached an agreement with the Greek government and raised the needed capital from the European financial markets, work began in 1882. When the French company went bankrupt in 1890, Andreas Syngros and a group of investors formed a company called the Société Hellénique du Canal de Corinthe, which finished the job. All told it took over 4,000 workers labouring for eleven years to remove over 12 million cubic metres of soil and rock to produce a channel 6 kilometres in length, 80 metres below ground level, 26 metres across at the water surface and 8 metres below the waterline (Fig. 5.5). The total cost in today's dollars was approximately half a billion. The savings to maritime transportation were considerable. The length of the trip from Piraeus to Patras was cut from

295 to 100 nautical miles, from Piraeus to Kerkira from 370 to 237 and from Piraeus to Brindisi in Italy from 464 to 333. Moreover, it saved ships from having to navigate the treacherous waters off of the southern Peloponnesos. So, though its cost was prohibitively high, the Corinth Canal contributed significantly to the country's economic development (Sinarelli 1989).

Echoing back to Korais, Trikoupis believed in advancement through education and it was an issue very dear to his heart. Throughout his years in office, he pursued an aggressive policy of expanding Greece's education system. Previously, this issue had received little attention, either legislatively or bureaucratically. For most of the nineteenth century, Greece had neither a fully financed, comprehensive public-school system nor a standardised programme of teacher preparation. Schools were locally funded – if they were funded at all – and the Lancastrian model was the norm (Nikolakaki 2013; Harlan 2011). It was not, however, the English model but the French one developed by the Sociète pour l'Instruction Public that most Greek communities adopted.

The most ambitious of the educational reform laws was introduced in 1889 by Yiorgos Theotokis, Trikoupis's Minister of Education. It mandated, for example, the construction of no fewer than 217 new primary schools. In addition to there being more schools, they were now staffed by more (the same bill called for the hiring of 675 new people) and better-trained teachers. In a far-sighted move, he even introduced equal pay for both men and women teachers. Central control over the educational system was now firmly vested in the Ministry of Education and a special fund made up of public finances and private donations (called the Treasury for Primary Education) was created to support it (Damianakos 1977: 146–7; Dimaras 2003; 2006). Under Trikoupis's leadership, then, public education expanded greatly: the number of university students between 1860 and 1900, for example, rose from 1,100 to 3,300; boys attending high school went from 6,000 to 24,000; boys enrolled in primary schools increased from 44,000 to 178,000 and girls from a mere 8,000 to over 82,000. Trikoupis, then, far-sightedly saw that social modernisation hinged on education.

In regard to the national issue and irredentism, Trikoupis had to confront them in the context of a rapidly changing international climate. Though he was not in power when the Plovdiv Revolution, the Bulgarian-Serbian war and the unification of Bulgaria occurred (1886), he still had to confront the challenges that a newly resurgent

Bulgaria posed. He responded by modernising the armed forces and by trying to build closer ties to the Ottoman Empire. In regard to the latter, one of his novel policies, even though it failed, stands out as an important precedent. In 1890, Trikoupis proposed a law that called for the government to provide to the Muslim community, free of charge, state property in Piraeus that would be used for the construction of a mosque and its attendant buildings. This proposal was part of a package of confidence building measures that he was undertaking to try to ameliorate tensions between Athens and Istanbul. While the national question placed the two at loggerheads, the emergence of an aggressively irredentist Bulgaria threatened them both.

Moreover, after 1882, when Greece acquired a sizable Muslim population in Thessaly, the Porte made clear that how the kingdom treated it would be closely watched. Initial opposition to the legislation quickly abated when the government announced that the law was tied to an agreement that had been reached with the Ottoman Empire. First, Istanbul would pay the cost for the construction of the mosque. Second, it further agreed that the Ottoman state would provide land free of charge to the Patriarchate to build churches in the empire. The legislation even specified where the mosque was to be built and provided additional land to be used for the new Muslim cemetery. 'In the end, the mosque in Piraeus was never built because the money which the High Porte had provided for its construction was "lost" somewhere between Constantinople and Athens' (Glavinas 2013: 1). Domestically, other developments would soon sweep this legislation from the public eye. Internationally, the failure of this initiative only exacerbated the growing tensions between Greece and the empire over the treatment of Muslims in the kingdom and over the fate of Macedonia and Crete.

The single greatest challenge facing Trikoupis and his administrations was how to finance their programmes of reform. Like his predecessors he had to chart a treacherous course between the need to raise revenues and the danger of strangling economic growth in the process. Foreign debt, as we saw earlier, was the engine that drove his reform programme. Between 1879 and 1890, six major foreign loans were arranged totalling 630 million drachmas; by 1887, 40 per cent of total government expenditure went to servising the national debt. The size of Greek public debt rose from 95 drachmes per person in 1869 to 363 in 1893 (Kostis 2013: 475). Internally, sources of revenue that did not have a direct deleterious impact on one sector of society or another were simply not available. In the end Trikoupis had to tax the Greek populace heavily in order to pay the bills. He levied taxes on wine, tobacco, sheep, goats, oxen and donkeys; the tithe on all agricultural produce was increased, as was the tax on land holdings. He established state monopolies on salt and matches, and the prices of both soared. High import tariffs raised revenues and prices, but failed to abate the people's appetite for foreign goods. Export duties consequently had to be raised on precisely those commodities that formed the economy's lifeblood. The impact of Trikoupis's fiscal policies on the average Greek citizen was profoundly negative. And still the debt grew. The sustained deficits evident through the 1880s caused the collapse of the 1890s (for a comparative perspective onnational debt among the Balkan states, see Bernholz 2008).

The Greek economy had been buoyed for some time by the rapid expansion of the international market in currants following the phylloxera epidemic that had destroyed many of the vineyards of France, Spain and Italy. Throughout the 1870s and especially during the 1880s Greek exports of currants soared as prices on the international market rose.[2] Cultivation expanded as demand grew. Profits from agricultural exports were converted into investment capital. Government revenues derived from export duties were a critical component in financing the reform programme. Many of the foreign loans that Trikoupis contracted were guaranteed by the revenues from currant exports. It is not going too far to say that the financing of his entire programme was underwritten by a raisin. So long as these conditions of high prices and great demand for Greek grapes lasted, the precarious position of the public fisc could be maintained; but in 1893 the bottom fell out of the Greek economy. Due to the confluence of numerous factors, laid out in detail on pages 266–7, currant prices plummeted and as a consequence so did government revenues. A massive budget deficit loomed, but the final nail in the budgetary coffin was that a number of major bond issues were becoming due at precisely the same moment. And Greece did not have the money to pay back the bondholders, let alone to service the annual interest on the other outstanding loans. In what was one of his shortest and surely his most memorable speech to Parliament, on 10 December 1893, Trikoupis informed his colleagues, 'Regretfully, we are bankrupt [Δυστυχώς επωχεύσαμεν].' The boom times were over and Greece's dark *fin-de-siècle* had begun.

Notes

1. Though Konortas's observation refers to Thrace, the same situation held true in Ottoman Macedonia.
2. The currant grape boom and its bust are discussed in detail in Chapter 8.

CHAPTER 6

The social history of everyday life

The painting in Figure 6.1 depicts a family gathered together in the living quarters of their house to dine; we will discuss this painting in more detail below. The image is so vivid that the viewer can almost feel the heat from the fire and enjoy the aroma of the meal, though probably not the musty smell from the animals penned up next to the dining area. We can use our imagination to craft a story about the people in the scene. A careful visual analysis of the painting, then, can tell us a great deal about social history and material culture. But we need to exert some caution. Images like this painting have to be evaluated carefully before we can analyse them. In this chapter, we explore Greek social history during the long nineteenth century of existence and in doing so, we run up against the problem of sources.

Common people in the past were mostly illiterate and so left us few direct testimonies about their lives. Consequently, we must rely on sources that indirectly give insights into their world. One important source is government records. Throughout their lives people interacted with the state and records were kept when people were born (birth certificates), when they married, and when they died. They also had economic dealings with the state, like paying taxes, which provide us with data about their economic activities. But these are just dry numbers. Other sources enable us to explore their lives more vividly.

Visual materials, like the painting, and the numerous drawings and photographs presented elsewhere in the book, inform us about how they lived and their material culture. A third social history source is the written accounts by Greek and foreign travellers who visited rural villages and left us their observations and impressions. Lastly, archaeology provides us with a great deal of information about the material world. All of these sources have their strengths and their weaknesses, and it is not possible to write a social history using just one of them. But, if we analyse them jointly, we can minimise their weaknesses and capitalise on their strengths, and by so doing we can

Figure 6.1 *The interior of a Greek peasant house during dinner © Pierre Peytier.*

gain valuable insights into everyday life and the cultural realities of Greek society during the long nineteenth century.

In this and the next chapter, we discuss how people in the past lived and worked. The aim is to reconstruct their lived reality. In doing so we explore aspects of their material culture and their experiences of everyday life. Two themes run through Chapters 6 and 7. The first one is the persistent tension between continuity and change in the face of an ever-evolving world. The second relates to the remarkable diversity that characterised Greek society and culture in the kingdom of Greece, the Ottoman Empire and the diaspora. When one thinks of Greek culture today, a relatively few iconic food dishes and cultural customs come to mind, which create an image of a very homogeneous society. This seeming homogeneity of the present stands in marked contrast to the exceptional diversity of the past. The language, culture and lifestyles of communities and regions were markedly different even within the borders of the nascent Greek state, let alone in the wider Greek world. House designs, material culture such as pottery and dress, and even speech varied widely and markedly from region to region and from place to place. Continuity, change and diversity are the key themes, then, that frame our discussion of Greek culture, society and economy.

This chapter begins with an examination of the basic structures of Greek society during the nineteenth century, such as demography and household structure. Since Greece was predominantly a rural society, we shall next move on to discuss various aspects of peasant society and material culture. Then, using gender as our organising axis, we can explore the social worlds of men and women. In the final section of the chapter, we move from the country to the city.

The Greek world was interconnected by a network of urban centres. Many of these were port cities that played an important role in the economic life of the region. These grew substantially over the course of the long nineteenth century and they became more structurally complex and wealth-stratified.

Demography and society

The War of Independence had been a long and bloody affair. Caught between the savage scorched-earth policy of Ibrahim Paşa and the continual depredations of the Greek irregulars, the peasantry suffered horribly. Though it is impossible to determine the exact numbers of fatalities, we can be sure that tens of thousands died. Yet, if the earliest demographic data available after the war are to be believed, a combination of Greek in-migration from outside the kingdom and a vigorous rate of growth among the indigenous population largely recouped the war losses within a few decades. Take the case of the village of Maryveli in Messenia (southwestern Greece) located not far from where the Battle of Manitaki took place. Before the war, it had a population of 230 people; wartime losses reduced this to 80 and it took thirty years for it to reach pre-war levels (Lee 2001: 55). The same is true for the large and prosperous village of Dimitsana, located in the uplands of Arkadia. Before the war, it had a vibrant population of over 6,000 people, only to see it fall to 1,750 after the conflict. By 1861, its numbers had risen to close to 5,000 but the village never fully recouped its losses. The same picture holds for the rest of the country. Table 6.1 provides an overview of population growth from 1833 to 1901 (for discussions of the sources and the current state-of-play in Greek demographic history, see Chouliarakes 1988; Hiondiou 2006; Kallivretakis 1995; Marre 2010; Petmezas 1999b).

Focusing first on the kingdom as a whole, it appears that the years immediately after the war, roughly from 1832 until 1835, witnessed a modest but steady growth in population. This was followed but a

Table 6.1   Population growth in Greece, 1821–1920.

Population	Country	Peloponnesos	Central Greece	Aegean Islands	Ionian Islands	Thessaly
1821	766,477	389,709	206,356	161,412		
1828	600,000					
1835	674,185					
1843	915,000					
1848	987,000					
1853	1,036,000					
1861	1,096,810	552,414	318,535	225,861		
1870	1,436,141	611,861	356,865	238,784	228,631	
1879	1,638,850	709,245	441,033	259,056	229,516	
1889	2,187,308	813,154	556,254	235,050	238,783	344,067
1896	2,434,000	902,181	758,385	234,747	235,973	385,520
1907	2,632,000	937,366	897,773	230,378	254,494	448,618
1920	5,021,790	915,204	1,125,073	222,347	224,189	491,159

Gallant 2001: 77

very sharp increase during the late 1830s and 1840s, that saw population size expand from about 650,000 in 1835 to almost one million in 1848. Indigenous growth rates remained at moderate to high levels for the remainder of the nineteenth century. All told, these figures suggest a 295 per cent increase within the territory of the kingdom between 1832 and the 1910s. The actual growth rate was even higher than these figures suggest because they do not take into account the half a million Greeks who left the country between 1880 and 1920. To place the Greek case into a comparative framework, over the same period the population of Spain grew by 183 per cent and that of Italy by 185 per cent, while the major powers of France and Great Britain expanded by 127 per cent and 233 per cent respectively. The Greek population, then, was clearly one of the fastest growing in all of Europe for much of the nineteenth century.

A number of factors control the population growth rate. At a very basic level, of course, the primary one is the ratio of the birth rate to the death rate. Quite simply, if more people are born than die, population increases. The birth rate, using the standard measure of births per every 1,000 persons, in 1860 was 38.6, while the mortality rate was 26.5. The birth rate rose over the next few decades reaching its zenith during the 1880s (40.8/1,000), while the mortality rate fell at a corresponding rate, sinking to its nadir of 20.3/1,000 at the turn of the century. In the absence of national-level data before 1860 we have to rely on archival studies of specific localities, and the few studies that have been done suggest that figures of the same magnitude pertained before 1860 as well. So more Greeks were being born while the rate at which others died fell (Gavalas 2002; 2004; 2008a; 2008b; 2013; Hionidou 1995a; 1995b; 2006).

The key demographic variables controlling the birth rate is the female age at marriage, life expectancy, fertility rate, artificial fertility control, the percentage of women and men who marry, and the infant mortality rate. If, for example, few women marry and they marry late in life and die shortly thereafter, and if many of the children they give birth to die, then the birth rate will be low. What transpired in Greece during the nineteenth century was the development of a high-growth demographic regime.

One critical contributing factor to this development was the low age at marriage for women. From the available data, it appears that throughout the century women married in their early twenties. The average age at marriage for men was late twenties. Over the course of the century, both of these figures fluctuated, but the trend was for the vast majority of women, over 90 per cent, to be married by the age of twenty-six, while the average age for men declined to twenty-six or twenty-seven, with over 80 per cent of men having taken a bride for the first time by the age of thirty. The discrepancy in age at marriage between men and women was largely due to the fact that men could only marry when they had accumulated the wherewithal to start a new household. In nineteenth-century Greek society, marriages were not love affairs but material transactions (Fig. 6.2). Simultaneously, life expectancy for both men and women increased from 35.7 in 1860 to 45.2 by the 1920s. Effective artificial birth control was not widely practised by Greek couples and so a natural fertility rate predominated (Gavalas 2002; Hionidou 1998).

Two additional factors of importance were: first, that almost all Greek men and women married, meaning that everyone contributed to the reproducing population, and, second, that the infant mortality rate was falling. According to one study, for example, the infant death rate fell from 198.2 in 1860 to 148.1 by the 1920s. We can conclude, then, that almost all Greek men and women married; they married somewhat younger and lived longer than their forebears, and in the absence of birth control, they produced more children, a greater percentage of whom survived to adulthood.

The results of this confluence of factors was clearly attested to in the 1920 census, which showed that fully 42 per cent of Greek families had more than five children and 15 per cent had eight or

Figure 6.2 *Young bride with her family, Eleusis, 1903 © Library of Congress Prints and Photography Division.*

In the past, a marriage was not just a union between a man and a woman but also a transaction that bound two families and households together materially and socially. Matches back then were not made for love but for a variety of reasons, and it was not the couple that arranged them. A marriage was the result of a long and protracted negotiation between two households, often conducted by professional matchmakers. When a deal was finally reached, a legally binding contract was drawn up, and many of these are preserved in Greek archives. The contract specified the property that the bride would take into the marriage as her dowry. It usually consisted of her trousseau (clothes, linen and other items needed to start a new household), cash (often presented as a ceremonial necklace, like the one seen on the bride in this photograph – splendid examples of which can be seen at the Benaki Museum and National Museum of Folk Culture in Athens) and real estate in some parts of the Greek world. Bridewealth in the form of cash was given by the husband's family to his wife's household. Weddings were time for celebration, including as sumptuous a feast as the bride's family could afford, accompanied by music and revelry. In addition to the religious ceremony, the 'crowning' of the couple, there were various other traditional rituals.

more children, and both of these figures were substantially higher than in 1861. The population expanded and Greek families grew larger. It was the combined effects of the developments discussed above that created the engine of growth that produced the profound population increase in Greece during the nineteenth century. Some of the more important social consequences of this growth will be examined shortly. I want to turn next to an examination of the nature of family and household in nineteenth-century Greece.

The *spiti*: family and household structure

As in other agrarian societies, the household, called in Greek σπίτι (spiti), constituted the primary social and economic unit on which the communal and the national social structures were built. It was both the centre of production and reproduction, and the most basic unit for the socialisation of the young. The following observation about the importance of the household in the recent past holds equally true for the nineteenth century: 'A man's categorical obligations are ... to his family [spiti]. Outside his family he may have other roles ... Yet where there is conflict between loyalty to the family and duty to another group or service, the former has precedence' (Campbell and Sherrard 1968: 334; Campbell 1964). Household interests come before all others in the Greek peasant worldview. However, no household is an island unto itself. The spiti was also the locus for the union of two groups of kindred – the husband's and the wife's. We shall see repeatedly throughout this chapter just how central the spiti was in Greek society. It is important at this juncture to examine the structure of the household and processes by which it was formed.

The most basic question we need to answer about the household is, what did the average one look like? Was the typical Greek household large, consisting of many generations or groups of brothers and their families living under one roof? Or was it more like the structure normative today, in which the household usually consists of a married couple and their unmarried offspring? Answering this question is not as simple as it might initially appear. First, there is yet again the problem of the paucity of information. We need fairly detailed census data or other types of family records in order to reconstruct the structure of households. Second, we have to be aware that the final form the average household took may not have been what people in fact were aiming at but were unable to achieve because of demographic factors. Nonetheless, we can venture some generalisations. Table 6.2 presents a brief overview of key terms and concepts that anthropologists and social historians use to study households and kinship.

Table 6.3 presents the data derived from studies of different communities in Greece and the Ottoman Empire during the late eighteenth and nineteenth centuries.[1] Chronologically, these cases span from 1788 until 1915, and geographically they spanned from mountainous Epiros to Asia Minor. Also, the sample includes upland and lowland villages, islands and continental sites, and two towns. An immediate and important observation is that the normative household formation in the Greek world, just as it was in the rest of Europe, was the nuclear household. In some cases, over three-quarters of households consisted of a conjugal couple and their offspring. With two exceptions, nuclear was the norm.

The village of Aristi in Epiros was the only place studied where complex households (57 per cent) predominated. The people of Aristi were not pastoralists but agriculturalists in an area where arable land was scarce and what there was of it was of poor quality. Like many upland communities in the Balkans where a very delicate balance between people and resources existed, village men would temporarily migrate as itinerant labourers, artisans or merchants. In the case of Aristi, they specialised as innkeepers and bakers, and men from the village worked in cities all across the Balkans. The female-headed households of the absent men would combine with siblings or in-laws on a temporary basis or co-reside in some other arrangement that produced joint households (Caftanzoglou 1997).

The other exception was Çukur in Cappadocia. This village had a mixed population of Muslims and Orthodox Christians, and the group focused on in this study were the Karamali (Turkish-speaking Greek Orthodox people). The author of this study argues that a particular set of circumstances, in this case the paucity of land, the nature of the local rural economy and the threat of raids by Turkoman and Kurdish tribes, compelled kinsman to pool resources economically and to co-reside for defensive purposes (Renieri 2002).

In nineteenth-century Greek society, then, there were three predominant, normative forms of family structure. The most common pattern pertained among the Greek peasantry where the nuclear household was the normative form. Another pattern, not infrequent among pastoralists and sharecroppers, featured a greater proportion of extended or joint households. And finally, there was an urban pattern in which nuclear households were the overwhelming

Table 6.2 *Household forms, kinship and property devolution.*

Family forms
1. Singleton/Solitaries: person living on her/his own.
2. Nuclear/Conjugal: couple with or without children
3. Extended/Stem: a nuclear household plus other members, usually the head of the household's parents.
4. Multiple Joint: two nuclear households co-residing
5. Multiple Complex: two or more nuclear households plus other members, usually the head of the household's parents.

Lineage
1. Patrilineal: descent traced through male line
2. Matrilineal: descent through the female line
3. Bilaterial: descent through both lines

Kingroups
1. Affinal: blood kin
2. Agnatic: kin by marriage

Residence Patterns:

Neolocal: establish new household separate from parents
1. Virilocal: live in household owned/inherited by the husband
2. Uxorilocal: live in household owned/inherited by the wife

Non-neolocal: live with or near parents
1. Patrilocal: live in husband's father's household
2. Patri-virilocal: live in separate household near husband's father
3. Matrilocal: live in wife's mother's house
4. Matri-uxorilocal: live in separate household near wife's mother

Dowry (Direct): προίκα (prika) property given by bride's family to the groom; remains legally hers but husband has use-rights (usufruct).
Bridewealth (Indirect dowry): προγαμιαία δωρεά (progamiaia dorea): property given by the groom's family to the wife's family.

Inheritance:

1. Partible Inheritance
    1. Pure Partible: each inherits an equal share
    2. Partial Partible: one heir receives more than the others, usually in exchange for caring for parents

2. Unogeniture
    1. Primogeniture: Inheritance went to the eldest heir.
    2. Ultimogenture: Inheritance went to the youngest heir.

Table 6.3 *Household structure in various regions.*

	Syrrako 1905	Syrrako 1905	Aristi 1905	Hermoupolis 1879	Mykonos 1861	Kythera 1788	Preveza 1780	Krokylio 1915	Çukur 1884
	Pastoralists	Permanent							
Solitaries	2	12.6	8.8	13.6	11.2	14.4	36	2.6	1.5
No family	0.6	5.4	1.3	7.2	4	2.6	16	1.3	0
Nuclear	50.1	46.2	28.9	72.4	76.8	75.7	40	62.6	45.5
Extended	21.1	21.5	25.2	4.5	3.9	4.5	4	16.7	4.5
Joint	23.9	11.7	32	0.5	3.8	2.7	4	12.1	47.9
Other	2.3	2.7	3.8	1.8	0.3	0.2	0	5.6	0

favourite. Related to the structure of the household and to how the household operated as a social unit was the pattern of residence.

Three different types of postmarital residence pattern have been observed in Greece. Not too surprisingly each of them was related to a number of factors, such as household structure, the nature of the kinship system and the way property was transmitted to the next generation. One prominent postmarital residence pattern was virilocality, or patrivirilocality. In the regions where this was the custom, the newly married couple would set up residence either in the household of the husband's father (patrivirilocal), thus creating a complex household, or they would build a house in very close proximity to the father's abode, often even in the same compound. Over time, this custom produced a spatial geography characterised by clusters of men related to one another by blood. It was found most frequently among pastoralists and in other areas like Crete and Epiros, regions with a tradition of autonomy and militarism that placed a premium on having numerous fighting men connected to one another like the Mani and the central mountainous regions of the Peloponnesos, and in places such as the Ionian Islands where sharecropping created common economic interests between agnatic kinsmen.

This system placed great emphasis on the kinship relationship between men and agnatic kin groups often formed tightly organised groups. Property transmission focused on men as well. Upon the death or retirement of the *pater familias*, the adult sons would share equally in the inheritance, but there were considerable social pressures placed upon them to continue to operate their holdings as a unit. Women traditionally did not receive land as part of their dowries or share in any inheritance. Instead, they received their share of the parental estate in their dowry, usually in the form of a trousseau that included cash and moveable property (Caftanzoglou 1998; Papataxiarchis and Petmezas 1998; Karouzou 1998).

The second postmarital residence pattern practised in the past was uxorilocality. In this case, the married coupled went to live either with the wife's family or in close proximity to them. In other words, uxorilocality is more or less the mirror image of the system that we just discussed, only in this instance the focus was on kindred women rather than men. Kinship lines tended to be traced bilaterally, in other words along both the husband's and the wife's families, and strong bonds were formed between kinswomen. Regarding the inter-generational transmission of property, the custom was for one of the daughters to receive her parents' house as part of her dowry, but the practice regarding which girl, if there were more than one daughter, varied. In some places it was the eldest, in others the youngest, and in others it was decided on the basis of filial affection. This custom was seen most frequently on the Aegean islands or in other maritime communities where the men would be absent for long periods of time (Kasdagli 2004).

The third system fell somewhere in between the other two, and while it had a long history, it really developed into the predominant custom only during the nineteenth century. In this instance, couples practised neolocality, in which the newly weds would establish their own household spatially distinct from either's parents. Since the parents would more than likely be leaving behind a house, one of the children would receive it as their patrimony, usually in exchange for agreeing to care for the aged parents. Property transmission among agriculturalists tended to be partible, meaning that each child received an equal share of the parental estate, and women frequently received land as part of their dowry (Franghiadis 1993). This was the practice among the vast majority of peasant farming families across Greece. It became the custom in the newly emerging urban areas as well, with an apartment or a similar dwelling space substituting for arable land.

Whether large and complex or simple and nuclear, the spiti was at the centre of Greek life. Before examining the traditional social roles that men and women played in their household, I want to look at the place of the spiti in the material world by posing two questions: What sort of community did most Greeks live in, and how did the household operate as a unit of production in the past?

Houses and villages

The visitor to Greece today is immediately struck by the degree to which cities, especially Athens, dominate Greek society. Such an impression is amply supported by a glance at the most recent census figures, which show that over one half of the entire Greek population resides in the greater Athens area alone. The large swathes of the countryside that are today unoccupied reinforce the view of Greek society's urban orientation. Yet the predominance of cities and their urban lifestyles is a relatively recent phenomenon. For most of its history, Greece had been a country of rural folk who lived in villages. For example, according to the first census that recorded occupational

Table 6.4 *Distribution of population in Greece by settlement size, 1861.*

Size of settlement	Frequency	Population
0–1000	10,050	2,703,539
1001–2000	510	689,012
2001–3000	107	263,697
3001–4000	38	119,677
4001–5000	23	101,613
5001–10000	33	230,210
10001–50000	26	466,154
50001–100000	1	51,598
<100000	3	593,281
Totals	10,791	5,218,781

Gallant 2001: 86

information, that of 1861, 74 per cent of adult men were agriculturalists who earned their livelihood from working the land. Moreover, the pattern remained fairly consistent through time. Even as
late as the 1890s, the proportion of heads of households listed as
farmers had barely changed, dropping only to 70 per cent. Before
examining the agrarian systems of nineteenth-century Greece, we
need to make a few observations about where Greeks lived and
how the built environment of the village helped shape their social
world.

Table 6.4 shows the distribution of human settlements in Greece
before 1913. Almost 52 per cent of the entire population resided
in villages containing fewer than 1,000 individuals, and villages of
this size accounted for nearly 94 per cent of all human habitations.
Hidden within these aggregate figures is the fact that the majority of
villagers (approximately 35 per cent) lived in villages of fewer than
500 people, and over 150,000 people lived in settlements of fewer
than one hundred. The typical village had a population of either
200–300 or 600–700 people. If we consider that settlements with
between 1,000 and 5,000 inhabitants were also populated predominantly by peasant families, then over 70 per cent of the population
lived in villages. The data also suggests that by the 1910s, the population distribution of Greece was sharply divided between rural
villages and larger cities, and that towns (that is, settlements with
between 5,000 and 10,000 people) were of relatively modest importance. Moving back in time, the picture of the region as a land of rural
villages only becomes more apparent. As a consequence of this, the

physical and social environment that shaped peoples' lives was that of the small face-to-face community.

It is impossible to describe the typical Greek village. Village design varied from region to region and from place to place within regions depending on a variety of localised factors. The same can be said for house design. In addition to the purely physical factors, there were social ones as well, especially wealth, that influenced village and house construction. We can, however, posit some generalisations regarding the common factors that influenced the physical layout of villages.

First, given that so much of the Greek landscape is hilly or mountainous and that arable land was at such a premium, villages tended to be built on hillsides and slopes rather than on farmland. Second, because of the very hot, dry summers, villages were sited with an eye to water sources. Some other recurring features were the presence of a church and an open space or square around which the village's houses would be clustered. Regarding house design, the fact that these were functioning farms also created some recurring features, such as storage facilities, spaces for penning animals, and areas reserved for food preparation.

Here is a lengthy description of a typical peasant household:

> The house in which we stopped was a good example of the houses of the villages amongst the mountains of the better kind. It had been built thirty years, as an inscription in front indicated. It consisted of two storeys, and, with the outhouses, formed a hollow square. The entrance was by an arched way, in which were small ornamented niches for holding water-vessels. On the ground floor were the sleeping apartments, in each of which was a good bed, without curtains; and in one of them, besides the bed, there was a loom. They had separate entrances, so as to be well adapted for different families. On the upper floor, approached by a flight of stone steps, was a large hall, containing one or two presses, several large chests, and a sufficient number of chairs and tables, all in pretty good order, and of tolerable quality; and ranged round the wall were pictures of the Virgin, of saints, and monasteries, and opposite the principal picture a lamp was suspended, and kept constantly burning. Off this hall, and communicating with it, there were four small bed-rooms, well provided with beds. In none of the rooms were there any fireplaces. The kitchen was a large room, a separate building in the rear, well provided, as it appeared, with culinary utensils, as spits, pots, &c. It had two ovens, one large, the other small, of the common construction, provided with holes below for holding ashes, with small recesses above, with a

shelf on each. In another part of the room was the hearth, with low seats on each side of it, forming a square.

The fire was kindled in the middle of the enclosed space, and the smoke had no vent, excepting through the door, as there was no opening in the roof above, and, if I recollect rightly, no windows. The firewood was piled on the other side of the room. The only utensil that attracted my attention particularly was a small hand-mill, composed of two circular pieces of rough sandstone from Cephalonia [Kefalonia], used to grind grain for soup, similar in construction to the hand-mill of Ceylon and of the continent of India, and to the quern of old of England and Scotland, and which is still in use in some parts of the Highlands. In another building adjoining was an olive press, exactly of the same kind as that used in the town; and in a third building there was a cornmill, of the common construction, which the proprietor let out, receiving in payment a certain portion of the grain ground. It was at work at the time; two women, in a kind of harness, assisted a horse in turning it. The sight was sufficiently degrading; it was, however, a labour they were accustomed to, and they did not seem to mind it; their hands were busily employed at the same time in spinning. This was not the only time and place where we saw women so occupied; at Oxicora [a nearby village on the island] we first noticed it; there we witnessed six in harness, labouring at the mill, and spinning as they ran round ...

The women are even more busily employed than the men, and as variously; spinning, weaving, and knitting may be considered almost as their amusements and recreations, after the more important and laborious labours of the day. They spin both cotton and worsted thread, and also goat-hair; knit very good stockings; and weave haircloth for bags, cotton cloth for dress and household purposes, and some carpeting, of which I saw two or three very pretty samples in the form of rugs.

At dinner we were attended by the daughter-in-law of our host, a fine active young woman, perfectly modest, without being in the least bashful. Her easy manner indicated that it was the custom of the country,-that she considered it a duty, – and that she was used to it as well as not displeased with it. (Davy 1842: Volume II. 196–9; Davy was the physician for the British garrison on the island of Kefalonia. He lived there for seven years and travelled widely on the islands. This is a description of a house in a mountain village called Volimes on the island of Zakynthos.)

This description conveys important insights into the multifaceted functions that the house served. As with so many other elements of Greek material culture, there was a great diversity of house design

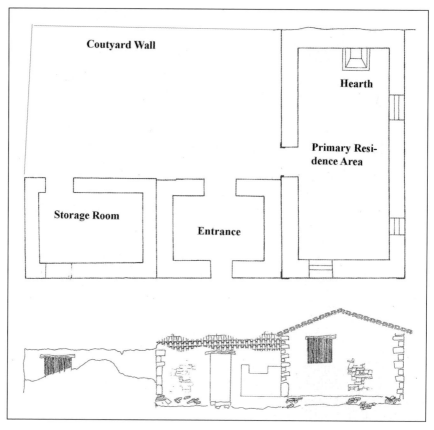

Figure 6.3 Drawing of a Peloponnesian peasant house © Thomas W. Gallant.

and construction styles. Some distinctions were regional and cultural, while others were based on material factors such as wealth. In spite of this variety, there were some central tendencies that most houses shared, and there are some forms that were more common than others. What we will do is highlight the key features of the most popular types of houses. In addition, using visual sources, like Figure 6.1, written descriptions, like the one above by Davy, and physical remains recorded by archaeologists, we can gain insights into the social history of the family.[2]

The most common form of rural dwelling was the so-called longhouse (Sigalos 2004: 61). At its simplest, it consisted of a single, elongated structure with only one or two interior rooms (Fig. 6.3). Frequently, however, one or two other buildings were attached to the primary dwelling, forming an L-shaped pattern, as evidenced in

Figure 6.4 *Women standing guard at the courtyard gate (Epiros, 1903)* © *Fred Boissonnas.*

the illustration. Quite frequently one of these ancillary rooms was a storage facility. Another recurring feature of this type of house was the addition of an exterior wall that connected the two ends of the 'L' to form a square-shaped dwelling with a courtyard. Houses tended to be inward-looking, and through their design they demarcated sharply between domestic and public space. The house provided the family with protection from the outside world, but it also articulated them to it. As Figure 6.4 shows, the courtyard gate provided a formidable barrier, and as the stern contenance of the women in the photograph suggests, gaining entry into the courtyard was not easily accomplished.

Davy's description and Figure 6.1 allows us to make some observations about what life was like in houses like this. The first thing to note is that the main residential area was a relatively large undifferentiated space. Their houses were not divided into separate rooms, but instead all inside activities took place in a single area. During the course of a day, then, the same space served as the dining room, as in Figure 6.1, a workshop, especially for women's work, and as the bedroom. Reflecting that this was a multi-activity space is the lack of furniture. Conspicuously absent are storage cupboards, tables, chairs and even beds. The furniture that is present is portable and can be removed quickly. So, the communal dining table consists of a large, round metal plate that rests on a short wooden base. The family sits around it on the floor, making it easy to convert the area into the bedroom when the meal was finished. The tray and its base would be stored, probably hung on the wall, and then sacks filled with straw were laid on the floor and covered with cloth and blankets. The family slept together in this communal area, along with some of their livestock. Domestic goods that needed to be stored were hung on the wall, from the rafters, or placed on shelves. The residential area was heated either with a fireplace, as shown in Figure 6.3, or with a portable brazier, like the one shown in Figure 6.1. Dark, smoke-filled and redolent with a variety of scents and smells, this type of house was at the centre of Greek life.

The other major domestic activity area was the courtyard. Like the house, it was also a multi-use space. Figure 6.5 lets us peer into the courtyard of a relatively affluent Ottoman Greek rural household. It was a place where children played, where women baked bread and casseroles, and where members of the household socialised. At different times of the day, the courtyard was gendered as a male or female space. It would be where the household goat was tethered so that women could milk it. It also contained areas for storing tools and equipment, as well as foodstuffs. Many courtyards contained a small room, the walls of which were plastered with lime to keep them dry and in which grain and other cereals were stored.

Contrasting with the simple one-story longhouse were the larger and more elaborate houses found among more affluent peasants. Whether in the mountains or on the plains, peasants who had the wherewithal to do so, tended to build more elaborate, larger and more complex houses. In mountainous or hilly regions, the houses were well-built, with stone masonry, usually two or more storeys in height, and the space within them tended to be divided into separate activity zones, often based on gender. The ground floor was reserved for keeping animals and storing equipment; the first floor was the primary dwelling space for the family, and the third storey usually

Figure 6.5 A woman, with her family, baking bread in an oven in the courtyard
of her house in a village in Asia Minor, Illustrated London News, *no. 2022,*
vol. Lxxii, Saturday, 30 March 1878, p. 301 © Mary Evans Picture Library.

contained more storage space and the sleeping quarters. In some
regions, this basic form was augmented by a stone tower or some
other similar type of defensive structure, and it usually incorporated
a walled-off courtyard. A hybrid form of house combined a tower
with the longhouse. On the island of Andros, for example, the typical
rural dwelling was a variant of the longhouse with a tower built over
only one section of it, usually over the storerooms. No matter
whether it was a simple one-room dwelling or a complex multi-storey
one, the house was the single most important element in Greek rural
society.

The social world of men and women

> The household, everyone says, is the kingdom of the wife and no one
> would think to raise any objections to this view. But the household is
> a word that encompasses a great deal: spouses, children, domestic
> servants, furniture, movable and immovable property. We ask there-
> fore: does the wife rule over her spouse in the household? No, because

the husband is its absolute master. ('Οι νόμοι μας και τα βασίλεια της γυναικός.' Εφημερίς των Κυριών, 23 June 1891)

This passage captures the paradox at the heart of gender relations in traditional Greek society: the distinction between public and private and between the formal and informal. The first part of the quote describes the situation that everyone knew: that it was women who essentially ran the household. The last sentence, however, asserts something that everyone also knew, and that was that the husband was the absolute master of the household. The key to understanding the paradox is the article's title: 'Our laws and the kingdom of women.' Formal legal power over the household and everyone and everything in it was vested solely in the man. Women were denied an autonomous legal existence; they were, in essence, property and throughout their life women were placed under the legal guardianship of a man, be it her father or later in life her husband, as reflected in the quote at the start of the section. It also captures the fundamental and central role that gender played a traditional Greek society. I begin with the world of men.

At the core of nineteenth-century notions of masculinity was the concept of *timi*. This term is usually translated as 'honour.' Honour has become such a loaded term that we must employ it with care. A better way of conceptualising timi is as reputation. A man of honour or timi was someone who was held in high esteem by his peers, by the other men in his community. And it appears the attribute that more than any other provided the yardstick by which a man's reputation was measured was control. A man should demonstrate at all times a firm command over all of those things that mattered in lives of Greek peasant men: land and property, animals and the people in his household. We should also add that he needed to demonstrate control over himself as well. Exercising control of resources defined his role as *nikokyris* (literally, lord of the household). He was to see to the material needs of those residing in his household. This included the mundane wherewithal of daily existence, but also it entailed ensuring that there would be enough goods to vouchsafe the future survival of his sons and daughters.

A man was to use every means at his disposal – deception, prevarication, intimidation and even violence, to defend the social standing and enhance the material welfare of his household. A popular metaphor at the time compared the plebeian household to the celestial order, with the head of the household playing the role of the Supreme Being. In carrying out his 'divine' duties, a man was to manifest complete control of everything in his spiti, and he was to ensure harmony within it as well. His reputation among his peers was based on their collective assessment of how well he lived up to this culturally inscribed set of expectations.

To be sure, the ideal of a man as absolute master of the domestic realm, and of the household as harmonious a realm as the celestial order was often far from reality. As in any society, conflicts between family members were not uncommon occurrences, and the court records are replete with examples of litigation between members of the same household and even of homicidal violence in the house.

Take the case of a young man on the island of Zakynthos in 1863. On Tuesday, 26 May, Ioannis Markoussas put a bullet into the head of his young wife, Maria Pagnopoulou, and then set her body on fire. He killed her because his father, who objected to the marriage, was about to disinherit him. His attempt to destroy the evidence of his foul act failed and the police eventually arrested him for murder. The evidence against him was overwhelming and as a result he was convicted and sentenced to fifteen years at hard labour (Gallant 2012: 141–2). Money, so it would it seem, triumphed over love. When violence and conflict within the household did occur, it was socially reprehensible. Violence directed from the spiti outward in defense of its interests, however, was not only acceptable, but even mandatory, if a man did not want to lose face.

A central element of nineteenth-century masculinity, then, was the ethos of vengeance. Charles Tuckerman, the United States Minister to Greece in the 1860s, captures well the essence of this ethos:

> [To a Greek man,] a wound of honor or a family insult burns like a compressed and slow consuming tow. In coarser natures it urges to desperate measures, and the traveler in the interior of Greece some-times sees men with their hair and beards growing long in token that the wearer has an enemy to meet; nor will it be cut or shaved until he has met insult with insult, or blood with blood. (Tuckerman 1872: 340)

This ethos meant that if a man or his family were insulted or wronged in any way, he had to respond with aggression or risk seeing his reputation diminished. But the type and the amount of socially accepted violence differed depending upon the context. One of the most common forms of honour-related violence was the knife fight, the essence of which is captured in the following tale.

On a hot summer's eve in 1836 Tonia Theodoros was sitting in the wineshop of his small village on the island of Kerkira. Men gathered, as was their wont for a few glasses and some conversation. Theodoros and a co-villager named Mokastiriotis, to whom he was not related, got into an argument, the cause of which none of the five witnesses could remember. Suddenly, Theodoros called Mokastiriotis a fool and a braggart. Mokastiriotis loudly replied that he would rather be a fool than 'the lord of a house full of Magdalenes'. Theodoros erupted from his chair, drew his pruning knife, and demanded that Mokastiriotis stand and face him like a man. None of the other men in the room intervened as the knife-fighters traded parries and thrusts. Finally, Theodoros with a flick of his wrist delivered a telling blow that cut his victim from the tip of his chin to half way up his cheek. As blood flowed from his face, Mokastiriotis fell to his knees cursing his assailant. When asked by the presiding magistrate at the Police Magistrate's court in the town of Kerkira why he caused the fight, Theodoros sternly replied that no man would call his wife and daughters whores and get away with it. His reputation would not allow it. As a man, he would not stand for it (Gallant 2000b: 359–60).

Thousands of similar episodes took place all across Greece. Men engaged in ritualised knife duels in order to defend their reputation. Most frequently the insult that inaugurated a duel was to call a man a cuckold or to brand his wife as a Magdaleni (a word in Greek that could mean either an adulteress or a prostitute), which would, of course, make the man a cuckold. Calling into question a woman's sexual reputation cut so deeply in this culture because it struck at the heart of masculinity: a man's ability to control the most important element in his household – his wife's or his daughter's reproductive behaviour. A man who could not control that aspect of his domain was, in their view, no man at all.

When confronted with such an insult or any imputation that the women of his household were anything less than chaste, a man either had to rise to the challenge and fight, or be humiliated. This form of violence was socially sanctioned and accepted. Take this episode from 1852 involving a flower vendor in Athens who, while selling flowers at the parade grounds one Sunday afternoon, saw a man approach his wife, and make advances to her. Grabbing his knife, he confronted the man and in the ensuing fight stabbed him through the heart.

Not only did the assembled crowd not intervene in the fight, they made no effort to stop the vendor and his wife from leaving, and some of the male onlookers even commended the man for the precision of the fatal stroke. Finally, by allowing two men to settle their dispute with a *mano-a-mano* duel served another function as well: it prevented disputes over honour between two men from expanding into violence that would involve all of their kinsmen. Another consequence of the ethos of vengeance was the vendetta.

In the world of Greek men during the nineteenth century, the shedding of the blood of another initiated a vendetta in which the family and the kin of the deceased were required to shed the blood of the killer or one of his kinsmen. The following case from the 1850s is not atypical.

For over three years, the Marandas and the Petas families from the village of Kaliteros on Zakynthos had been in blood, that is, feuding. The two families had a number of fields adjacent to one another and according to the police report there had been 'family differences … that have given rise to ill will and revenge'. On the night of 10 September 1856, Nikolaos Petas and his sister were guarding some of the family's vineyards when two men attacked them. One, wielding an axe, killed Nikolaos, while the other beat the girl with a stick. She identified their assailants: they were Tasos Marandas and his cousin Vassilis. But the prosecution found insufficient evidence and the case was dismissed. On 12 April 1857, Dionysios Marandas was shot and wounded in the shoulder while walking back from his fields to the village. Dimitrios Petas was accused but the case was dismissed for lack of proof. Attempted payback came eight months later when Marandas fired upon Petas as he was walking from the village to the town of Zakynthos. The next episode in the feud came two years later when Theodoros Marandas, Dionysios's cousin, was shot in the head. The police believed that Panagiotis Petas, cousin of Dimitrios Petas, had done the deed but could not prove it. So in an attempt to end the feud, they arrested and charged with murder Panagiotis and his four sons, Nikolaos, Ioannis, Antonios and Christos. Feuds like this one were common all across the Greek world (Gallant 2008: 82–3).

In theory a feud would persist until the men on both sides, save one, were killed. Few did though. Usually a form of arbitration would take place and one side would pay blood money to other, and not infrequently the families would exchange marriage partners to seal the pact. The vendetta and the feud, even as the state authorities tried to stop them and the urban bourgeoisie denounced them, remained features of Greek society well into the twentieth century.

There was one other circumstance in which the community of men absolutely demanded blood: seduction and betrayal. Panagiotis Plarinos had been conducting an illicit affair with his cousin's wife. Few were surprised, therefore, when on the night of 15 June 1859 the cuckolded husband and his wife's brother gunned him down. While pasturing her family's cattle in a field, Katerina Vlassis was assaulted by Nikolaos Sabatis. When she returned to her village without her 'girdle', her brother armed himself with two pistols and a knife and swore not to return until blood had been spilt. He was home in time for dinner and Sabatis's body was found in a field with a bullet in his heart (Gallant 2008: 81).

These cases involved men slaying other men who had committed sexual transgressions with another man's kinswoman. But women as well met with brutal ends at the hands of their kinsmen if they violated communal norms. On 3 January 1864, the body of 30-year-old Katerina Rapsomarikis was found in a well close to the village of Katastari on Zakynthos. The police arrested her four brothers, Yiorgos, Evstathis, Arvanitakis and Dimi, and Andreas Rapsomarikis, her husband. It took the police only a few minutes to learn what everyone in the village seemed to know: Katerina had committed adultery. She had brought dishonour on her husband and her family. Because of the extended period of time that the body had been submerged, the police surgeon was unable to determine whether they had killed her and then dumped her body in the well or whether she had been thrown in the well while still alive (Gallant 2012: 148).

From the foregoing one gets the impression that violence was highly prevalent during the nineteenth century, and compared to most other areas of Europe at the time, it was. Even concerted attempts by the state to curtail violence failed to diminish it. Figure 6.6, for example, depicts men in the prison on Zakynthos, all of whom have been sentenced to death for murder. Yet it was not violence so much as it was aggression that was crucial to honour. A related dimension to the code was that a man should act on his own to achieve his goals. To rely on agents of the state, like the police and courts, was seen as a sign of weakness, was 'to be like a woman'. Yet the reality, of course, was that such a situation was impossible. Wealth and class stratified Greek society by the nineteenth century. Even within the hamlets and small villages and certainly within the large ones, there were households that were larger and wealthier than the others. So while men shared an ethical system that emphasised equality, their world was one rife with inequalities.

Figure 6.6 '*Murderers' Row*' © *Percy Falcke Martin (1913). This photograph shows the men incarcerated in the British prison on the island of Zakynthos in 1899. They have all been sentenced for murder or attempted murder, mostly the result of knife fights. Those seated in the front row are awaiting execution. In a cross-section of Greek plebian culture, many are attired in characteristic peasant garb, while the man seated in the front right is in a shepherd's goatskin cloak (*capote); standing next to him is an urban dandy.*

How did they reconcile ideology and reality? One mechanism involved honour itself. As I mentioned earlier, a man's reputation was made or lost through the assessment of his peers, that is, those co-villagers and neighbours and kinsmen who subscribed to the same ethical system. This process determined boundaries between those who were part of the group that mattered: Us, and those that did not: Them – the bourgeoisie, the landlords, the bureaucrats, and so on. The ideology of equality pertained to those in the group. Peasants coped with the reality of inequalities in a number of ways.

One was to make useful outsiders insiders through the practice of fictive kinship, blood brotherhood and godparenthood, for example. Reliance on men who shared the same blood, even metaphorically, did not diminish a man's reputation. Finally, men formed strategic alliances with those from the higher strata of society, in which they willingly adopted the subservient position in order to obtain material benefit and protection. These bonds between a client and his patron provided the weaker partner with an important insurance policy in the unsure environment of rural Greece. Because the dominant party came from a higher social class and because the client benefited from the arrangement, to become a client did not diminish a man's stature among his peers. The key here was that the client obtained goods and services that increased his family's fortunes, and so it enhanced his reputation as a man who could take care of his own. Thus, there was often intense competition between peasant men to forge a bond with a powerful figure.

The social world of men, then, was marked by intense and often violent contests over goods, resources and reputations. But what of the social world of women?

> Man is endowed with strength to meet life's challenges whereas a woman's strength is toward the tending and feeding of the child. Powerful is the man who takes risks; weak and cautious the woman. He is clever and has imposing and sweeping plans. She is a demon and loses herself in details.

This is how a late nineteenth-century woman's periodical, Ευρήδικη, summarised some of the differences between men and women (21 November 1870). During the nineteenth century the roles and prescribed behaviours of men and women were sharply defined, in theory at least. As examinations of gender roles in more recent times have suggested, there is often a gap between what the cultural rules mandate and how real people act in their daily lives. This certainly seems to hold true for the past as well. Let us look first at the ideal.

The first element that stands was the spatial segregation of women from the outside world. The house was the domain of women, and especially if they were young and unmarried, they were not to leave it without good cause. Second, modesty and shame provided the moral framework that dictated women's comportment, and the Virgin Mary (in Greek, the Panayia) was supposed to be her model. Third, the woman was to be the source of sustenance in the household; it was her job to prepare the food and to see the material needs of her family. Fourth, she was also to be the source of spirituality, and women were supposed to keep the family icons and attend church. All of these aspects emphasise the positive roles that woman played in society. But men believed there was a dark side as well. Women were believed to be closer to nature and to have the ability to perform magic and witchcraft. Since women lacked self-control, they were always at risk of falling to prey to their baser, sexual instincts. Thus, the great concern among men about their wives' reputations. In short, women's roles in society were shaped by their domestic duties and their need to ensure that their reputations remained unsullied.

The reality of women's lives was more complex and varied greatly between classes. The daily life of peasant women was dominated by domestic duties. Preparing her family's food, especially bread, took up a considerable portion of her day. Fetching water was also a very time-consuming task that was gendered as women's work. The care and nurturance of children was obviously of importance as well. The women of the household were also to spin and weave the cloth consumed in the household and they were to produce the goods that constitute the trousseau that the daughters of the house would include in their dowries. And while these activities were mainly conducted within the house, there were a variety of activities that took them out into the world.

The labour needs of the peasant household, for example, invari-ably required women's participation. In large villages and in towns, unmarried women were often employed as domestic servants and per force had to venture out into public. Lastly, there were a whole variety of female-dominated social gatherings that took place in public. Female seclusion, then, was an unrealisable ideal, except perhaps among the upper classes for whom women's labour was not vital. What was crucial was that women comported themselves in public in a way that conformed to cultural expectations and that the reason she was out in public needed to be related to one of her domestic roles.

Finally, women were supposed to be active defenders of their own and their family's reputations. There was an ethical code for women similar to men's honour, and like men, women engaged in contests over reputations. But whereas men often waged their combat with knives, women employed words. Gossip and slander were the weapons of choice and the stakes were high. If a woman did not contest malicious gossip about sexual comportment, the cleanliness of her house, or her devotion to the church, her sons might have a harder time to find a good match, her daughters might require a much larger dowry to secure a husband, or her spouse might find himself drawing the blade to defend her and his reputation.

In sum, the social world of the little communities of Greece in the past was shaped by the gendered roles of men and women. But in many ways, those roles served a common purpose – enhancing the material wealth and social reputation of the households that men and women made together (Gallant 2002: 149–74; 2012).

So far we have examined how rural people lived, and given that throughout the nineteenth century, Greeks were predominantly village dwellers, that is appropriate. But there was another important development during the long nineteenth century that had a profound impact on society and that was urbanisation. By the 1910s, a sizable portion of the Greek population in Greece, the Ottoman Empire and Russia resided in cities, and so we now need to explore how city folk lived.

Urban lifestyles

> Tell me if you have ever see viler pig breeding villages than the slums of Athens, or another such Vatheia? In the summer, dust by the ladle full. Pools of water in mud up to the knee, if they have been dripped on at all, and in every street a fenced – or unfenced – yard where you see the latrine for the whole neighbourhood? But where are they to go, those who go there, since the medical councillors, the architects, the police, the mayors, the prefect all regard you as necessary dross. (Emmanuil Roidis 'The Gravedigger's Pain', p. 90, describing a scene from a working-class neighbourhood called Metaxourgeion in Athens)

> In the immense room they called the buffet, tables as long as railway lines were set. There, atop embroidered linen table cloths lay rows of faience platters laden with delicacies I had never before laid eyes on – black caviar, fish-roe, salad, hams, pickles, stuffed roast fowl, oysters, lobsters, shrimp, fish covered with rich mayonnaise and home-baked white bread flavoured with mastic. Crystal goblets sparkled as they were filled with the beverage that foamed like breaking waves and popped like firecrackers when the bottles were opened. Carriages drew up at the gate, there depositing gentlemen in evening dress and top hats, some wearing monocles – just how do they keep them from popping out? I wondered. They were the foreign consuls and the Greek bankers, merchants, landowners, doctors, lawyers, journalists and local dignitaries – 2 high ranking clergyman even put in an

appearance. And the women what a sight they were! (Sotiriou 1991:55, describing a dinner party at the home of a wealthy Greek merchant in Smyrna)

These two passages capture two diametrically opposed aspects of urban life. No social history is complete without discussion of life in the cities. Until the annexation of Salonika there was really only one urban complex in the kingdom and that was Athens with its port, Piraeus. But in the broader context of the Greek world, it has to be analysed with other cities like Smyrna, Istanbul and Alexandria, where there was a substantial Greek population. Moreover, we should not discuss them in isolation, but rather as elements of a network and along whose nodes there was a constant flow of goods and people. We begin with the numbers.

Greece and the Ottoman Empire experienced major urban growth during the second half of the nineteenth century (Freitag et al. 2011). Athens, for example, had a population of approximately 17,000 when the Bavarians made it the capital in 1834. By 1860, it had grown to just over 40,000, and then massive immigration from the countryside buoyed its numbers to 84,903 by 1880 and 114,355 by 1890. Perhaps even more impressive was the expansion of Piraeus. It went from being a sleepy little coastal community of just over 1,000 people at the time of independence to being home to over 50,000 by the end of the century (Gallant 2001: 108). The port city of Patras grew during the boom years of the 1880s and 1890s from a modest 15,000 in 1850 to over 50,000 by the turn of the century. Ottoman cities, as well, experienced similar magnitudes of growth. The population of Istanbul, for example, burgeoned from 391,000 in 1844 to close to one million by 1890, of which close to one-quarter were Greeks (Çelik 1986: 37–9; Mutlu 2003: 11). Smyrna's vibrant population stood at 800,000 in 1914, whereas only seventy years earlier it was home to 145,000 people. According to the 1914 census, 34 per cent of the city's population were Ottoman Greeks (Mutlu 2003: 21). I could provide figures from the other major cities of the empire, but they would tell the same story.

Urban expansion at such levels opened up new opportunities for masses of people, but it raised numerous problems as well. Some, like fire, water supply, sanitation and crime, threatened lives, whereas others, such as dogs and dust, mostly just irritated and inconvenienced (for Athens: Miller 1905: 202; for Istanbul: Boyer and Fleet 2010: 187). National governments and municipal councils had to take expensive action to deal with them. They established fire

Figure 6.7 Poultry vendor in Athens © 1895 Library of Congress Prints and Photography Division. *This photo captures the dynamic tension in late nineteenth-century Athens between the old and the new. We see an elderly man in traditional costume selling fresh chickens on the street, while behind stand two schoolboys in Western-style suits and straw hats.*

departments to deal with that serious issue; Athens, for example, got its first fire department in 1854. Costly infrastructure projects were inaugurated to bring safe drinking water to neighbourhoods and sewerage lines were laid to take waste away. Nonetheless, diseases such as cholera, as well as tuberculosis, remained serious problems, especially in the poorer parts of the city. According to William Miller, a long-term resident of Athens, in 1904 over one-third of all deaths in Athens were the result of consumption (1905: 195). Ensuring that people had access to plentiful and safe food supplies was also difficult. Figure 6.7 depicts a poultry vendor hawking his birds in one of Athens's nicer neighbourhoods. Daily, farmers tramped along the city's streets selling fruit and vegetables grown in their nearby villages. Shepherds traipsed about with their flocks, providing fresh, but unpasteurised milk. Food safety was a persistent problem. Lastly,

Figure 6.8 *Young men drinking in a taverna, Athens 1888, photographer unknown © Thomas W. Gallant Photograph Collection.*

probably the most visible of the urban ills were crime and public disorder.

Take the case of Athens and Piraeus, for example. Their rates of crime and violence soared. During the 1880s and 1890s, when the homicide indictment rates in cities like London, Paris, Berlin and Amsterdam were fewer than two killings for every 100,000 people, Athens recorded a rate of 107 (Gallant 1998: 12; Gallant 2000a). Young men, like those depicted in Figure 6.8, gathered in the cities' taverns, wine shops and tekes (drug emporia), bringing with them hair-trigger sensibilities to any slights along with guns and knives. The result was drunken brawls and lethal encounters of such a magnitude that one of Athens's leading newspapers, *Aion*, proclaimed after the deadly Easter weekend of 1891, 'More Greeks than Lambs Slaughtered' over the holiday (cited in Gallant 1998: 15). None of the cities in the region was spared from the onslaught of violence (for Istanbul, see Deal 2010). In Smyrna in 1892, one contemporary noted:

the young men ... drink and often after nocturnal orgies they come home drunk, breaking the shop windows and using knives from time to time. They are the plague of the whole quarter. Consequently, the brawls are frequent ... and not a Saturday afternoon passes without noise and confusion and without the police being obliged to intervene to reestablish order' (cited in Gallant 2009: 21–2)

The other public order issue that dominated the times was prostitution (Gallant 2009: 24–6; Yanitisiotis: 2006: 246). As with the other urban problems, the state had to expend valuable resources to deal with them.

Another consequence of growth was the development of greater structural differentiation among the urban population. In other words, as they grew in size the cities became more socially complex with the dominant trend seeing the rich grow richer and the poor grow poorer as well as more numerous (Kechriotis and Fuhrmann 2009). All of the major cities of the region became showplaces for the rich. Along Stadiou, Panapistemiou and Ermou Streets in Athens, one can still see the magnificent townhouses that were once the homes of the city's elite. Alongside them there soon developed an Athenian petite bourgeoisie as well (Potamianos 2013). The same is true in the old Rom neighbourhoods of Istanbul, and, but for the ravages of horrendous fires in 1917 and 1923, that would have been the case in Salonika and Smyrna. Moreover, as the description of the sumptuous banquet quoted at the start of this section indicates, they lived a grand lifestyle, and were not averse to showing it off. Not far from these luxurious abodes of the rich, however, were other neighbourhoods, where the well-off seldom went.

Every major city also had its slums and less savoury neighbourhoods. In Athens, they tended to be on the west side of the city because that was where the factories and workshops were. In port cities, the tougher neighbourhoods tended to cluster near the waterfront. As the other quote reproduced at the start of this section describes, there were few urban amenities in the slums and people lived in dirty and often squalid conditions. Men, many of whom had only recently migrated from the countryside, had to scramble to find the wherewithal to take care of their families. Most of the jobs in manufacturing paid little and required hard labour. Industry was unregulated and so employers forced long hours on their workers and provided no security. Underemployment was also a persistent problem. Young, unmarried men, who made up a large part of the

Figure 6.9 *Photograph of women sewing clothing in an alley* © *Library of Congress Prints and Photography Division. Taken from the entrance of one of the myriad alleyways that characterised urban space in the old city of Athens, this photograph vividly captures the manifold realities of working women's lives. One of the first things to note is that there is not a single adult male in the picture. During the day, these public urban spaces were gendered female and became an extension of the domestic realm. The culturally constructed practice of gender segregation, which we discussed earlier in regards to rural society, persisted even after migration to the city. Indeed, the separation between men's and women's worlds was even wider in the city than in the countryside. Note as well the very large number of children in the photograph. The population of Greece was rapidly growing and becoming younger, creating numerous problems that we will refer to as the 'urban ills'. Notice also what many of the women are doing. They are hard at work sewing. Historians using official government statistics maintain that women played a very small role in Greek manufacturing. Largely absent from the factory floor, it is argued that there were only two non–domestic labour sectors for women: domestic service as maids, and prostitution. What the 'official' statistics do not capture is the unreported work that women undertook. Mill owners turned textiles into finished products through the practice of hiring poor women to sew cloths, like shirts, trousers and linens, on a piecemeal basis. Manufacturers exploited women like the ones in the picture. Not covered by any labour regulations, these women worked long hours for meagre wages in order to generate even a modest income to help feed their families. Women in the city, then, bore a double burden: they had to manage their household and take on wage labour to make ends meet.*

labour force, not surprisingly flocked to bars and taverns when their working day was done.

The transition from rural to city life was especially difficult for working-class women. Young, unmarried women who migrated to the regions cities found employment, as discussed in Chapter 7, primarily as domestic servants in the homes of the wealthy, or as prostitutes, and very frequently girls started as the former and ended up as the latter. Life was hard for married women as well. In large part this was because people in the cities still subscribed to the gender system, discussed above. In fact many of the strictures dictated by that ideology, such as segregation and domesticity, were more rigorously enforced in the city. Simple household economics meant that many women had to take on whatever work they could find to help make ends meet. Figure 6.9 and the accompanying caption vividly capture the grim reality that many women in urban working-class neighbourhoods faced.

So far we have discussed the region's cities individually, but it is important to emphasise that they were part of an integrated network. Historians often use the term 'cosmopolitan' to describe Mediterranean port cities, and there are good reasons for doing so. The culture of the elite was certainly urbane and sophisticated and in touch with the latest fads and fashions from the West. They wore the latest fashions, dined off imported china and decorated their mansions with *objets d'art* from around the world. Moreover, they were a very mobile group. Some families had homes (and businesses) in other cities and they moved freely and frequently between them. It would not be going too far to speak of there being a transnational Greek elite.

We can also describe the Greek working class in the same way. Greeks featured prominently in working population of every Mediterranean port city, taking their place in the diverse body of people of various nationalities, ethnicities and religions. Take the case of Yiorgos Mandiras. Born on Kerkira, his parents apprenticed him to a cobbler in Smyrna. After working two years there, his master sold his contract to a cobbler in Salonika, and he spent much of the rest of his life there, with intermittent sojourns back to his previous haunts. Or that of Andreas Mavroioannis, a part-time labourer and thief who in the course of his working life resided in Kerkira, Hermoupolis, Smyrna, Alexandria and Constantinople. Many women also led itinerant lives. Theoni Galati was a prositute, who over the course of her 28-year-long career plied her trade in

Hermoupolis, Constantinople, Smyrna, Malta, Beirut and Salonika (Gallant 2009: 22–7).

At any given moment, then, the urban population of Mediterranean port cities contained a palimpsest of residents: some of them had lived there their entire lives, others would have been there for only a matter of days, while still others had come to the city and would live there for time spans varying from a few months to a few years before moving on elsewhere. In sum, the port city working-class population was characterised by high degrees of mobility, fluidity and transiency. Put another way, there was a human river of Greek workers that flowed through the region and connected the waterfronts and darker neighbourhoods of Mediterranean port cities.

Notes

1. The data in this table were taken from: Syrrako (Caftanzoglou 1994), Aristi (Caftanzoglou 1997), Hermoupolis (Hionidou 1999; Loukos 2004), Mykonos (Hionidou 1995a; 1995b; 1998), Kythera (Hionidou 2011), Prevesa (Komis 2004), Krokylio (Papathanassiou 2004), Çuker (Renieri 2002).
2. Recently, historians and archaeologists have begun to pay much more attention to the study of villages and domestic remains as a source for social history. See Bintliff 2012: 460–88; Cooper and Kourelis 2002; Dimitropoulos 2011; Marmaras 2008; Papaïoannou 2003; Sigalos 2004; Vionis 2005; 2013.

CHAPTER 7

The economy between traditional and modern

Figure 7.1 captures Greeks at work during the nineteenth century. It shows men and women harvesting grain in the fields of Argos. Labouring under the sweltering Mediterranean sun and in sight of the great fortress of Larissa, there is almost a timelessness quality to the image. Utilising the same implement that Greeks had used to cut grain for centuries, the viewer feels that this was a picture that could have come from any time in the past, dating all the way back to ancient times. The image, however, is somewhat deceptive. The seemingly static and unchanging nature of the countryside and of agricultural technology is misleading. As we will see, the rural economy of Greece and the wider Greek world was incredibly diverse and dynamic during the long nineteenth century (Kallivretakis 1999). Likewise, even though industrialisation remained an impaired and incomplete process, with older forms of manufacturing remaining important if not predominant, fundamental and important changes in manufacturing did take place. This chapter, then, examines Greek economic history, endeavouring to capture the tensions that existed during this period between persistence of the old and transition to the new, or to put it another way, to explore the contestation between tradition and economic modernity.

This chapter on the economy is divided into four sections. The first focuses on the natural environment, which, after all, played a significant role in shaping the contours of the rural economy. Section two examines the rural sector of the economy, as it should, because this was the single largest component of the nineteenth-century economy and the one that involved the largest number of people. The third section discusses industrialisation. As will be explained in more detail later, much of the current literature castigates the Greek and Ottoman industrial economies as being ' backward' or 'under-developed' when compared to Western Europe. That they never attained the level of industrialisation that Great Britain or the United States did, is certainly correct. But our goal is not to focus on what

Figure 7.1 Greek peasants harvesting grain on the plains of Argos, 1901
© Library of Congress Prints and Photography Division.

did not happen but instead try to understand the changes that did take place in the manufacturing sector and how those changes impacted people's lives. Lastly we explore the marketing system and the commercial networks that underpinned the economy.

The natural environment

The natural environment, especially topography, geography and climate, exerts a powerful influence over human societies, and particularly on pre-industrial ones because they depend so heavily on the environment for the production of their basic foodstuffs. The natural environment impacts people's lives at multiple levels, from the intensely local to the macro regional. It is in the process of adapting and exploiting the conditions around them that cultures devise multiple, diverse, and different economic strategies. These in turn profoundly shape culture and society. At the macro level, the Greek world was influenced by two powerful countervailing sets of geographical factors, one of which we can call the centrifugal tendency and the other the centripetal tendency.

Greece, the rest of the Balkans and much of Asia Minor are lands of mountains. Indeed, almost all of the landmasses along the northern Mediterranean are highly mountainous in nature (McNeill 1992; Grove and Rackham 2001; Vogiatzakis 2012). Over 70 per cent of the surface area of contemporary Greece, for example, is categorised as mountainous and it has twenty mountain peaks higher than 2,000 metres above sea level. The same is true for much of the rest of the Balkan peninsula. Mediterranean mountain building occurred during the Pleistocene era when three tectonic plates, the European, the Asian and the African, collided and produced what is now the Mediterranean basin. As the tectonic plates collided, tremendous pressure was exerted, with the result that successive waves of up-thrusts produced mountains while corresponding down-thrusts created deep valleys. Because of the way the tectonic plates collided, the resultant mountain ranges trend from northwest to southeast. These forces not only shaped the Mediterranean landmasses, but also the nature of the sea itself. The Mediterranean is extremely deep in many places because of the down-thrusts, and its numerous islands are nothing but the tops of mountains.

The Mediterranean, then, is a land of mountains and they exert a very powerful influence on almost all aspects of human life in the region, and one of these is the centrifugal tendency. This term refers to the ways that the mountainous topography of the region tends to separate and isolate people and settlements. Perched on a mountainside or nested in an upland basin, mountain villages seem cut off from the outside world, connected only by narrow, rugged tracks cut into the sides of ravines (Fig. 7.2) or filtered through narrow passes. As one mountain man himself noted 'there are Greek villagers who do not know of any village more than an hour away from their own' (Kolokotronis 1977 [1844]: 144). What is not stated here is that it would have taken more than an hour to walk to an adjacent village that was only a kilometre or so away as the crow flies. As we will see later in this chapter, Kolokotronis's assessment overstates the case that the ruggedness of the mountainous terrain does exert powerful forces that tend to isolate people and to foster the development of diverse lifeways.

If mountains isolate, the sea connects. Three bodies of water interconnect the Greek world: the Black Sea, the Aegean Sea and the Mediterranean. These create a centripetal tendency that facilitates the flow and the movement of peoples and goods across vast expanses. As the map of the Greek world shows, outside of those territories where Greeks constituted the majority of the population, they tended to settle along the coast. The sheer magnitude of the maritime coastline of the Greek world meant that access to the sea was almost ubiquitous. Greece, for example, has a coastline that

Figure 7.2 *Muleteer and his caravan crossing the main road over Mount Tayetos, Lakonia, 1903* © *Fred Boissonnas*, Photos (1903).

extends for over 15,000km, giving it one of the highest ratios of coast to landmass of any country in the world. In the Greek world one is never far from the sea and access to it is everywhere. In addition, there are over 2,000 islands in the Aegean and the Eastern Mediterranean, and they create a dense network of nodes that makes island-hopping easy. These two tendencies, the centripetal and the centrifugal, have throughout history deeply influenced the development of Greek society.

The next macro-level geographical factor of importance is what I refer to as corridors of connectivity. These are the natural features that connected the Greek world to other regions of the globe. Beginning in the northeast, the first of these corridors runs from the Sea of Azov along the basin of the River Don, providing entry on to the steppes of Eurasia. The second one is located on the eastern side of the Black Sea. This corridor follows the Danube River into central Europe. The third avenue of connectivity is the Mediterranean itself, articulating the Greek world with North Africa, Italy and Spain and from there to the Atlantic World. The fourth corridor is located in the southeastern Mediterranean and it extends by water through the Red Sea and from there to the Indian Ocean, and on land it follows the Nile River into Africa. These four corridors of connectivity articulated the Greek world to the rest of the globe and the movement of people and goods along them played a critical role in of the history of the Greeks.

No assessment of the natural environment would be complete without a discussion of the climate. Mentioning the climate of Greece brings to mind clear blue skies, golden sunshine and sweltering heat, usually seen and experienced from a beach. While this cliché captures one climate reality, it is not the whole story. The core area of the Greek world, in fact, falls under three distinct climatic zones: the Mediterranean, the Alpine Mediterranean and the Trans-continental Mediterranean. The Mediterranean zone is the one typically associated with Greece. It is characterised by hot temperatures during the summer, accompanied by extreme drought, and what little precipitation there is tends to fall in extreme downpours. Winters are characterised by mild temperatures, overcast skies and moderate levels of more consistent precipitation. Snow falls in the mountainous areas regularly and occasionally in more lowland areas, including Athens. This climate regime encompasses the Peloponnesos, Attica and eastern central Greece and the islands. Much of central Greece and Epiros, as well as lands further north that are not part of Greece now but were part of the Greek world in the past, have an Alpine Mediterranean climate. The main characteristics of this include higher levels of precipitation during the summer months, especially along the west coast, and less extreme summer temperatures. These areas experience severe winter conditions and heavy snowfalls, with snow remaining on the ground in some areas until May, and harsh, low temperatures; some villages at the highest elevations are actually cut off from the outside world for weeks or even months because the snow makes the roads impassable. Trans-continental Mediterranean is the climate regime of Thessaly, Macedonia, Thrace and much of Asia Minor. It falls in between the other two, with summers that are not as hot, but prone to extreme but brief heatwaves, and with higher levels of rainfall that tends to come in thunderstorms or showers.

Winters have milder temperatures than in the alpine zone and high levels of precipitation that falls mostly as rain; snowstorms are not uncommon but the snowpack usually does not last for long.

Another important element of climate is its variability. Climate change occurs at two levels temporarily, a short-term and long-term one. The climate of Greece generally experiences high levels of inter-annual variability. What this means is that from year to year elements like rainfall can fluctuate radically. It is this level of climate variability that people experience and have to deal with. All across the Greek world the yields of the major subsistence crops varied greatly from year to year. Greek farmers had to gear their agricultural practices to this crucial fact (Gallant 1991: 60–112). Climate also changes on a longer-term basis: one extended climate epoch, the Little Ice Age, came to an end during the time period that we are studying and its termination impacted Greek rural economy and society. The Little Ice Age covered a period extending from approximately 1500 to the 1870s, during which annual average temperatures were lower and levels of precipitation were higher. The shift, as we will see, had an impact especially in the mountainous regions of the Greek world (Tabak 2008; White 2012; 2013; Mikhail 2011a; 2011b; 2012).

The natural environment impacts almost all aspects of human material life. This was especially true in the case of pre-industrial, agrarian societies. Basic elements of how people lived, such as domestic architecture, clothing and attire, and material culture, evolved as adaptations to meet peoples' needs. Environmental conditions influenced what crops they grew, how they grew them, and the environment set the rhythms of everyday life. Even critical aspects of the community's cultural life were connected to the cycles of nature. Having delineated the environmental conditions of the Greek world, we can now turn to a discussion of the most important element of the Greek economy, which was agriculture.

The rural sector

> Το βασικό του άνθρωπου ήταν τα έχεις στο σπίτι το λάδι και το ψωμί. [The main thing in life was to have in the house olive oil and bread.] (Cretan-peasant saying, cited in Blitzer 2004: 113)

This aphorism captures an enduring truth about the overarching economic goal of the family farm. Peasant households sought to ensure that there was always on-hand sufficient food to sustain the members of the household through good times and bad. Though their aim was self-sufficiency, Greek farmers always had to produce above the subsistence level. That was because there were always entities, like the state and the church, which staked a claim to some of the family's production in the form of taxes or a tithe. Also, there were basic commodities that any household needed to survive and that they could not produce themselves, such as salt, tea and a variety of other tools and objects. Nonetheless, this did not change the fact that their production goal was to be as self-sufficient as possible, making them market averse and inhibiting the development of a more market-orientated rural economy.

This image of the Greek rural population is the dominant one in both scholarly literature and in popular culture. But it is not the whole story. At the other end of the spectrum, there were farms both large and small that were geared to the production of commercial crops, such as cotton, tobacco and currant grapes, aimed primarily at secondary production or foreign markets. As with so much else about the Greek world, the agricultural countryside was characterised by great diversity; by region, by category and across time. Both inside the kingdom of Greece and in the Ottoman Empire throughout the nineteenth century, the vast majority of Greeks were agriculturalists, and so if we are to understand their way of life, then we must begin an examination of the rural economy.[1]

Two qualifications are needed before beginning our discussion of the Greek countryside. The first refers to the data. While abundant econometric information about the Greek and the Ottoman economies exists, there is a problem with the congruity between it and the object of our study. Economic statistics tend to be recorded at the state level, and so the problem is not with Greece but with the Ottoman Empire. Greeks made up only one element in the economy of the vast and multi-ethnic Muslim empire and Ottoman economic records do not distinguish between national or religious groups. This means that it is exceedingly difficult to disentangle information about Greeks from other groups, such as Turks, Arabs, Jews or Armenians, for example. What we can do, however, is to examine the dominant trends within the Ottoman economy and then to highlight wherever possible the Greek component. The second qualification refers to the categories employed in government records. People and their activities were slotted into discrete categories such as 'agriculturalist' or 'artisan' or 'merchant'. While the categories might be distinct, the people performing those tasks were often the same. Because of the challenges of eking out a living in the Greek countryside, especially in the mountainous areas, most men had to perform pluriactivities (Argyrou 2006; Brunnbauer 2004; Kizos 2010; Nitsiakos and Kasimis 2008). What this means is that people had to undertake numerous economic activities in order to make ends meet. So, for example, for part of the year a man might have worked his land as a farmer, but he would also supplement his household's income by undertaking other tasks such as making shoes, cutting and selling timber, making charcoal, or selling his labour as a carter or farm labourer. What this means is that in order to get at the lived reality of Greek peasants, we have to look beyond the cold numbers in the state's ledger books, which show us only the big picture. Instead, we must peer into peasant houses to see what they ate and what they grew, how they lived and how they worked. We need, in other words, to explore the food system of the Greek world during the nineteenth century (Coclanis 2010).

Any society's food system is based upon a number of factors, but the two most important are the natural environment (climate, soil types, topography and others) and dietary preferences. The relationship between the two is interactive, meaning that people choose what they wish to eat, and thus grow, but their choices are constrained by environmental variables. To take an extreme example, a society living in the Arctic that wanted to live primarily by consuming oranges would probably not last very long. In the case of the Greek world, it would seem intuitively obvious that at the core of their food system would be the famous Mediterranean diet. After all, the canonical Mediterranean diet was defined on the basis of a study on Crete in the 1950s (Allbaugh 1953). In its most general form, the diet calls for heavy reliance on cereals and plant products, moderate consumption of wine, very low consumption of saturated fats and high levels of ingestion of monounsaturated fats. Total fat in this diet is 25–35 per cent of calories, with saturated fats at 8 per cent or less of calories. The amount of red meat people eat is small, seafood plays only a minor, subsidiary role, and consumption of dairy products, mostly cheese and yogurt, is moderate to high (Gallant 1991). While this description is mostly accurate, we also have to appreciate that there was a very wide degree of variability and diversity amongst Mediterranean cultures and regions both in the present and in the past (Damianakos 1997 on variability and diversity; regarding the types of sources we can use to reconstruct diets in the past, see Balta 1992; Garvie-Lok 2001). In other words, within the parameters of the Mediterranean diet there was a great deal of variability. One recent study, for example, suggests that olive oil consumption in Greece in the nineteenth century was substantially lower than it is today (Matalas 2001; 2006a, 2006b). Nonetheless, the Mediterranean diet as described and observed during the mid-twentieth century does capture the essential nature of the Greek food system in the past, and thus, we will begin our examination of rural society by describing briefly the plants that produced the foods at the core of their diet.

Cereal grains, especially wheat, contributed the single largest percentage of calories to the typical Greek peasant family, and thus were the most important food crops they produced. Two types of wheat predominated, one that was better suited for making bread and the other for producing pasta. Other cereal grains of importance were barley, rye and oats. Along with wheat, each of these were well suited to the natural environment of Greece, while occupying slightly different ecological niches. All of them were sown in the autumn, usually in September or October, and reaped in May or June. They had to be cultivated during the winter months because that was when the rains necessary for their growth fell. Each of them required slightly different amounts of moisture; wheat needed the most and barley and rye the least. Ideally then, farmers would plant some of each of them, thus having a buffer in case of drought or drier conditions. Another practice that farmers adopted to cope with risk was to sow seeds from the different plants together on the same plot of land; this mixture of grains was referred to as maslin (Jones and Halstead 1995).

One other cereal that was critical to the Greek rural economy was maize or Indian corn (Fig. 7.3). This, along with the other New World plants introduced to Europe during the sixteenth century, spread rapidly through the Ottoman world and soon became a mainstay of the rural economy (Andrews 1993). Corn was perfectly adapted to the Mediterranean natural environment and became especially important because it could grow at very high altitudes, where other cereal grains could not. It became a mainstay of mountain communities and lowland areas as well. It was often grown adjacent to vineyards because it flourishes on the same types of soils as grapes and, because it requires peak labour at same time as the vines, farmers could tend to both crops at the same time. Even though it was considered in some circles as the least desirable food grain, a food for the poor as it were, maize cultivation in the kingdom expanded dramatically, nearly doubling over the course of the nineteenth century (Franghiadis 1990: 49). According to the 1860

Figure 7.3 *Girl shucking maize* © National Geographic.

agricultural census, maize was the second largest cereal crop after wheat (Petmezas 2003: 173). Taken as a group, cereal grains accounted for somewhere between 60 and 70 per cent of the daily caloric intake of the typical Greek peasant.

These cereals, then, were the mainstay of the Greek rural economy. In addition to producing the bulk of the food that people consumed, they provided them with other key resources as well. For example, the stocks left after stripping the heads of grain could be used as animal fodder or mixed with mud to produce mud bricks for building. The stubble left in the field after harvesting the grain could be used as pasturage for sheep, goats and other animals (see Fig. 7.12). In thinking about how much of their land they would cultivate under cereal grains farmers had to consider the quantity they would need to feed their family, the percentage of the crop they would need to set aside as seeds for next year, and the amount that they would have to pay out for various taxes and other exactions. For much of the nineteenth century, for example, both in Greece and the Ottoman Empire, farmers had to pay to the state a percentage of their wheat crop as a tithe.

The next most important family of plants was pulses and legumes. Various beans and vetches were essential foods for both people and animals. Critical to the Greek diet, then and now, were chickpeas, broad beans, fava beans, peas and lentils. Farming families tradition-ally grew small quantities of all of them, not only because they gave versatility and variety of taste to the bland cereal-dominated diet, but also because they helped restore valuable nutrients to the soil. Other pulses such as bitter vetch, common vetch, grass peas and lupine were cultivated primarily as animal feed, though humans could consume them in times of scarcity. Like cereals, most of the pulses and legumes were grown over the winter months, but some of them could grow during the dry months of summer and so were especially valuable. In addition to providing valuable food and natural fertiliser, they also required most attention at times of the year when the other more important crops did not. As a group, they were intended almost exclusively for domestic consumption, finding markets only locally. Nonetheless, the contribution they made to the Greek rural economy was significant.

A diet based solely on bread and beans would not only be monot-onous but also nutritionally deficient. Farming households, therefore, grew a wide variety of other crops, usually cultivated in gardens located close to the farmhouse or on the outskirts of the village. Among the most commonly grown foods were onions and garlic, potatoes, tomatoes, cucumbers, a variety of leafy plants such as cabbage, lettuce, and kale, fennel, endive, asparagus, watermelon and a variety of squashes. An early twentieth-century study of family farms in the Argolid recorded how one household in a small village cultivated no less than eighteen different plants on less than one and a half hectares of land, and this was not uncommon (Karouzou 2000: table 5; see also Blitzer 2004: 161–7 for a discussion of similar practices in the Mesara region of Crete). Just as every household had its garden, it also grew a number of different trees, some produc-ing fruits, like pears, plums, cherries, apples and figs, while others produced nuts such as almonds and walnuts. Most frequently house-holds had only one or two of these at best; wealthier households of course grew more, including a few citrus trees (oranges and lemons most often). Gardens and orchards, then, provided Greek households with a variety of foodstuffs that added taste and vitally needed calories and nutrients.

The two other components of the famous Mediterranean triad of foods were, of course, olives and grapes. In addition to being important elements of the Greek diet, both of these were also major cash crops whose commercial export contributed significantly to the economy. We need, therefore, to talk about them in two contexts: their role in daily diet and their role in the larger economic system. Here we will focus on the former of these two.

The olive and Greece are practically synonymous, and there are many good reasons why that is so. Certainly, since antiquity, the olive tree has been cultivated all across Greece and its products have been mainstays of the rural economy. This does not mean, however, that there have not been important changes over time as to the extent of olive cultivation and the role of olives in the Greek diet. The olive is ideally suited to the Mediterranean natural environment. It needs abundant sunlight, is relatively drought resistant and can flourish in a variety of soils and at different altitudes. It is well suited to lowland areas, and most importantly for the Greek world, it does well in hilly and mountainous areas. It can also tolerate some cold temperatures and, in fact, requires a short, cool period in order to produce a full crop, which it does in alternate years.

Given how long and how widely olives have been cultivated in Greece, it is not surprising that there is a large number of various types. In the region of Laconia alone, for example, there are cultivated no fewer than seven different varieties of olives, and in other areas, there are even more than that. In general terms, however, farmers divided trees into two broad groups regardless of the exact type of olive grown on them: those that produced small olives ideal for grinding for oil and those with larger, so-called 'fat' olives, best suited for human consumption. The cultivation process for both was pretty much the same (Beneki 2007; Perdicoulias 2007; Kamilakis and Karapidakis 2003; for regional variations, see Adiyeke and Adiyeke 2006 (Crete); Balta 2007 (Peloponnesos); Blitzer 2004: 150–8 (Crete); Brumfield 2002 (Crete); Chatziioannou 2007 (Peloponnesos); Couroucli 2008 (Kerkira); Kizos and Koulouri 2005; 2006; 2010 (Lesbos); Sifneos 2004 (Lesbos); Theodossopoulos 1999 (Zakynthos)).

The growth cycle and the labour requirements of olive cultivation fit perfectly into the Greek agricultural calendar. After ploughing and sowing their grain fields, farmers cleared the land beneath the trees in anticipation of the harvest, which began in October. In many areas, they laid out nets on which to collect the olives. Both men and women were involved in the harvest. In many areas, men would beat the tree branches with long sticks to knock down the ripened fruit, and so prized was this skill, that there were actually experts at it who travelled around the countryside offering their services for hire. Moreover, they were very highly paid for their efforts. While men worked up in the trees, women laboured below.

During the day, women would pick through the stuff that had fallen onto the nets, pulling out and discarding sticks, branches and other unwanted things. Periodically they would fill baskets with the ripened olives and place them on donkeys, which would take the fruit back to the farm. At the end of the day, the nets would be rolled up and transported there as well. At night, working by candle or lamp-light, women would sort the olives, pulling out those that were not fully ripe, and then dividing the rest into those earmarked for grinding and those destined for human consumption. When sufficient quantities of the latter had been gathered, men dumped them into huge wooden vats into which salt and fresh water were added. Brining the fruit was essential for making the olives palatable. The harvest extended over a number of months, beginning in October and extending in some areas to as late as February. In the spring, the trees would be pruned and cuttings from wild olive trees grafted onto those designated for cultivation. The areas underneath the trees would then be ploughed and, depending upon the area and the amount of winter rainfall, some of the trees would be selectively irrigated. Almost all the tasks described above were done at a time when most of the other major crops required little attention.

The olive was so important to the Greek rural economy and society because it provided households with numerous essential products. First and foremost was olive oil. Through a process that we will examine shortly, crushed olives exuded oil that could be put to a variety of uses. Olive oil was a nutritional mainstay of the Greek diet. Though some studies have suggested that olive oil consumption was actually lower in the nineteenth century than in the twentieth century, it was still critically important, providing the bulk of daily fat intake, especially of important monounsaturated fat, as well as vitally important vitamins, minerals and nutrients (Matalas 2001; 2006a, 2006b). It was used in other ways as well.

For example, olive oil was burnt in clay or metal lamps that provided households with light. In many cities and towns, including

Athens and Istanbul, until well into the nineteenth century street lamps were fuelled by olive oil. So important was olive oil that both in the Ottoman Empire and in the kingdom of Greece a special tax was levied upon it, and households were frequently ordered to pay their taxes in oil rather than wheat or cash. In addition, oil was the basic raw material from which soap was made. Finally, olive oil was also a key commercial crop that households depended on for generating a cash income. In terms of the diet, brined olives were also important, providing both gastronomic variety and nutrition. Another great advantage of olives and olive oil was their storability. If treated properly, they could be stored for extended periods of time, usually in large clay storage jars called pithoi. These vessels were so important that households routinely expended considerable sums of cash to purchase them. No part of the olive tree went to waste. Cuttings from the trees provided building material such as girders and joists, roof frames, floors, beams and door lintels. Even the leaves from the trees could be put to use as fodder and feed for domestic animals (Halstead 2009). In sum, the olive amply deserves the privileged place it holds in Greek society.

Almost as important and as emblematic of Greece as the olive is the grape. Like the olive, the vine has a long and famous history in the region, and like it as well, it also produced numerous resources vital to the household economy. Grapes were divided into two broad groups, those destined to be consumed as table grapes or to produce wine and those that were to be dried as raisins. The most important of the latter, and the most important commercial crop in Greece, was the currant grape. The currant is a small but sweet grape that when dried into a raisin was much favoured in places like England as a staple ingredient in fruit cakes. It was also fermented into a delicate, sweet wine. As we will see, almost the entire Greek currant crop was destined for export to foreign markets. The growth cycle of both types of vines was roughly the same, with the main difference being that currants were harvested later than the others. Vines required substantially more labour than olives, cereals, pulses or gardens; by one estimate, vineyards required fifty man-days per year, which was eight to ten times as much labour as was needed to cultivate the equivalent area under cereals.

The production calendar for grapes began in October, when the farmers would dig around each individual plant exposing the roots so that they could absorb the winter rains, while at the same time they supplied animal manure. From November through January, the delicate process of pruning the vines took place. This was an extremely important task and there were well-compensated specialists who migrated across the countryside offering their skills. Hoeing was done to allow the soil to aerate and to better absorb the rain. It also helped to destroy weeds and bury the fallen leaves, which, when they rotted, enriched the soil. Hoeing was very labour-intensive, and wage labourers were often hired to augment the family workforce. The workers lined up in rows across the vineyard, and moved across it in ranks. In late March–early April, farmers began harrowing: piles of earth formed during hoeing were pulverised into a fine powder and pressed up against the base of the stock, forming hillocks around each plant. These mounds protected the roots and the base of the plant from the summer heat. Harrowing was probably the most important step. Peasants had a saying that 'even pigs may hoe, but harrowing must be done by the landlord himself' – a clear reflection of just how important this process was.

In spring, farmers applied sulphur to their vines two or three times, the first being right after the harrowing was finished. In mid-May came the next vital stage in the process: ring-cutting. This was done when the first blossoms appeared. Ring-cutting prevents unwanted vegetative growth and encourages the formation of the fruit. It was a difficult task that required specialised skill. Probably the most highly paid agricultural hired labourers were the ring-cutting specialists. An experienced ring-cutter (called in Greek a χαρακότης) could do 0.13 hectares per day, and an entire vineyard had to be done within ten days, otherwise the fruit would not ripen uniformly.

Late July–August was the time for harvesting, drying, cleaning and gathering the grapes. Large groups of workers, including women, would perform the harvest. Harvesting did not last more than six days, and a team of seven people could harvest 1.2 hectares; accordingly, since the average vineyard was 2.4 hectare, the labour of 14 people was required. So, unless the household had only a very small vineyard, a single family would have had extreme difficulty completing the harvest on their own, and so they needed to call on the services of wage labourers.

After harvesting, grapes that were to be dried into raisins or currants would be laid out on threshing floors for seven to ten days, depending upon the weather, to dry. Once they were desiccated, the currants were collected and any impurities that had become mixed in with them were picked out. This was also a crucial moment. The dried currant grapes generated the critically important cash income that a family needed to survive, and the exposed fruit was extremely vulnerable. An untoward rainstorm, for example, could destroy the entire crop. Growing vines, then, was a long and complicated process, but the variety of products they produced was essential to the existence of the Greek agrarian household (Franghiadis 1990: 201–19; Pizanias 1988; Psychogios 1995; Blitzer 2004: 158–60; Agriantoni 1988).

Both olive trees and vines produced fruit and other products that were critical to a household's subsistence and that could be sold commercially. With olives, it was primarily oil and from vineyards it was largely the currant grape. A few other crops were grown widely across the Greek world that were geared exclusively for non-subsistence, commercial purposes. The most important of these were mulberry trees for the production of silk, cotton and tobacco. While some peasant farms grew these crops, they were mostly cultivated on large estates or plantations, and these tended to cluster in just a few regions. Map 7.1 shows the spatial distribution of the major commercial crops in Greece and the Ottoman Empire. Currant production was densely concentrated in the northern and western Peloponnesos and the Ionian islands of Zakynthos and Kefalonia. The major centres for export-oriented olive production were, within the kingdom of Greece, the southern Peloponnesos, and in particular Sparta and Messenia, Attica, and after 1864 Kerkira; within the Ottoman Empire, those areas where Greeks played an especially important role in olive production were Pelion, southern Macedonia, northwestern Anatolia, the area around Smyrna, some of the Aegean islands (most importantly Lesbos) and Crete.

For much of the nineteenth century, tobacco was not a major commercial crop in the kingdom of Greece, except to a limited extent in the province of Aitolia-Akarnannia. This changed with the signing in 1884 of the Greece-Egypt Tobacco Convention that gave Greek tobacco preference over Ottoman tobacco by levying import tariffs on the former at a rate one-third lower than the latter. Accordingly, tobacco production in Greece took off, especially in Thessaly and Boiotia (Birdal 2010: 151–2). Within the Ottoman Empire, however, it was an important crop in eastern Macedonia and Thrace, and the western coast of Anatolia (Dagkas 2007; Neuburger 2013). All of those were areas with substantial Greek populations and they played important roles in the tobacco industry, as they did in Egypt (Shechter 2003; 2006: 31–6; see Karanasou 1999 and Kitroeff 1989 for overviews of the history of Greeks in Egypt).

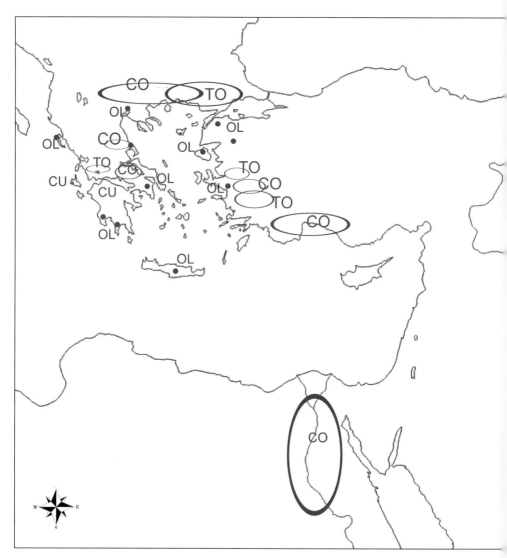

Map 7.1 Distribution of commercial crops in Greece and the Ottoman Empire.

Cotton cultivation was concentrated in Boiotia, Thessaly, Macedonia, central western Anatolia, southern Anatolia, in particular in the area around Mersin, and Egypt (Teoman and Kaymak 2008). In addition to mulberries, which were grown widely in numerous areas, other cash crops of importance were madder, a perennial herbaceous shrub the roots of which were used for the production of red dye, and valonia, an essential ingredient in leather production extracted from raw acorns and from acorn cups. These, in conjunction with the more subsistence-orientated crops discussed above, constituted the essential core of Greek agriculture. But in order to understand fully the rural economy of nineteenth-century Greece, we have to understand how these crops were integrated into a coherent food system, and in order to do that we have to analyse three interrelated topics: land, labour and farm organisation.

After the actual crops that they grew, the next two most important factors in determining the nature of an agrarian system were land and labour. The two of them are intimately connected, both were in short supply in the nineteenth century, and each underwent significant changes in both Greece and the Ottoman Empire. To help guide us in our discussion, Figure 7.4 presents a typology of farms based on the combination of land and labour. Like any ideal schema, these represent archetypes and most real-world farms fell somewhere in between. At one end of the spectrum were estates (also referred to as plantations or latifundia), which in the Ottoman Empire were called çiftliks. These were the largest and wealthiest farms in the Greek world. They consisted of large tracts of land on which were cultivated a variety of crops, including both subsistence crops for sale in local markets and, in particular, commercial products intended for export. The owners of such estates, of course, supplied no labour of their own and in many cases they were absentee landowners, who spent only part of the year actually living on their estates. The work on the plantation was done by a combination of peasant families, who were employed on a full-time basis and who resided on the estate, and seasonal labourers, who were retained as needed. These plantations also included warehouses, mills and other types of agricultural production facilities.

At the opposite end of the spectrum were the poorest of households, whose land-holdings are sometimes referred to as minifundia. These families possessed little or no land, and so they had to rely on a variety of activities to make ends meet. These included hiring themselves out as wage labourers, entering into a sharecropping arrangement with a large landowner whereby they would farm parcels of his land in exchange for a percentage of the crop, undertaking petty manufacturing of commodities for sale, and/or undertaking periodic labour migrations to gain a cash income. In between latifundia and minifundia were the most common types of households, and these were small or middling farms. On a small household farm, the family owned sufficient land to provide for their subsistence needs, as well

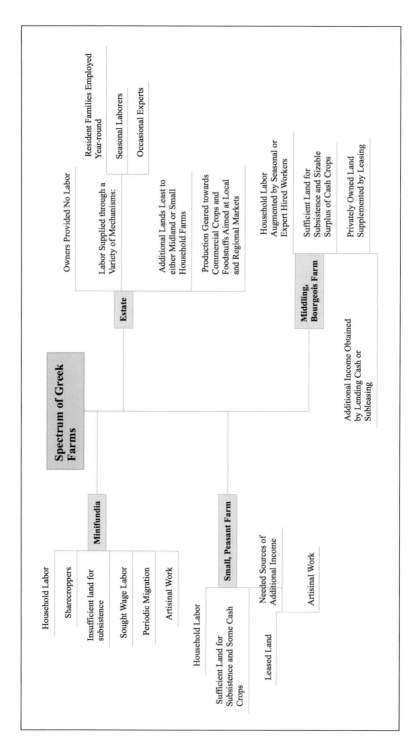

Figure 7.4 Graph showing spectrum of Greek farms.

as to produce some cash crops for sale. The labour supply came from family members, augmented seasonally by specialists, like the vine ring-cutters discussed above. Some years, when the crop yields were lower than expected, members of this type of household would have to seek additional income either by selling their labour or by undertaking other productive activities to raise cash. The middling household farm was distinguished by its size, possessing more land, and by the labour regime it employed. On this type of farm, the owners might or might not participate in direct culti-vation. They therefore had to hire seasonal labourers or lease some of their land to poorer families. The owners of both middling farms and large estates were often a critically important source of credit to poor families. A few real, historical examples of each of these ideal types can give us a better sense of how they functioned in Greek society.

An impressive, but not atypical, example of the large plantation-type estate was one that belonged to P. I. Halikiodopoulos from Pyrgos. He was a Member of Parliament and sat on the board of directors of the National Bank of Greece. An absentee landlord who nonetheless took great interest in agrarian pursuits (he edited the *Journal of Greek Agriculture*), he paid great attention to his beloved plantation. His estate covered 50.2 hectares that were divided into three sectors connected by roads. The first of these consisted of 9.4 hectares of arable land along the slope of a hill. On top of the hill, occupying one-third of a hectare, was his magnificent manor house. It had eleven rooms, forty-five doors and windows, and was beauti-fully embellished in marble. The estate also had four other houses, each approximately 1,650m², where the estate's sharecroppers and their families lived. There were two warehouses, numerous outbuild-ings, a mill and three animal folds. The lands adjacent to the house were planted with currant vines; just beyond them were groves and orchards covered with 890 olive trees, 300 pear trees, 100 fig trees, 80 almond trees, and 40 mulberry trees. The second major plot of land measured 19.2 hectares on the flatlands northwest of the main estate and it was devoted to currants, citrus trees and vegetable gardens. There was also a cistern, enclosed and stone-paved areas for drying the currants, and another warehouse for storing them. The third sector of the estate consisted of 21.5 hectares, almost all of which were devoted to grain cultivation; as was often the case, the fields devoted to cereal cultivation were located the furthest away from the estate's centre (Franghiadis 1990: 166, footnote 5).

The plantation of Sotiris Sotiropoulos provides us with another example of a great estate. Sotiropoulos came from a wealthy family and was very active in national politics, holding various ministerial portfolios during his career, including that of Prime Minister. In his account of the thirty-six days that he spent with a bandit gang as its hostage, he gave a detailed description of his plantation. It was in Messenia and it consisted initially of fifteen hectares, twelve of which were planted with currant vines; in 1861 he acquired an additional nine hectares through a combination of purchases and debt fore-closures. On his plantation were also 250 mulberry trees for the production of silk, forty pear trees, and three vegetable gardens. He grew wine grapes on another hectare plot and set aside half a hectare as a drying ground for his currants. On another part of the grounds he had built a villa where his family resided during the summer months. Sotiropoulos was an absentee landlord. In comparison to the latifundia of Sicily or southern Spain, this was a small plantation; nonetheless within a Balkan context, it was a sizable estate, worked by hired labourers.

Like Halikiodopoulos, he employed an overseer who, along with his family, lived on the estate all year round. They were permitted to grow food crops in their gardens, were provided with a house, and were paid a monthly wage. Two unmarried hired workers also lived on the estate with them. The job of the three men was to tend the vines and the other tree crops throughout the year as well as tending to the villa. A gang of fifteen workers was hired for a two-week period during the spring to assist with hoeing the vineyards, and a group of thirty or more was employed in July and August to harvest the grapes. Plantation owners like these two men often hired small gangs of armed guards to protect their fields during the summer months and to protect their estates from bandits (Sotiropoulos 1866).

At the opposite end of the spectrum was the destitute household of Aunt Achtitsa, the lead character in Alexandros Papadiamantis's short story 'The Gleaner' (Papadiamantis 1987 [1894]). Following the tragic deaths of her husband and eldest son in a shipwreck, of her daughter in childbirth, and the migration of her youngest son to America, she lost all of the family's land to rapacious creditors. Left with two young grandchildren, she eked out a meagre existence by gathering wild herbs and grasses and selling them in the market, and by working as a seasonal labourer harvesting wheat and other grains on nearby islands. After visiting an estate on the island of Euboea,

Eunice Felton penned this moving description of the lives of women like Aunt Achtitsa:

> Their supper consisted only of a piece of bread beside some soup; and this diet has but few variations, such as black olives, salad, and fruit in season. Meat is a great rarity; many ate it but once a year, at the feast of Lambri, or Easter. Then everyone eats roast spring lamb; and if one is too poor to buy it, he will be sure to find somebody to give it to him. (Felton 1882: 681)

Most Greek rural households, however, belonged to either the small or middling category. Here is an example of the latter. Theodoros Papailiou was a bourgeois lawyer from the Peloponnesian town of Pyrgos. He acquired eight hectares of national land in accordance with the 1871 land-distribution act, discussed below; he acquired sixteen more by purchasing parcels of land from poor farmers who had fallen so deeply in debt that they could not repay their creditors. He thus controlled twenty-four hectares of land, 11.6 of which he then rented to two peasant households from a mountain village in Mantineia and another 6.5 to a family with a father and two adult sons from a mountain village near Kalavryta. These families then undertook to prepare the vineyards and build threshing floors. He advanced them interest-free loans of 2,135 drachmas and 1,257 drachmas respectively. After five years, the lawyer received back half of the vineyards and the threshing floors, while full ownership of the remaining land was ceded to the peasant renters on two conditions: one was that they had to repay the advance and two that they would have to cultivate the lawyer's vineyards. One of the families could not make the repayment, and he charged them 12 per cent interest over a five-year period, during which time they could not sell their portion of the vineyard to anyone but him. The peasant owners also became responsible for paying the taxes and the installments for the mortgage on the estate in accordance with the land-tenure laws. In addition they had to maintain Papailiou's fields, outbuildings and his farmhouse.

Konstantinos Roinitios's farm in the province of Iliadas in the western Peloponnesos provides us with a good example of the typical small family farm. At the core of his household was a farmhouse in the village of Palaiochori that he had inherited from his father. For reasons unknown to us, he seems not to have received any land in his patrimony nor did his wife bring any land into the marriage as part of her dowry. For that reason he had to acquire land using a variety of mechanisms. With funds from the 1871 land-redistribution programme, he purchased three hectares of arable land. He obtained access to another 1.8 hectares of vineyards planted in currant grapes, which he worked on a sharecropping basis; in exchange for cultivating the vines, he received one half of the crop. He rented another 1.6 hectares of land on which he grew wine grapes; unfortunately, we do not know the precise terms of his lease agreement. Finally, he purchased half a hectare of arable land distant from the village where he grew cereal grains. Altogether, then, Roinitios worked 6.9 hectares of land in plots widely distributed across the countryside, and over which he had sole control of only 3.5 hectares. This would have provided him with sufficient food and an income to sustain his family, but with neither a cushion in case of a bad year nor with much of a profit in a good one. He, like 80 per cent of other Greek peasant farmers, had access to additional land through joint ownership or collaborative cultivation with kinsman. It was extremely common for clusters of related men to accumulate plots of land in the same area and to work them jointly. This, then, was the most common form of Greek household: landholdings of approximately four to five hectares, some owned, some rented and some leased, and worked with labour from the household, with supplemental support from nearby kinsman or specialists if the family budget could afford it (Franghiadis 1990: 286, note 7; see also pp. 97–100; Gallant 1991: 101–12).

The development of the types of farms discussed above was shaped in numerous and important ways by legal changes that took place in both Greece and the Ottoman Empire that impacted land ownership and land tenure. During the summer of 1858, the Ottoman government issued a 132-article Land Code that superseded all previous laws and practices and introduced a modern, comprehensive and universally applicable land-tenure law. 'The Code recognized private property rights, significantly enlarged liberties of landholders, pushed inheritance rules further towards gender equality, and included some clauses that favored landed interests' (Aytekin 2009a: 936; 2009b; İslamoğlu 2011). Many Ottoman Greeks were able to take advantage of the opportunities opened up by the new legislation and acquired landed holdings, including in some areas very large estates.

In the kingdom of Greece, as we saw in Chapter 4, the 1835 land-reform programme was fraught with difficulties and susceptible to corruption, and its implementation, though woefully incomplete – only 10 per cent of national lands were actually sold (Franghiadis

2011: 114) – still produced a stark disparity between a relatively small number of sizable estates, middling bourgeois farms, and a much larger number of peasant minifundia. In addition, because the scheme was so poorly implemented, only a fraction of national lands ended up being distributed, leaving huge tracts in the hands of families who had no legal claim to them (Petmezas 2003: 4–5, 7). Because these holdings were undocumented, they were largely untaxed, and so in 1845 the government passed a law basically giving the squatters *usufruct* rights to the land that they occupied. The next major redistribution of national lands occurred in 1871, and as we saw in Chapter 5, it greatly expanded the amount of land under cultivation.

The 1871 law was largely successful in creating new peasant farms. But some of the old problems persisted. Corruption by assessors led to a maldistribution in some areas. Even where the system worked fairly, this second round of land distribution still left thousands of households in possession of land holdings insufficient to meet their basic needs. The great interannual variability of crop yields in Greece meant that even farms that could sustain a family during a good year soon fell prey to debt and all that went with it after any one of numerous bad years. Rural indebtedness remained a huge problem. 'The usury market was the only capital market accessible for peasant family production units' (Franghiadis 2011: 122; for a more general discussion of peasant indebtedness in the region, see Aytekin 2008). They had to borrow, and they were in no position to object to whatever terms were attached to the loans. With interest rates pegged at between 20–30 per cent, numerous families fell into a debt trap from which there was no escape' (Franghiadis 1990: 133–9, 224).

When looking at rural poverty, we have to pay attention not only to who owned the land, but, more importantly, who controlled the surplus production from that land. In the case of commercial crops, smallholders had to transform their product into a marketable commodity, usually abroad. The local bourgeoisie, then, did not need to own the land to control the profits that it produced. Interest rates on family farms ranged from 20 to 24 per cent on commercial crops and 30–40 per cent on subsistence cultivation. In the Ottoman Empire, as well, rural debt weighed heavily on the peasantry while providing a generous income to the wealthy. In the vilayets of northwestern Anatolia, where there was a dense concentration of Rom, the kocabaşi Salmaslı Kevork, from the town of Mihalic, had a credit portfolio which included seven nearby villages that owed him over

Figure 7.5 *Agricultural terracing on the island of Andros © Thomas W. Gallant Photographic Collection.*

10,000 piasters. The Rom family of Yorapoğulları, also from Mihalic, had extended fourteen major loans to six nearby villages, totalling more than 20,000 piasters and the Cağaloğulları family was owed more than 10,000 piasters in outstanding debts (Aytekin 2008: 301). The consequences of the continuing small size of the average peasant holding and a household's continued vulnerability to debt were that, first, some members had to undertake pluriactivities, and, second, many families had to cede part of their harvest to creditors, effectively becoming sharecroppers on their own land.

While changes in the legal framework gave more people access to land than ever before, farming families adopted a number of other practices to deal with the challenges posed by the Greek natural environment and by their specific economic conditions. The first of these was terracing. Even the casual visitor to Greece today will be struck by the near ubiquity of terraces, while travelling around the country. Almost every hill and mountainside has been carved out with narrow terraces that allow some form of arable cultivation (see Fig. 7.5, depicting terraces of the island of Andros). Dating Greek terraces precisely is exceptionally challenging and archaeologists and historians are still hard at work devising ways to do so. What is clear is that new terraces were built and old ones were restored during the nineteenth century in response to the need to acquire more arable

Figure 7.6 Intercropping on the island of Kefalonia © Thomas W. Gallant Photographic Collection.

land. While expanding the cultivated area, terracing did so at a marginal cost. What that means is that families invested much greater labour in constructing or restoring terraces then they earned from them. That was because terraces were built on marginal land and so produced much lower yields. Nonetheless, terraces were a vital necessity (Bevan and Conolly 2011; Bevan et al. 2012; Kizos and Koulouri 2005, 2006; Krahtopoulou and Frederick 2008; Petanidou, Kizos and Soulakellos 2008; Zgaier 2008).

Another widespread practice was multicropping (Fig. 7.6). Farmers would cultivate more than one crop on the same piece of land, usually some mixture of olives, vines, cereals or pulses. As we saw earlier, each of these plants occupied a different niche in the Greek agricultural calendar, drawing on human manpower, as well as moisture and nutrients from the soil at different times. In other words, the different crops complemented rather than competed for resources (Kizos and Koulouri 2010; Forbes 2007: 189). Multicropping allowed farmers to maximize the number of different cultigens they could produce on limited landholdings. But at a cost: this practice maximised economic security but reduced productivity. Another way that farmers tried to gain economic security was through the practice of land fragmentation (Adams 2000; Gallant 1991; Forbes 2000; 2007: 190–9). Rather than having all of their

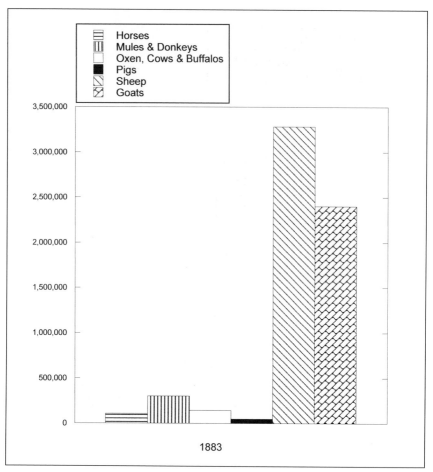

Figure 7.7 Farm animals in Greece 1883 (Petmezas 2003: figure 4.20, p. 20).

family's land concentrated in one place, households divided their landholdings into numerous, small parcels distributed widely across the countryside. This enabled them to take advantage of the intense microspatial variability of climate and soils in Greece, as well as increasing their economic security by minimising the risk that any single environmental crisis would wipe out all of their crops. The manpower cost of travelling from parcel to parcel of land was more than offset by the economic security they obtained. All of these strategies aimed at ensuring that households produced a steady and secure source of subsistence. While they were effective at that, they had the side effect of reducing economic productivity (Petmezas 2009b: 355).

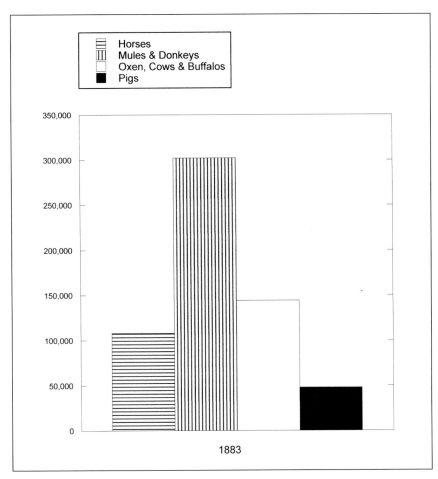

Figure 7.8 *Farm animals in Greece minus sheep and goats, 1883 (Petmezas 2003: figure 4.20, p. 20).*

No farm could operate and no rural family could get by without a host of animals. They were sources of energy for working the land, foods like meat and diary products, and raw materials such as wool and hides. Figure 7.7 shows the distribution of animals according to the 1883 agricultural census (Petmzas 2003: 133–44). As it graphically demonstrates, sheep and goats by far made up the largest sector of the livestock population in the kingdom. This figure is so large because it captures two different elements of the rural economy; one, and the one we are interested in here, relates to the family farm on which people kept a few sheep and goats for their milk and their wool, and another, which we will discuss shortly, which is connected

Figure 7.9 Boy ploughing a field with oxen, Thessaly, 1903 © Library of Congress Prints and Photography Division.

to large-scale animal husbandry. Tethered in the courtyard or corralled in pens adjacent to their houses, Greeks kept nearby a few sheep and goats to supply them with milk.

In order to get a clearer picture of the distribution of animals on a typical farm, Figure 7.8 shows the results of the 1883 census with sheep and goats removed. Nearly half of the remaining animal population consisted of mules and donkeys, followed by an almost equal percentage of horses and bovines such as oxen, cows and buffaloes. These animals were used for their traction power to plough fields and do other agricultural tasks, and as beasts of burden for transportation (Fig. 7.9). These national figures, however, mask local level variations. In lowland areas and on plains, such as in the Argolid or in Boiotia, cattle and horses were more prevalent because they could provide greater power that was necessary to plough the heavier lowland soils and because there was more plentiful fodder to feed them (see Fig. 7.10 and Karouzou 2000: table 4). In upland areas, by contrast, mules and donkeys were more prevalent, especially for ploughing on rough and rocky parcels of land and on agricultural terraces. Every household needed at least one, and preferably two or more, of these vitally important animals. They were so vital to a

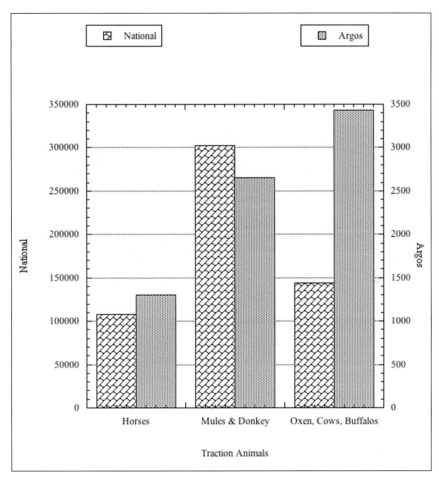

Figure 7.10 *Traction animals on Greek farms, 1861 (Karouzou 2000: table 4).*

household's continued existence that we know from iconographic depictions (see Fig. 6.1) and archaeological data that it was extremely common for people to keep these animals in their houses, often in areas adjacent to the family's living quarters. There were, of course, other animals kept in Greek households, such as pigs, chickens and dogs, and in many areas even insects such as bees were important to the rural economy.

In Figure 7.8, we saw how overwhelmingly the largest number of animals kept by Greeks was sheep and goats, and, as was suggested above, every family sought to own at least a few to provide milk and wool. But the sheer number of flocks recorded indicates that

Figure 7.11 *Transhumant shepherds with their flocks, 1909 © Library of Congress Prints and Photography Division.*

shepherding was also a large-scale, almost industrial, endeavour. Animal husbandry on this scale could not have been sustained by family farms. Thus, one of the enduring features of the pastoral economy in Greece has been the practice of transhumance. Each year shepherds, mostly belonging to one or two ethnic groups such as the Sarakatsani and Vlachs, would undertake biennual migrations. In Figure 7.11, we can see shepherds, both men and women, leading their flocks along a country road.

During the summer the lowland areas were parched, making water and pasturage scarce, and most of the arable land was under cultivation. So, shepherds would move their flocks up into the mountains. There they found plentiful food and water to sustain their animals. In winter, when the mountains would be covered in snow and ice, the shepherds migrated to the lowland areas. A symbiotic relationship developed between the pastoralists and the lowland farmers. The farmers would earn a small income from the rent they charged the shepherds and their fields would be fertilised by animal

Figure 7.12 *Shepherds and their flocks on the Argive plain, 1906* © *Library of Congress Prints and Photography Division.*

droppings (manure), as Figure 7.12 shows. This arrangement worked very well for the shepherds, of course, because it sustained their animals through the winter months. Moreover, it brought them into closer proximity to lowland villages and market towns in which they could sell dairy products, wool, and in the spring, animals to be consumed as part of the Greek Easter celebration. Map 7.2 shows the major routes traversed by transhumance shepherds and their flocks. As it clearly shows, these annual treks spanned the entirety of the southern Balkans and Greece. The character and the magnitude of transhumance, however, changed over time. The imposition of national boundaries, like the 1832 Greek-Ottoman border, had a profound impact on their movements. In addition, market demands and changing economic conditions also had an impact on large-scale shepherding. Nonetheless, throughout much of the nineteenth century, dairy products such as milk and cheese, and wool, were provided by transhumant shepherds and their flocks.

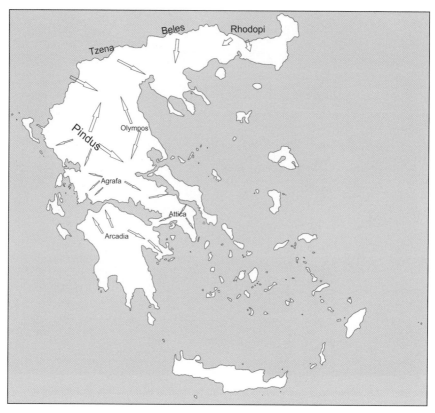

Map 7.2 *Migration routes of Balkan transhumant shepherds.*

Mills and milling

Another necessary, and thus ubiquitous, feature of the Greek countryside was the mill. Two of the most important elements of the Greek rural economy and diet, grains and olives, needed to be crushed before they could be consumed. Prior to being ground into flour, cereal grains and maize kernels were dried and cleaned. When ready, they were ground into flour using a very simple hand-operated grinder, which consisted of two circular stones attached by a central wooden post. We know from archaeological excavations that such hand-operated grinders had been in use in Greece from ancient times. The problem with flour produced from a hand grinder was that it was extremely coarse and difficult to digest. Because a rotary motion was required, grinding stones were attached to wind or water mills in order to turn them. Both types of mill were widely distributed across Greece (see Map 7.3). An excellent example of a nineteenth-century

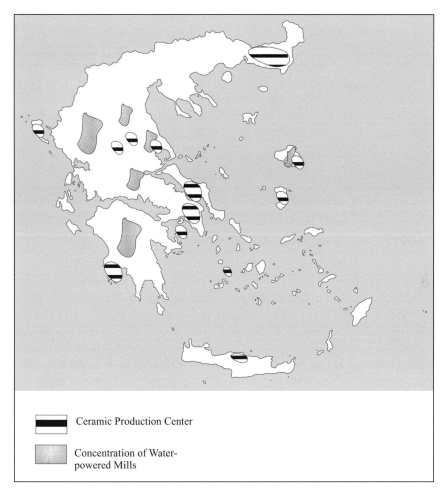

Map 7.3 Selected centres of manufacturing in Greece and the Ottoman Empire.

water-driven grain mill can be visited at the Waterpower Museum in Dimitsana. The flour produced at water mills was of a far superior quality than that produced by grinding by hand. The usual practice was for farmers to bring their grain to the mill, where it was ground into flour; as payment for their services, millers usually retained 10 per cent of the flour. By the end of the nineteenth century, steam-driven grain mills had been built in the vicinity of all of the major eastern Mediterranean cities, including Athens and Salonika. None-theless, in the countryside wind and water mills still predominated.

Figure 7.13 provides us with a view of a traditional olive mill; the example seen here dates to the 1830s. In order to extract oil from the

Figure 7.13 *Traditional Greek olive mill © Mary Evans Picture Library.*

olives, the kernels must first be crushed and then the resulting pulp pressed. On the right-hand side of the drawing, we see a labourer placing the olives on a stone platform. Two large crushing stones rotate on top of the platform, driven by a donkey that pushes a wooden frame that is attached to a central post, which in turn rotates the crushing stones. Once the olives have been crushed the resulting pulp was collected in baskets and then dumped into coarse fabric sacks. These are then placed underneath a manually operated wooden screw press. The first pressing produces the best quality of olive oil, called virgin oil. The oil is then strained and is ready for human consumption. The sacks of pulp, however, are pressed at least one more time to extract every bit of oil from it. The oil from the second, and certainly the oil from the third, pressing is of lesser quality and is used for other purposes, such as making soap.

Note a few things about the traditional olive mill. First, all of the machines were made out of wood and stone. The wooden-frame crusher and screw press have limited tensile strength, and so are not particularly efficient at extracting the maximum amount of oil from the fruit and the olive pits. Noteworthy as well is that all of the energy driving these machines is animate, that is, either human or animal power. This places a very low ceiling of potential productivity on the traditional mill, and it produces a relatively poor-quality oil. Because of the increasing demand for Greek and Ottoman olive oil, and in particular for higher-quality oils, important improvements were made to olive milling. First, the productive capabilities of crushers and screw presses were improved by making them out of metal. The major change to the technology of pressing involved replacing the stone platform with an iron basin. This provided a far more efficient and productive surface for crushing the olives, producing an even finer pulp and releasing more of the essential oils. Iron, or wood and iron, screw presses were also introduced and because they could exert much higher levels of pressure, more and purer oil was now extracted. The introduction of metal machinery also made it possible for millers to employ far more efficient and stronger sources of power: first, wind and water mills and then, most importantly, steam engines. By the end of the century, steam-driven olive mills were built in the major olive oil-producing areas, such as Lesbos and Crete, and in the industrialised zones of cities like Athens. Having now examined the food system and rural productive practices in the Greek world, we can now turn to how the rural economy as a whole developed during the long nineteenth century.

The big picture

At the macro level the single most important development impacting the rural economy of the Greek world was the rapid, sustained and great expansion of the production of commercial crops. These products were almost exclusively geared for the international export markets, primarily in Western Europe. The economies of both Greece and the Ottoman Empire, therefore, became integrally connected with world markets. The results of this asymmetrical relationship included the enrichment of some sectors of society, particularly Greeks in the Ottoman Empire who largely controlled international maritime trade, but at the same time, it made their economies much more vulnerable to the vagaries of international markets (Kasaba 1998; Petrakis and Panorios 1992).

In the kingdom of Greece one commercial crop more than any other predominated: the currant grape. Between independence and the 1890s, currant production increased sixty-four fold, with the largest expansion of production occurring after 1870. Figure 7.14 vividly captures the dramatic increase in the production of currants. The chart shows the annual production figures for currants; I have also plotted five-year moving averages, which show even more clearly the pace of growth. In the 1870s and into the early 1880s, it would not be going too far to speak of a 'currant mania' in some parts of Greece. What caused this exceptional transformation of the rural

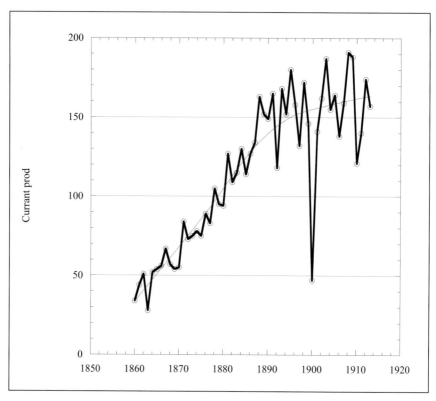

Figure 7.14 *Currant production, 1860–1913 (Franghiadis 1990).*

economy? The answer to this question lay not in the eastern Mediterranean but further to the west.

Sometime during the mid-1850s, a deadly stowaway arrived in France. Aphids, probably originating from the southern US, rapidly spread throughout the country, as well as into parts of Italy and Spain. The favourite food for this insect was the sap in vine roots. Between 1860 and 1875, 60 per cent of all the vineyards in France were devastated, and in some places the destruction was almost complete. For some unknown reason, the aphid infestation never crossed the Adriatic and, so the entire Balkan peninsula, including Greece, was spared. Total European vine production plummeted, while demand remained buoyant, resulting in a huge increase in the price buyers were willing to pay for grapes, and, in particular, the sweet currant grape. For Greeks, there was now a huge market for their grapes in France, on top of the always-vibrant demand from England. Driven by high prices and market demand, and assisted by

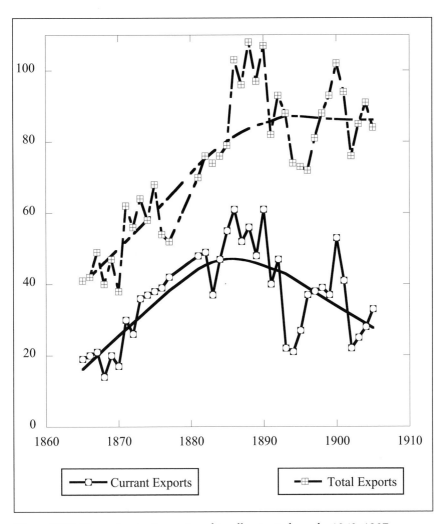

Figure 7.15 *Currant exports compared to all exported goods, 1863–1907 (Franghiadis 1990: 22).*

the 1871 land-distribution law, large and small Greek farms began planting new vineyards. In low-lying areas, previously uncultivated land was drained and planted with vines. Terraces rendered steep hillsides cultivable and, because of the high profit margin, planting them with grapes now made sound economic sense. In some areas, we know that farmers even converted land previously used to grow food crops into vineyards. It seemed to be a win-win situation. Agricultural incomes rose dramatically and the Greek state profited handsomely by levying duties on exported grapes. As Figure 7.15

shows, the income from currant exports accounted for the lion's share of Greek total exports. The currant boom transformed Greek agriculture and rural society (Petmezas 2000, 2011).

There were, however, some important consequences to this transformative development. First, it led to a major shift in the distribution of the rural population. Previously, large swathes of the lowland areas of the Peloponnesos had remained unoccupied. A lengthy description in the Greek government's *Journal of Greek Agriculture* explains why:

> Greece is surrounded by lakes and swamps from all sides. Lakes and marshes cover an area of almost 230,000 hectares, which favour the propagation of fevers and other diseases which torment the already scarce population of Greece. The lowlands suffer more. The swamp fevers are more injurious to those coming from the healthier climate of the mountains to the plains to pass the winter. That is the reason why entire populations lived in a state of continuous migration, similar to herds of sheep, and cannot settle in the empty plains. Hunger and snow chased them away from the mountains during the whole winter; fevers drove them out of the plains back to the mountains for six months, as if they were in a state of siege. Those obliged to pass the summer in the plains, when they fall ill, instead of searching for another remedy, turned back to the Highlands; those who insist on staying, run the risk of catching chronic diseases due to swamp fevers. (Εφεμερίς της Ελλάδος Γεωργίας, November 1855 [cited in Franghiadis 1990: p. 76, note 1])

Pressure to increase grape production led to the agricultural colonisation of the lowlands. Numerous families acquired land in the lowland districts on which they planted vineyards. Large landowners, like the ones we discussed earlier, created huge estates and plantations in the lowland areas, and then brought in families from the upland districts to work them. As one Greek historian has noted, 'agricultural colonisation [of the lowlands] has rightly been considered the major trend in nineteenth-century Greek social history' (Franghiadis 2011: 120). In addition to founding new villages, many sites that were formerly used by mountain villagers as temporary workstations were converted into permanent villages through agricultural colonisation (Stamatoyannopoulou 1993).

Second, the currant boom led to a great increase in the demand for labour, but mostly for seasonal workers at harvest time. Child labour became increasingly important because there were many tasks involved in producing currants that could be done by small children.

This development, as we saw in the previous chapter, may have had an impact on Greek peasant families' reproductive strategies. Third, it had a knock-on effect that created demand for other goods and supplies, such as wood to be used for staves in the vineyards and for making barrels to hold the grapes for export. Timber cutting and lumber milling, especially through the use of water-driven sawmills, flourished as economic activities in the upland areas, providing income and employment for mountain villagers. Fourth, as we saw in Chapter 5, the need to lower transportation costs was one of the driving forces behind Trikoupis's programme of road and railway construction. These infrastructure projects also provided labour opportunities for Greek men, and because there was an insufficient supply of them, workers from the Ottoman Empire and Italy as well. These labourers generated demand for locally grown Greek food products. The repercussions, then, of the rapid and huge expansion of vine production were manifold and important.

But they were not equally distributed across country. The areas that witnessed the greatest growth in vine cultivation were the Ionian islands of Zakynthos and Kefalonia and parts of the Peloponnesos. The currant growing areas of the latter are divided into three regions, the North that included Patras, Aigialeia and Corinth, the West consisting of Ilia and Trifilia and the South made up of Pilia, Messenia and Kalamata. Figure 7.16 shows the shifting configuration of currant cultivation in these three areas between 1860 and 1888; as it shows the greatest expansion was in the South. In other regions of Greece and in the Ottoman Empire, the cultivation of commercial crops also took off during the last few decades of the nineteenth century, though not the scale as currant cultivation.

The next most important commercial crop was olives and olive oil. Olive oil production in the kingdom of Greece from 1860 to 1913 expanded dramatically, and followed a very similar developmental arc to currant grape production, with the highest rate of growth occurring in the 1870s and 1880s followed by a levelling out in the early twentieth century (Fig. 7.17; a similar growth pattern has been recorded for Spain as well (Infante-Amate 2012). Unlike the currant grape, however, because of the nature of the growth cycle of olives, there was more marked interannual variability. The greatest market demand was for olive oil both as an item for consumption and as the raw material for making soap. Within Greece the areas that experienced the greatest expansion of production were Sparta, Kerkira, Attica and Messenia (see Fig. 7.18).

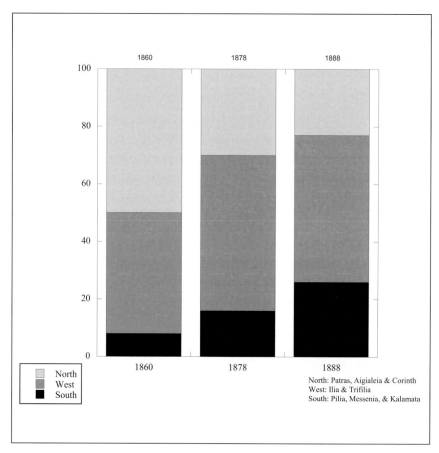

Figure 7.16 *Comparison of currant production in the Peloponnesos (Franghiadis 1990: 22).*

In the Ottoman Empire, olive cultivation took off most dramatically in areas such as Pelion in Thessaly, Lesbos and Crete where Greeks were the majority population. On Lesbos, for example, by the end of the nineteenth century, olive groves covered over 75 per cent of the island's cultivated surface area – a twenty-fold increase since the early 1800s. By the 1890s, the island was exporting over 25,000,000 kilos of olive oil annually, on top of which a prodigious amount remained on the island and was used to produce 4,000,000 kilos of olive oil soap. Two-thirds of the entire tax base of the island was derived from the olive (Kizos and Koulouri 2005: 186–7). A not dissimilar picture is seen on the island of Crete (Adiyeke and Adiyeke 2006). By the 1890s olive oil accounted for almost half of the total

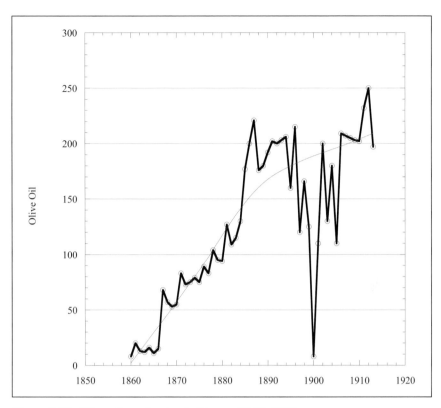

Figure 7.17 *Olive oil production in Greece, 1860–1913.*

exports from the island, with the vast majority of the oil going to, in order of importance, Marseille, Trieste, Salonika, Istanbul, and then Alexandria, Odessa and London. In addition to oil, Crete also became a major producer of olive oil soap that was largely intended to satisfy domestic markets in the Ottoman Empire.

The last two important commercial crops were cotton and tobacco. Like the others, production took off dramatically during the 1860s and continued through the 1880s, and then after a slight decline during the depression of the 1890s they both recovered admirably during the twentieth century (Fig. 7.19; for a discussion of the global economic crisis and its implications for the region, see Pamuk 1984; 1987; Pamuk and Williamson 2000; 2011). Neither cotton nor tobacco, of course, produced any subsistence products and so their production was geared solely for secondary use. Most of the cotton grown within Greece and the Ottoman Empire served the needs of the nascent textile industry (see below), while tobacco

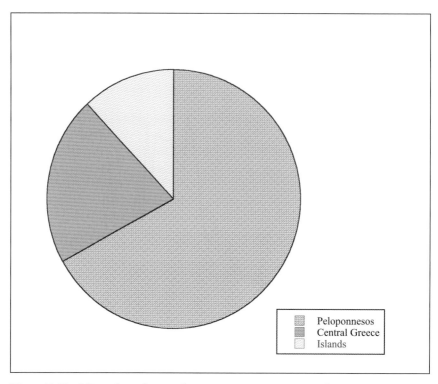

Figure 7.18 *Olive oil production by region, 1860 (Yiannopoulou 2007: 107).*

became the staple product for the emerging cigarette industry (on tobacco see especially Neuberger 2013; Chaker 2012, and Dagkas 2007. For an overview of the Mediterranean cotton industry in a more global context, see Gekas 2007). While the introduction of cigarette-rolling machines created greater demand for Greek and Ottoman tobacco, the cotton supply crisis created by the American Civil War spurred the expansion of cotton cultivation in the region (Kallivretakis 1987). Within Greece, the primary cotton-producing area was Boiotia in the central part of the country (see Map 7.1). There were numerous sites where cotton production flourished within the Ottoman Empire and, in almost all of them, Greeks played an important role both in the production and the marketing of raw cotton.

Two regions exemplify well what transpired. Before the 1860s, cotton production at Mersin and its surrounding territory in southern Anatolia was minimal, but by the 1890s it was a major producer and exporter of fine cotton. As cotton prices rose, farmers

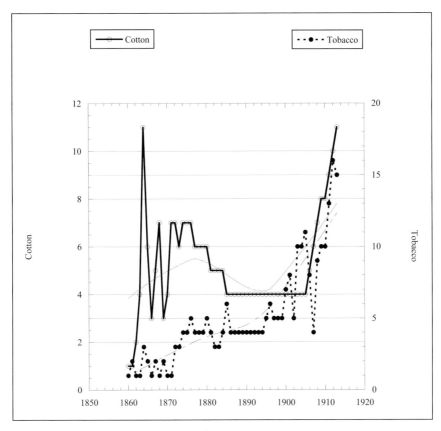

Figure 7.19 *Cotton and tobacco production, 1860–1913.*

and merchants moved to this largely underdeveloped area where land was cheap and local ecology amenable to growing cotton. Joining Muslim immigrants who came from various places in the empire were large numbers of Greek Aegean islanders and Cypriots. As production and trade took off, one family, the Mavromatis from Cyprus, came to dominate the cotton economy of the region (Toksöz 2010; 2011). Greeks played a major role in the cotton industry of Egypt. The most highly prized cotton in the world, the so-called Sakel cotton, was developed by Ioannis Sakellerdis. Greeks played only a minor role in the cultivation of cotton in Egypt, instead they controlled the processing of raw cotton (by 1900 over 75 per cent of the cotton gins in Egypt were owned by Greeks) and its marketing (Greeks owned 25 per cent of all the brokerage houses in the country and 30 per cent of the non-Greek owned houses were operated by

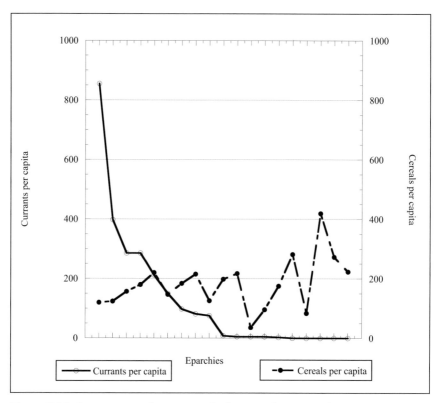

Figure 7.20 *Comparison of currant and wheat production in the Peloponnesos by region (Franghiadis 1990: 56, table 1.5).*

Greeks). Many Greek family fortunes were made with Egyptian cotton.

Much the same happened with tobacco. Greeks came to play a leading role in the growth of the tobacco economy in Macedonia, Thrace, Smyrna and Egypt. The tremendous increase in the production of commercial crops, then, was the single most important development in the last quarter of the nineteenth century with regard to the rural economy. But, in spite of the many benefits this brought, there were some negative consequences as well.

As the extent of land devoted to the production of commercial crops expanded, the amount available for growing subsistence crops contracted. Figure 7.20 compares currant production per capita with cereals production in each of the eparchies of the Peloponnesos. Clearly, there was an inverse correlation between vine and cereal production. In other words, in those areas where significant amounts

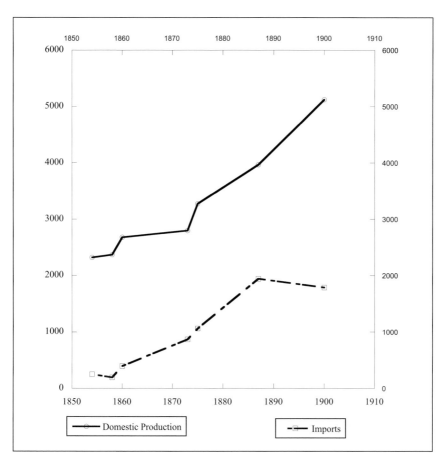

Figure 7.21 *Comparison of domestic wheat production and grain imports.*

of land were devoted exclusively to the production of grapes, per capita production of cereals fell. This, combined with a shift in population to the cities that created even more demand for bread and other cereal products, meant that even though domestic production of grains increased, particularly in Boiotia and after 1881 in Thessaly, Greece increasingly had to import wheat and other cereals (see Fig. 7.21).

In 1850, approximately 80 per cent of the wheat consumed in Greece was produced domestically, whereas by the 1890s almost 50 per cent of it was imported (Table 7.1). Some of the imported grain came from the Ottoman Empire but the bulk of it was shipped from Russia. According to one study, on average, each year between 1881 and 1913 Greece imported 129,272,727 kilos of wheat from

Table 7.1   *Imported foreign and domestic wheat consumption,
1850–1900.*

Decade	Domestic wheat	Imported wheat
1850s	80%	20%
1806s	71%	29%
1870s	59%	41%
1880s	54%	46%
1890s	53%	47%

Petmezas 2004b: 9

Russia (Falkus 1966: 423). This meant that the income derived from the export of commercial crops was counterbalanced by expenditures for foreign imported foodstuffs. When combined with the massive trade imbalance in finished products and machinery, the result was that Greece suffered from a seriously debilitating foreign trade deficit.

Another negative consequence of the over-reliance on the production of commercial crops geared for export was that it made the Greek and the Ottoman economies vulnerable to the vagaries of international markets, and the most dramatic and profoundly important example of this was the collapse of the Greek currant economy during the 1890s. As we saw in Chapter 5, the fiscal crisis this event triggered resulted in Greece going bankrupt. Essentially what happened was that a series of interrelated developments combined to bring down the economy. First, the vineyards of France began to recover from the phylloxera blight, and in order to protect this still-vulnerable agricultural sector like it did with other crops, the French government levied stiff tariffs on imported products (Bassino and Dormois 2010). It then took even more deleterious direct action aimed at the importation of currant grapes, by first putting restrictions on imports from Greece and, then, by banning them altogether (Petmezas 2013; Pizanias 1988). Second, it was precisely at this time that California became a major player in the international dried fruits industry. California raisins were of high quality and, because of developments in the industry particularly related to the drying process, they were cheaper (Morilla, Olmstead and Rhode 1999). The results of these interrelated developments were a huge drop in prices and a tremendous fall off in demand for Greek raisins. In addition to bankrupting the country, this crisis devastated the Greek countryside with far-reaching consequences. The vine industry would recover, but it would never again occupy the primacy of place in the rural economy that it did during the late nineteenth century (Schönhärl 2013).

I want to end this discussion of the rural economy of the Greek world, however, on a more positive note. It stood at a critical cross-roads by the time the world was plunged into war in 1913. The crises of the 1890s brought to an end a four- to five-decade-long period of expansion and development. The crisis did not destroy the rural economy, but it certainly led to major modifications. Looking at the history of the countryside in the long-term, it is clear that the rural economy was at its height during the boom period of the last quarter of the nineteenth century. Standing as stark reminders of how extensive and vibrant the economic life of the Greek countryside was at that time are the hundreds of deserted villages, the thousands of hectares of abandoned land, and the uncultivated terraces that litter the landscape today. Greece's rural economy would only attain the level of production achieved during this period after the introduction of agricultural machinery in the post-World War II era.

Industry and manufacturing

Did Greece and the Ottoman Empire experience the Industrial Revolution? The usual answer provided by historians is decidedly 'yes', but then there usually follows a series of qualifiers of this development such as 'incomplete', 'impaired', or 'unfinished', to cite but a few. Overall, the economies of the region are most frequently described with adjectives such as backwards or semi-peripheral, or some other one that connotes that they did not attain the level of industrialisation that Great Britain or Germany did (Kostis and Petmezas 2006; Ianeva 2011; Kostelenos 2006). And while that is factually true, what this assessment leaves out is that nowhere else in Europe did either. Moreover, by focusing on the narrow question of the extent of modern industrialisation, it diverts our attention from what I consider to be the most important questions, which relate to what changes and developments did take place within the more traditional manufacturing sectors and their relationship to the advent of the modern steam-powered factory. In other words, just because the mechanisation and industrialisation of manufacturing did not attain the production or productivity level of the most economically advanced regions of the world, it does not mean that there were not substantive and important developments in the manufacturing sectors that had profound impact on people's lives.

Throughout the nineteenth century, as they had for centuries before, Greek rural households produced not only the foodstuffs that they consumed but also many of the other goods and commodities that their families required. The most important of these were wooden objects and textiles. Men hand-carved out of wood furniture such as chairs, beds, dowry chests, tables and even babies' cradles, as well as tools and eating utensils, barrels and bins, and even machines such as spinning wheels and looms. Most of these were crude utilitarian objects, but some men became so skilled at woodworking that they produced finely decorated products that could even be considered works of art. But the single most important sector of domestic manufacturing was textiles. Utilising time-honoured technologies, the women of the household aimed to produce all of the woollen and cloth goods that their families needed. They spun by hand raw cotton, silk or wool into thread or yarn that they then worked on a hand-carved loom into bolts of fabric. Next they dyed, embroidered and sewed the cloth into the various textiles used by the family on a daily basis; things such as sheets, coverlets, towels, tablecloths, and, most importantly, clothing (see Quataert 1988 for a discussion of the persistence artisanal manufacturing). As with woodworking, some women became so skilled in embroidery that their finished products became highly prized commodities (many exquisite examples of women's embroidery and men's woodwork can be viewed in the superb collection of the Benaki Museum in Athens). From childhood, women spent countless hours daily working with textiles, and one of the most important tasks of unmarried women was the production of the woven goods that they would bring into their marriage as part of their dowry. Domestic manufacturing continued to thrive but that does not mean, as we shall see, that there were not important changes to it as well (for an excellent and copiously illustrated examination of the material culture of traditional Greek households, see Totsikas 2008).

There was, however, a wide variety of tools and objects that a household needed to survive and that could not be made in the home. The most important of these were tools and other objects made out of metal and a whole host of ceramic goods. Even the poorest farmers and landless labourers needed iron agricultural implements. Artisan blacksmiths were to be found in every town and in many large villages producing plough shares, sickles, and all of the other iron tools and bladed implements needed to work a farm. Smiths were tied into market network both as buyers and sellers, and they needed large quantities of charcoal, which, in turn, provided part-time employment for rural villagers who knew how to make it. Before glass became cheap and plastic was invented, most items in a rural household were made out of clay. The list of ceramic objects found in every rural farmhouse is incredibly long. People ate from clay plates and drank out of ceramic cups. They poured their wine and olive oil from ceramic jugs, and they lit their houses with pottery lamps. Generations of their children played with toys made out of clay. As a walk through the excellent collections of traditional ceramics on display in the Kyriazopoulos Ceramic Collection in the Tzitserakis Mosque and the Centre for the Study of Modern Ceramics in Athens show, there was practically no object in traditional society that was not made out of clay. Most important of all, perhaps, were storage vessels.

The family's continued survival depended upon their ability to store and preserve vital foodstuffs over extended periods of time. Grains and pulses, oil and wine, and just about everything else, were stored in clay pithoi of various shapes and sizes (see Fig. 7.22). Some Greek storage vessels, such as the famed Koroneika pithoi from Messenia in the southeast Peloponnesos, were greatly prized and were shipped throughout the Mediterranean. Ceramic workshops were widely spread across the Greek world, clustering of course around the areas where rich clay deposits were to be found. Even though workshops tended to be modest in size, often comprised of a master potter and apprentices; in aggregate they produced pottery on an industrial scale (see Map 7.3 for the locations of the major pottery production centres). In addition to the productive sector that manufactured these more utilitarian goods, during the nineteenth century there still flourished one that put out exquisite finely decorated glazed wares. Greek artists and artisans, both in the kingdom and the Ottoman Empire, produced fine wares in Çanakkale style and domestic wares in variations of it or in other regional styles, while some artisans continued to manufacture beautiful fine ware in Kütahya and even in Iznik styles. Throughout the nineteenth century, pottery remained essential to the Greek way of life. The pottery industry then, even though it remained rooted in a predominately pre-industrial mode of production, expanded greatly and contributed in important ways to the economies of Greece and the Ottoman Empire (Blitzer 1990; Kardulias 2000; Kalentzidou 2000a; 2000b; Psaropoulou 1988; 1990; Kardoulias 2000).

The types of manufacturing we have examined so far certainly

Figure 7.22 *Traditional olive oil storage jars (pithoi), Sparta © Thomas W. Gallant Photographic Collection.*

achieved significant increases in overall production during the nineteenth century, and in some cases, the manufacturing units even expanded in size to resemble small factories, but they did not experience a major jump in productivity. They remained pre-industrial in the sense that they continued to rely primarily on animate sources of power. The greater use of, first, water and then steam power and the shift from wooden to iron machinery would occur in the textile industry, in the manufacturing of secondary agricultural products, such as olive oil, soap, and, to a lesser extent, in the tobacco industry and in tanning (Zarkia 1997). The most critical elements of industrialisation, then, were the concentration of labour in factories and the replacement of animate sources of power with steam engines. Let us look at how these two developed in Greece (any discussion of industrialisation in Greece must rely heavily on the seminal scholarship of Christina Agriantoni (1999, 2003, 2006b, 2006c, 2009)).

Between 1865 and 1893, the total amount of steam power applied to manufacturing doubled (Dertilis 2009: 669). The sector of the population involved in manufacturing had risen from 12 per cent. Table 7.2 shows the distribution of steam-driven engines, number of factories and number of workers employed by industry. Food production accounted for over 50 per cent of the total number

Table 7.2   Steam-driven factories in Greece, 1900.

Industry	Factories (%)	Steam engines (%)	Workers (%)
Food production	52.0	43.3	21.5
Textiles	16.6	33.1	45.9
Metals	12.1	9.6	14.7
Tanneries	2.2	1.1	2.5
Chemical	9.9	6.0	5.7
Other	7.2	6.9	9.7

Agriantoni 2010: 366

Table 7.3   Expansion of steam-driven factories in Greece, 1874/5 to 1890/1.

Industry	1874/75	1882/83	1890/91
Food production	100	146	155
Textiles	100	76	70
Metals	100	150	250
Tanneries	100	133	133
Chemical	100	125	200
Other	100	125	150

Agriantoni 2010: 253

of factories, utilised over 40 per cent of steam engines, but only employed about one-fifth of the industrial workforce. Textiles while accounting for only 17 per cent of the number of factories, utilised one-third of all of the steam engines in Greece and employed 46 per cent of the industrial workforce. What this reflects is the fact that the textile industry was more steam engine driven, yet also required a large number of workers using older technologies. Table 7.3 tracks the expansion of steam power from 1870–90. In relative terms, the greatest increase occurred in the chemical and the metal industries. Food production expanded by 50 per cent, whereas textile manufacturing actually decreased, reflecting again the persistent and important role of hand manufacturing in that industry. Table 7.4 shows the spatial distribution of steam-driven factories in Greece. As it makes clear, Piraeus and Hermoupolis were home to the largest number of factories using steam and employing the most workers. Lastly, Table 7.5 chronicles the growth of factories between 1875 and 1900. What it clearly shows is that, while most factories tended to be

Table 7.4   *Distribution of steam-driven factories in Greece by city, 1875.*

City	Factories (%)	Steam engines (%)	Workers (%)
Piraeus	28.0	40.3	34.0
Hermoupolis	13.1	13.8	25.4
Patras	12.2	9.3	8.2
Athens	7.5	6.5	5.3
Kalamata	5.6	3.7	9.5

Agriantoni 2010: 227

Table. 7.5   *Distribution of steam-driven factories in Greece by size.*

Size of labour force	Percentage by industry		Percentage of workers		Average size (workers per factory)	
	1875	1900	1875	1900	1875	1900
1–5	6	2	1	1	3–4	5
6–25	43	40	14	9	15–16	16–18
26–100	43	43	55	32	56–7	51–4
>100	8	15	30	58	157–62	264–70
Total	100	100	100	100		

Agriantoni 2010: 211

small manufacturing units, with fewer than 100 workers, by 1900 a small number of factories had had grown quite large, with over 58 per cent of the industrial workforce working in plants with more than 100 workers, and the average size of such factories rose from 162 to 260 employees. There were, in conclusion, dramatic changes in manufacturing in both Greece and the Ottoman Empire during the last quarter of the nineteenth century. We need now to look at a couple of the key developments in more detail.

As we just saw, the two most important sectors were textiles and secondary agricultural production. There had been a long tradition in some parts of Ottoman Europe of producing finely dyed cotton thread and woollen yarn for export to Western Europe. In some instances, for example in a few Greek villages in Thessaly, production rose to a proto-industrial level (Petmezas 1990; Katsiardi-Hering 2008; for the situation in the Ottoman Empire generally, see Quataert 1993: 36–8). But it was really only in the second half of the nineteenth century that textile manufacturing took off. Initially, production was still proto-industrial, in the sense that it relied on older technologies and human power. In Greece, the Athanassios Douroutis & Co. silk factory (popularly referred to the Metaxourgeio) provides a good example of the industrialisation process. Originally built in fields located west of Athens in 1836, it was primarily a mulberry orchard with a number of small buildings where women, using wooden spinning wheels turned the raw fabric into silk thread; spindles of the finished product were then loaded onto carts and transported to Piraeus. Then, in 1852, the company was purchased by a British firm, Wrampe & Co., and larger spinning machines were installed.

In 1857 work began on the new gasworks (called *Gazi*), which were completed in 1862, and in the same year construction of a railway line to the port of Piraeus began. The gasworks required huge amounts of coal and the railway made it easier and cheaper to move bulk commodities from the factory to the port. These two concerns, the gasworks and the silk mill, attracted other manufacturing to the west side of Athens. The final phase of the industrialisation of the silk mill took place in 1884 when the entire factory was converted to metal-framed machines powered by steam engines (Agriantoni and Chatziioannou 1997). The developmental process, then, consisted of a shift from domestic manufacturing to factories that concentrated the labour force but still employed pre-industrial technologies utilising traditional sources of power, and this was followed by the replacement of human or animal power with steam engines. The process, as this example shows, was incomplete and textile mills continued to be a blend of the old and the new. This was the case not only with silk but with cotton manufacturing as well (Figs 7.23 and 7.24).

Cotton, even more than silk, was the fabric of the Industrial Revolution. During the 1870s, Piraeus and Hermoupolis in Greece, and Naoussa, Edessa, Veroia and Salonika in Ottoman Macedonia, and Smyrna, Adana, Damascus and Alexandria in other regions of the Ottoman Empire began to emerge as major textile-producing sites. We will focus primarily on developments in Greece and Macedonia. In Greece, cotton spinning expanded considerably, as measured by the number of spinning mills and the number of spindles they produced (Table 7.6). Take the example of the Retsinas brothers. They built their first mill in Piraeus in 1872. It imported cotton, mostly from the Ottoman Empire, and employed a workforce of 150 people, who, utilising hand-powered spinners, produced a

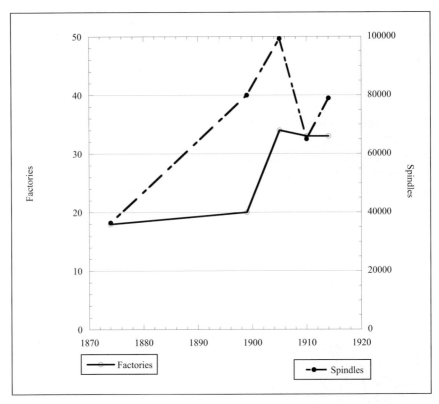

Figure 7.23 *Greek textile production (Papastefanaki 2004: 2).*

Table 7.6 *Greek cotton production, 1874–1914.*

Year	Factories	Spindles	Looms
1874	18	36,468	—
1899	20	80,000	1,050
1905	34	99,300	1,165
1910	—	65,000	—
1914	33	78,975	1,561

Papastefanaki 2004: 2

modest number of spindles (Papastefanaki 2009: 143; 2004, 2006). By 1905 the brothers had expanded their operation to include three steam-driven mills, one that produced cotton thread and yarn, another that wove so-called 'American cloth' (plain white cotton sheeting), and a third that used power-looms to weave multicoloured finished cloth. All told, the Retsinas mills operated 30,000 steam-

Figure 7.24 *Men and women working in a textile mill, postcard 1901*
© *Thomas W. Gallant Photographic Collection.*

driven spinning machines and 400 power-looms (Clark 1905: 23). The Retsinas brothers' story captures well the experience of the Greek textile industry as a whole.

In the Ottoman Empire, Macedonia, and in particular the area around Naoussa, emerged as a major production centre. By 1900, for example, almost one-third of all cotton spinning was located there (Lapavitsas 2004: 2; 2006). Greek Ottoman families, like the Lappas-Hajdimoulases, owned and operated water-driven textile mills in Naoussa and Salonika, importing raw material from both

Greece and other areas of the Ottoman Empire (Quataert 2011). They sold their finished product mostly to domestic markets. Almost all of the mills built and operated before 1900 were primarily powered by water, and it was only in the early twentieth century that steam began to take over. With the introduction of steam, the locus of production shifted from southern Macedonia to Salonika. Between 1906 and1909 alone, for example, the number of spindles produced rose from 42,900 to 60,000 and the total output of yarn increased from 2,900,000 to 5,000,000 kilos (Quataert 1993: 44). Though still caught between tradition and modernity, the textile industry clearly underwent important changes during the late nineteenth century (Pamuk 1986).

The same can be said, perhaps even more emphatically, for the processing of secondary agricultural products, and in particular in the production of olive oil. The two most important stages in the production of olive oil, crushing the olives into pulp and then pressing it to extract the oil, were both readily amenable to the application of steam power. The rotary motion needed to rotate the crushing stones was easily generated by a steam engine and, since it put out much greater levels of power, the size of the crushing unit (including the stones and the iron basin in which they sat) could be much larger, causing a dramatically high jump in productivity. Olive pressing as well was fully mechanised. Now, instead of utilising a simple screw press, a steam engine propelled a piston-like presser that extracted much more oil than was the case with the older technology. In addition, these new iron machines made it possible for the first time to extract oil from olive kernels. Kernel oil, while not suitable for human consumption, was excellent for making soap. The greater productivity achieved in steam-driven olive mills helps to explain why these types of factories employed fewer workers than textile mills (see Table 7.2).

The number of steam-driven mills rose dramatically in the key olive oil-producing areas of Greece and the Ottoman Empire during the last twenty years of the nineteenth century and the early twentieth century. By 1913 on Lesbos, for example, there were 113 steam-driven olive oil mills and six mills producing kernel oil, whereas a few decades earlier there was only a handful (Table 7.7; Sifneos 2002: 69). Much the same happened on Crete. But in spite of these advances in mechanisation, across the region generally, the older water- or animal-powered mills still predominated. According to one estimate, in the late nineteenth century on Crete, there were

Table 7.7   *Mechanised factories on Lesbos, 1913.*

Manufacturing sector	Number of factories	Percentage of factories
Olive oil mills	113	70%
Flour mills	15	9%
Soapworks	14	9%
Olive kernel oil mills	6	4%
Tanneries	3	2%
Machine-shops	2	1%
Textile mills	2	1%
Other	7	4%
Total	162	100%

Sifneos 2002: 77

Table 7.8   *Soapworks in Greece and selected areas of the Ottoman Empire, 1896.*

	Number of factories	Percentage of factories
Lesbos (OE)	42	40%
Crete (OE)	29	27%
Zakynthos (GR)	14	13%
Piraeus (GR)	4	4%
Kerkyra (GR)	4	4%
Phthiotida (GR)	2	2%
Elefsian (GR)	2	2%
Remainder of Greece	8	8%
Total	105	100%

Sifneos 2002: 77

well over 3,000 olive mills and only around 120 were powered by steam (Adiyeke and Adiyeke 2006: 160).

This was the case in soap manufacturing as well. The domestic and international demand for olive oil soap rose dramatically in the late nineteenth century, and these burgeoning markets were the driving force behind the expansion of olive cultivation and the establishment of more productive olive mills. It also led to, of course, the building of factories to produce soap. Table 7.8 records the distribution of soapworks in Greece and the Ottoman Empire; as it shows, 67 per cent of them were located on Lesbos and Crete, while in Greece the major sites of production were Zakynthos, Piraeus and Kerkira. Soapworks were frequently built adjacent to olive mills, and this made sense for a number of reasons. It reduced transportation costs, and with the introduction of steam, the two mills could share the same engines. Only one stage in the production of soap, that of cutting the huge slabs of soap into bars, could be mechanised, but what these factories did need was huge quantities of boiling water, which could of course be obtained from the same boilers that drove the engines. In spite of the relatively significant increase in mechanisation, just as with olive milling, soap manufacturing remained caught between older and newer modes of production. On Lesbos in 1913, for example, of the fifty-three soap factories operating on the island, only fourteen employed steam engines.

So far this section has emphasised the positive and quantitatively significant strides that the manufacturing sector made. But it needs to be made abundantly clear that both Greece and the Ottoman Empire remained primarily agrarian societies. If we look at the distribution of the labouring population by the sector they worked in, we see only a modest shift from agriculture to industry. According to the 1861 Greek census, 74 per cent of the working population worked in farming or activities related to the rural economy, while industry accounted for only 8 per cent. By 1907, the relative proportions had shifted to 65 per cent and 15 per cent. The overwhelming majority of men, then, continued to work the land. And, even among those men who were listed as working in 'industry', only a fraction of them worked in manufacturing (for a discussion of wage labour during this period, see Fountanopoulos 1999: 86–121). The census lumped together occupations such as construction, transportation, and other types of manual labour as industry. Of course, many of these jobs were related to the expansion of manufacturing and its related sectors, such as building houses in the expanding cities and towns.

The labour picture in regard to women looks even more traditional. First, the overwhelming majority of them (approximately 90 per cent) did not work outside the home, according to the official data. As we saw in the last chapter, many women in rural areas and particularly in the cities, like Athens and Piraeus, worked at home to produce goods, especially finished textiles, intended for the market. Women, of course, also provided essential labour in agriculture. But in the eyes of the state, they were categorised as non-employed. In regard to female labour sectors outside the home, the most important in order of magnitude were: domestic service, manufacturing (overwhelmingly in the textile industry) and prostitution (see Table 7.9; on domestic service, see Hantzaroula 2010; 2012; Hionidou 2005; Sant

Table 7.9   *Women working in domestic service and manufacturing,*
1870–1907.

	1870		1879		1907	
	Number	%	Number	%	Number	%
Domestic service	10,808	65	15,598	77	19,458	49
Manufacturing	5,735	35	4,732	23	19,708	51
Total	16,543	100	20,330	100	39,166	100

Hantzaroula 2012: 156

Cassia and Bada 1992; on prostitution, see Gallant 2009; Drikos 2002). We do not have any accurate figures regarding the number of prostitutes in Greece during the nineteenth century, but, based on the studies that have been done, it was probably quite considerable. In regard to the other two sectors, what we see is that by 1907, women workers were split almost evenly between working in factories and in domestic service. Labour, then, like manufacturing, experienced important changes but remained closely tied to traditional patterns.

Significant strides were made in regard to economic modernisation and industrialisation but at a significant macroeconomic cost: national trade imbalance. Figure 7.25 quantifies the total value of Greek imports and exports from 1850 to 1909. As the chart clearly shows, Greek exports rose dramatically from 1850 onwards and, even with the depression years of the 1890s, the overall trajectory continued upward. However, as it also shows, imports closely paralleled exports, except at a much higher level. In other words, the value of exported commercial crops to Western markets could not even come close to offsetting the amounts expended on foreign imports, the vast majority of which came from Europe. As we have seen, each year Greece expended enormous sums importing consumables, most especially wheat. European consumer goods deeply penetrated Greek markets. Lastly, huge sums of capital were expended abroad to import the machinery and the technology needed to mechanise manufacturing and modernise transportation. The steam locomotives and the tracks on which they ran were all imported.[2] The steam engines needed to power the textile factories and the olive mills were almost all imported from abroad and Greek businessman had to expend huge sums annually to purchase the coal to run them. There were no viable coal sources inside of the kingdom of Greece and so all of it had to be imported: coal imports to Greece

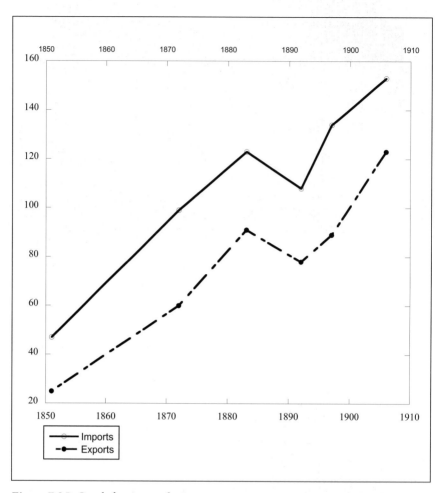

Figure 7.25 Greek foreign trade: imports vs. exports

rose from 76,000 tons in 1872 to 341,000 tons by 1911, with most of it coming from the Ottoman Empire. Greek entrepreneurs were thus caught in a developmental dilemma: 'revolutionising' industry meant increasing the already yawning national trade deficit.

The following example captures the paradox of economic modernisation in the Greek world. Beginning in the late nineteenth century and continuing well into the twentieth century, Greek consumers purchased huge numbers of Singer sewing machines. Here was a commodity that was quintessentially the product of the Industrial Revolution. Made out of iron and mass-produced in factories, it increased substantially the rate at which a worker could sew textiles

Figures 7.26a and 7.26b 'The
graceful national costume is dis-
appearing throughout Greece.
Today it is worn only by peasants
in and around Athens and it is
predicted that in another generation
it will entirely disappear in favour
of French styles made on Singer
sewing machines from English and
American materials.

In 1894 these three peasants were
photographed near Athens for the
Singer National Costume Series.
The woman on the left wears the
purely Greek dress, consisting of
a heavy cotton skirt with a deep
border of coarse embroidery. Over
this is worn a cloak of the same
material reaching to the knees and
made stiff, as are the sleeves, with
bands of embroidery. A narrow
apron worked with bright colours,
a thin white veil over the head and
neck, and bangles in oriental
fashion complete the costume.

The picturesque dress of the men is familiar to many people. Over the tight-
fitting shirt and white trousers is worn a full, loose, white garment reaching almost
to the knees. This is girdled at the waist by a silk sash used often as a pocket. Over
this is worn a short, richly-embroidered jacket, with sleeves open from shoulder
to waist.' (Singer National Costume Series, advertisement © Review of Reviews
Magazine *(May 1899), 70).*

into clothing. For women, owning a Singer sewing machine became an emblem of modernity. Singer aggressively marketed the product around the world. In Greece, it ran a national competition that included a huge cash prize to the woman who could sew the best traditional costumes on a Singer sewing machine. More importantly, they dispatched teams of women and men to visit rural villages to give demonstrations to the local women on how to use them (Figs 7.26a–b). The paradox, of course, is that the wildly successful marketing of Singer sewing machines actually impaired the development of the Greek national economy by contributing to the trade imbalance and by perpetuating domestic production of textiles. Whether in the courtyard of their village house or in the alleyways of working-class Athens (see Fig. 6.9), women produced clothing both for their families and for domestic markets that inhibited the demand for mass-produced factory goods. In other words, here was a modern product that in important ways insured the continuation of traditional modes of production.

Markets and maritime

The last aspect of the economy that we need to examine relates to markets and marketing. Internally, the Greek world was interconnected by a dense network of markets that served local needs, while externally, a well-developed system of maritime commerce connected it to foreign markets. Scattered across Greece and Ottoman Europe were market towns that served the surrounding hinterland. In the Peloponnesos, for example, there were numerous market towns, like Sparta, Argos, Tripolis, Kalamata and many more. Farmers came to town to sell and buy goods, and to acquire specialised services only available there. Fig. 7.27 captures the hustle and bustle of the *agora* (market) in Argos in the late 1800s. We see vendors hawking their goods, and men and women picking through piles of vegetables. Scenes like this could be found in any one of the towns listed above. But in addition to the town, rural villages were connected to the market via periodic market fairs. In 1862 there were no less than twenty-two such market fairs in the kingdom of Greece, mostly taking place during spring and summer, and especially at harvest time (Chatziioannou 2003: 78; also Parveva 2003; 2009; Razhdavichka 2006; Toksöz 2010: 114).

Merchants selling various wares, artisans offering their services to make tools or other items that rural folk needed, along with

Figure 7.27 *Market day in Argos, 1907 © Library of Congress Prints and Photography Division.*

musicians, singers, and others providing entertainment annually traversed a circuit that spanned the southern Balkans. Tramp shipping played at sea the same role as market fairs on land. Because of the overwhelming presence of the sea and the region's extensive coastline, it was easier and cheaper to move bulk goods and commodities on small boats. Fig. 7.28 captures a moment on the waterfront of Aegina, as a boatload of the island's prized ceramic products were loaded onto boats to be shipped to markets in Greece and the Ottoman Empire. For much of the year, then, the countryside was alive with movement. There was the constant and regular comings and goings of people with their goods and their animals travelling to local markets and towns, or to other parts of the Greek

Figure 7.28 *Tramp shipping of ceramics from Aegina, early twentieth century, postcard © J. Bouchard & Sons, 1901.*

world, as part of the larger caravans that interconnected the region through periodic market fairs.

'There should be no doubt that shipping had an important role in the Greek development process of the nineteenth century' and 'that shipping along with agriculture can be regarded as the leading sectors in the development of the Greek economy in the period' (Haralaftis and Kostelenos 2012: 1426). The type of shipping they are referring to differed from the type we just discussed in that this shipping was international in character. As we saw earlier, Greeks had played a major role in Mediterranean maritime shipping since the late eighteenth century and their presence only grew greater during the next century. After the foundation of the kingdom of Greece, there were three major centres of Greek shipping: Russia, centred around the port cities of Odessa, Taganrog and Mariupol on the Black Sea and the Sea of Azov (Sifneos 2005; 2011; 2013; Shliakhov 2013); the Ottoman Empire's major port cities of Salonika, Istanbul, Smyrna, Trabzon and Alexandria (Frangakis-Syrett 1998) and, of course, Piraeus, Patras and Hermoupolis, and after 1864, the Ionian Islands, in Greece (Harlaftis 2003; 2006; Gekas 2009).

With the introduction of large, open-water steamships during the latter part of the century, Greek shipping really took off (Kardasis 1997). As the recent, detailed study by Harlaftis and Kostelenos shows, the net tonnage of Greek-owned steamships rose from practically nothing in the late 1870s to over 700,000 tons by 1910 (2012: 1406, fig. 1). Maritime shipping, then, constituted one of the most important economic elements in the Greek world. It was the means by which imports and exports of the commodities we discussed earlier were transported. It had the knock-on effect of creating employment opportunities for men as ship captains and seamen, as dockworkers and as shipbuilders. Greek sailors were a ubiquitous feature of every Mediterranean port city, so much so that the common language of waterfront communities was a dialect of Greek (Gallant 2009; 2015 forthcoming). Just as the traditional triad of olives, grapes and cereals remained at the heart of the Greek diet, so too did the trinity of farming, shepherding and sailing persist as the fundamental basis of the economy. There were, as we have seen, significant strides taken toward the modernisation of the economy and the Industrial Revolution left its mark on the Greek world. But it did so in a way that left the economy poised between tradition and modernity.

Notes

1. For a general discussion of Greek rural society, see Bournova and Progoulakis 2001; 2006; Franghiadis 2006; 2007; 2011; Kostis 2006; Petmezas 1999a; 2003; 2006; 2009b.
2. Many of the earliest steam engines used in Greece are on display in the Railway Museum in Athens, which is well worth visiting. All of them were foreign imports.

CHAPTER 8

The Greek fin-de-siècle *(1893–1913)*

The *fin-de-siècle* (1895–1913) was a tumultuous, confusing and conflicted time for Greeks, to say the least. The two images opposite (Figs 8.1a and 8.1b) capture all of these elements. In one, we see Greeks in the kingdom of Greece flocking to the banner of war against the Ottoman Empire in 1897. In the other, produced only eleven years later, we see an Ottoman soldier and Macedonian Greek insurgent shaking hands to celebrate what promised to be a new era of multicultural peace and democracy in the Ottoman Empire following the Young Turk revolution of 1908. The country of Greece would witness some incredible highs, such as the Olympic Games of 1896 and the addition of Epiros and Macedonia in 1913, and some astonishing lows, like bankruptcy in 1893, a humiliating defeat on the battlefield in 1897, and the collapse of parliamentary democracy in 1909. It was also a time of increasing social polarisation. Some people, as we saw earlier, both inside and outside the kingdom were growing phenomenally rich. Like the famous robber barons of the United States at the same period, Ottoman Greek entrepreneurs, financiers and industrialists were taking advantage of the increasingly interconnected global markets to gain great wealth. Meanwhile poverty, both in the cities and in the countryside, spread deeply and widely. One result of this was a massive exodus of Greeks from the kingdom and from the Ottoman Empire, with the vast majority of emigrants settling in the US.

Also casting a pall over the entire region were ongoing and increasingly virulent episodes of violence. This was the case in the areas where competing Balkan irredentisms clashed, like Macedonia. Intercommunal unrest was also occurring in the newly created independent Balkan states, where exclusionary nationalist policies were making life more difficult for minority populations. Lastly, in areas of the Ottoman Empire further to the east there were escalating tensions between Muslims and non-Muslims that would soon explode into some of the worst episodes of civilian violence in

Figure 8.1a *Recruits for the Greek army gather before the Thesseion in Athens (1897) © Library of Congress Prints and Photography Division.*

Figure 8.1b *Greek and Muslim fighters after the Young Turk revolution (1908) © Greek National History Museum.*

modern times. By the end of the period, the partitioning of the Ottoman Empire in Europe would be nearly complete; Bulgarian, Serbian, and especially Greek irredentism would experience their greatest gains; the Greek world would have expanded to now encompass North America; and the situation of Ottoman Greeks within the empire was growing increasingly precarious.

The political fallout of bankruptcy

King George I appointed a caretaker government under the leadership of veteran economist Sotiris Sotiropoulos and it proved incapable of dealing with the economic crisis. In spite of his long service as Minister of Finance and his international name-recognition, Sotiropoulos was widely known in Western Europe because of the memoir he penned about his experience of having been kidnapped by bandits and which had been translated into English (Sotiropoulos 1866; Bagdon's translation was published in 1868), Sotiropoulos was unsuccessful in his attempts to renegotiate the terms of the Greek debt with its foreign creditors. They rejected his plan, which was to offer payment in promissory notes rather than in hard currency. The paper was worthless and everyone knew it, and if anything it highlighted Greece's destitute state. Nor was he able to make much headway in enacting internal reforms. Since he had been appointed without having won an election, he enjoyed little to no support in parliament, even amongst members of his own National Party. His six-month term of office came to an end in November 1893 when Trikoupis reasserted his right as head of the party with the largest contingent in parliament to lead the new government.

This was to be his seventh and final term of office, and it lasted sixteen months (from November 1893 to January 1895). The challenges his government faced were formidable and the opposition to his administration was intractable. Greece's economic situation continued to deteriorate. Globally, the Great Depression worsened as markets continued to contract and as more countries found themselves on the verge of bankruptcy. Thus, the prices for dried fruits on world markets, especially for currants, continued to plummet (Morilla, Olmstead and Rhode 1999: 327). The French legal proscriptions on Greek imports hit hard, with the value of Greek exports to French markets falling in value by over 70 per cent of what they had been as recently as in 1893 (Bassino and Dormois 2010). Correspondingly, Greek government revenues from the tariffs on exports fell precipitously. Trikoupis endeavoured to make up the difference by borrowing from international financial markets but his entreaties fell on deaf ears, especially after he proposed imposing a 70 per cent reduction, or haircut, on the existing foreign debt (*The Times* of London, Monday, 2 September 1895; p. 9; issue 34671; col G). Not even Ottoman Greek entrepreneurs and financiers, who had played so important a role during the 1880s, would lend to Greece in the face of such economic uncertainty. He had, then, to address the financial situation internally. This meant dramatic spending cuts and a firm policy of austerity. All sectors of government felt the axe, but none more so than the military. On the revenue side, the government raised almost all of the existing taxes, thus rendering even more onerous the burden on Greek taxpayers, who had already seen their taxes double over the previous decade. Then he introduced other fiscal exactions, and none that was more despised than the new property tax. It is fair to say that Trikoupis's financial policies managed to alienate almost every sector of Greek society.

Other issues loomed large as well. Prominent among these were the Olympic Games; more will be said about them shortly, but the point to be made here was that Greece had to incur the financial burden of preparing the facilities for the games. Trikoupis thought that Greece should withdraw its offer to host them, considering them to be an 'expensive frippery' (quoted in Lewellyn Smith 2004: 3), but this suggestion met with fierce opposition from the monarchy and from society as a whole. The other momentous issue of the day was the National Question. The situation in Macedonia was deteriorating rapidly and on Crete whispers of revolution were in the air once again. As important as these were, for Trikoupis they were secondary to the financial crisis. Deliyiannis and the National Party obstructed Modernist initiatives at every juncture. Inside parliament, they used the filibuster and any other tactic they could think of to delay the passage of legislation. Pro-Nationalist media excoriated the government for its policies. Opposition groups took to the streets staging demonstrations and protests against the government. Armed gangs attacked the offices of pro-Modernist newspapers and periodicals. Even more ominously, new radical nationalist organisations formed. The most important of these was the Ethniki Etaireia (Nationalist Society). Founded by disgruntled military officers during the summer of 1894 it was dedicated to the cause of raising the country's morale and of supporting initiatives to free the 'enslaved' Greeks of the Ottoman Empire. Lastly, Trikoupis continuously found himself at loggerheads with King George I. For decades their relationship had been frosty at best but now it had become downright hostile.

Finally, the strain of having to deal with parliamentary gridlock and opposition from the monarchy proved to be too much. When Prince Constantine appeared at a public rally in opposition to the government's real-estate tax, Trikoupis formally protested to the king and when he was summarily rebuffed, on 24 January 1895, he tendered his resignation. He would take his case to the people and let them decide. The result was not what he expected. After a bitter campaign marked by massive demonstrations and violence, the election in April saw the National Party under Deliyannis win 68 per cent of the seats in parliament, while the Modernist Party came in a distant third, gaining only 18 per cent. Most insulting of all, Trikoupis himself lost. Upon learning that he had been defeated, he sent a curt note to his staff, stating: 'Instead of us, Mr. Goulimis will be the member of parliament. Good night.' [Άνθ ημών λοιπόν Βουλευτής ο κύριος Γουλιμής. Καληνύχτα σας.] (Triha 2001: 26). And with this electoral defeat the political career of the greatest Greek politician of the nineteenth century came to an end. Trikoupis went into self-imposed exile in Cannes, France, where he died the following spring (1896). Greece's fortunes would go from bad to worse under the leadership of his longtime rival.

Deliyannis and the National Party may have been in power but they were not fully in charge. Internally, the relationship with the monarchy was not much better than it had been under the previous administration and radical, nationalist extra-parliamentary organisations, like the National Society, were growing in power and popularity. Externally, the Great Powers increasingly looked upon the Eastern Question as one of the great issues of the day, largely because it had the potential to ignite a conflict between them. Pan-Slavism and an increasingly aggressive Bulgarian irredentism threatened Greece's national interests in Macedonia and the Cretan issue was stretching Greek-Ottoman rapprochement to the breaking point. Finally, the country's economic situation remained grim and showed no prospects of improving. Shortly before the new Conservative government took power, Greece experienced one of the few bright spots in an otherwise dark time: the 1896 Olympics.

The idea of reviving the Olympic Games and of staging them in Greece had been around since the 1830s. The initiative did not get very far until a wealthy Rom merchant, Evangelis Zappas[1] stepped forward and provided the funds to begin the renovation of the old

Panathenaic Stadium, which was located outside Athens on the far side of the Ilisos River. The bridge to the stadium had been destroyed during the War of Independence and a new one had to be built. The stadium itself was nothing but a grassy shell and so it had also had to be modified to accommodate spectators. The first games, at which only Greeks participated, took place in 1858. Upon his death in 1865, Zappas left a very generous bequest to fund future games, and these took place in 1870 and 1875. It was only in the 1890s, however, that the movement for a truly international modern Olympics gained traction. Under the leadership of a French nobleman, Baron Pierre de Coubertin, an International Olympic Committee was formed for the purpose of organising the games. When a dispute erupted over where the inaugural game should be held, Coubertin and a diaspora Greek, Dimitrios Vikelas, proposed Athens as a compromise site. Vikelas was elected the first president of the IOC and the announcement that the games would be held in Athens was met with an overwhelming display of support, especially from the Greek monarchy. A local organising committee was established and Crown Prince Constantine chaired it. Funding the games, however, would prove to be a real challenge (Llewellyn Smith 2004; Koulouri 2004).

The cost of the games was projected to be 3.7 million drachmas, which the destitute Greek state could ill afford. Consequently, other means had to be found to raise the needed money. Public subscriptions were started, special stamps were issued for public consumption, and the sale of tickets raised funds but they were insufficient. Once again Greece had to rely on private benefactors. Konstantinos Zappas, Evangelis's cousin and executor of his estate, had also bequeathed funds to support the games; this was on top of the monies that he had expended to build the Zappeion Exhibition Hall. Another Rom millionaire, Giorgios Averoff, provided nearly one million drachmas to complete the construction in of the stadium in marble.[2]

On 6 April 1896 (25 March or Greek Independence Day in the old calendar) at a magnificent ceremony King George I officially declared the games open. For the next nine days athletes from fourteen different countries representing four continents competed. Interestingly, the Greek 'national' team consisted not just of athletes from the kingdom but also of Ottoman Greeks. For Greece the highlight of the games was Spiros Louis's victory in the marathon. On the morning of 9 April, the runners set off from the site of the ancient Battle of Marathon, and over 100,000 people stood along the route to cheer

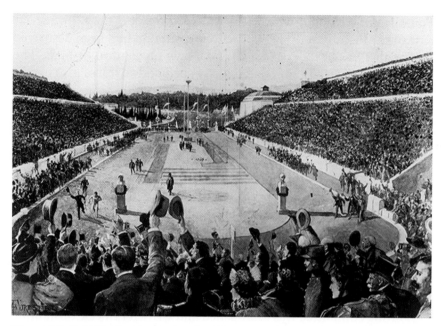

Figure 8.2 *Spiridon Louis entering the Olympic stadium at the end of the marathon © Albert Meyer, Wikimedia Commons. Running alongside him are Princes Constantine and George.*

on the runners. Halfway through the race, Louis stopped to eat an orange and drink a glass of cognac before getting back into the contest. When word reached the stadium that a Greek runner was in the lead, the crowd began to chant 'Hellene, Hellene' and it went wild when Louis entered the stadium. Unable to contain themselves, the royal princes, Constantine and George, leapt out of the royal box and ran with Louis to the finish line (Fig. 8.2). The games came to a close on Wednesday, 15 April, with a sumptuous closing event hosted and paid for by the royal family. The Athens games were widely considered to be a great success and went some way towards rehabilitating Greece's reputation internationally. Whatever goodwill the games had generated, however, would soon be lost when the country was plunged into an ill-fated and disastrous war of its own making.

While Athens was basking in its 'golden' Olympic moment, ominous developments were occurring in the Ottoman Empire – specifically in Macedonia and Crete – that would soon overshadow it. The National Question once more came to dominate public discourse and drive government policy, and the government found itself hostage to the very nationalist forces that it helped foster. Ever the populist, Deliyiannis still believed that he could play the nationalist card as a means to stay in power and yet still remain in control of the situation. But times had changed.

In Greece, the National Society became even more influential. Its leaders used the opportunity of the Olympics to recruit new members and supporters, some of whom were very influential men like Dimitrios Vikelas, president of the IOC. By the summer of 1896 it had established over 130 chapters in Greece and abroad and had recruited thousands of members. It organised massive public demonstrations and mobilised sympathetic media to demand that the government and the monarchy either take action in Crete and Macedonia or step aside. Even more ominously there were those who thought that the National Society was too moderate in its stance and they established even more radical nationalist organisations. The following proclamation by one of these far right-wing groups, the Bloody Committee, shows how incendiary the rhetoric had become:

> The time for salvaging the honour of the Greeks, who have been overwhelmed with wickedness, has come. The nation must shake off the innumerable disgraces, to which they have been subjected for so long and rise up. Let us rise up altogether. Let us get ready to make every kind of sacrifice. Let us decide to cleanse our nation of the stains of evil and disgrace by washing them away in a flood of blood from an honourable war. The King, the Prime Minister, the leader of the opposition, ministers, members of the Parliament and owners of wealth: unite for this movement as it will bring to you fame and honour. War, war again, and war forever! (Quoted in Ekinci 2009: 20; a copy of this proclamation was attached to a confidential report sent by the Ottoman Empire's ambassador in Athens to the Porte.)

Romantic nationalism was reaching a fever pitch and, as a consequence, for Deliyiannis and King George I, it was increasingly clear that external conflict in the name of the Megali Idea was the only way to avoid internal unrest. And developments in Macedonia and Crete provided them with the *casus belli*.

The 'struggle for hearts and minds' in Macedonia had by the 1890s reached an impasse. In spite of the construction of thousands of Exarchate, Patriarchate, Serbian and Ottoman schools that were educating tens of thousands of students, only limited headway had been made in converting Orthodox Christians in the vilayets of Salonik, Kosova, Edirne and Thrace into Bulgarians, Greeks, Serbians or Ottomans (Blumi 2001; Fortna 2002; Lory 2011;

Papadakis 2006). Many people, regardless of whether they were Slavophones or Grecophones, still held on tenaciously to pre-national identities, seeing themselves as simply 'Christians' (Christianoi, Rom or Romioi) or espousing a more localised identity. Moreover, new nationalist movements amongst Albanians and Vlachs were making an already complex situation even more compli-cated (Arslan 2004). New organisations emerged that believed that conversion at gunpoint could succeed where casual persuasion had failed. None was more important than the Internal Macedonian Revolutionary Organisation (IMRO).

Founded in Salonika in 1893, the organisation's stated goal initially was to foment revolution against the Ottoman Empire result-ing in the creation of an autonomous province of Macedonia and Thrace. Though the province would be multinational and multi-denominational, it would be predominantly a Bulgarian-controlled entity aligned with the Exarchate. Soon, there was a split in the organisation with one faction espousing unification with Bulgaria. Moreover, IMRO adopted revolutionary violence as the tactic to achieve its goals. This militarisation of the Macedonian question triggered an escalation of violence as both Serbia and Greece responded. The National Society in Athens raised funds to purchase arms and supplies for paramilitary groups that would infiltrate the Ottoman provinces to advance the Greek national cause. Beginning in 1896 and increasing in frequency in early 1897, armed bands based in Thessaly crossed the border into the Ottoman Empire. These activities would help to trigger the 1897 Greek-Ottoman War, but it was developments on Crete that really drove the Greek government into that disastrous conflict.

An insurrection broke on Crete in 1889 and it had come to a bloody end with martial law being lifted in 1892. As punishment for what it saw as unreasonable behaviour by a privileged group, Christian Cretans, the Porte refused to enforce many elements of the Chalepa Convention. In response Christian Cretans refused to par-ticipate in the remaining areas of communal governance, arguing that to do so would lend credibility to the regime. Even the appointment of an Ottoman Greek governor, Alexandros Karatheodori Paşa, in 1895 failed to break the political gridlock. Indeed, in some ways it made it even worse because the Cretan Muslim community refused to cooperate with him. Raising temperatures further were develop-ments on the ground. A *de facto* population exchange was taking place, as Muslims fled the countryside seeking refuge in Rethymno

Figure 8.3a *Muslim child survivor from the massacre of his village © Library of Congress Prints and Photography Division. This little Muslim boy was the sole survivor of an attack on his village by Orthodox Cretan insurgents. Over 350 civilians were massacred in the village near Hania.*

and Hania, while Christian town dwellers left either for the mountain villages or for Greece (Poulios 2013; Perakis 2011). Intercommunal relations had completely broken down and the swelling number of refugees called on Athens or Istanbul to help them. Each side formed armed gangs to protect their communities. In December, a new Muslim governor was appointed with a mandate to stabilise the situation. He failed (Şenışık 2010; 2011).

The National Society began to ship arms and equipment to Crete, while daily the Athens newspapers printed horror stories about the massacre of Cretan Christians accompanied by first-hand accounts from the refugees. On 18 May 1896 Christian rebels slaughtered the Ottoman garrison at Vamos, and in retaliation Ottoman troops and Cretan Muslim militias devastated numerous Christian villages. In an attempt to ease the tensions, Great Britain sent warships to patrol the island. The Ottoman response was to send military reinforcements, primarily from Syria. Violence escalated (see Figs 8.3a and 8.3b). The Great Powers demanded that Ottoman forces stand down and

Figure 8.3b *A Christian Cretan surveying the ruined streets of Hania, Crete, after the city was razed by Cretan Muslims during the 1896 insurrection © Library of Congress Prints and Photography Division.*

that the Porte agree to enforce the Chalepa Convention, which it did. They likewise ordered the Greek government to stop the arms shipments, which it did not.

A key moment came in July. The Christian Cretan assembly passed a resolution demanding autonomous status for the island, and the Porte responded favourably. It proposed that henceforth the island would have a Christian governor appointed for a five-year term; there also would be a freely elected assembly, two-thirds of whose members would be Christians. It also promised that the legal system and the police would be reformed and placed under international supervision. The conservative Cretan Christian party accepted this offer, but Athens and the Cretan unionists did not. As a result, the Great Powers began to see the Greek government as the main stumbling block to a solution to the Cretan problem. And the situation rapidly got worse. Under intense internal pressure both Deliyiannis and King George I adopted a more strident stance. In early February, the Greek flag was raised at Chalepa, and then a few weeks later a Greek military contingent led by Colonel Timoleon

Vassos, the king's aide-de-camp, landed at Hania and unilaterally declared the unification of the island with Greece. Sultan Abdulhamid could not let such provocation go unanswered. The empire began to mobilise its forces along the Thessalian frontier. Only the Great Powers could avert a war but they were divided over how to respond. The Germans and the Austrians pushed for punitive measures to be taken against Athens, while Russia and Britain opted for a more moderate response. But nothing would stop the slide to war.

1897 War

The 1897 Ottoman-Greek War was one that the Ottoman Empire did not want, the Great Powers tepidly sought to prevent and the Deliyiannis government in Athens could not stop. Abdulhamid's government found itself in a quandary. A war with Greece that would inevitably result in Great Power intervention and that was the last thing it wanted. The recent episodes of anti-Armenian violence had already brought on international opprobrium. Plus, the empire's financial situation had only recently begun to improve. War would jeopardise those gains. But national honour and international credibility were on the line. On the other side, *The Times* captures well what was going on in Athens: 'The destinies of Greece are now in the hands neither of the Government nor of the King, but of a violently excited democracy' (*The Times*, Tuesday, 2 March 1897; p. 5; issue 35140; col B). War fever gripped the country and there was no stopping it. Peasants from the countryside flocked to Athens to join the reserves. Throngs gathered in Sintagma Square daily exhorting the government to act. Even the royal family joined in the clamour for war. There was a mania bordering on blind faith stoking the belief that a war of liberation against the Ottoman Empire would cure all of the country's ills. Thus, Greece entered into a fray that would see the nation's fortunes turned upside down in a matter of weeks. The Thirty Days' War had begun.

If war fever had infected the Greek body politic, the same could not be said for the Rom in the Ottoman Empire. Of course, given how large and diverse the Greek Orthodox population was, we should not expect there to have been a monolithic response to the threat of war. Certainly, the Rom who held high positions in the Ottoman government were against the war, and some of them conveyed these sentiments to the government in Athens. The leadership of the various communal organisations in cities such as Istanbul and Smyrna were anti-war, fearing a Muslim backlash against their communities. Economically, while war profits would have flowed into the pockets of some Rom merchants and land-owners, they would have been offset by the economic disruption the war would cause, especially to the hundreds of firms that did business in both the kingdom and the empire. Among the rank and file, as well, there was little support for war. Few Greek Orthodox Christians in the Ottoman territories along the border joined, or even supported, the armed bands sent by the Athens government. Else-where in the empire, we know that many Rom who were eligible for conscription into the Ottoman army either migrated or found other ways to avoid serving. Their motivations for doing so, however, remain unclear. Some, perhaps, did not want to fight against fellow Greek Orthodox Christians, whereas others may simply have wanted to evade any military service. The bottom line is that in the empire, this was an unwanted conflict.

The war was fought along two fronts on the Ottoman-Greek border: Epiros and Thessaly. The latter would be the more important of the two. Under the leadership of Crown Prince Constantine, Greece mobilised three divisions, two of which were dispatched to the Thessalian front. The Greek forces in this critical area consisted of 45,000 infantry, 500 cavalry and 96 small field-artillery pieces. From his headquarters at Elassona, the Ottoman commander, Edhem Paşa, marshalled 58,000 infantry, 1,500 cavalry and 190 pieces of artillery. The Ottoman numerical advantage in numbers, especially in cavalry, proved decisive. But numbers alone did not account for the Greek defeat.

The Ottoman army was equipped with newer and better arma-ment. The infantry, for example, now carried German smokeless Mauser repeater rifles, whereas the Greek infantry still used much inferior single shot French Gras carbines. The German Empire had also sold to the Ottomans far superior modern field artillery. In addi-tion to logistical superiority, the Ottoman forces were much better organised, trained and led. A German military mission under the leadership of General Baron von der Glotz had reorganised the Ottoman army and had trained most of the new Ottoman general staff. On the other side, from the very beginning there were problems in the Greek military leadership. The professional soldiers, such as Colonel Constantine Smolenskis, had little confidence in the royal princes and their reservations proved well founded. Prince

Constantine and his staff made numerous critical errors that cost the Greek side dearly. Outmanned, outgunned, and poorly led, the Greek forces were quickly routed.

In order to get his army across the mountain ranges that separated Thessaly and the empire, Edhem Paşa had to force two passes – the Nezeros Pass to the east and the Melouna Pass in the centre. Both mountain defiles witnessed some of the fiercest fighting of the war. Of the two passes, Melouna was the more important because it guarded the main road from Elassona, Ottoman HQ, and Larissa, where Prince Constantine had his command centre. For four days, the two sides ferociously contested every inch of the pass, until finally on 21 April the Ottoman infantry broke the Greek defences. The Greek army regrouped and made a stand at the village of Tyrnavo but it soon also fell. With a secure beachhead and the mountain passes in his hands, Edhem Paşa marched the main army on to the Thessalian plain, where his numerical superiority in cavalry gave him a marked advantage. Larissa was indefensible and so the Greeks evacuated. Thus, after only a span of less than two decades, the city was back in Ottoman hands.

Prince Constantine retreated, dividing his army in two. One group marched to Farsala, where it could use the hillier topography to its advantage and also defend the mountain passes that protected the city of Lamia. The other sector of the army regrouped at Velestino, a site that controlled the main passage southward to the coastal road, along which the modern national highway runs, and that protected the main route to the critically important city of Volos. In response, Edhem divided his forces in three. Two followed the Greek forces southward, while the third marched to the city of Trikala to the west. By seizing it, he could threaten the rear of the Greek forces in Epiros. Ottoman forces were successful in all three areas. Smolenskis, Greece's most able commander, devised a brilliant plan and his forces put up fierce resistance at the Battle of Velestino before finally being defeated on 30 April. Just over a week later, Volos was taken. The Greek army was now cut off from the sea. On 5 May, the forces at Farsala were beaten. Constantine fled to Lamia to regroup, and then, following the advice of his staff, he marched the remnants of his army south to make a final stand at Thermopylai. He would not have the chance to see if he would be modern Greece's equivalent to the Spartan King Leonidas, leader of the famous 300, because on 20 May, under pressure from the Great Powers, an armistice was declared. The war was over after only thirty days.

Chaos and despair

The groundswell of patriotic fervour that helped drive Greece into war now turned into anger and rage. While the war was in progress, daily thousands gathered in public places to hear the latest news from the front. As telegraph reports continually brought news of military defeats and retreats, and then as refugees from Volos and elsewhere poured into Athens, making starkly manifest the magnitude of the defeat, the restive crowds increasingly looked for someone to blame for the debacle. The spectre of riots, revolts or even a military coup loomed. One of the war's first political casualties was Deliyiannis. Even before the ceasefire, King George demanded his resignation, and when he refused to tender it, the king fired him. The veteran Athenian politician, Dimitrios Rallis, became the new prime minister and his government had the unfortunate task of picking up the pieces. After lengthy negotiations conducted under the auspices of the Great Powers and complicated by the political situation in Athens, a peace was finally signed in December. Considering that Greece had instigated the war, it got off relatively lightly and this was due primarily to the intercession of Queen Victoria and Tsar Nicholas II.

First, Greece was not forced to cede significant territories to the empire. Some modifications to the border were made but they were minor. Second, Greece had to pay a war indemnity amounting to two million pounds and since it did not have the money, it had to borrow it from the Great Powers. This was an enormous sum, especially when we take into consideration Greece's already dire economic situation and that it had only worsened because of the war. Third, the international community used this opportunity to try to bring closure to the Cretan Question. The island would remain in the Ottoman Empire but as an autonomous province under the rule of a high commissioner selected by the Powers. As the first holder of this post they selected Greece's Prince George. The Porte objected to this choice but could do little to stop it. Consequently, Ottoman troops were removed and in their wake there followed a mass exodus of Cretan Muslims (Poulios 2013; Perakis 2011). Many others remained, however, and tried to continue on in a now Christian-controlled state. Both communities had suffered terribly during the rebellions and massive humanitarian relief was needed to provide basic necessities. But, for the first time in years, peace reigned on the great island, though not for long (on the Cretan Question, see Şenışık 2010; 2011; Rodogno 2012; Kallivretakis 2006; on Prince George's term as High Commissioner, see Holland 1999 and Holland and Makrides 2006 for the narrow British perspective on the issue).

With the war against the empire ended and at least one of the national questions closed – albeit temporarily – Greece had to confront its economic troubles. In 1898, Greece was placed into receivership. Great Britain, France, Germany, Austria, Russia and Italy jointly created the International Financial Commission and gave it the mandate to oversee the Greek economy to ensure the payment of the country's debts.

The commission was given the power to collect and then expend monies to retire the following financial obligations: (1) the 1833 guaranteed loan on which Greece had defaulted in 1843, (2) all of the foreign loans contracted between 1881 and the default of 1893, (3) the loan Greece had taken out to pay the indemnity for the 1897 war. The IFC retained a Greek company to collect and to convey to it these revenues: the customs duties of the ports of Piraeus, Volos, Kerkira, Lavrion and Patras; taxes from state monopolies over salt, matches, playing cards, cigarette paper, kerosene and emery from Naxos; various 'sin taxes', especially on tobacco products. The IFC laid out the repayment schedule, and any revenues collected that exceeded the stipulated amount was transferred to the National Bank of Greece to be used to service internal loans and other purposes. But, to be sure, the foreign bondholders came first. Lastly the commission had considerable input on Greek internal taxation and fiscal policies. In the long-term, IFC policies stabilised the drachma on the foreign exchange markets and allowed Greece to re-enter the international bond markets, and by so doing helped to foster economic growth during the first premiership of Eleftherios Venizelos. In the short-term, however, the commission's austerity regime further depressed agricultural exports, triggered a rise in the prices of imports, including foodstuffs, and thus drove the economy further into depression, all of which inflicted great pain on the Greek people (Andreopoulos 1988; Stassinopoulos 2006; 2011; Kostis and Petmezas 2006).

The decade following the war was also marked by political instability and turmoil. A large sector of the population blamed the monarchy for defeat in the war. When members of the royal family ventured into public or rode through Athens in their carriages, they were ridiculed and derided. One day in February 1898, an assassin even opened fire on the carriage carrying King George and his daughter Marie. It was not only the general public that blamed the monarchy. Both inside and outside of the military there were calls for the royal princes to lose their commissions. And the monarchy was not the only institution called into question in the aftermath of the national humiliation. The old political parties were also beset by difficulties. The Modernist party after the death of Trikoupis fragmented into competing factions, none of which could command a majority in parliament for long. The war triggered the breakup of the Nationalist Party, and the conservatives spilt into competing factions. When, on 13 June 1905, an unemployed gambling-house bouncer struck down Deliyiannis on the steps of parliament, the political scene was shaken up even further. None of the old parties seemed capable of addressing the nation's pressing needs. Consequently, new ideas and movements emerged that challenged the old political order.

One such movement was the Japan Party, or the Team of the Japanese. Founded in 1906, it consisted of seven members of parliament; they were mostly younger men who bridled against what they saw as the impotence and corruption of the old political parties. They took their inspiration from the Meiji Restoration in Japan. When this small island country thrashed the Russian Empire in the war of 1906, it became evident to many that there was an alternative to the Western path to modernisation. The Japanese experience showed that social and economic development could be achieved without sacrificing a commitment to militarisation in furtherance of the national cause. The Japan Party worked for nothing less than the complete revitalisation of the Greek body politic in a way that combined progressive socialism with fervent nationalism, especially in regard to Macedonia. In short, they wanted to replicate the Meiji modernisation miracle in Greece. Their message resonated particularly among university students and they attracted the support of many of the best and the brightest of the new generation, though it never began a mass party.

At the same time new ideologies and new political organisations from the Left gained traction in society as well. Established in 1902, the Sociological Movement rapidly emerged as the leading voice of a new socialist movement in Greece. Trade unions had also made significant strides in organising Greek workers. Labour confederations, for example, united working men in most of the major cities and towns, and especially in Volos. An organisation called the Radical Movement led by Yiorgos Skleros started to gain momentum as a political movement, especially after it combined with the Sociological Movement to form the Panhellenic Labour

Confederation. The spectre of socialism was rising and it terrified the old political order.

The humiliation of the 1897 war had other profound consequences for Greek society as well. It triggered an existential angst among intellectuals. As Peter Mackridge has noted: 'After the 1897 defeat the intelligentsia lost faith in the laos [folk] and turned to super-human Nietzschean ideals, using the popular language without its social content' (Mackridge 2009: 243). During the heyday of roman-tic nationalism, many intellectuals accepted that all of the virtues that they believed constituted the true and authentic Hellenic character were preserved in the peasantry. This led them to privilege the spoken vernacular of rural folk overthe official language of the state, *katharevousa*. The failure in the war revealed to some not just military weakness but a fundamental character flaw in the Hellenic *laos*. Disillusioned intellectuals looked for answers. Many common people believed that the crises were divine in nature, seeing the defeat of 1897 as nothing less than God's retribution on the Greeks for having strayed from the path of true Orthodoxy. Still another measure of the profound impact of the national humiliation was the marked increase in suicides (Margaritis 1997; Peckham 1999). A cultural malaise had set in that, in the view of many, infected the body politic.

The war of 1897 even impacted Greek feminism and the move-ment for female emancipation. For feminists, the war was both a blessing and a curse. On the one hand, the very important role that women's charitable organisations and nursing groups had played during the war, especially in dealing with the refugees and in helping to reform shattered families, demonstrated the contribution that women could make to the national cause. Led by Kallirroi Parren, Greek feminists defined a gendered discourse about the 'Greek character' that privileged the 'female' and that called for the legal emancipation of women. They wanted nothing less than a renego-tiation of the 'social contract' between the sexes and women's acquisition of political rights as 'active citizens'. On the other hand, the speed and the thoroughness of the military's defeat, especially when contrasted with the success of 1821, highlighted for many, mostly conservative and religious men, the degeneration of Greek masculinity. They blamed Greek women for this enfeeblement. Too many of 'the weaker sex', critics riled, had been corrupted by trends and fashions from the West. European feminism, with its excessive emphasis on individualism, had led them astray from their traditional role as the breeders and rearers of sons for the nation. In their view, the decline of traditional femininity and domesticity had contributed to the Greek defeat at the hands of the Ottoman army (Anastasopoulou 1997a, 1997b; Avdela 2005; Avdela and Psarra 2005; Psarra 2006; 2007; Tzanaki 2007; 2009; Varikas 1993).

All of these different currents of discontent and discord merged in Athens, leading to recurrent episodes of civil unrest and violence. The largest and most famous episode took place in 1901 and is called the Gospel Riot. It was sparked off by the publication of two translations of the New Testament into vernacular Greek. One translation had been commissioned by Queen Olga, who had become interested in this issue when, during the 1897 war, she visited military hospitals and refugee shelters and found that the poor people could not read the New Testament in its original *koine*, or church, Greek. But to many nationalists, any change to the original Greek text jeopardised the essential Hellenic character of Orthodoxy and thus lent legitimacy to the Bulgarian Exarchate Church, which used a Bulgarian version of the New Testament. That Olga was the daughter of Russian Grand Duke Constantine, who was one of the foremost leaders of the pan–Slavist movement and supporter of Bulgaria, only made them more suspicious over her motives. That the venture was the work of two women also made it suspicious to many. At the same time, a noted diaspora intellectual, Alexandros Pallis, also published excerpts of his translation of the New Testament:

> Most of all his [Pallis] translation of the Gospels aim[ed] to foster national moral and political regeneration after the 1897 defeat, both by enhancing the prestige of the colloquial modern language and by democratizing and modernizing national culture and opening it up to the broad masses of the population. (Mackridge 2009: 249)

In spite of their seemingly benign intent, both translations were perceived by some as threats to the nation. The Ecumenical Patriarch, Konstantinos V, for example, refused to recognise the translations as legitimate. In early November, the theological faculty at the University of Athens officially condemned all translations of the New Testament into the common language. On 5 November, university students broke into the offices of the newspaper that had published excerpts of the translation. Soon the Holy Synod of Athens also condemned all such translations. The riots erupted over 7–8 November. The students, led by a prominent history professor, demanded that the Archbishop of Athens not only condemn but excommunicate anyone who translated the Bible. They were soon joined by artisan guilds. They also demanded that all copies of the translations be confiscated and burned. Eight demonstrators were killed in clashes with the police while trying to reach the archbishop's residence. As a consequence, he resigned two days later and the government itself would fall shortly after that (Carabott 1993; Mackridge 2009: 244–54). A few years later another riot would erupt over language; in this instance it was over the performance of an ancient Greek play in the modern vernacular. In between, numerous other demonstrations and violent outbursts took place over seemingly trivial issues. What they all reflected was the deep crisis of identity and purpose that had infected Greek society since 1897.

Going to America

One of the major developments that was triggered by the crises and that helped reshape the Greek world was the massive emigration of Greeks from the kingdom and from the Ottoman Empire. Between 1890 and the 1920, over half a million Greeks, almost 90 per cent of them men between the ages of 18 and 35, left their homelands and migrated to almost every corner of the globe. Some crossed the Mediterranean and moved to Ethiopia, the Sudan, Tanganyika, and South Africa; others gravitated to places where long-standing Greek communities existed like Britain and Russia; but the vast majority looked to both the northern and southern hemispheres of the New World, and above all the other places combined, they emigrated to the United States. During the decades around the turn of the century, more than 500,000 men moved to the United States. Many returned to Greece; few returned to the Ottoman Empire. Most stayed and carved out a living, eventually bringing over a bride from their homeland (Kitroeff 1999).

The factors driving the exodus are for the most part the same ones that caused the shift in population from the countryside to the cities. Relative rural overpopulation, a scarcity of labour and low wages made it simply impossible for households with more than one or two sons to make ends meet and to provide for the continuation of the family into the next generation by providing dowries and inheritances that could sustain new households (Fig. 8.4). The 1890s collapse of the currant market, which pushed Greece into bankruptcy devastated the rural economy. Larger estates that employed thousands of wage labourers either went out of business or dramatically

Figure 8.4 *Greek emigrant crossing the Corinth Canal © Library of Congress Prints and Photography Division. This picture aptly captures the two sides to the Trikoupis reform era. Here is a poor countryman migrating to Athens, and maybe even after that to the USA, crossing one of Trikoupis's major successes: the Corinth Canal. Such capital expenditures, however, led to the financial crisis that drove many peasants, and most likely the man in the picture, into destitution, forcing them to migrate.*

scaled back production, thus putting more people out of work. Sharecroppers who paid their rents in currants now found themselves defaulting on their payments, and many were evicted. Small, private landholding peasants who grew currants as their cash crop with which to pay their taxes and to meet household expenses were devastated. A new wave of men and women were driven out of the countryside looking for work. The slow pace of industrialisation meant that there were not sufficient jobs in the cities to absorb the rural refugees. In addition, many of those who had been part of the migration flow to Athens and Piraeus during the 1870s and 1880s and who found jobs and established families suffered as well during the depression of the 1890s. Some determined to stay and fight for better conditions by joining the labour movement or one of the emerging left wing political parties. Others chose to seek a better life in America.

Four different migration flows took people from Greece to the United States. The largest one consisted of men and a few women who had either already lived in cities for some time or who had recently arrived there but could not make ends meet. According to the best available figures over 63 per cent of the immigrants to the United States were either unskilled workers or servants. Another stream swept up people who moved abroad directly from the countryside. Included in this group were the sixteen per cent who considered themselves to be farmers and some of those who listed their occupation as labourers. There was a third and smaller group that consisted of merchants and skilled workers. Most of these people moved from the city and constituted the majority of those who moved as couples or as complete families. The fourth migration stream emanated from the Ottoman Empire.

The move abroad was financed in one of three ways. In some cases, men paid for their own passage with funds that they had been able to save or to borrow from kinsmen. In many instances agents called padrones would make an agreement with young men whereby the agent would provide them with passage to America. In return, the men would be obligated to work for whomever the padrone contracted them out to. Obviously this system was susceptible to corruption and abuse, and many Greek migrants recalled the horrors of the transatlantic crossing that were only compounded when they arrived in the United States to be shipped in cattle cars to the western frontier to work laying railroad track or digging in mines.

The last mechanism for emigration consisted of chain migration. In these cases, one member of a family, who had made the sojourn previously, would send money back to Greece to pay the passage of a kinsman. In this way more than one member of a kin-group could move abroad without falling into the clutches of a padrone. As men from the same or nearby communities migrated and settled near one another, they largely replicated their natal communities in America. Greeks from certain regions thus became closely associated with specific locations in America. People from Epiros, for example, settled in certain mill towns, like Manchester, New Hampshire, and dominated Greek immigrant life there.

The mass migration of the late nineteenth–early twentieth century had a profound impact on the development of Greek society. The consequences of the exodus were both positive and negative. The most important of the positive results was the massive amount of money injected into the Greek economy by remittances sent home by foreign emigrants. It is estimated that on average Greeks sent home approximately five million dollars each year between 1903 and 1914. The huge outflow of people relieved the population pressure and underemployment in the countryside: perhaps too much so. Some large landowners found themselves having to bring in migrant farm workers from Albania to meet their labour needs. Wages in some industries also rose as companies competed for workers. The levels of interpersonal violence were reduced substantially as the most violent-prone sector of society migrated to the United States, where they were equally violent. But there were numerous negative consequences. Factory owners and others replaced male workers with women or children, to whom they paid low wages. The demographic growth of the country slowed. The number of men in their prime eligible for service in the military fell. Large sections of the countryside went out of cultivation, and numerous small villages became deserted. The massive emigration of Greeks was just one more manifestation of the crisis at the turn of the century and it set in motion one of the most important transformations of the Greek world globally.

Goudi

On 28 August 1909, an organisation called the Military League staged a takeover of the Greek government. The Goudi Coup, as it is usually refereed to in English, was an intervention in the political life of the nation that compelled the monarchy to suspend parliamentary democracy and to accede to major modifications to the political system. The coup set in train a series of developments that set the country on a new path and that ushered onto the national scene Greece's greatest modern political leader, Eleftherios Venizelos. What factors prompted the military to intervene once again and why did that intervention occur in 1909? Certainly at one level, the League was responding to the general sense of crisis and disorder that we discussed earlier in this chapter. But there were also a number of specific developments in Greece and the Ottoman Empire that helped trigger the putsch. Some of them were peculiar to the military and others were not. We begin with the external events (Maroniti 2009; 2010; Papacosma 1977).

One major factor contributing was the ongoing struggle in Macedonia (Kostopoulos 2006; Livianos 1999). As we saw earlier, the multisided conflict in the region was one of the causes of the 1897 war. With that conflict's end, the situation deteriorated quickly. IMRO, in particular, stepped up its efforts to instigate a conflict with the Ottoman Empire that would lead to either the formation of an independent Macedonian state or the incorporation of the area into Bulgaria. Their efforts came to a head on 2 August 1903 when the organisation inaugurated a widespread rebellion.

The Ilinden Uprising began in the area around Monastir (also known as Bitola) but it quickly spread southward into Western Macedonia and then eastward, with coordinated attacks erupting in the area around Serres and in Thrace. Though ostensibly a rebellion against the Ottoman state, it quickly took on sectarian dimensions. A pro-IMRO mob in Monastir, for example, burnt down the Greek quarter of the city. In the countryside, Muslim villages were attacked and their populations massacred. Greece and Serbia joined Istanbul in warning Bulgaria not to intervene. In the absence of support from Sofia, the Ottomans were able to suppress the rebellion within a few months (the fighting ceased in October) – but not before horrendous damage had been done. In the span of a few months, over 200 villages were destroyed and at least 14,000 homes wrecked. According to one estimate, over 12,000 people were massacred and over 3,000 rapes took place. Before the rebellion had ended, tens of thousands of people migrated from the region; most of them were Muslims who fled to the Anatolian parts of the empire. The Great Powers, led by Austria and Germany intervened and a series of reforms known as the Mürzsteg Programme were imposed that ended the rebellion but did not solve the Macedonia Question (Brown 2003; Yosmaoğlu 2014, especially 209–88 on the logic of ethnic violence).

In the aftermath of Ilinden, sectarian violence became even more pronounced. Serbia and Greece both proactively took measures to protect their 'unredeemed brothers' from IMRO and Bulgarian atrocities. In Greece an organisation called the National Society (Εθνική Εταιρεία) was formed in 1894 to funnel fighters and funds to Greek Macedonian warrior bands. The Society's aim was to protect the Rom population while at the same time evicting non-Greeks from what they claimed as Greek national territory. The society acted with the implicit consent of the Greek government, which itself undertook explicitly to support their activities through the Greek consulates in

Ottoman Macedonia and Thrace. Led by fighters like Pavlos Melas, the National Society provided the Greek people with a rare beacon of light in a dark time, as they were seen to be acting in the national interests at a time when the state seemed impotent to do so. When he died in October 1904, Melas became a national hero and a martyr for the nation. The failure of Greek governments to make much headway in the Macedonian conflict after 1904 contributed to an escalating disillusionment with the old political parties. It also contributed to the growing sense of disillusionment within the military. In the view of many – particularly junior – officers, the lack of political leadership was the only thing restraining them from open action in furtherance of the national cause.

An event of major importance in the Ottoman Empire also helped to spark the Goudi Coup. On 3 July 1908, the Committee of Union and Progress (CUP) seized the government and deposed Sultan Abdulhamid. They replaced him with Mehmet V, who agreed to the restoration of the 1876 constitution. The CUP brought together young intellectuals, many of whom had studied abroad, who shared a vision of creating a liberal, multi-ethnic, multidenominational and democratic state. They found inspiration in what the Meiji dynasty had done and so one of their stated goals was to make the Ottoman Empire the Japan of the Near East: economically vibrant, militarily strong and freed from dependency on the West. Through their publication 'The Young Turk', their vision of a modern and liberal Ottoman state became widely known, and its message resonated with peoples of all faiths and nationalities. It also found favour with many junior officers in the Ottoman military. Under the leadership of officers loyal to the CUP, Ottoman forces from Salonika marched on the capital and overthrew the old regime.

Euphoria swept the empire. In the first elections under the restored constitution an Ottoman parliament was convened in which all of the different groups were represented. Rom leaders played prominent roles in both the coup and in the new government. The Young Turk Revolution stood as an example and as a model for how a small group of dedicated activists could overthrow the old corrupt political order and by so doing usher in an era of national regeneration. It is not a coincidence that within a few months after the CUP's coup, a group of Greek military officers formed their own secret society: the Military League.

In October 1908, two small groups of junior officers met and decided to organise for action. Over the next few years, they recruited over 1,300 members drawn from all branches of the military and the gendarmerie. A series of events beginning in 1907 led to the decision of the League's leadership that the intervention of the military into politics was required. The first of these was the situation regarding Macedonia. Britain was continuing to put pressure on Greece to stop the activities of the Greek bands. When, during the summer of 1907, Britain entered into a pact with Russia, fears were raised that a solution unfavourable to Greece and advantageous to Bulgaria would be forthcoming (Dialla 2009). The following year, the new CUP government promised major modifications to the administration of the region. This held out the promise of ending the troubles that beset the region and could lead to Macedonia remaining as an integral part of the empire.

The radical nationalist turn of the Young Turk government in the spring of 1909 threatened to plunge the region back into sectarian violence at a time when it was clear to the Greek military leadership that the current government in Athens was unprepared to deal with it. These events came on the heels of another disastrous year economically and the consequent increase in civil unrest. Finally, the impending trials in a court martial of some of their colleagues in the military for having presented the government of Prime Minister Dimitrios Rallis with a list of demands provided the final pretext for action. Rebuffed yet again by the government, Colonel Nikolaos Zorbas and First Lieutenant Theodore Pangalos, prominent members of the League, gathered 5,500 troops at the garrison at Goudi and on 28 August 1909 used them to stage a *coup d'etat*. After bloodlessly overthrowing the government, the Military League issued four demands:

1. a written acknowledgement from the government that it had received and accepted the memorandum of reforms which they had issued;
2. formal assurance that the parliament would not be dissolved;
3. amnesty for all those who had taken part in the coup or who had been dismissed for political reasons in the months leading up to it;
4. the dismissal from the military of those officers who had opposed the League.

Rallis refused to accept these terms and resigned. King George appointed a caretaker government and did the best that he could to keep up the appearance that the monarchy was still in charge, but the Military League held the reigns of power. It had a very narrow agenda, limited primarily to issues involving the armed forces and irredentism. The coup initially met with wide support, not because the League furthered the interests of a single class, but rather because it symbolised action at a time of national malaise. Once in power, it became apparent that the League leaders were unsure how to proceed. King George was very concerned about his position; the Great Powers had never supported the coup and reiterated their firm support of the monarchy. Moreover, the coup imperilled Greece's relationship to the international financial community. As a consequence of these developments, the leadership of the Military League finally recognised that it needed to return the reins of power to civilian politicians. The dilemma for them was to find a politician who was not tainted by association with the old political parties, who had credibility on the national issues, who could command popular support, and who could thus oversee the regeneration of Greece. They found him on Crete.

Venizelos ascendent

Eleftherios Venizelos was born in the city of Hania on the island of Crete in 1864. His family fled during the 1866 rebellion and settled in Hermoupolis on the island of Syros (the collection of essays by Kitromilides (2006) provide the best assessment of Venizolos life and career). Reared in a middle-class family, he became a lawyer, as well as a journalist and a politician. Possessing an agile mind, a deep intellect and a charismatic personality, 'he was alternatively an audacious revolutionary and a thorough constitutionalist, liberal by education and principles but intolerant by temperament, a popular agitator and a sober statesmen, an outlaw and a prime minister' (Macrakis 1982: 85; 2006). Not surprisingly, he quickly became a leading figure in the Cretan liberation movements. He entered politics in 1889 as an assemblyman in the short-lived Cretan assembly. Between that date and the second Cretan revolution of 1896–7, discussed earlier, Venizelos was very active writing articles and making fiery speeches in the cause of unification. While the end was always clear, his views on the means for achieving them were not. He opted for a strategy of 'guns and negotiations', though how these two were to be balanced and carried out was never really clear. Even after Crete had been granted limited autonomy, Venizelos continued the struggle for full unification to the point of being declared an outlaw and a rebel.

He proved to be a thorn in the side of Prince George, the first High Commissioner of autonomous Crete, because he felt that the prince was bypassing Crete's democratic institutions and was ruling like an autocrat. Even after the prince was replaced by a more amenable Athenian politician Venizelos continued to push for unification with Greece.

In 1908, he was a member of the five-person executive committee that essentially staged a *coup d'état* and that would govern the island until such time as that responsibility would be taken over by the Greek government. Venizelos entered the stage of Greek politics more broadly in 1910 when he answered the call of the Military League. Since the coup in 1909, relations between the military leadership, the caretaker civilian government and the monarchy had deteriorated radically. The League's leadership began to look for a politician who was sympathetic to their cause and who could oversee the transition back to parliamentary democracy. Their gaze increasingly turned to the south (Gardikas-Katsiadakis 2006).

Venizelos supported the military seizure of power. In a series of newspaper articles, he applauded the League of Officers' efforts to clean up the old corrupt political system. They also looked favourably on him and in December 1909 asked him to come to Athens to assume political control. He was adamant, however, that he would not form a new government without receiving first a popular mandate and that meant contesting an election. So, together with his closest advisors, he founded a new party that drew supporters from across the political spectrum: the Liberal Party. After some initial political machinations, Venizelos won two resounding victories in national elections, winning 260 out of 346 (75 per cent) seats in the first election of January 1911 and 145 of 181 (80 per cent) in the second election fourteen months later.

The period from 1911 to 1916 is often referred to as the 'First Golden Age' because of the striking successes that Venizelos and the Liberals would achieve both domestically and abroad. The popular base of the Liberal Party was diverse. It drew on younger, educated professionals seeking advancement, as well as Trikoupists who saw the party as a continuation of their old movement, urban merchants and artisans, industrial workers and factory owners. The party's evident nationalist orientation helped to solidify support across the board. Unlike the conservative Nationalist Party that refused to recognise that class divisions had developed in Greece during the previous twenty years and the various parties of the Left that adopted an explicitly class-based orientation, the Liberal Party recognised class differences but endeavoured in some way to address the needs of all of them (see Agriantoni 2006a for an assessment of Venizelos's economic programme). Thus, in the period between 1910 and 1912, Venizelos set in motion his reform programme by passing a bevy of legislation at a frantic pace.

During the first six months of 1911, for example, no less than fifty-three constitutional amendments were passed dealing with the procedures and powers of the judiciary, the legislature, and even the monarchy. New bureaucratic organisations, most importantly a new council of state and a consultative committee for drafting legislation, were established. The eligibility requirements for parliament were altered; the age of qualification was lowered; commissioned officers in the armed forces were barred from holding office, as were civil servants and directors of banks and public companies. The powers of the state were expanded. The administration of public education was taken out of the hands of local authorities and placed under central control. The state's ability to confiscate private property was eased, requiring only that the state show 'public benefit' rather than compelling 'public need'. One amendment rendered to the state the capacity to suspend fundamental civil rights, such as protection from arbitrary seizure, the right to a trial by jury, the need to show cause for a search of a person's body or premises, the freedom of the press, and the right to public assembly. These amendments show the autocratic side of the charismatic Cretan.

In the months that followed, Venizelos demonstrated his populist side by pushing through an impressive array of social legislation. One package of laws attempted to regulate workplace conditions and delineate workers' rights. For example, legislation was passed which fixed wages for women and children, regulated child labour, established the six-day working week, and created a labour relations board. Trade unions were legalised and joint trade associations (these were management-controlled workers' unions which employees had to join as a condition of employment) were outlawed. Dealing with workers' issues was clearly one of his top priorities, and as he later recalled, 'there are few of my acts in government of which I am so proud as I am of the pro-worker legislation which we passed' (quoted in Anzoulatou-Retsila and Lovi 1992: 144). 'Feudalism' and the archaic law of summary seizure for debt were abolished. He legislated for the creation of a national health insurance system. Land reform and land redistribution schemes were passed and implemented. He attempted to simplify the Byzantine tax system by introducing a graduated income tax; many of the most onerous and regressive indirect taxes were removed from the books. Seen as a whole, this was the single most comprehensive agenda of social reform legislation in Greek history. Moreover, it had something for everybody, and so stole the thunder of the parties both to the Left and the Right.

Recognising the circumstances that had brought him to power, Venizelos was careful to address the needs of the armed forces. Not only was he cognisant of the potential interference of the military, but he saw clearly that Greece needed strong armed forces both to achieve his own dream of Cretan unification and to further the cause of Greek irredentism elsewhere. Consequently, he embarked on a programme of reform and restructuring of the military. He introduced compulsory military service and increased the size of the army to 150,000. Massive expenditures were made on the latest armaments from Germany and elsewhere. French advisors had been brought in to staff the new officer-training college he founded. The monarchy was allowed to continue its traditional relationship with the army, but its role become more ceremonial than real. The Greek fleet was expanded and modernised, and its officers sent to study with English Royal Navy experts.

Paying for the reforms and the military expansion was made possible through the financial management skills of Stefanos Dragoumis. He managed to raise revenues through tax reform which, when combined with new loans and renegotiated terms on existing loans alongside higher revenues, led to cash surpluses in the treasury by 1912. The nation had been rearmed and Venizelos would soon put the refurbished military to use. In his first years of office, he oversaw the reinvigoration of Greece after the financial collapse of the 1890s, the national humiliation of the Greek military on the plains and hills of Thessaly, and the malaise and discontent of 1900s. His social reforms addressed fundamental questions and problems that, if left unanswered, threatened to erupt in massive unrest – as had occurred in many other parts of Europe. His fiscal reforms brought a semblance of financial stability in the wake of the chaos of the previous decade. His military reforms had rearmed the nation and set it on a footing to compete for power in the Balkans.

The Balkan Wars

The Balkan Wars of 1912–13 ushered in a decade of conflict and violence that would completely transform the region. By its end, the Ottoman Empire after 600 years no longer existed. The Balkan Christian states had completed the 100-year-long process of partitioning the empire in Europe and creating their own exclusivist nation-states, while managing to stifle the nationalist ambitions of smaller groups. The Greek world, not surprisingly, was also completely transformed.

The Kingdom of Greece experienced both incredible highs, like almost fulfilling the Megali Idea in 1919, and catastrophic lows, such as its humiliating defeat at the hands of the Turkish National Army in 1922. Greek Russia was profoundly impacted by World War I and the Russian Revolution and would never be the same. Ethnic cleansing and population exchanges had caused one of largest forced migrations of people in human history. The Rom population of the Ottoman Empire largely ceased to exist, with only a few pockets of them remaining in what was now the Turkish Republic, the rest having been reduced to refugee status in Greece. Migration and massacres decimated the large Muslim population that had for centuries dwelt all across the Balkans to fraction of its pre-war size. In sum, by 1923, Southeastern Europe was a very different place. What caused these conflicts and why did they have such horrendous consequences?

The Balkan Wars were caused by a number of factors, some internal to the region and some that emanated from outside (see the collection of essays in Yavuz and Blumi (2013) and Hall (2000) for a general account of the conflict; see, Erickson (2003) for the military history, especially from the Ottoman perspective, and Aksakal (2008) for the political background). Internally, the driving force behind the conflict were the unresolved irredentist ambitions of Bulgaria, Greece and Serbia that produced interstate tensions between them and the Ottoman Empire and amongst themselves. Through the first decade of the twentieth century the problem of Macedonia and Thrace had remained an issue of national and international significance.

As discussed previously, during the late nineteenth and early twentieth centuries rival factions, in particular IMRO and the Ethniki Etaireia, struggled to define the ethnic and cultural identity of the region. Language and education were for a period the chosen battleground in the struggle to get Orthodox Christians to declare themselves either as supporters of the Patriarchate or the Exarchate. Many people, however, remained resistant to the attempts to get them to declare a national identity (Farrar 2003; Ginio 2005). They continued to adhere to the old ways and to define themselves by their religion and their ethnicity while eschewing a national identity. So, for example, there were large numbers of people living in Bulgaria who had no difficulty reconciling a Greek ethnic identity and adherence to the Patriarchate with being good citizens of the Bulgarian state (Dragostinova 2011: 31; see also Ploumidis 2005).

The persistence of intercommunal and interdenominational co-existence led to a change of tactics toward violence and coercion and this complicated matters immensely. The political situation was equally complex: some groups wanted total unification with Greece, others wanted a separate Macedonian state, and still others wanted Macedonia to be included in a Serbian or Albanian or Bulgarian state. Villages and even households were split, and deciding which cause one espoused was increasingly a matter of life or death. Greek guerrilla warriors from all around the Greek world flocked to Macedonia to join the fighting. Matching them were fighters from the other countries. Athens was actively supporting the irredentist movement in Macedonia. Money, materials and men were being surreptitiously sent northwards. Greek bands totalling approximately 2,000 men waged constant guerrilla war against IMRO and other Exarchist bands. Terror was a tactic used by both sides against non-combatants. In spite of the hyperbolic propaganda produced by the various factions, it is clear that atrocities were being committed and that no one group was any more guilty than the others.

The escalating violence in Macedonia and Thrace had ramifications for ethnic minority populations elsewhere that further escalated interstate tensions. In Bulgaria, for example, reports of Greek bands slaughtering Macedonian Exarchists led to reprisals against the Greek minority population. On a number of occasions this took the form of economic boycotts against Greek businesses (Lyberatos 2013). On others, it manifested itself in violence, the worst episode of which happened on 30 July 1906 when a mob burnt down the majority Greek town of Anhialo/Anchialos (Dragostinova 2011: 44–5; Avramov 2013). In the Ottoman Empire as well, Greek actions in Macedonia and Thrace instigated action against the Rom. On a number of occasions there were successful calls for boycotts of Rom businesses in Istanbul and Smyrna (Çetinkaya 2013: 39–88). By punishing Rom communities for deeds done by Greeks in the name of Hellenic irredentism, Muslims were counterproductively pushing Orthodox Christians to reject Ottomanism and to identify their own communal interests more closely with those of the Greek state.

The Cretan problem also continued to stew through the first decade of this century. The protectorate status of the island was simply unacceptable to the nationalists who wanted enosis at any cost. The matter came to a head with the accession to power of Venizelos. The Ottomans threatened war when he took up the office of prime minister. Tensions increased further when the Assembly on Crete voted to send representatives to the new parliament in 1912. The British fleet intervened to stop them from reaching Athens, and after they were released, Venizelos forbade their admission into the session. Nonetheless, the response from the Porte was clear: the disposition of Crete could lead to war.

The Great Powers were also becoming more involved in the region because of Crete and the Macedonian conflict. Britain in particular endeavoured to find a workable solution to the question. Russia had expressed continued interest in the Slavic cause, which in turn caused concern in Austria regarding its ongoing difficulties with Serbia. The Anglo-Russian Entente of 1907 only elevated their suspicions, as well as generating fear in Athens that Britain would be less supportive. And they were right to be concerned. Pressure was brought to bear on Greece to curb the activities of the bands. British Foreign Secretary Sir Edward Grey, in a series of speeches in the British Parliament, began to explore the idea of an independent Macedonia.

The Young Turk Revolution of 1908 changed the situation dramatically. The initial response to the coup and the restoration of the constitution was very favourable. The first post-revolution election produced a truly multi-ethnic, multidenominational parliament that was led by the CUP. The party's promise to democratise rule and to create a truly integrated multi-ethnic state generated great enthusiasm initially. But that soon changed. Internally, the Rom, the Armenian and the other non-Muslim communities found that democratic pluralism in fact meant the loss of much of the autonomy they had had over their own communities. In cities like Smyrna, where Rom leaders had previously controlled their own affairs, they now found themselves marginalised on Muslim-dominated city councils (Kechriotis 2009). Centralisation and political equality threatened to diminish autonomous communal authority and to reduce the Rom, and the other non-Muslim groups, to the status of marginalised minorities; in other words, if the electoral system was based on a simple one-person, one-vote system, then Muslims would dominate every election. In the end that did not happen – all of the major groups were fairly represented in every freely elected parliament – but the fear remained, and this stoked intercommunal tensions.

The CUP was also committed to maintaining intact the empire's territorial integrity. For one sector of the Young Turk movement, this issue was paramount. Christians and Jews, Albanians and Bulgarians, Rom and Arabs and everyone else were now all free and equal members of the Ottoman nation-state and, consequently, not another piece of imperial land would be ceded to any of the separatist states. This stance, of course, meant an end to the irredentist ambitions of Athens, Sofia and Belgrade, because if they persisted in their activities, then the result would be war. Externally, rather than abating outside interference in the empire's affairs, the revolution seemed, if anything, to accelerate it. The perception that the revolution showed Ottoman weakness led some European states to act aggressively towards it. Italy, for example, launched a campaign against the empire in North Africa that resulted in the loss of its provinces in Libya. In response to dissension from within and attacks from without, the military faction of the CUP gained the upper hand and so the government became less liberal, more autocratic, less tolerant of opposition and more belligerent. Increasingly a Balkan war looked inevitable.

That certainly was the perception in the capitals of the independent Balkan states. Internationally the situation had changed dramatically. The ambitions of imperial newcomers like Italy, and the vacillations of older empires like Russia and Britain, convinced Greece, Bulgaria and Serbia that they needed to act, but none of them could go it alone. A series of bilateral treaties created an alliance system referred to as the Balkan League. On 13 March 1912, Serbia and Bulgaria signed a mutual defence pact, obligating each to assist the other in case of war. The treaty also divided northern Macedonia between them. It assumed that the fate of southern Macedonia would be decided between Bulgaria and Greece. The response in Athens to this development was to open negotiations with both Serbia and Bulgaria, and the eventual signing of a bilateral pact with Sofia in May. The Bulgarian treaty was particularly important because, in spite of long negotiations and agreement on numerous other issues, no consensus could be reached on the fate of Macedonia. Greece and Serbia never signed a formal treaty, though they did have an understanding about how they would cooperate in case of war. Treaties between Serbia, Montenegro and Bulgaria sealed the deal. Essentially, the Balkan states agreed to cooperate militarily against the Porte, but after that each was expected to grab what they could, any way they could. While the treaties set the stage for war against the Ottoman Empire, they also left too many vital issues unresolved for peace to endure.

The Balkan Wars lasted from October 1912 until August 1913. On 18 October 1912, Montenegro declared war on the Ottoman government and when it responded in kind, the mutual defence clauses of the treaties kicked in and the Balkan League went to war. The war was fought across a broad front that spanned the peninsula. The Serbian and Montenegrin armies seized the Adriatic coast so as to prevent the Ottoman navy from landing reinforcements and supplies. The main contingent of their armies attacked the major cities in western Macedonia where the Ottoman garrisons were. The Bulgarian army invaded the empire on two fronts. One marched southeastward, aiming to capture Edirne/Adrianopolis and then to continue on and threaten Istanbul. A second contingent marched south toward the Aegean; its strategic goal was to isolate the largest force in the Ottoman army stationed at Salonika and, if possible, to capture the city itself. The Greek army also launched its invasions along two fronts – one to the northwest into Epiros with the aim of capturing Ioannina, and the other into southern Macedonia. Prince Constantine was once again in command of the Greek army, though this time his actions would bring him acclaim rather than opprobrium. By attacking on multiple fronts, the armies of the Balkan League isolated the widely scattered Ottoman forces and either defeated them in battle or compelled them to surrender.

The war effort went incredibly well. By early November, the Bulgarian army in Thrace had driven back Ottoman forces and was besieging the city of Edirne. In a short time they hoped to threaten Istanbul itself. Inclement weather that rendered the roads impassable and an outbreak of cholera stopped the Bulgarian army in its tracks. The Ottomans dug in for a last ditch effort to protect the capital, and a form of trench warfare that would later characterise the campaigns of World War I commenced. Neither side could gain a strategic advantage, and by early December there was gridlock and stalemate. The Bulgarian invasion of Macedonia was a complete success and by early November advanced forces were rapidly closing in on Salonika. By then, so was the Greek army. Venizelos's modernisation plan paid rich dividends. Within a matter of weeks, the Greek army pushed back the Ottoman army, taking Katerini, Elassona and Kozani by 25 October. The path to Salonika was now open and the race was on with the Bulgarians to see who could get there first. The commander of the Ottoman forces, Hassan Tahsin Paşa, saw that his position was hopeless and so he commenced negotiations with both sides. The Greeks offered more favourable capitulation terms and so, on 8 November, he agreed to surrender the city to them. Within a matter of hours of the Greeks occupying the city, the Bulgarian army arrived. Its commander claimed the city to be under his control, going so far as to telegraph Tsar Ferdinand that the city was his. A tense standoff ensued, but the Greeks clearly had the upper hand. In the west, Greek forces laid siege to Ioannina. But the Ottoman garrison put up stiff resistance and the city held out. It would take a long campaign before the city surrendered.

It is fair to say that by the end of November 1912, the armies of the Balkan League had attained almost all of their strategic goals. But it had taken an enormous effort, and all sides were near exhaustion. Negotiations commenced that ended with the declaration of an armistice on 3 December. Two weeks later in London a conference began to hammer out the peace treaty, with Venizelos representing Greece. Bulgaria and Serbia were ready to sue for peace. Greece, however, was reluctant to do so because Ioannina had yet to capitulate. Negotiations dragged on through January, but then broke down and the fighting recommenced. Of the three Balkan powers, Bulgaria was faring the worst in this second phase of the conflict. It had overextended its forces to the northeast and so had lost a valuable opportunity to stake a claim to Macedonia. Greece's stock soared when its fleet scored stunning victories over the Ottoman Navy in January 1913. Greece controlled the Aegean. This meant that the Porte was unable to move forces from the Levant or North Africa to assist in the Balkan campaigns. In addition, the Greek Navy could even threaten to blockade the Dardanelles. Greek success at sea more than any other factor perhaps compelled the empire to capitulate. A few weeks later Greece gained the other prize that it sought. On 6 March 1913, the Ottoman commander of Ioannina surrendered the great city to Prince Constantine. Greece could now go back to the negotiating table with a much stronger hand to play.

On 30 May, the Treaty of London was signed and Ottoman Europe largely ceased to exist. The big winner at the peace table was Bulgaria. Its redrawn borders now encompassed almost all of Thrace, placing the border with the Ottoman Empire only a few miles away from Istanbul. It also received much of eastern Macedonia and drew the boundary with Greece only a few miles north of Salonika, which had gone to Greece as part of the negotiations. Northwestern Macedonia and Albania were divided between Serbia and Montenegro. The treaty also established a minuscule independent Albania. No one was particularly pleased with the treaty. Serbia and Greece thought that their national ambitions had been thwarted and that Bulgaria had received far too much. Bulgaria, on the other hand, felt aggrieved because Salonika had gone to Greece. Tensions rose in the region, especially after Greece and Serbia negotiated a bilateral agreement in which they proposed to redraw the map of Macedonia.

The Bulgarian response was to attack both, with disastrous consequences. On the night of 29–30 June, Bulgaria attacked Serbia and triggered the second Balkan War. It would not last long. Greece and Romania entered the fray, invading Bulgaria from the south and the north respectively. The Ottoman Empire, now under the leadership of a military dictatorship, launched a counterattack of its own driving back the Bulgarian army. By the end of July the Bulgarian situation was hopeless and it capitulated. Three agreements: the Treaty of Bucharest (10 August), the Treaty of Istanbul (30 September) and the Treaty of Athens (14 November) ended the Balkan Wars and redrew the map of the Balkans. Bulgaria lost significant territories, and correspondingly Greece, Serbia, the Ottoman Empire and Romania gained them. The boundaries of Albania were expended. In sum, the map of the Balkans took on a more recognisable form (Map 8.1).

The Balkan Wars were a watershed moment in the history of the region and they had manifold consequences – both good and bad. Across the board, the war was a humanitarian nightmare. The military forces of all of the combatant states through deaths in battle and disease had suffered horrendous casualties. According to Hall, the Bulgarian losses alone totalled 66,000 dead and 110,000 wounded (Hall 2000: 135). More appalling, but less susceptible to quantification, were civilian deaths. During the war, each side mobilised paramilitary groups whose task it was to ethnically cleanse the territory seized by the national armies. They hoped to strengthen their claims to an area but by proving that their co-nationals predominantly occupied it, and removing all others was the most straightforward way to do so. People of all ethnicities and faiths suffered, but the axe fell especially heavily on the Muslim population (Hall 2000: 136–7;

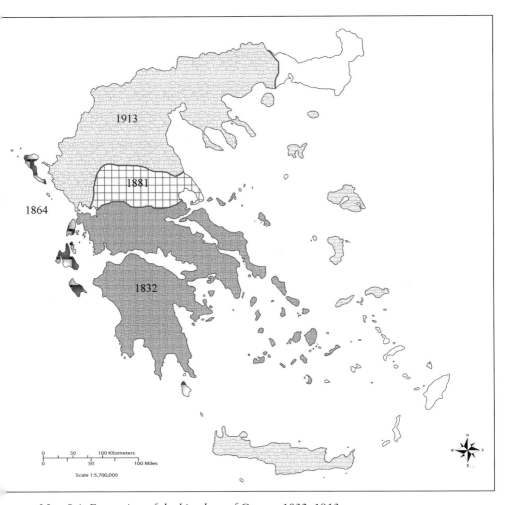

Map 8.1 Expansion of the kingdom of Greece, 1832–1913.

Kostopoulos 2007; Papaioannou 2012). Thousands were massacred and tens of thousands fled the region to be resettled as refugees elsewhere in the Ottoman Empire. Traumatised and eager for revenge they would become a powerful destabilising factor in the empire.

Under Venizelos's skillful guidance, Greece scored some notable successes in the international arena. With the addition of southern Epiros, Macedonia, Crete and some of the Aegean Islands, the size of the country was increased by 68 per cent, including some of the richest agricultural land on the peninsula. The population rose from 2,700,000 to 4,800,000. The great cities of Ioannina and Salonika (now called Thessaloniki, its ancient name) were incorporated into the kingdom. Indeed, the Balkan War had brought the Megali Idea closer to realisation than ever before. Territorial expansion, however, brought with it new challenges. First and foremost was the humanitarian challenge of dealing with huge numbers of people who had been left destitute and homeless by the war. Second, for the first time in its history, the Greek state had to confront the issue of how to incorporate into the nation-state very large numbers of people who did not possess a consciousness or a national identity that was Greek. In the new territories, there were still substantial populations of Muslims, Jews, Vlachs, Bulgarians, Albanians and others. Some, like the Jews of Salonika, manifestly did not want to be incorporated into the Greek state and in fact were terrified at the prospect (Theologou and Michaelides 2010; Fleming 2008; Mazower 2005). Others, like the sizable Slavic-speaking population, looked on Greece as the enemy, while still others, like Albanians and Vlachs, sought either inclusion in another state or a country of their own (Arslan 2003; 2004; Kahl 2003).

For the more than three million 'Greeks' outside the kingdom's boundaries the war was a disaster. While no one could have predicted that within a decade after the Balkan Wars the Rom presence in the Ottoman Empire would be virtually nil, many communal and religious leaders feared dark days ahead. Defeat in war and the loss of its European territories unleashed a wave of anger and dismay that shook the empire to its foundations. For the Ottoman political elite, most of whom originated in the European provinces, it was as if the beating heart of the empire had been ripped out. Mustafa Kemal, a prominent military and future founder of the Turkish Republic, for example, broke down in tears when he was informed that his home city of Salonika had fallen to Greece. Psychological trauma turned to outrage. The military dictatorship now in control of the CUP declared the experiment in democratic pluralism failed, concluding that the non-Muslim populations had made it clear that their loyalties lay elsewhere.

Turkish nationalism replaced Ottomanism as the dominant ideology of political discourse. Stoked by the reports of persecution, massacres and forced evictions, Ottoman Muslims looked to take revenge against non-Muslims, especially the Rom – now increasingly castigated as being 'Greeks' (Yunani) – and Armenians. Balkan Muslim refugees who were settled in areas where there was a significant Rom population, like the region along the coast of the southern Marmara (the vilayet of Hüdavendigar), sought vengeance. The

Figure 8.5 *The assassination of King George I in Salonika, 1912* © La Dominca del Corriere, *XV, 18 (30 March–6 April 1912), p. 1.*

decade after 1913 saw widespread and horrendous violence against the non-Muslim population of the empire, culminating with the genocide of the Armenians. From a Greek Ottoman perspective, then, the future looked bleak (Doumanis 2013; Gingeras 2009; Ozil 2013; Reynolds 2011).

That was assuredly not the case in Athens. The dark days of the *fin-de-siècle* seemed to be over. Even the assassination of King George I (Fig. 8.5) could not dampen the public's enthusiasm and unbridled optimism. With the coronation of King Constantine a new rallying cry was heard: 'A Constantine founded it [the Byzantine Empire]. A Constantine lost it [Constantinople]. And a Constantine will get it back.' The 'it' referred to in this slogan is, of course, the great city of Constantinople/Istanbul.

The Greeks' long nineteenth century had come to an end. Forces let loose in the 1770s inaugurated changes that completely reshaped the Greek world, redefining and reframing the place of Orthodox Greeks within the Ottoman Empire and expanding the boundaries of the diaspora outside it, especially into Russia. The bloody civil war of the 1820s resulted in the formation of the first independent Greek state. This was a seminal event and, though the new nation–state was small, impoverished and dependent on the Great Powers, that it existed at all marked a major turning point in the history of Southeastern Europe and the Eastern Mediterranean. The main themes that dominated the long nineteenth century – internal state-formation, transnational nation-building, expansion of the diaspora and irredentism (expanding the borders of the Greek state to encompass the entirety of the Greek nation) – seemed to have come to fruition in 1913. The twentieth century dawned with the promise of continued success. Such, however, was not to be. Within a matter of months after its moment of great triumph the Greek world would once more be plunged into crisis.

Notes

1. Zappas belong to a well-known family from Epiros and he had made a fortune in the Danubian Principalities by becoming one of the major suppliers to the Russian army during the numerous wars that raged across that region.
2. Fitting out the entire stadium in marble, however, was not completed in time for the games. Only the first six rows were marble. The remainder of the seating was constructed out of wood but was painted white to resemble marble. The stadium, as it looks now, was only completed in time for the 1906 Athens Olympic Games.
3. The pound, or lira, had been adopted by the Ottoman Empire in 1844. Since 1881, the lira was a gold currency. So, Greece had to make the payment in gold (see Eldem 2011 for a discussion of the Ottoman monetary system at this time).
4. It takes its name from the neighbourhood called Goudi where the military garrison from which they launched their coup was located. The name actually refers to the family who owned the area where the military barracks were.
5. The Balkan Wars would barely be over when World War I erupted, plunging the region into conflict until 1918. Then, Greece and the Ottoman Empire would fight for control of Asia Minor until 1922. In total, war reigned over the region for a full decade.
6. We will discuss here the first part of this story; for a detailed discussion of the developments after 1913, see the next volume in the Edinburgh University Press series by Antonis Liakos and Nicholas Doumanis.

Timeline

1768	The Ottoman-Russian War, 1768–74
1770	The Orlov Rebellion
1774	Treaty of Küçük Kaynarca
1789	The French Revolution
1792	Treaty of Jassy
1774–90s	Greek settlement in South Russia
1796	Rigas Velestinlis published his 'New Greek Constitution'
1798	Rigas Velestinlis executed in Belgrade
1798	Napoleon's invasion of the Ottoman Empire
1805–15	The Serbian Revolt
1814	The Philiki Etaireia established in Odessa
1817	Establishment of the United States of the Ionian Islands
1820	Civil war between Tepedelenli Ali Paşa and Sultan Mahmud II
1821	The Greek War of Independence
1822	The first Greek constitution
1824	The Greek Civil War
1825	Ibrahim Paşa's invasion of the Peloponnesos
1827	The Battle of Navarino
1830	The London Protocol establishes independent Greece
1831	President Ioannis Kapodistrias assassinated
1832	The Treaty of Constantinople
1833	Arrival of King Otho in Greece
1834	Athens became the capital of Greece
1839	The Rose Garden Decree inaugurates the Tanzimat
1843	Military intervention forces Otho to accept constitutional rule
1844	New constitution passed
1848	European revolutions
1854	The Crimean War begins and Greece occupied by British and French forces
1856	The second phase of the Tanzimat begins
1862	King Otho forced to abdicate
1863	Prince William Christian becomes ruler of Greece as King George I
1864	New constitution passed
1866–9	Rebellion on Crete
1870	The Bulgarian Exarchate established
1875	King George accepts the principle of Dedilomeni; Harilaos Trikoupis emerges as a major political figure

1876	Ottoman constitution enacted, and then suspended
1877–8	The Ottoman-Russian War
1881	Incorporation of Thessaly into the Greek kingdom
1880–93	The era of Harilaos Trikoupis in power
1893	Greek declares bankruptcy
1895	Trikoupis defeated and retires from politics
1897	The Greco-Ottoman War
1905	The Ilinden Uprising
1908	The Young Turk Rebellion
1909	The Goudi Coup in Athens
1910	Eleftherios Venizelos comes to power and launches his reform programme
1912–13	The Balkan Wars

Guide to Further Reading

For readers who are interested in following up on the history of Greece and the Ottoman Empire, there is no other book in English like this one that tells the story of the Greeks in both places over the course of the nineteenth century. There are, however, a number of good general surveys that focus on one or the other.

For Greece, most of the general books available today cover from 1821 to the present. Here are some of the best:

Calotychos, V. (2003), *Modern Greece: a Cultural Poetics*, London: Berg.

Clogg, R. (2013), *A Concise History of Greece*, 3rd edn, New York: Cambridge University Press.

Gallant, T. (2001), *Modern Greece*, London: Arnold.

Kalyvas, S. (2014), *Modern Greece: What Everyone Needs to Know*, New York: Oxford University Press.

Koliopoulos, J. S. and T. Veremis (2002), *Greece: the Modern Sequel: from 1821 to the Present*, London: Hurst & Co.

Koliopoulos, J. S. and T. Veremis (2010), *Modern Greece: a History since 1821*, Malden, MA: Wiley-Blackwell.

Kostis, K. (2013), *'Τα κακομαθημένα παιδιά της ιστορίας'. Η διαμόρφωση του νεοελληνικού κράτους, 18ος–21ος αιώνας*, Athens: Polis.

For the Ottoman Empire, there are also a number of very good surveys, including:

Faroqhi, S. N. (ed.) (2006), *The Cambridge History of Turkey: the Later Ottoman Empire, 1603–1839*, New York: Cambridge University Press.

Finkel, C. (2005), *Osman's Dream: The History of the Ottoman Empire*, New York: Basic Books.

Hanioglu, M. (2008), *A Brief History of the Late Ottoman Empire*, Princeton: Princeton University Press.

Kasaba, R. (2008), *The Cambridge History of Turkey: Turkey in the Modern World*, New York: Cambridge University Press.

Quataert, D. (2000), *The Ottoman Empire, 1700–1922*, New York: Cambridge University Press.

Bibliography

Abu-Manneh, B. (2010), 'Mehmed Ali Pasa and Sultan Mahmud II: The Genesis of a Conflict', *Turkish Historical Review*, *1* (1), pp. 1–24.

Adams, K. W. (2000), 'Mutable Boundaries: Subdivision and Consolidation in a Greek Village, 1936 –1978.' In S. B. Sutton (ed.), *Contingent Countryside: Settlement, Economy, and Land Use in the Southern Argolid Since*, Stanford: Stanford University Press, pp. 228–40.

Adanir, F. (2005), 'Turkey's Entry Into the Concert of Europe', *European Review of History*, *13*, pp. 395–417.

— (2006), 'Semi-autonomous Forces in the Balkans in Anatolia', in S. N. Faroqhi (ed.), *The Cambridge History of Turkey: The Later Ottoman Empire, 1603–1839*, New York: Cambridge University Press, pp. 157–85.

Adiyeke, N. and N. Adiyeke (2006), 'Olive Production in Crete in 19th Century', *Bulgarian Historical Review*, *3–4*, pp. 155–67.

Adiyeke, N. (2008), 'Multi-dimensional Complications of Conversion to Islam in Ottoman Crete', in V. Demetriades, E. A. Zachariadou, and A. Anastasopoulos (eds), *The Eastern Mediterranean under Ottoman rule: Crete, 1645–1840*, Rethymno: Crete University Press, pp. 203–9.

Agriantoni, C. (1988), 'Μεσογειακά αγροτικά προϊόντα: Η ελιά, η μουριά, και το αμπέλι την ώρα της βιομηχανίας', *Τα Ιστορικά*, *8*, pp. 69–84.

— (1999), 'Βιομηχανία', in C. Hatziiosif (ed.), *Ιστορία της Ελλάδας του 20ού αιώνα. Οι παρχές 1900–1922. Α' τόνος, μέρος 1ο*, Athens: Bibliorama, pp. 72–221.

— (2003), 'Η ελληνική οικονομία στον πρώτο βιομηχανικό αιώνα', in V. Panagiotopoulos (ed.), *Ιστορία του νέου ελληνισμού 1770–2000. 4ος τόμος. Το ελληνικό κράτος, 1833–1871: Η εθνική εστία και ο ελληνισμός της Οθωμανικής Αυτοκρατορίας*, Athens: Elliniki Grammata, pp. 61–74.

— (2006a), 'Venizelos and Economic Policy', in P. M. Kitromilides (ed.), *Eleftherios Venizelos: The Trials of Statesmanship*, Edinburgh: Edinburgh University Press, pp. 284–318.

— (2006b), 'Βιομηχανία', in K. Kostis and S. Petmezas (eds), *Η ανάπτυξη της ελληνικής οικονομίας κατά τον 19ου αιώνα*, Athens: Alexandreia, pp. 219–52.

— (2006c), 'Οικονομίακη εκβιομηχάνισμη στην Ελλάδα του 19ου αιώνα', in V. Kremmydas (ed.), *Εισαγωγή στη νεοελληνική οικονομική ιστορά (18ος–20ος αιώνας)*, Athens: Typotheto, pp. 145–76.

— (2009), *Οι απαρχές της εκβιομηχάνισης στην Ελλάδα τον 19ο αιώνα*, Athens:

Istoriko Arheio Emboriki Trapeza tis Ellados.

Agriantoni, C. and M. M. C. Chatziioannou (eds) (1997), *Metaxourgeion: The Athens Silkmill*, Athens: National Hellenic Research Foundation.

Akhund, N. (2009), 'Muslim Representation in the Three Ottoman Vilayets of Macedonia: Administration and Military Power (1878–1908)', *Journal of Muslim Minority Affairs*, 29 (4), pp. 443–54.

Aksakal, M. (2008), *The Ottoman Road to War in 1914: The Ottoman Empire and the First World War*, Cambridge: Cambridge University Press.

Aksan, V. H. (1993), 'The One-Eyed Fighting the Blind: Mobilization, Supply, and Command in the Russo-Turkish War of 1768–1774', *The International History Review*, 15 (2), pp. 221–38.

— (1998), 'Whatever Happened to the Janissaries? Mobilization for the 1768–1774 Russo-Ottoman War', *War in History*, 5 (1), p. 23.

— (2007), *Ottoman wars 1700–1870: an Empire Besieged*, Harlow: Longman/Pearson.

— (2009), 'Ottoman Military and Social Transformations, 1826–28: Engagement and Resistance in a Moment of Global Imperialism', in Streeter, Weaver, and Coleman (eds), *Empires and autonomy: moments in the history of globalization*, Vancouver, BC: University of British Columbia Press, pp. 61–78.

Alexander, J. C. (1974), 'Some Aspects of the Strife Among Moreot Christian Notables, 1789–1816', *Epetiris Eterias Stereo Elladikon Meleton*, 5, pp. 473–504.

— (1985), *Brigandage and Public Order in the Morea, 1685–1806*, Athens: Paragoge.

— (2010), 'Yusuf Bey Al-Moravi on the Siege of Tripolitsa in 1821', in K. Lappas, A. Anastasopoulos, and I. Kolovos (eds), *Μνήμη Πηνελόπης Στάθη. Μελέτες ιστορίας και φιλολογίας*, Herakleion: University Press of Crete, pp. 139–54.

Alivisatos, N. K. (2003), 'Τα συντάγματα του Αγώνα, 1821–1828', in V. Panagiotopoulos (ed.), *Ιστορία του νέου ελληνισμού 1770–2000. 3ος τόμος. Η ελληνηκή επανάσταση 1821–1832. Ο αγώνας της ανεξαρτησίας και η ίδρυση του ελληνικού κράτους*, Athens: Elliniki Grammata, pp. 171–84.

— (2011), *Το σύνταγμα και οι εχθροί του: Στη νεοελληνική ιστορία, 1800–2010*, Athens: Polis.

Allbaugh, L. G. (1953), *Crete. A Case Study of an Undeveloped area*, Princeton: Princeton University Press.

Anastasiadou, I. (2005), *National and International Considerations in the Building of the Greek Railroads*, Athens: unpublished manuscript.

Anastasopoulos, A. (2005), 'Crisis and State Intervention in Late Eighteenth Century Karaferye (mod. Vidin)', in *Ottoman Balkans, 1750–1830*, Princeton: Markus Weiner Publishers, pp. 11–34.

— (2006), 'Building Alliances: A Christian Merchant in 18th-century Karaferye', *Oriente Moderno*, 25 (86) (1), pp. 65–75.

— (2007), 'Karaferye (Veroia) in the 1790s: How Much Can the Kadı Sicilleri Tell Us?', in A. Anastasopoulos and E. Kolovos (eds), *Ottoman Rule and the Balkans, 1760–1850: Conflict, Transformation, Adapta-*

tion, Rethymno: University of Crete, pp. 45–60.

— (2010), 'Albanians in the Eighteenth-century Ottoman Balkans', in E. Kolovos and P. H. Kotzageorgis (eds), *The Ottoman Empire, the Balkans, the Greek lands: toward a social and economic history*, Istanbul: Isis Press, pp. 37–48.

Anastasopoulou, M. (1997a), 'Feminist Awareness and Greek Women Writers at the Turn of the Century: The Case of Kallirroe Parren and Alexandra Papadopoulou', in P. Carabott (ed.), *Greek Society in the Making, 1863–1913: Realities, Symbols and Visions*, Brookfield, VT: Ashgate, pp. 161–77.

— (1997b), 'Feminist Discourse and Literary Representation in Turn-of-the-Century Greece: Kallirrhoe Siganou-Parren's "The Books of Dawn"', *Journal of Modern Greek Studies*, 15, pp. 1–28.

Anastassiades, G. (1982), 'Interpretations of Nineteenth-century Constitutional History', in *New Trends in Modern Greek Histiography*, New Haven, CT: Modern Greek Studies Association, pp. 61–8.

Anderson, M. S. (1954), 'Great Britain and the Russo-Turkish War of 1768–74', *English Historical Review*, 69 (270), pp. 39–58.

Anderson, Rufus (1830), *Observations upon the Peloponnesus and the Greek Islands, Made in 1829*, Boston: Crocker and Brewster.

Andreopoulos, G. J. (1988), 'The International Financial Commision and Anglo-Greek Relations (1928–1933)', *Historical Journal*, 31 (2), pp. 341–64.

Andrews, J. (1993), 'Diffusion of Mesoamerican Food Complex to Southeastern Europe', *Geographical Review*, 83 (2), pp. 194–204.

Andriotis, N. (2003), 'Τα πολεμικά γεγονότα. Η επανάσταση στην Κρήτη και την Κύπρο', in V. Panagiotopoulos (ed.), *Ιστορία του νέου ελληνισμού 1770–2000. 3ος τόμος. Η ελληνηκή επανάσταση 1821–1832. Ο αγώνας της ανεξαρτησίας και η ίδρυση του ελληνικού κράτους*, Athens: Elliniki Grammata, pp. 119–24.

Angelomatis-Tsougarakis, E. (2008), 'Women in the Greek War of Independence', in M. Mazower (ed.), *Networks of power in modern Greece: essays in honor of John Campbell*, New York: Columbia University Press, pp. 45–68.

— (2010), *1821 Η γέννηση ενός έθνους-κράτους. Α τόμος. Η προεπαναστατική Ελλάδα*, Athens: National Bank.

Anscombe, F. F. (2006), 'Albanians and "Mountain Bandits"', in F. F. Anscombe (ed.), *The Ottoman Balkans, 1750–1830*, Princeton: Markus Wiener Publishers, pp. 87–114.

— (2010), 'Islam and the Age of Ottoman Reform', *Past and Present*, 208 (1), pp. 159–89.

Antiç, Ç. (2007), 'The Formative Years of the Principality of Serbia (1804–1856): Ottoman Influences', in A. Anastasopoulos and E. Kolovos (eds), *Ottoman Rule and the Balkans, 1760–1850: Conflict, Transformation, Adaptation*, Rethymno: University of Crete, pp. 243–5.

Antzoulatou-Retsila, E. and L. Lovi (eds) (1992), *Μουσείο <<Ελευθέριος Κ. Βενιζέλος>>*, Athens: The Cultural Centre of the Municipality of Athens.

Argyrou, E. (2006), 'Μηχανισμοί ενίσχυσης οικογενειών με ανδρονικό εργατικό δυναμικό', *Τα Ιστορικά, 45* (Δεκ), pp. 281–314.

Aroni-Tsihli, K. (1989), *Αγροτικές εξεγέρσεις στην παλιά Ελλάδα, 1833–1881,* Athens: Papazisi.

Aroni-Tsihli, K., and L Triha (eds) (2000), *Ο Χαριλάος Τρικούης και η εποχή του: Πολιτικές, επιδοχείς και κοινωινικές σύνθεκες,* Athens: Ekdoseis Papazese.

Arsh, G. (1985), 'On the Life in Russia of the Greek Patriotic Family of Ypsilanti', *Balkan Studies, 26* (1), pp. 73–90.

Arslan, A. (2003), 'Greek-Vlach Conflict in Macedonia', *Etudes Balkaniques, 39* (2), pp. 78–102.

— (2004), 'The Vlach Issue During the Late Ottoman Period and the Emergence of the Vlach Community (millet)', *Etudes Balkaniques, 40* (4), pp. 121–39.

Augustinos, G. (1992), *The Greeks of Asia Minor: Confession, Community, and Ethnicity in the Nineteenth Century,* Kent, OH: Kent State University Press.

Avdela, E. (2005), 'Between Duties and Rights: Gender and Citizenship in Greece, 1864–1952', in *Citizenship and the Nation State: Greece and Turkey,* New York: Routledge, pp. 117–43.

Avdela, E. and A. Psarra (2005), 'Engendering "Greekness": Women's Emancipation and Irredentist Politics in Nineteenth-Century Greece', *Mediterranean Historical Review, 20* (1), pp. 67–79.

Avramov, R. (2013), 'Anchialo, 1906: The Political Economy of An Ethnic Clash', in A. Lyberatos (ed.), *Social Transformation and Mass Mobilization in the Balkan and Eastern Mediterranean Cities, 1900–1923,* Herakleion: Crete University Press, pp. 195–228.

Aytekin, E. A. (2008), 'Cultivators, Creditors and the State: Rural Indebtedness in the Nineteenth Century Ottoman Empire', *Journal of Peasant Studies, 35* (2), pp. 292–313.

— (2009a), 'Agrarian Relations, Property and Law: An Analysis of the Land Code of 1858 in the Ottoman Empire', *Middle Eastern Studies, 45* (6), pp. 935–51.

— (2009b), 'Historiography of Land Tenure and Agriculture in the Nineteenth Century Ottoman Empire', *Asian Research Trends-New Series, 1,* pp. 1–19.

Badem, C. (2010), *The Ottoman Crimean War, 1853–1856,* Boston: Brill.

Baer, M. (2010), *The Dönme: Jewish converts, Muslim revolutionaries, and secular Turks,* Stanford: Stanford University Press.

Baker, L.-C. (1837), 'Memoir on the Northern Frontier of Greece', *Journal of the Royal Geographical Society of London, 7,* pp. 81–94.

Balta, E. (1992), 'The Bread in Greek Lands during the Ottoman Era', *TAD, 26/27,* pp. 199–226.

— (2006), 'The Insular World of the Aegean (15th to 19th Century)', in E. Özveren, O. Özel, S. Ünsal, and K. Emiroglu (eds), *The Mediterranean World. The Idea, The Past and Present,* Istanbul: Iletisim, pp. 97–106.

— (2007), 'Η ελαιοκαλλιέργεια στον τουρκοκρατούμενο Μοριά', in E. Beneki (ed.), *<<Ο δε τόπος ... ελαιοφόρος>> Η παρουσία της ελιάς στην*

Πελοπόννησο, Athens: Bank of Piraeus Cultural Foundation, pp. 90–105.

— (2008), 'The Perception and Use of Religious Otherness in the Ottoman Empire: Zimmi-Rums and Muslim Turks', in P. M. Kitromilides (ed.), *The Greek world under Ottoman and Western domination: 15th–19th centuries*, New York: Alexander S. Onassis Public Benefit Foundation (USA), pp. 40–7.

Bartlett, R. P. (1979), *Human Capital: the Settlement of Foreigners in Russia, 1762–1804*, New York: Cambridge University Press.

Bassino, J.-P. and J.-P. Dormois (2010), 'Rainfall, the Méline Tariff and Wheat Production in Mediterranean France, 1885–1914', *Australian Economic History Review*, 50 (1), pp. 23–38.

Beaton, R. (2013), *Byron's War: Romantic Rebellion, Greek Revolution*, New York: Cambridge University Press.

Beneki, Eleni (ed.) (2007), *<<Ο δε τόπος ... ελαιοφόρος>> Η παρουσία της ελιάς στην Πελοπόννησο*, Athens: Bank of Piraeus Cultural Foundation.

Bernholz, P. (2008), *Government Bankruptcy of Balkan Nations and Their Consequences for Money and Inflation Before 1914: A Comparative Analysis*, Athens: Bank of Greece.

Bevan, A. and J. Conolly (2011), 'Terraced Fields and Mediterranean Landscape Structure: An Analytical Case Study From Antikythera, Greece', *Ecological Modelling*, 222, pp. 1303–14.

Bevan, A., J. Conolly, S. Colledge, C. Frederick, C. Palmer, R. Siddall, et al. (2012), 'The Long-Term Ecology of Agricultural Terraces and Enclosed Fields From Antikythera, Greece', *Human Ecology*, pp. 1–18.

Bierman, Irene A. (ed.) (2003), *Napoleon in Egypt*, Los Angeles: Gustave E. von Grunebaum Center for Near Eastern Studies.

Bintliff, J. (2012), *The Complete Archaeology of Greece: From Hunter-gatherers to the 20th Century AD*, Malden, MA: Wiley-Blackwell.

Birdal, M. (2010), *The Political Economy of Ottoman Public Debt: Insolvency and European Financial Control in the Late Nineteenth Century*, New York: I. B. Tauris.

Bitis A. (2006), *Russia and the Eastern Question: Army, Government, and Society: 1815–1833*, New York: Oxford University Press.

Black, J. (2003), 'The Mediterranean As a Battleground of the European Powers: 1700–1900', in D. Abulafia (ed.), *The Mediterranean in history*, Los Angeles: J. Paul Getty Museum.

Blitzer, H. (1990), 'ΚΟΡΩΝΕΙΚΑ: Storage-jar Production and Trade in Traditional Aegean', *Hesperia*, 59 (4), pp. 675–711.

— (2004), 'Agriculture and Subsistence in the Late Ottoman and Post-Ottoman Mesara', in L. V. Watrous, D. Hadzi-Vallianou, and H. Bliter (eds), *The Plain of Phaistos: Cycles of Social Complexity in the Mesara Region of Crete*, Los Angeles: The Costen Institute of Archaeology, pp. 111–217.

Blumi, I. (2001), 'Teaching Loyalty in the Late Ottoman Balkans: Educational Reform in the Vilayets of Manastir and Yanya 1878–1912', *Comparative Studies of South Asia, Africa and the Middle East*, 21 (1 and 2), pp. 15–23.

Boissonnas, F. (1903), *Photographies: 1) Corfu, Athenes, 2) Peloponnese*

3) *Akrata, Ithaque. Voyage en Grece du 13 Avril au 6 Juin 1903, 3 volumes*, Geneva: privately published.

Bournova E. and G. Progoulakis (2001), 'The World of Rural Greece, 1830–1912', *Ruralia*, (8), pp. 1–18.

Bournova, E. and G. Progoulakis (2006), 'Ο αγροτικός κόσμος 1830–1940', in I. Kremmydas (ed.), *Εισαγωγή στη νεοελληνική οικονομική ιστορά (18ος– 20ος αιώνας)*, Athens: Typotheto, pp. 45–104.

Bower, L., and G. Bolitho (1939), *Otho I: King of Greece*, London: Selwyn & Blount Ltd.

Boyar E., and K. Fleet (2010), *A Social History of Ottoman Istanbul*, New York: Cambridge University Press.

Bozikis, S. (2011), 'The Political Demarcations and the Tax Mechanism During the Greek Revolution of 1821', in P. Pizanias (ed.), *The Greek Revolution of 1821: A European Event*, Istanbul: The Isis Press, pp. 181–96.

Brown, K. (2003), *The past in question: modern Macedonia and the uncertainties of nation*, Princeton: Princeton University Press.

Brumfield, A. (2002), 'Agriculture and Rural Settlement in Ottoman Crete, 1669–1898', in Carroll and Baram (eds), *A Historical Archaeology of the Ottoman Empire*, New York: Springer, pp. 37–78.

Brunnbauer, U. (2004), 'Environment, Markets, and the State: Human Adaptation in the Balkan Mountains, 19th and Early 20th Centuries', *Ethnologia Balkanica*, 8, pp. 129–54.

Burrows, M. (1986), 'French Cultural Policy in the Middle East, 1860–1914', *The Historical Journal*, 29 (1), pp. 109–35.

Caftanzoglou, R. (1994), 'The Household Formation Pattern of a Vlach Mountain Community of Greece: Syrrako 1898–1929', *Journal of Family History*, 19 (1), pp. 79–98.

— (1997), 'Shepherds, Innkeepers, and Census-takers: The 1905 Census in Two Villages in Epirus', *Continuity and Change*, 12 (3), pp. 403–24.

— (1998), 'Domestic Organization and Property Devolution in a Mountain Community of Epirus During the Late 19th Century', *Mélanges De L'Ecole Française de Rome. Italie et Méditerranée*, 110 (1), pp. 181–6.

Campbell, J. K. (1964), *Honour, Family and Patronage. A Study of Institutional and Moral Values in a Greek Mountain Community*, Oxford: Oxford University Press.

Campbell, J. K, and P. Sherrard (1968), *Modern Greece*, New York: Praeger.

Carabott, P. (1993), 'Politics, Orthodoxy and the Language Question in Greece: The Gospel Riots of November 1901', *Journal of Mediterranean Studies*, 3 (1), pp. 117–38.

Castanis, Christophoros Plato (2002 [1851]), *The Greek exile: or, A narrative of the captivity and escape of Christophorus Plato Castanis, during the massacre on the island of Scio, by the Turks, together with various adventures in Greece and America*, New York: Cultural Chapter of the Chian Federation.

Cazanisteanu, C. (1982), 'The Consequences for the Rumanian Principalities of the Ottoman Wars with Austria and Russia', in *East Central European Society and War in the Pre-Revolutionary Eighteenth Century*,

New York: Atlantic Research and Publications, pp. 387–400.

Chaker, J. E. (2012), *Eastern tobacco and the Ottoman Regie: a history of financiers in the age of Empire*, PhD dissertation, Beirut: American University of Beirut.

Chatziioannou, M. C. (2003), 'Το ελληνικό εμπόριο. Το παλαιό καθεστώς και το νέο διεθνές περιβάλλον', in V. Panagiotopoulos (ed.), *Ιστορία του νέου ελληνισμού 1770–2000. 4ος τόμος. Το ελληνικό κράτος, 1833–1871: Η εθνική εστία και ο ελληνισμός της Οθωμανικής Αυτοκρατορίας*, Athens: Elliniki Grammata, pp. 75–84.

— (2007), 'Από την κορινθιακή σταφίδα στις ελιές καλαμών: Προϊόντα της Μεσογείου με τοπική διάσταση', in E. Beneki (ed.), <<*Ο δε τόπος ... ελαιοφόρος*>> *Η παρουσία της ελιάς στην Πελοπόννησο*, Athens: Bank of Piraeus Cultural Foundation, pp. 132–45.

— (2013),'War, Crisis and Sovereign Loans: The Greek War of Independence and British Economic Expansion in the 1820s', *The Historical Review*, X, pp. 33–55.

Chatziioannou, M.C. and D. Kamouzis (2013), 'From a Multiethnic Empire to Two National States: The Economic Activities of the Greek Orthodox Population of Istanbul, ca. 1870–1839', in D. Reuschke, M. Salzbrunn, and K. Schönhärl (eds), *The Economies of Urban Diversity: the Ruhr Area and Istanbul*, New York: Palgrave Macmillan, pp. 119–43.

Chouliarakes, M. (1988), *Evolution of the Population of the Rural Areas of Greece*, Athens: National Centre of Social Research.

Clark, W. A. G. (1905), *Cotton Textile Trade in Turkish Empire, Greece, and Italy*, Washington, DC: Department of Commerce and Labor, Bureau of Manufacturers.

Clay C. G. A. (2000), *Gold for the Sultan: Western Bankers and Ottoman Finance 1856–1881: A Contribution to Ottoman and to International Financial History*, New York: I. B. Tauris.

Coclanis, P. A. (2010), 'Breaking New Ground: From the History of Agriculture to the History of Food Systems', *Historical Methods: A Journal of Quantitative and Interdisciplinary History*, 38 (1), pp. 5–13.

Cole, J. R. (2007), *Napoleon's Egypt: invading the Middle East*, New York: Palgrave Macmillan.

Cooper F. A., and K. Kourelis (2002), *Houses of the Morea: vernacular architecture of the Northwest Peloponnesos (1205–1955)*, Athens: Melissa.

Couroucli, M. (2008), *Έργα και ημέρες στην Κέρκυρα. Ιστορική και ανθρωπολογία μιας τοπικής κοινωνίας*, Athens: Alexandreia.

Cowles, L. (1990), 'The Failure to Restrain Russia: Canning, Nesselrode, and the Greek Question, 1825–1827', *The International History Review*, 12 (4), pp. 688–720.

Çelik, Z. (1986), *The Remaking of Istanbul: Portrait of an Ottoman City in the Nineteenth Century*, Berkeley: University of California Press.

Çetinkaya, D. (2013), *The Young Turks and Boycott Movement: Nationalism, Protest and the Working Classes in the Formation of Modern Turkey*, London: I. B. Tauris.

Dagkas, A. (2007), 'Peasants and Workers in Tobacco Production in Greece,

Nineteenth and Twentieth Centuries: Social and Cultural Lives', in E. Close, Tsianakas, and G. Couvalis (eds), *Greek Research in Australia*, Adelaide: Department of Languages-Modern Greek, pp. 313–22.

Dakin, D. (1973), *The Greek struggle for independence, 1821–1833*, Berkeley: University of California Press.

Damianakos, A. N. (1977), *Charilaos Trikoupes and the Modernization of Greece, 1874–1894*, New York: New York University.

Damianakos, S. (1997), 'The Ongoing Quest for a Model of Greek Agriculture', *Sociologia Ruralis*, 37 (2), pp. 190–208.

Darling, L. T. (2006), 'Public Finances: The Role of the Ottoman Centre', in S. N. Faroqhi (ed.), *The Cambridge history of Turkey: the later Ottoman Empire, 1603–1839*, New York: Cambridge University Press, pp. 118–33.

Davies, B. (2013), *Empire and Military Evolution in Eastern Europe: Russia's Turkish Wars in the Eighteenth Century*, New York: Continuum.

Davison R. H. (1976), 'Russian Skill and Turkish Imbecility: The Treaty of Kuchuk Kainardji Reconsidered', *Slavic Review*, pp. 463–83.

— (1979), 'The "Dosografa" Church in the Treaty of Küçük Kaynarca', *Bulletin of the School of Oriental and African Studies, University of London*, 42 (1), pp. 46–52.

Davy, J. (1842), *Notes and Observations on the Ionian Islands and Malta*, London: Smith, Elder & Co.

Deal, R. A. (2010), *Crimes of Honor, Drunken brawls and murder: Volence in Istanbul under Abdülhamid II*, Osmanbey, Istanbul: Libra Kitapçılık ve Yayıncılık.

De Groot, A. H. (2010), 'Dragomans' Careers: Change of Status in Some Families Connected with the British and Dutch Embassies at Istanbul 1785–1829', *Turkology Update Leiden Project Working Papers Archive*.

Deringil, S. (2012), *Conversion and apostasy in the late Ottoman Empire*, New York: Cambridge University Press.

Dertilis, G. (2009), Ιστορία του ελληνικού κράτους, 1830–1920, Athens: Estia.

Dialla A. (2009), Η Ρωσία απέναντι στα βαλκάνια ιδεολογία και πολιτική στο δεύτερο μισό του 19ου αιώνα, Athens: Alexandria.

Dimaras, A. (2003), 'Εκπαίδευση 1833–1871. Η διαμόρφωση του εκπαιδευτικού συστήματος', in V. Panagiotopoulos (ed.), Ιστορία του νέου ελληνισμού 1770–2000. 4ος τόμος. Το ελληνικό κράτος, 1833–1871: Η εθνική εστία και ο ελληνισμός της Οθωμανικής Αυτοκρατορίας, Athens: Elliniki Grammata, pp. 177–94.

— (2006), 'Modernization and Reaction in Greek Education During the Venizelos Era', in P. M. Kitromilides (ed.), *Eleftherios Venizelos: The Trials of Statesmanship*, Edinburgh: Edinburgh University Press, pp. 319–45.

Dimitropoulos, D. (2011), 'On the Settlement Complex of Central Greece: An Early Nineteenth-century Testimony', *The Historical Review*, 7, pp. 323–46.

Doumanis, N. (2013), *Before the Nation: Muslim-Christian coexistence and its destruction in late Ottoman Anatolia*, Oxford: Oxford University Press.

Doxiadis E. (2011), 'Legal Trickery: Men, Women, and Justice in Late Ottoman Greece', *Past and Present, 210* (1), pp. 129–53.

— (2012), *The Shackles of Modernity: Women, Property, and the Transition from the Ottoman Empire to the Greek state (1750–1850)*, Cambridge, MA: Harvard University Press.

Dragostinova, T. (2011), *Between Two Motherlands: Nationality and Emigration Among the Greeks of Bulgaria, 1900–1949*, Ithaca, NY: Cornell University Press.

Drikos, T. (2002), *Η πορνεία στην Ερμούπολη το 19ο αιώνα*, Athens: Elliniki Grammata.

Droulia, L. (2003), 'Ο φιλελληνισμός. Φιλελεύθερο και ριζοσπαστικό πολιτικό κίνημα', in V. Panagiotopoulos (ed.), *Ιστορία του νέου ελληνισμού 1770–2000. 3ος τόμος. Η ελληνική επανάσταση 1821–1832. Ο αγώνας της ανεξαρτησίας και η ίδρυση του ελληνικού κράτους*, Athens: Elliniki Grammata, pp. 267–88.

Dümler, Christian, and Kathrin Jung (eds) (2002), *Von Athen nach Bamberg: König Otto von Griechenland*, München: Bayerische Schlösserverwaltung.

Ekinci, M. U. (2009), *The Unwanted War: the Diplomatic Background of the Ottoman-Greek War of 1897*, Saarbrücken: VDM.

Eldem, E. (2011) 'Chaos and Half Measures: the Ottoman Monetary "System" of the Nineteenth Century, in E. Eldem and S. Petmezas (eds), *The Economic Development of Southeastern Europe in the 19th Century*, Athens: Alpha Bank, pp. 231–305.

Erdem, Y. H. (1996), *Slavery in the Ottoman Empire and its Demise, 1800–1909*, New York: St Martin's Press.

— (2005), '"Do Not Think of the Greeks As Agricultural Labourers": Ottoman Responses to the Greek War of Independence', in T. Dragonas and F. Birtek (eds), *Citizenship and the Nation-State in Greece and Turkey*, New York: Routledge, pp. 67–84.

— (2007), '"Perfidious Albanians" and "Zealous Governors": Ottomans, Albanians, and Turks in the Greek War of Independence', in A. Anastasopoulos and E. Kolovos (eds), *Ottoman Rule and the Balkans, 1760–1850: Conflict, Transformation, Adaptation*, Rethymno: University of Crete, Department of History and Archaeology, pp. 67–84.

— (2011), 'The Greek Revolt and the End of the Old Ottoman Order', in P. Pizanias (ed.), *The Greek Revolution of 1821: A European Event*, Istanbul: The Isis Press, pp. 257–64.

Erickson, E. J. (2003), *Defeat in Detail: the Ottoman Army in the Balkans, 1912–1913*, Westport, CT: Praeger.

Exertzoglou, H. (2010), *Οι <<χαμένες πατρίδες>> πέρα από τη νοσταλγία. Μια κοινωνική-πολιτισμική ιστορία των Ρωμίων της Οθωμανικής Αυτοκρατορίας (μέσα 19ου–αρχές 20ού αιώνα)*, Athens: Nefeli.

Fahmy K. (1997), *All the Pasha's Men: Mehmed Ali, His Army, and the Making of Modern Egypt*, New York: Cambridge University Press.

Falkus, M. E. (1966), 'Russia and the International Wheat Trade, 1861–1914', *Economica, 33* (132), pp. 416–29.

Farrar, L. L. (2003), 'Aggression Versus Apathy: The Limits of Nationalism

During the Balkan Wars, 1912–1913', *East European Quarterly*, 37 (3), pp. 257–80.

Felton, E. (1882), 'Domestic Country Life in Greece', *Contemporary Review, November*, pp. 675–85.

Figes, O. (2010), *The Crimean War: a History*, New York: Metropolitan Books.

Finkel, C. (2005), *Osman's Dream: The History of the Ottoman Empire*, New York: Basic Books.

Finlay, G. (1971 [1861]), *History of the Greek Revolution and the Reign of King Otho*, London: Zeno Reprints.

Fisher, A. W. (1970), *The Russian Annexation of the Crimea, 1772–1783*, Cambridge: Cambridge University Press.

Fleming, K. E. (1999), *The Muslim Bonaparte: Diplomacy and Orientalism in Ali Pasha's Greece*, Princeton: Princeton University Press.

— (2008), *Greece – a Jewish history*, Princeton: Princeton University Press.

Forbes, H. (2000), 'Dowry and Inheritance: Their Relationship to Land Fragmentation and Risk Reduction on Methana', in S. Sutton (ed.), *Contingent Countryside Settlement, Economy, and Land Use in the Southern Argolid since 1700*, Stanford: Stanford University Press, pp. 200–27.

— (2007), *Meaning and Identity in a Greek Landscape: an Archaeological Ethnography*, New York: Cambridge University Press.

Fortna, B. C. (2002), *Imperial classroom: Islam, the state, and education in the Late Ottoman Empire*, New York: Oxford University Press.

Fotopoulos, A. T. (2005), *Οι κοτζαμπάσηδες της Πελοποννήσου κατά τη δεύτερη τουρκοκρατία 1715–1821*, Athens: Erodotos.

Fountanopoulos, K. (1999), 'Μισθωτή εργασία', in C. Hatziiosif (ed.), *Ιστορία της Ελλάδας του 20ού αιώνα. Οι απαρχές 1900–1922. Α' τόμος, μέρος 1ο*, Athens: Bibliorama, pp. 86–121.

Frangakis-Syrett, E. (1998), 'Commerce in the Eastern Mediterranean from the Eighteenth to the Early Twentieth Centuries: The City-Port of Izmir and Its Hinterland', *International Journal of Maritime History*, 10 (2), pp. 125–54.

— (2006), 'Market Networks and Ottoman–European Commerce, c. 1700–1825', *Oriente Moderno*, 25 (86) (1), pp. 109–28.

— (2009), 'Banking in Izmir in the Early Twentieth Century', *Mediterranean Historical Review*, 24 (2).

Frangakis-Syrett, E. and J. M. Wagstaff (2004), 'The Port of Patras in the Second Ottoman Period: Economy, Demography and Settlements, c. 1700–1830', *Revue Des Mondes Musulmans Et De La Méditerranée*, 23, pp. 79–94.

Franghiadis, A. (1990), *Peasant Agriculture and Export Trade*, PhD dissertation, Florence: European University Institute.

— (1993), 'Dowry, Capital Accumulation and Social Reproduction in 19th Century Greek Agriculture', in *The World of the Peasantry*, Florence: European University Institute, pp. 129–53.

— (2006), 'Αγροτική Οικονομία και Εξώτερικό Εμπόριο', in K. Kostis and S. Petmezas (eds), *Η ανάπτυξη της ελληνικής οικονομίας κατά τον 19ου αιώνα*

(1830–1914), Athens: Alexandreia, pp. 153–74.

— (2007), *Ελληνική οικονομία 19ο–20ος αιώνας*, Athens: Nefeli.

— (2011), 'Land Tenure Systems, Peasant Agriculture and Bourgeois Ascendancy in Greece, 1830–1914', in E. Eldem and S. Petmezas (eds), *The Economic Development of Southeastern Europe in the 19th century*, Athens: Alpha Bank, pp. 101–36.

Frank, A. (2012), 'The Children of the Desert and the Laws of the Sea: Austria, Great Britain, the Ottoman Empire, and the Mediterranean Slave Trade in the Nineteenth Century', *The American Historical Review*, *117* (2), pp. 410–44.

Frazee, C. (1969), *The Orthodox Church and Independent Greece 1821–1852*, Cambridge: Cambridge University Press.

Freitag, U., M. Fuhrmann, N. Lafi, and F. Riedler (eds) (2011), *The City in the Ottoman Empire: Migration and the Making of Urban Modernity*, New York: Routledge.

Galani, K. (2011), 'The Napoleonic Wars and the Disruption of Mediterranean Shipping and Trade: British, Greek and American Merchants in Livorno', *The Historical Review/La Revue Historique*, 7 (0), pp. 179–98.

Gallant, T. W. (1991), *Risk and Survival in Ancient Greece: Reconstructing the Rural Domestic Economy*, Stanford: Stanford University Press.

— (1998), 'Murder in a Mediterranean City: Homicide Trends in Athens, 1850–1936', *Journal of the Hellenic Diaspora*, *24* (1), pp. 1–27.

— (1999), 'Brigandage, Piracy, Capitalism, and State-formation: Transnational Crime From a Historical World Systems Perspective', in J. M. Heyman (ed.), *States and Illegal Networks*, London: Berg, pp. 25–61.

— (2000a), 'Crime, Violence, and Reform of the Criminal Justice System During the Era of Trikoupis', in K. Aroni-Tsili and L. Triha (eds), *Ο Χαρίλάος Τρικούης και η εποχή του: Πολιτικές, επιδοχείς και κοινωινικές σύνθεκες*, Athens: Papazisis, pp. 401–10.

— (2000b), 'Honor, Masculinity, and Ritual Knife-fighting in Nineteenth Century Greece', *American Historical Review*, *105* (2), pp. 359–82.

— (2001), *Modern Greece*, New York: Oxford University Press.

— (2002), *Experiencing Dominion: Culture, Identity and Power in the British Mediterranean*, Notre Dame: University of Notre Dame Press.

— (2008), '"When Men of Honor" Met "Men of Law": Violence, the Unwritten Law and Modern Justice' in S. d'Cruze, E. Avdela, and J. Rowbotham (eds), *Crime, Violence and the Modern State, 1780–2000*, London: Edwin Mellen, pp. 69–92.

— (2009), 'Tales From the Dark Side: Transnational Migration, the Underworld and The "Other" Greeks of the Diaspora', in D. Tziovas (ed.), *Greek diaspora and migration since 1700: society, politics and culture*, London: Ashgate, pp. 17–29.

— (2012), 'Women, Crime and the Courts on the Ionian Islands During the Nineteenth Century', *Historein*, *11*, pp. 1–32.

— (2015), 'All Unquiet on the Waterfront: Eastern Mediterranean Port-cities As Sites of Working-class Cosmopolitanism', *Journal of Social History, Under Review*, pp. 1–28.

Gardika, K. (2008), 'Η Ελλάδα και ανατολικό ζήτημα (1821–1923)', in

K. Gardika, V. Kechriotis, C. Loukos, C. Lyrintzis, and N. Maroniti (eds), *Η συγκρότηση του ελληνικού κράτους. Διεθνές πλαίσιο, εξουσία και πολιτική τον 19ο αιώνα*, Athens: Nefeli, pp. 149–78.

Gardikas-Katsiadakis H. (2006), 'Venizelos' Advent in Greek Politics, 1909–1912', in P. M. Kitromilides (ed.), *Eleftherios Venizelos: The Trials of Statesmanship*, Edinburgh: Edinburgh University Press, pp. 87–114.

Garvie-Lok, S. J. (2001), 'Diet and Mobility in Medieval Greece Based on Bone Stable Isotope Ratios', *American Journal of Physical Anthropology*, 68.

Gavalas, V. S. (2002), 'Fertility Transition on a Greek Island', *Continuity and Change*, 17 (01), pp. 133–60.

— (2004), 'Family Formation and Dissolution in An Aegean Island', *Journal of Biosocial Science*, 37 (3), pp. 351–70.

— (2008a), 'Island Mortality in the Past: Some Evidence From Greece', *Journal of Biosocial Science*, 40 (02), pp. 203–22.

— (2008b), 'Marriage Patterns in Greece During the Twentieth Century', *Continuity and Change*, 23 (03), pp. 509–29.

— (2013), 'The History of Family and Community Life Through the Study of Civil Registers: Paros in the 20th Century', *The History of the Family*, pp. 1–20.

Gavrilis, G. (2008a), *The Dynamics of Interstate Boundaries*, Cambridge: Cambridge University Press.

— (2008b), 'The Greece–Ottoman Boundary As Institution, Locality, and Process, 1832–1882', *American Behavioral Scientist*, 51 (10), p. 1516.

— (2010), 'Conflict and Control on the Ottoman-Greek Border', in I. W. Zartman (ed.), *Understanding Life in the Borderlands: Boundaries in Depth and in Motion*, Athens, GA: University of Georgia Press, pp. 40–57.

Gazi, E. (2000), *Scientific National History: the Greek Case in Comparative Perspective (1850–1920)*, Frankfurt am Main: Peter Lang.

— (2009), 'Revisiting Religion and Nationalism in Nineteenth-Century Greece', in D. Ricks and R. Beaton (eds), *The Making of Modern Greece: Nationalism, Romanticism, and the Uses of the Past (1797–1896)*, London: Ashgate, pp. 95–108.

Gekas, A. (2007), 'A Global History of Ottoman Cotton Textiles, 1600–1850', in *EUI Working Papers*, Florence: European University Institute.

— (2009), 'Class and Cosmopolitanism: The Historiographical Fortunes of Merchants in Eastern Mediterranean Ports', *Mediterranean Historical Review*, 24 (2), pp. 95–114.

— (2013) 'The Crisis of the Long 1850s and Regime Change in the Ionian State and the Kingdom of Greece', *The Historical Review*, X, pp. 57–84.

Gingeras, R. (2009), *Sorrowful Shores: Violence, Ethnicity, and the End of the Ottoman Empire, 1912–1923*, Oxford and New York: Oxford University Press.

Ginio, E. (2005), 'Mobilizing the Ottoman Nation During the Balkan Wars (1912–1913): Awakening From the Ottoman Dream', *War in History*, 12 (2HAA57I3), pp. 156–77.

Glavinas, Y. (2013), 'Οι πρώτες προσπάθειες ανέγερσης τζαμιού στην Αθήνα:

Από τον Τρικούπη στον Ελευθέριο Βενιζέλο', Εφημερίδα των Σύντακτων, *172* (June), pp. 1–3.

Gordon, T. (1832), *History of the Greek Revolution*, Edinburgh and London: W. Blackwood; T. Cadell.

Gounaris, B. C. (1985), 'Greco-Turkish Railway Connections: Illusions and Bargains in the Late Nineteenth Century Balkans', *Balkan Studies*, 26, pp. 311–32.

— (1993), *Steam over Macedonia, 1870–1912: Socio-economic Change and the Railway Factor*, New York: Eastern European Monographs, distributed by Columbia University Press.

— (2007), *Τα Βαλκανία των Ελλήνων. Από το διαφωτισμό έως τον Α' Παγκόσμιο Πόλεμο*, Athens: Epikentro.

Gradeva, R. (2005), 'Osman Pazvanoglu of Vidin: Between Old and New', in F. Anscombe (ed.), *Ottoman Balkans, 1750–1830*, Princeton: Markus Wiener Publishers, pp. 115–62.

— (2007), 'Secession and Revolution in the Ottoman Empire at the End of the Eighteenth Century: Osman Pazvanoğlu and Rhigas Velestinlis', in A. Anastasopoulos and E. Kolovos (eds), *Ottoman Rule and the Balkans, 1760–1850: Conflict, Transformation, Adaptation*, Rethymno: University of Crete, pp. 73–94.

Grant, J. (2005), 'Rethinking the Ottoman "Decline": Military Technology Diffusion in the Ottoman Empire, Fifteenth to Eighteenth Centuries', *Journal of World History*, 10 (1179185), pp. 179–201.

Grove, A. T., and O. Rackham (2001), *The Nature of Mediterranean Europe: an Ecological History*, New Haven, CT: Yale University Press.

Güthenke C. (2008), *Placing Modern Greece: the Dynamics of Romantic Hellenism, 1770–1840*, Oxford: Oxford University Press.

Hadziiossif, C. (1997), 'Class Structure and Class Antagonism in Late Nineteenth-century Greece', in P. Carabott (ed.), *Greek Society in the Making, 1863–1913: Realities, Symbols and Visions*, Brookfield, VT: Ashgate, pp. 3–19.

— (1993), *Η γηραιά σελήνη. Η βιομηχανία στην ελληνική οικονομία, 1830–1940*, Athens: Themlio.

Hall, R. C. (2000), *The Balkan Wars, 1912–1913: prelude to the First World War*, London and New York: Routledge.

Halstead, P. (2009), 'Studying the Past in the Present: Archaeological Engagement with Modern Greece', in Llewellyn Smith, Kitromilides, and Calligas (eds), *Scholars, travels, archives: Greek history and culture through the British School at Athens*, London: British School at Athens, pp. 201–16.

Hannell, D. (1989), 'Lord Palmeston and the "Don Pacifico Affair" of 1850: The Ionian Connection', *European History Quarterly*, 19, pp. 495–507.

Hantzaroula, P. (2010), 'Public Discourses on Sexuality and Narratives of Sexual Violence of Domestic Servants in Greece (1880–1950)', *Journal of Mediterranean Studies*, 10, pp. 2–27.

— (2012), *Σμιλεύοντας την υποταγή: Οι έμμισθες οικιακές εργάτριες στην Ελλάδα το πρώτο μισό του εικοστού αιώνα*, Athens: Papazisi.

Harlaftis, G. (1996), *A history of Greek-owned shipping: the making of an*

international tramp fleet, 1830 to the present day, New York: Routledge.
— (2003), 'Ιστοφόρος ναυτιλία. Η περίοδος της μεγάλης ακμής, 1833–1871', in V. Panagiotopoulos (ed.), *Ιστορία του νέου ελληνισμού 1770–2000. 4ος τόμος. Το ελληνικό κράτος, 1833–1871: Η εθνική εστία και ο ελληνισμός της Οθωμανικής Αυτοκρατορίας*, Athens: Elliniki Grammata, pp. 105–18.
— (2006), 'Ναυτιλία', in K. Kostis and S. Petmezas (eds), *Η ανάπτυξη της ελληνικής οικονομίας κατά τον 19ου αιώνα (1830–1914)*, Athens: Alexandreia, pp. 421–62.
Harlaftis, G. and G. Kostelenos (2012), 'International Shipping and National Economic Growth: Shipping Earnings and the Greek Economy in the Nineteenth Century 1', *The Economic History Review*, 65 (4), pp. 1403–27.
Harlaftis, G. and S. Laiou (2008), 'Ottoman State Policy in Mediterranean Trade and Shipping, c. 1780–c.1820: The Rise of the Greek Owned Ottoman Merchant Fleet', in M. Mazower (ed.), *Networks of power in modern Greece: essays in honor of John Campbell*, New York: Columbia University Press, pp. 1–44.
Harlan, D. (2011), 'British Lancastrian Schools of Nineteenth-century Kythera', *The Annual of the British School at Athens*, 106, pp. 325–74.
Hatzidimitriou, C. G. (1999), *Founded on Freedom and Virtue: Documents Illustrating the Impact in the United States of the Greek War of Independence, 1821–1829*, New York: Aristide D. Caratzas.
Hatziiosif, C. (1999), 'Η Μπελ Επόκ του Κεφαλαίου', in C. Hatziiosif (ed.), *Ιστορία της Ελλάδας του 20ού αιώνα. Οι Απαρχές 1900–1922. Α' Τόμος, Μέρος 1ο*, Athens: Bibliorama, pp. 308–49.
Hatzopoulos, M. (2011), 'Oracular Prophecy and the Politics of Toppling Ottoman Rule in South-east Europe', *Historical Review*, viii, pp. 95–116.
— (2009), 'From Resurrection to Insurrection: "Sacred" Myths, Motifs, and Symbols in the Greek War of Independence', in R. Beaton and D. Ricks (eds), *The Making of Modern Greece: Nationalism, Romanticism, and the Uses of the Past (1797–1896)*, London: Ashgate, pp. 81–94.
Hering, G. (1992), *Die politischen Parteien in Griechenland 1821–1936*, Munich: R. Oldenbourg Verlag.
Herlihy, P. (1979), 'Greek Merchants in Odessa in the Nineteenth Century', *Harvard Ukrainian Studies*, 3, pp. 399–420.
Hicks, G. (2004), 'Don Pacifico, Democracy, and Danger: The Protectionist Party Critique of British Foreign Policy, 1850–1852', *The International History Review*, 26 (3), pp. 515–40.
Hionidou, V. (1995a), 'The Demographic System of a Mediterranean Island: Mykonos, Greece 1859–1959', *International Journal of Population Geography*, 1 (2), pp. 125–46.
— (1995b), 'Nuptiality Patterns and Household Structure on the Greek Island of Mykonos, 1849–1959', *Journal of Family History*, 20 (1), pp. 67–103.
— (1998), 'The Adoption of Fertility Control on Mykonos, 1879–1959: Stopping, Spacing or Both?', *Population Studies*, 52, pp. 67–83.
— (1999), 'Nineteenth-century Urban Greek Households: The Case of Hermoupolis, 1861–1879', *Continuity and Change*, 14 (3), pp. 403–28.

— (2005), 'Domestic Service on Three Greek Islands in the Later 19th and Early 20th Centuries', *The History of the Family*, 10 (4), pp. 473–89.

— (2006), 'Δημογραφία', in K. Kostis and S. Petmezas (eds), *Η ανάπτυξη της ελληνικής οικονομίας κατά τον 19ου αιώνα (1830–1914)*, Athens: Alexandreia, pp. 39–80.

— (2011), 'Independence and Inter-dependence: Household Formation Patterns in Eighteenth Century Kythera, Greece', *The History of the Family*, 16 (3), pp. 217–34.

Holland, R. F. (1999), 'Nationalism, Ethnicity and the Concert of Europe: The Case of the High Commissionership of Prince George of Greece in Crete, 1898–1906', *Journal of Modern Greek Studies*, 17 (2), pp. 253–76.

Holland, R. F., and D. W. Markides (2006), *The British and the Hellenes: Struggles for Mastery in the Eastern Mediterranean 1850–1960*, Oxford: Oxford University Press.

Ianeva, S. (2011), 'Main Characteristics of and Changes in Industrial Activity in the Central Balkans During "the Long 19th Century"', in E. Eldem and S. Petmezas (eds), *The Economic Development of Southeastern Europe in the 19th Century*, Athens: Alpha Bank, pp. 197–224.

Ilicak, S. (2009), 'The Revolt of Alexander Ipsilantis and the Fate of the Fanariots in Ottoman Documents', in P. Pizanias (ed.), *Η ελληνική επανάσταση του 1821. Ένα Ευρωπαϊκό γέγονος*, Athens: Kedros, pp. 320–34.

Infante-Amate, J. (2012), 'The Ecology and History of the Mediterranean Olive Grove: The Spanish Great Expansion, 1750–2000', *Rural History*, 23 (02), pp. 161–84.

Inglesi, A. (2004), *Βορειοελλαδίτες έμποροι στο τέλος της Τουρκοκρατίας. Ο Σταύρος Ιωάννου*, Athens: Ιστορικό Αρχείο. Πολιτιστική Συμβολή της Εμπορικής Τράπεζας της Ελλάδος.

Islamoğlou, H. (2011), 'Property As a Contested Domain: Makings of Individual Property in Law and Through Land Registration in the 19th Century Ottoman Empire', in E. Eldem and S. Petmezas (eds), *The Economic Development of Southeastern Europe in the 19th Century*, Athens: Alpha Bank, pp. 47–100.

Jenkins, R. (1999), *The Dilessi Murders*, London: Prion Press.

Jones, G. and P. Halstead (1995), 'Maslins, Mixtures and Monocrops: On the Interpretation of Archaeobotanical Crop Samples of Heterogeneous Composition', *Journal of Archaeological Science*, 22 (1), pp. 103–14.

Kahl, T. (2003), 'Aromanians in Greece. Minority or Vlach-speaking Greeks?', *Jahrbücher Für Geschichte Und Kultur Südosteuropas*, 5, pp. 205–19.

Kalentzidou, O. (2000a), 'Discontinuing Traditions: Using Historically Informed Ethnoarchaeology in the Study of Evros Ceramics', *Journal of Archaeological Method and Theory*, 7 (3), pp. 165–86.

— (2000b), 'Pots Crossing Borders: Ethnic Identity and Ceramics in Evros, Northeastern Greece', *Near Eastern Archaeology*, 63 (2), pp. 70–83.

Kalligas, P. (2000), *Thanos Vlekas*, Evanston, IL: Northwestern University Press.

Kallivretakis, L. (1987), 'Το ελληνικό βαμβακί στη συγκυρία του αμερικανικού

εμφυλίου πολέμου', *Τα Ιστορικά*, 7, pp. 81–102.
— (1990), *Η Δυναμική του αγροτικού εκσυγχρονισμού στην Ελλάδα το 19ου αιώνα*, Athens: The Agricultural Bank.
— (1995), 'Geographie et demographie historiques de la Grèce: le probleme des sources', *Histoire et Mesure*, 10 (1–2), pp. 9–23.
— (2003), 'Η Κρήτη 1829–1869. Μεταξύ δύο επαναστάσεων', in V. Panagiotopoulos (ed.), *Ιστορία του νέου ελληνισμού 1770–2000. 4ος τόμος. Το ελληνικό κράτος, 1833–1871: Η εθνική εστία και ο ελληνισμός της Οθωμανικής Αυτοκρατορίας*, Athens: Elliniki Grammata, pp. 373–89.
— (2006), 'A Century of Revolutions: The Cretan Question Between European and Near Eastern Politics', in P. M. Kitromilides (ed.), *Eleftherios Venizelos: The Trials of Statesmanship*, Edinburgh: Edinburgh University Press, pp. 11–35.
Kamilakis, P., and L. Karapidakis (eds) (2003), *Η ελιά και το λάδι από την αρχαιότητα έως σήμερα*, Athens: The Greek Folklore Research Centre.
Karanasou, F. (1999), 'The Greeks in Egypt: From Mohammed Ali to Nassar', in R. Clogg (ed.), *The Greek Diaspora in the Twentieth Century*, New York: St Martin's Press, Inc., pp. 24–57.
Kardasis, V. A. (1987), *Σύρος, σταυροδρόμι της Ανατολικής Μεσογείου (1832–1857)*, Athens: Morfotiko Idrima Ethnikis Trapezas.
— (1997), 'Greek Steam Liner Companies, 1858–1914', *International Journal of Maritime History*, 9 (2), pp. 107–27.
— (1998), *Έλληνες ομογενείς στη Νότια Ρωσία 1775–1861*, Athens: Alexandreia.
— (2001), *Diaspora merchants in the Black Sea: the Greeks in southern Russia, 1775–1861*, Lanham, MD: Lexington Books.
— (2006), 'Διασπορά', in K. Kostis and S. Petmezas (eds), *Η ανάπτυξη της ελληνικής οικονομίας κατά τον 19ο αιώνα (1830–1914)*, Athens: Alexandreia, pp. 409–20.
Kardulias, P. N. (2000), 'The "Traditional" Craftsman As Entrepreneur: A Potter in Ermioni', in S. Sutton (ed.), *Contingent countryside settlement, economy, and land use in the southern Argolid since 1700*, Stanford: Stanford University Press, pp. 275–89.
Karouzou, E. (1998), 'Système d'héritage et formation de la propriété familiale dans la région d'Argos (deuxième moitié du XIXe siècle)', *Mélanges De L'Ecole Française De Rome. Italie Et Méditerranée*, 110 (1), pp. 205–10.
— (2000), 'Le paysan individualiste: marché et systèmes d'exploitation de terre dans la Grèce du sud (fin du XIXe–début du XXe siècle)', *Ruralia. Sciences Sociales et Mondes Ruraux Contemporains*, 7.
Kasaba, R. (1988), *The Ottoman Empire and the World Economy: The Nineteenth Century*, Albany, NY: State University of New York Press.
— (2009), *A Moveable Empire: Ottoman Nomads, Migrants, and Refugees*, Seattle: University of Washington Press
Kasdagli, A. E. (2004), 'Family and Inheritance in the Cyclades, 1500–1800: Present Knowledge and Unanswered Questions', *The History of the Family*, 9 (3), pp. 257–74.
Katsiardi-Hering, O. (2008), 'The Allure of Red Cotton Yarn, and How It

Came to Vienna: Associations of Greek Artisans and Merchants Operating Between the Ottoman and Habsburg Empires', in S. Faroqhi and G. Veinstein (eds), *Merchants in the Ottoman Empire*, Paris: Peeters, pp. 97–132.

— (2011), 'City-ports in the Eastern and Central Mediterranean From the Mid-sixteenth to the Nineteenth Century: Urban and Social Aspects', *Mediterranean Historical Review*, 26 (2), pp. 151–70.

Katsiardi-Hering, O., A Kolia-Dermitzaki and K. Gardkia (eds) (2011), *Ρωσία και Μεσόγειος. Πρακτικά Α' διεθνούς συνεδρίου*, Athens: EKPA/ Herodotos Publications.

Kechriotis, V. (2008), 'Ρέκβιεμ για την Οθωμανική Αυτοκρατορία', in K. Gardika, V. Kechriotis, C. Loukas, C. Lyrintzis, and N. Maroniti (eds), *Η συγκρότηση του ελληνικού κράτους. Διεθνές πλαίσιο, εξουσία και πολιτική τον 19ο αιώνα*, Athens: Nefeli, pp. 17–52.

— (2009), 'Protecting the City's Interest: The Greek Orthodox and the Conflict Between Municipal and Vilayet Authorities in Izmir (Smyrna) in the Second Constitutional Period', *Mediterranean Historical Review*, 24 (2), pp. 207–22.

— (2013), 'Civilization and Order: Middle-class Morality Among the Greek-Orthodox in Smyrna/Izmir at the End of the Ottoman Empire', in A. Lyberatos (ed.), *Social Transformation and Mass Mobilization in the Balkan and Eastern Mediterranean Cities, 1900–1923*, Herakleion: Crete University Press, pp. 115–32.

Kechriotis, V. and M. Fuhrmann (2009), 'The Late Ottoman Port-Cities and Their Inhabitants Subjectivity, Urbanity, and Conflicting Orders', *Mediterranean Historical Review*, 24 (2), pp. 71–8.

Khoury, D. (2006), 'The Ottoman Center Versus Provincial Power-holders: An Analysis of the Historiography', in S. N. Faroqhi (ed.), *The Cambridge history of Turkey: the later Ottoman Empire, 1603–1839*, New York: Cambridge University Press, pp. 135–56.

Kitroeff A. (1989), *The Greeks in Egypt, 1919–1937*, London, Atlantic Highlands: Ithaca Press.

— (1999), 'Υπερατλαντική μετανάστευση', in C. Hatziiosif (ed.), *Ιστορία της Ελλάδας του 20ού αιώνα. Οι απαρχές 1900–1922. Α' τόμος, μέρος 1ο*, Athens: Bibliorama, pp. 122–71.

Kitromilides, P. M. (1992), *The Enlightenment as Social Criticism: Iosipos Moisiodax and Greek Culture in the Eighteenth Century*, Princeton: Princeton University Press.

— (ed.) (2006), *Eleftherios Venizelos: the trials of statesmanship*, Edinburgh: Edinburgh University Press.

— (ed.) (2010), *Adamantios Korais and the European Enlightenment*, Oxford: Voltaire Foundation.

— (2013), *Enlightenment and Revolution: the Making of Modern Greece*, Cambridge, MA: Harvard University Press.

Kitromilides, P., and H. S. Ilicak (2010), *1821 Η γέννηση ενός έθνους-κράτους. Ε τόμος. Ιδεολογικά ρεύματα: Έλληνες-Οθωμάνοι. α. Νεοελληνικός Διαφωτισμός. β. Η άλλη όχθη*, Athens: National Bank of Greece.

Kizos, T. (2010), 'Multifunctionality of Farm Households in Greece', *Norsk*

Geografisk Tidsskrift – Norwegian Journal of Geography, 64 (2), pp. 105–16.

Kizos, T. and M. Koulouri (2005), 'Economy, Demographic Changes and Morphological Transformation of the Agri-Cultural Landscape of Lesvos, Greece', *Problems in Human Ecology*, 12 (2), pp. 182–92.

Kizos, T. and M. Koulouri (2006), 'Agricultural Landscape Dynamics in the Mediterranean: Lesvos (Greece) Case Study Using Evidence From the Last Three Centuries', *Environmental Science and Policy*, 9 (4), pp. 330–42.

Kizos, T. and M. Koulouri (2010), 'Same Land Cover, Same Land Use at the Large Scale, Different Landscapes at the Small Scale: Landscape Change in Olive Plantations on Lesvos Island, Greece', *Landscape Research*, 35 (4), pp. 449–67.

Klein, N. (2000), *L'humanité, le christianisme, et la liberté: Die internationale philhellenische Vereinsbewegung der 1820er Jahre*, Berlin: von Zabern.

Kokosalakis, N. (1987), 'Religion and Modernization in 19th-Century Greece', *Social Compass*, 34, pp. 223–41.

Koliopoulos, J. S. (1987), *Brigands with a Cause: Brigandage and Irredentism in Modern Greece, 1821–1912*, Oxford: Clarendon.

Kolokotronis, T. (1977 [1844]), *Απομνημονεύματα*, Athens: Tolmidi.

Kolovos, E. (2006), *Η νησιωτική κοινωνία της Ανδρου στο Οθωμανικό πλαίσιο: Πρώτη προσέγγιση με βάση τα οθωμανικά εγγραφα της Καϊρείου Βιβλιοθήκης (1579–1821)*, Andros: Kaireiou Library.

— (2007), 'Insularity and Island Society in the Ottoman Context', *Turcica*, 39, pp. 49–122.

Komis, K. (2003), 'Προσφυγικές μετακινήσεις. Πολεμικές καταστροφές και νεές εγκαταστάσεις', in V. Panagiotopoulos (ed.), *Ιστορία του νέου ελληνισμού 1770–2000. 3ος τόμος. Η ελληνηκή επανάσταση 1821–1832. Ο αγώνας της ανεξαρτησίας και η ίδρυση του ελληνικού κράτους*, Athens: Elliniki Grammata, pp. 235–46.

— (2004), 'Demographic Aspects of the Greek Household: The Case of Preveza (18th Century)', *The History of the Family*, 9 (3), pp. 287–98.

Konortas, P. (1998), *Οθωμανικές θεωρήσεις για το οικουμενικό πατριαρχείο 17ος–αρχές 20ού αιώνα*, Athens: Alexandreia.

— (2010), 'Nationalism Vs Millets: Building Collective Identities in Ottoman Thrace', in N. P. Diamandouros, T. Dragona, and C. Keyder (eds), *Spatial Conceptions of the Nation: Modernizing Geographies in Greece and Turkey*, London: I. B. Tauris, pp. 161–80.

Kostantaras, D. J. (2006), *Infamy and Revolt: The Rise of the National Problem in Early Modern Greek Thought*, New York: Columbia University Press.

— (2013), 'Christian Elites of the Peloponnese and the Ottoman State, 1715–1821', *European History Quarterly*, 43 (4), pp. 628–56.

Kostelenos, Y. (2006), 'Μακροοικονομικά μεγέθη', in K. Kostis and S. Petmezas (eds), *Η ανάπτυξη της ελληνικής οικονομίας κατά τον 19ου αιώνα (1830–1914)*, Athens: Alexandreia, pp. 39–80.

Kostis, K. P. (2005), 'The Formation of the Greek State', in F. Birtek and

T. Dragonas (eds), *Citizenship and the Nation-State in Greece and Turkey*, New York: Routledge, pp. 18–36.

— (2006), 'Δημόσια οικονομία', in K. Kostis and S. Petmezas (eds), *Η ανάπτυξη της ελληνικής οικονομίας κατά τον 19ου αιώνα (1830–1914)*, Athens: Alexandreia, pp. 293–336.

— (2013), *'Τα κακομαθημένα παιδιά της ιστορίας'. Η διαμόρφωση του νεοελληνικού κράτους, 18ος–21ος αιώνας*, Athens: Polis.

Kostopoulos, T. (2006), 'Ο εμφύλιος Μακεδονικός Αγώνας (1904–1908): Εκδοχές του κρατικού μονοπωλίου της συλλογικής μνήμης', *Τα Ιστορικά, 45* (Δεκ), pp. 393–432.

— (2007), *Πόλεμος και εθνοκάθαρση: η ξεχασμένη πλευρά μιας δεκαετούς εθνικής εξόρμησης*, Athens: Bibliorama.

Koulouri, Christina (ed.) (2004), *Athens: Olympic City, 1891–1906*, Athens: International Olympic Academy.

Krahtopoulou, A. and C. Frederick (2008), 'The Stratigraphic Implications of Long-term Terrace Agriculture in Dynamic Landscapes: Polycyclic Terracing From Kythera Island, Greece', *Geoarchaeology, 23* (4), pp. 550–85.

Kremmydas, V. (2006), 'Το Εμπόριοκαιη Ναυτιλία 1775–1835', in V. Kremmydas (ed.), *Εισαγωγή στη νεοελληνική οικονομική ιστορά (18ος–20ος Αιώνας)*, Athens: Typotheto, pp. 13–44.

Küçükkalay, A. M. (2008), 'Imports to Smyrna Between 1794 and 1802: New Statistics From the Ottoman Sources', *Journal of the Economic and Social History of the Orient, 51* (3), pp. 487–512.

Kyrkini-Koutoula, A. (1996), *Η οθωμανικη διοικήση στην Ελλάδα. Η περίπτωση της Πελοποννήσου (1715–1822)*, Athens: Arsenidi.

Laiou, S. (2009), 'Η ελληνική επανάσταση στην Πελοπόννησο σύμφωνα με την περιγραφή ενός ντόπιου οθωμανού λογίου', in P. Pizanias (ed.), *Η ελληνική επανάσταση του 1821. Ενα ευρωπαϊκό γέγονος*, Athens: Kedros, pp. 307–19.

— (2011), 'The Greek Revolution in the Morea According to the Description of An Ottoman Official', in P. Pizanias (ed.), *The Greek Revolution of 1821: A European Event*, Istanbul: The Isis Press, pp. 241–56.

Lapavitsas, C. K. (2004), *Social Origins of Ottoman Industrialisation: Evidence from the Macedonian Town of Naoussa*, University of London: School of Oriental and African Studies.

— (2006), 'Social and Economic Underpinnings of Industrial Development: Evidence From Ottoman Macedonia', *Journal of European Economic History, 35* (3), pp. 661–710.

Lazaretou, S. (1993), 'Monetary and Fiscal Policies in Greece: 1833–1914', *Journal of European Economic History, 22* (2), pp. 285–312.

— (2005), 'The Drachma, Foreign Creditors, and the International Monetary System: Tales of a Currency During the 19th and the Early 20th Centuries', *Explorations in Economic History, 42* (2), pp. 202–36.

Lee, W. E. (2001), 'Pylos Regional Archaeological Project, Part IV: Change and the Human Landscape in a Modern Greek Village in Messenia', *Hesperia, 70* (1), pp. 49–98.

Lekas, P. E. (2008), 'The Greek War of Independence From the Perspective of Historical Sociology', *The Historical Review, 2*, pp. 161–83.

— (2009), 'Nationalism Qua Modernization: The Greek War of Independence', in P. Pizanias (ed.), *Η ελληνική επανάσταση του 1821. Ενα ευρωπαϊκό γέγονος*, Athens: Kedros, pp. 267–78.

Levy, A. (1971), 'The Officer Corps in Sultan Mahmud II's New Ottoman Army, 1826–39', *International Journal of Middle East Studies*, 2 (1), pp. 21–39.

— (1982), 'Military Reform and the Problem of Centralization in the Ottoman Empire in the Eighteenth Century', *Middle Eastern Studies*, 18 (3), pp. 227–49.

Liakos, A. (1985), *Η ιταλική ενοποίηση και η Μεγάλη Ιδέα*, Athens: Themelio.

Livianos, D. (1999), '"Conquering the Souls": Nationalism and Greek Guerrilla Warfare in Ottoman Macedonia, 1904–1908', *Byzantine and Modern Greek Studies*, 23 (195–221).

Llewellyn Smith, M. (2004), *Olympics in Athens 1896: the invention of the modern Olympic Games*, London: Profile Books.

Lory, B. (2011), 'Schools for the Destruction of Society: School Propaganda in Bitola 1860– 1912', in H. Grandits, N. Clayer and R. Pichler (eds), *Conflicting Loyalties in the Balkans: the Great Powers, the Ottoman Empire and Nation-building*, London: I. B. Tauris, pp. 46–63.

Loukos, C. (2003), 'Κυβερνήτης Καποδίστριας. Πολιτικό έργο, συναίνεση και αντιδράσεις', in V. Panagiotopoulos (ed.), *Ιστορία του νέου ελληνισμού 1770–2000. 3ος τόμος. Η ελληνική επανάσταση 1821–1832. Ο αγώνας της ανεξαρτησίας και η ίδρυση του ελληνικού κράτους*, Athens: Elliniki Grammata, pp. 185–216.

— (2004), 'Families and Family Structure in a Neo-Hellenic City: Hermoupolis in the Mid-19th Century', *The History of the Family*, 9 (3), pp. 317–24.

— (2007), 'Some Suggestions for a Bolder Incorporation of Studies of the Greek Revolution of 1821 into their Ottoman Context', in A. Anastasopoulos and E. Kolovos (eds), *Ottoman Rule and the Balkans, 1760–1850: Conflict, Transformation, Adaptation*, Rethymno: University of Crete, pp. 195–204.

— (2008), 'Η Επανάσταση Του 1821', in K. Gardika, V. Kechkriotis, C. Loukos, C. Lyrintzis, and K. Maroniti (eds), *Η συγκρότηση του ελληνικού κράτους. Διεθνές πλαίσιο, εξουσία και πολιτική τον 19ο αιώνα*, Athens: Nefeli, pp. 53–68.

Louvi, L. (2003), 'Το πολιτικό πλαίσιο των πρώτων βηματισμών', in V. Panagiotopoulos (ed.), *Το ελληνικό κράτος, 1833–1871: Η εθνική εστία και ο ελληνισμός της οθωμανικής αυτοκρατορίας*, Athens: Elliniki Grammata, pp. 9–26.

Lyberatos, A. (2010), 'Men of the Sultan: The Beglik Sheep Tax Collection System and the Rise of a Bulgarian National Bourgeoisie in Nineteenth-century Plovdiv', *Turkish Historical Review*, 1 (1), pp. 55–85.

— (2013), 'Confronting the Urban Crowd: Bulgarian Society and the 1906 Anti-Greek Movement', in A. Lyberatos (ed.), *Social Transformation and Mass Mobilization in the Balkan and Eastern Mediterranean Cities, 1900–1923*, Herakleion: Crete University Press, pp. 177–94.

Lyrintzis, C. (2008), 'Κράτος, εξουσία, πολιτική (1830–1880)', in K. Gardika, V. Kechriotis, C. Loukos, C. Lyrintzis, and N. Morinitii (eds), *Η* συγκρότηση του ελληνικού κράτους. Διεθνές πλαίσιο, εξουσία και πολιτική τον 19ο αιώνα, Athens: Nefeli, pp. 69–91.

Mackridge, P. (2009), *Language and National Identity in Greece, 1766–1976*, New York: Oxford University Press.

Macrakis, A. L. (1982), 'Eleftherios Venizelos in Crete, 1864–1910: The Main Problems', in L. Macrakis and N. Diamandouros, (eds), *New Trends in Modern Greek Histiography*, New Haven, CT: Modern Greek Studies Association, pp. 85–104.

— (2006), 'Venizelos' Early Life and Political Career in Crete, 1864–1910', in P. M. Kitromilides (ed.), *Eleftherios Venizelos: The Trials of Statesmanship*, Edinburgh: Edinburgh University Press, pp. 37–86.

Makrides, V. (2009), *Hellenic Temples and Christian Churches: a Concise History of the Religious Cultures of Greece from Antiquity to the Present*, New York: New York University Press.

Maleševi , S. (September, 2012), 'Did Wars Make Nation-States in the Balkans?: Nationalisms, Wars and States in the 19th and Early 20th Century South East Europe', *Journal of Historical Sociology*, 25 (3), pp. 299–330.

Marangou-Drygiannaki, S. (2000), 'Orthodoxy and Russian Policy Towards Greece in the 19th Century: The Philorthodox Society's Conspiracy (1830–1840)', *Balkan Studies*, 41 (1), pp. 27–42.

Margaritis, G. (1997), 'The Nation and the Individual: Social Aspects of Life and Death in Greece (1896–1911)', in P. Carabott (ed.), *Greek Society in the Making, 1863–1913: Realities, Symbols and Visions*, Brookfield, VT: Ashgate, pp. 87–98.

Marmaras, E. V. (2008), 'Cycladic Settlements of the Aegean Sea: A Blending of Local and Foreign Influences', *Planning Perspectives*, 23 (4), pp. 503–20.

Maroniti, N. (2008), 'Βασιλευόμενη δημοκρατία: Λόγοι και πρακτικές (1864–1910)', in K. Gardika, V. Kechriotis, C. Loukas, C. Lyrsintzis, and N. Maroniti (eds), *Η συγκρότηση του ελληνικού κράτους. Διεθνές πλαίσιο, εξουσία και πολιτική τον 19ο αιώνα*, Athens: Nefeli, pp. 91–118.

— (2009), *Πολιτική εξουσία και εθνικό ζήτημα στην Ελλάδα. 1880–1910*, Athens: Alexandreia.

— (2010), *Το Κίνημα στο Γουδί εκατό χρόνια μετά. Παραδοχές, ερωτήματα, νέες προοπτικές*, Athens: Alexandreia.

Marre, S. (2010), 'La population du royaume de Grèce (1834–1914). Les sources et leurs rapports', *The Historical Review/La Revue Historique*, 6, pp. 207–42.

Marsot, A. L. (1984), *Egypt in the reign of Muhammad Ali*, New York: Cambridge University Press.

Marzagalli, S. (2005), 'Establishing Transatlantic Trade Networks in Time of War: Bordeaux and the United States, 1793–1815', *Business History Review*, 79 (4), pp. 811–44.

Masters, B. (2009), 'Mehmed Ali', in G. Ágoston and B. A. Masters (eds), *Encyclopedia of the Ottoman Empire*, New York: Facts On File, pp. 372–3.

Matalas, A.-L. (2001), 'The Mediterranean Diet: Historical Background and Dietary Patterns in Pre-World War II Greece', in A.-L. Matalas, V. Stavrianos, Zampelas, and I. Wolinski (eds), *Mediterranean Diet: Constituents and Health Promotion*, Boca Raton, FL: CRC Press, pp. 32–49.

— (2006a), 'Dietary Patterns in Pre-World War II Greece. Disparities Within Peasant and Urban Foodways', *Food and History*, 4 (1), pp. 237–53.

— (2006b), 'Disparities Within Traditional Mediterranean Food Patterns: An Historical Approach of the Greek Diet', *International Journal of Food Sciences and Nutrition*, 57 (7–8), pp. 529–36.

Mavromoustakou, E. (2003), 'Το ελληνικό κράτος 1833–1871. Πολιτικοί θεσμοί και διοικητική οργάνωση', in V. Panagiotopoulos (ed.), *Ιστορία του νέου ελληνισμού 1770–2000. 4ος τόμος. Το ελληνικό κράτος, 1833–1871: Η εθνική εστία και ο ελληνισμός της οθωμανικής αυτοκρατορίας*, Athens: Elliniki Grammata, pp. 57–70.

Mazower, M. (2005), *Salonica, City of Ghosts: Christians, Muslims, and Jews, 1430–1950*, New York: Alfred A. Knopf.

McGrew, W. (1985), *Land and Revolution in Modern Greece, 1800–1881. The Transition in the Tenure and Exploitation of Land from Ottoman Rule to Independence*, Kent, OH: Kent State University Press.

McNeill, J. R. (1992), *The Mountains of the Mediterranean World: an Environmental History*, New York: Cambridge University Press.

Menning, B. W. (May, 1984), 'Russian Military Innovation in the Second Half of the Eighteenth Century', *War and Society*, 2 (1), pp. 23–41.

Michailidis, I. D. (2006), 'The Formation of Greek Citizenship (19th Century)', *Citizenship in Historical Perspective*, pp. 155–62.

— (2010), *1821 η γέννηση ενός έθνους-κράτους. Γ τόμος. Ο αγώνας των ελλήνων. πολιτικές επιλογές και στρατιωτικές επεχειρήσεις 1821–1827*, Athens: National Bank of Greece.

Mikhail, A. (2011a), 'Global Implications of the Middle Eastern Environment', *History Compass*, 9 (12), pp. 952–70.

— (2011b), *Nature and Empire in Ottoman Egypt: an Environmental History*, New York: Cambridge University Press.

— (2012), 'The Middle East in Global Environmental History', in J. R. McNeill and E. S. Mauldin (eds), *A Companion to Global Environmental History*, Hoboken, NJ: Wiley, pp. 167–181.

Miller, J. P. (1828), *The condition of Greece in 1827 and 1828*, New York: J. & J. Harper.

— (1974 [1829]), *Letters from Greece*, Athenes: Historike kai Ethnologike Hetairia tes Hellados.

Miller, W. (1905), *Greek Life in Town and Country*, London: George Newnes, Ltd.

Minoglou, I. P. (2002), 'Ethnic Minority Groups in International Banking: Greek Diaspora Bankers of Constantinople and Ottoman State Finances, c. 1840–1881', *Financial History Review*, 9, pp. 125–46.

— (2007), 'Women and Family Capitalism in Greece, C. 1780–1940', *Business History Review*, pp. 517–38.

Morilla, J. M., A. L. Olmstead and P. W. Rhode (1999), '"Horn of Plenty": The Globalization of Mediterranean Horticulture and the Economic

Development of Southern Europe, 1880–1930', *Journal of Economic History*, 59 (2), pp. 316–52.

Mutlu, S. (2003), 'Late Ottoman Population and Its Ethnic Distribution', *Turkish Journal of Population Studies*, 25, pp. 3–38

Myrogiannis, S. (2012), *The Emergence of the Greek Identity (1700–1821)*, Newcastle: Cambridge Scholars.

Nagata, Y. (1995), 'Greek Rebellion of 1770 in the Morea Peninsula', in Y. Nagata (ed.), *Studies on the Social and Economic History of the Ottoman Empire*, Akademi Kitabevi: Izmir.

Neuburger, M. (2013), *Balkan Smoke: Tobacco and the Making of Modern Bulgaria*, Ithaca, NY: Cornell University Press.

Nikolakaki, M. (2013), 'Pedagogical Systems and the Construction of the Primary School Teacher in the Teachers Training Institution (Didaskalio) in Greece (1830–1933): Issues of Power and Governmentality', *Policy Futures in Education*, 11 (1), pp. 59–73.

Nitsiakos, Vassilis, Haralambos Kasimis (eds) (2008), *Ο ορεινός χωρός της βαλκανικής, συγκρότηση και μετασχηματισμοί*, Athens: Plethron.

Ollier, E. (1878), *Casssell's Illustrated History of the Russo-Turkish War*, 2 vols, London: Cassell Petter & Galpin.

Ozdemir, B. (2003), *Ottoman Reforms and Social Life: Reflections from Salonica, 1830–1850*, Istanbul: Isis Press.

Ozil, A. (2013), *Orthodox Christians in the Late Ottoman Empire: A Study of Communal Relations in Anatolia*, New York: Routledge.

Özdemir, B. (2003), 'Position of the Muslims in Salonica During the Reform Period: "Rulers" or "Ruled"?' in *Ottoman Reforms and Social Life: Reflections from Salonica, 1830–1850*, Istanbul: The Isis Press, pp. 1–7.

Özdeğer, M. (2011), 'Ayan Era in Government', *Manas*, 6 (1), pp. 29–42.

Pagratis, G. D. (2011), 'Greeks and Italians in the Italian Peninsula During the Napoleonic Period, From the Standpoint of the Septinsular Republic', *The Annals of the Lower Danube University of Galati, History*, 10, pp. 43–54.

— (2012), 'Shipping and Trade in the Ionian Islands: The Merchant Fleet of the Septinsular Republic', *Journal of the Oxford Historical Society*, 8, pp. 1–21.

Pamuk, S. (1984), 'The Ottoman Empire in the "Great Depression" of 1873–1896', *Journal of Economic History*, 44 (1), pp. 107–18.

— (1986), 'The Decline and Resistance of Ottoman Cotton Textiles 1820–1913', *Explorations in Economic History*, 23 (2), pp. 205–25.

— (1987), *The Ottoman Empire and European Capitalism, 1820–1913 Trade, Investment, and Production*, New York: Cambridge University Press.

Pamuk, S., and J. G. Williamson (2000), *The Mediterranean Response to Globalization before 1950*, London, New York: Routledge.

Pamuk, S. and J. G. Williamson (2011), 'Ottoman De-industrialization, 1800–1913: Assessing the Magnitude, Impact, and Response', *The Economic History Review*, 64, pp. 159–84.

Panagiotopoulos, V. (2003), 'Η Φιλική Εταιρεία. Οργανωτικές προϋποθέσεις της εθνικής επανάστασης', in V. Panagiotopoulos (ed.), *Ιστορία του νέου* ελληνισμού 1770–2000. 3ος τόμος. Η ελληνική επανάσταση 1821–1832. Ο αγώνας της ανεξαρτησίας και η ίδρυση του ελληνικού κράτους, Athens: Elliniki Grammata, pp. 9–32.

— (2011), 'The Filiki Etaireia (Society of Friends). Organizational Preconditions of the National War of Independence', in P. Pizanias (ed.), *The Greek Revolution of 1821: A European Event*, Istanbul: The Isis Press, pp. 101–28.

Panzac, D. (1992), 'International and Domestic Maritime Trade in the Ottoman Empire During the 18th Century', *International Journal of Middle East Studies*, 24 (2), pp. 189–207.

Papacosma, S. V. (1977), *The Military in Greek Politics: The 1909 Coup d'Etat*, Kent, OH: Kent State University Press.

Papadakis, L. (2006), *Teaching of the Nation; Greek Nationalism and Education in Nineteenth Century Macedonia*, Thessaloniki: Institute for Balkan studies.

Papadiamantis, A. (1987 [1894]), *Tales from a Greek Island*, Baltimore: Johns Hopkins University Press.

Papadopoulos, S. A. (1971), *Liberated Greece and the Morea Scientific Expedition: The Peytier Album in the Stephen Vagliano Collection*, Athens: National Bank of Greece.

Papageorgiou, S. P. (2003), 'Η στρατιωτική διοργάνωση. Πολεμικές επιχειρήσεις στα χρόνια του Καποδίστρια', in V. Panagiotopoulos (ed.), Ιστορία του νέου ελληνισμού 1770–2000. 3ος τόμος. Η ελληνική επανάσταση 1821–1832. Ο αγώνας της ανεξαρτησίας και η ίδρυση του ελληνικού κράτους, Athens: Elliniki Grammata, pp. 217–34.

— (2005), Άπο το γένος στο έθνος. Η θεμελίωση του ελληνικού κράτους, 1821–1862, Athens: Papasisi.

— (2011), 'Attempts to Strengthen Centralized Power. The Capodistrian Political Model', in P. Pizanias (ed.), *The Greek Revolution of 1821: A European Event*, Istanbul: The Isis Press, pp. 171–9.

Papaioannou, S. S. (2012), *Balkan Wars between the Lines: Violence and Civilians in Macedonia, 1912–1918*, PhD Dissertation, College Park, MD: University of Maryland.

Papaïoannou, K. S. (2003), Το ελληνικό παραδοσιακό σπίτι, Athens: University Press.

Papakonstantinou, K. (2008), 'The Pondikas Merchant Family From Thessaloniki, ca. 1750–1800', in S. Faroqhi and G. Veinstein (eds), *Merchants in the Ottoman Empire*, Paris: Peeters, pp. 133–50.

— (2011a), 'The Port of Messolonghi: Spatial Allocation and Maritime Expansion in the Eighteenth Century', *The Historical Review/La Revue Historique*, 7 (0), pp. 277–97.

— (2011b), 'Transport and Communication in Southeastern Europe in the 19th Century: The Impact of Trade', in E. Eldem and S. Petmezas (eds), *The Economic Development of Southeastern Europe in the 19th century*, Athens: Alpha Bank, pp. 349–96.

Papastamatiou, D. (2011), 'Tax–farming (litzam) and Collective Fiscal Responsibility (Maktu) in the Ottoman Southern Peloponnese in the 2nd Half of the 18th Century', in E. Kolovos and P. H. Kotzageorgis (eds),

The Ottoman Empire, the Balkans, the Greek lands: toward a social and economic history, Istanbul: Isis Press, pp. 289–305.

Papastefanaki, L. (2004), *From Industry to Services?*, Barcelona: Proceedings of the eighth annual conference of the European Business History Association.

— (2006), 'Μισθωτή εργασία', in K. Kostis and S. Petmezas (eds), *Η ανάπτυξη της ελληνικής οικονομίας κατά τον 19ου αιώνα (1830–1914)*, Athens: Alexandreia, pp. 253–92.

— (2009), *Εργασία, τεχνολογία και φύλο στην ελληνική βιομηχανία. Η κλωστοϋφαντουργία του Πειραιά, 1870–1940*, Herakleion: Crete University Press.

Papataxiarchis, E. and S. D. Petmezas (1998), 'The Devolution of Property and Kinship Practices in Late- and Post-Ottoman Ethnic Greek Societies. Some Demo-economic Factors of 19th and 20th Century Transformations', *Mélanges de l'Ecole Française de Rome. Italie et Méditerranée*, *110* (1), pp. 217–41.

Papathanassiou, M. (2004), 'Aspects of Childhood in Rural Greece: Children in a Mountain Village (c. 1900–1940)', *The History of the Family*, *9* (3), pp. 325–45.

Papatheodorou, G., M. Geraga and G. Ferentinos (2005), 'The Navarino Naval Battle Site, Greece – an Integrated Remote-Sensing Survey and a Rational Management Approach', *International Journal of Nautical Archaeology*, *34* (1), pp. 95–109.

Pappas, N. C. (1991), *Greeks in Russian Military Service in the Late Eighteenth and Early Nineteenth Centuries*, Thessaloniki: Institute for Balkan Studies.

Parveva, S. (2003), 'Agrarian Land and Harvest in South-West Peloponnese in the Early 18th Century', *Etudes Balkaniques*, *39* (1), pp. 83–123.

— (2009), *Village, Town and People in the Ottoman Balkans: 16th-mid-19th Century*, Istanbul: The Isis Press.

Patrinelis, C. G. (2001), 'The Phanariots Before 1821', *Balkan Studies*, *42* (2), pp. 177–98.

Peckham, R. S. (1999), 'Diseased Bodies of the Nation: Suicide in Fin-de Siècle Greece', *Journal of Mediterranean Studies*, *9* (2), pp. 155–74.

Pécout, G. (2004), 'Philhellenism in Italy: Political Friendship and the Italian Volunteers in the Mediterranean in the Nineteenth Century', *Journal of Modern Italian Studies*, *9* (4), pp. 405–27.

Perakis, M. (2011), 'Muslim Exodus and Land Redistribution in Autonomous Crete (1898–1913)', *Mediterranean Historical Review*, *26* (2), pp. 135–50.

Perdicoulias, P. (2007), *Museum of the Olive and Greek Olive Oil*, Athens: Piraeus Bank Group Cultural Foundation.

Perry, D. M. (1988), *The Politics of Terror: The Macedonian Revolutionary Movements, 1893–1903*, Durham, NC: Duke University Press.

Petanidou, T., T. Kizos and N. Soulakellis (2008), 'Socioeconomic Dimensions of Changes in the Agricultural Landscape of the Mediterranean Basin: A Case Study of the Abandonment of Cultivation Terraces on Nisyros Island, Greece', *Environmental Management*, *41* (2), pp. 250–66.

Petmezas, S. (1990), 'Patterns of Protoindustrialization in the Ottoman Empire: The Case of Eastern Thessaly, ca. 1750–1860', *Journal of European Economic History*, 19 (3), pp. 575–603.

— (1999a), 'Αγροτική οικονομία', in C. Hatziiosif (ed.), *Ιστορία της Ελλάδας του 20ού αιώνα. Οι απαρχές 1900–1922. Α' τόμος, μέρος 1ο*, Athens: Bibliorama, pp. 52–85.

— (1999b), 'Δημογραφία', in C. Hatziiosif (ed.), *Ιστορία της Ελλάδας του 20ού αιώνα. Οι απαρχές 1900–1922. Α' τόμος, μέρος 1ο*, Athens: Bibliorama, pp. 40–51.

— (2000), 'Export-dependent Agriculture, Revenue Crisis and Agrarian Productivity Involution', *Histoire et Mesure*, 15 (3), pp. 321–37.

— (2003), *Η ελληνική αγροτική οικονομία κατά τον 19ο αιώνα: Η περιφερειακή διάσταση*, Heraklio: University of Crete Press.

— (2006), 'Αγροτική οικονομία', in K. Kostis and S. Petmezas (eds), *Η ανάπτυξη της ελληνικής οικονομίας κατά τον 19ου αιώνα (1830–1914)*, Athens: Alexandreia, pp. 103–50.

— (2009a), 'From Privileged Outcasts to Power Players: The "Romantic" Redefinition of the Hellenic Nation in the Mid-19th Century', in R. Beaton and D. Ricks (eds), *The Making of Modern Greece: Nationalism, Romanticism, and the Uses of the Past (1797–1896)*, London: Ashgate, pp. 123–36.

— (2009b), 'Agriculture and Economic Development in Greece, 1870–1973', in P. Lains and V. Pinilla Navarro (eds), *Agriculture and Economic Development in Europe since 1870*, London: Routledge, pp. 353–74.

— (2011), 'Foreign Trade and Capital Flows in 19th-century Greece', in E. Eldem and S. Petmezas (eds), *The Economic Development of Southeastern Europe in the 19th Century*, Athens: Alpha Bank, pp. 447–92.

— (2013) 'L'Économie Agricole Grecque Face À La Longue Crise De La Première Globalisation', *The Historical Review*, X, pp. 85–105.

Petrakis, P. E. and H. Panorios (1992), 'Economic Fluctuations in Greece, 1844–1913', *Journal of Economic History*, 21 (1), pp. 31–47.

Petropoulos, J. A. (1968), *Politics and Statecraft in the Kingdom of Greece: 1833–1843*, Princeton: Princeton University Press.

Philliou, C. M. (2009), 'Communities on the Verge: Unraveling the Phanariot Ascendancy in Ottoman Governance', *Comparative Studies in Society and History*, 51 (01), pp. 151–81.

— (2011), *Biography of an Empire: Governing Ottomans in an Age of Revolution*, Berkeley: University of California Press.

Pissis, N. (2008), 'Investments in the Greek Merchant Marine (1783–1821)', in S. Faroqhi and G. Veinstein (eds), *Merchants in the Ottoman Empire*, Paris: Peeters, pp. 151–64.

Pizanias, P. (1988), *Οικονομική ιστορία της ελληνικής σταφίδας, 1851–1912*, Athens: Research and Educational Foundation of the Commercial Bank of Greece.

— (2003a), 'Επανάσταση και έθνος. Μια ιστορική -κοινωνιολογική προσέγγιση του 1821', in V. Panagiotopoulos (ed.), *Ιστορία του νέου ελληνισμού 1770–2000. 3ος τόμος. Η ελληνική επανάσταση 1821–1832. Ο αγώνας της ανεξαρτησίας και η ίδρυση του ελληνικού κράτους*, pp. 33–52.

— (2003b), 'Ο αγροτικός κόσμος. Το ζήτημα της ενσωμάτωσης στο νέο κράτος', in V. Panagiotopoulos (ed.), *Ιστορία του νέου ελληνισμού 1770–2000. 4ος τόμος. Το ελληνικό κράτος, 1833–1871: Η εθνική εστία και ο ελληνισμός της Οθωμανικής Αυτοκρατορίας*, Athens: Elliniki Grammata, pp. 85–104.
— (ed.) (2009a), *Η ελληνική επανάσταση του 1821. Ενα ευρωπαϊκό γέγονος*, Athens: Kedros.
— (2009b), 'Από ραγιάς στο έλληνας πολίτης. Διαφωτισμός και επανάσταση 1750–1832', in P. Pizanias (ed.), *Η ελληνική επανάσταση του 1821. Ενα ευρωπαϊκό γέγονος*, Athens: Kedros, pp. 13–78.
— (ed.) (2011a), *The Greek Revolution of 1821: A European Event*, Istanbul: The Isis Press.
— (2011b), 'From Reaya to Greek Citizen: Enlightenment and Revolution, 1750–1832', in P. Pizanias (ed.), *The Greek Revolution of 1821: A European Event*, Istanbul: The Isis Press, pp. 11–84.
Ploumidis, S. G. (2005), *Εθνοτική συμβίωση στη Βαλκάνια. Έλληνες και Βούλγαροι στη Φιλιππούπολη 1878–1914*, Athens: Pataki.
Potamianos, N. (2013), 'From the People to a Class: The Petite Bourgeoisie of Athens, 1901– 1923', in A. Lyberatos (ed.), *Social Transformation and Mass Mobilization in the Balkan and Eastern Mediterranean Cities, 1900–1923*, Herakleion: Crete University Press, pp. 313–46.
Poulios, S. (2013), 'The Muslim Exodus From Crete: Property Destruction, Urbanization and Counter Violence', in A. Lyberatos (ed.), *Social Transformation and Mass Mobilization in the Balkan and Eastern Mediterranean Cities, 1900–1923*, Herakleion: Crete University Press, pp. 245–66.
Prousis, T. C. (1992), 'Smyrna in 1821: A Russian View', *History Department Publications*, 16, pp. 145–68.
— (1994), *Russian Society and the Greek Revolution*, DeKalb: Northern Illinois University Press.
— (2010), *Lord Strangford at the Sublime Porte (1821): the Eastern crisis*, Istanbul: Isis Press.
Psaropoulou, B. (1988), *Last Potters of the East Aegean*, Nafplion: Peloponnesian Folklore Foundation.
— (1990), *Η κεραμική του χθες στα Κύθηρα και στην Κύθνο*, Athens: Centre for the Study of Modern Ceramics.
Psarra, A. (2006), '"Few Women Have a History": Callirhoe Parren and the Beginnings of Women's History in Greece', *Gender and History*, 18 (2), pp. 400–11.
— (2007), 'A Gift From the New World: Greek Feminists Between East and West (1880–1930)', in A. Frangoudaki and Keyder (eds), *Ways to modernity in Greece and Turkey: encounters with Europe, 1850–1950*, London: I. B. Tauris, pp. 150–75.
Psychogios, D. K. (1995), *Προίκες, φόροι, σταφίδα και ψωμί. Οικονομία και οικογένεια στην αγροτική Ελλάδα του 19ου αιώνα*, Athens: National Centre of Social Research.
Pylia, M. (2007), 'Conflits politiques et comportements des primats chrétiens en Morée, avant la guerre de l'indépendance', in A. Anastasopoulos and E. Kolovos (eds), *Ottoman Rule and the Balkans, 1760–1850:*

Conflict, Transformation, Adaptation, Rethymno: University of Crete, pp. 137–48.

Quataert, D. (1988), 'Ottoman Handicrafts and Industry in the Age of European Industrial Hegemony, 1800–1914', *Review (Fernand Braudel Center)*, pp. 169–78.

— (1993), *Ottoman Manufacturing in the Age of the Industrial Revolution*, New York: Cambridge University Press.

— (2011), 'Industry, Labor and Technology Transfer in the South Eastern Balkans and Aegean Coast of Anatolia and Istanbul, 1830–1922', in E. Eldem and S. Petmezas (eds), *The Economic Development of Southeastern Europe in the 19th Century*, Athens: Alpha Bank, pp. 173–96.

Razhdavichka, E. (2006), 'Nineteenth-century Balkan Fairs As Social Space: Hierarchy, Marginality, Ethnicity and Gender', *Etudes Balkaniques*, 1, pp. 125–48.

Reid, J. J. (1996), 'Irregular Military Bands and Colonies in the Balkans, 1769–1878', *Etudes Balkaniques, Cahiers Belon*, 3, pp. 131–65.

— (2000), 'Batak 1876: A Massacre and Its Significance', *Journal of Genocide Research*, 2 (3), pp. 375–409.

Rendall, M. (2002), 'Restraint or Self-Restraint of Russia: Nicholas I, the Treaty of Unkiar Skelessi, and the Vienna System, 1832–1841', *The International History Review*, 24 (1), pp. 37–63.

Renieri, I. (2002), 'Household Formation in 19th-century Central Anatolia: The Case Study of a Turkish-speaking Orthodox Christian Community', *International Journal of Middle East Studies*, 34 (3), pp. 495–517.

Repousis, A. (2009), 'The Devil's Apostle: Jonas King's Trial Against the Greek Hierarchy in 1852 and the Pressure to Extend US Protection for American Missionaries Overseas', *Diplomatic History*, 33 (5), pp. 807–37.

Reynolds, M. A. (2011), *Shattering Empires: The Clash and Collapse of the Ottoman and Russian Empires 1908–1918*, New York: Cambridge University Press.

Rizopoulos, C. A., and A. C. Rizopoulos (2008), *Φιλέλληνες και έλληνες τέκτονες το 1821*, Athens: Tetraktys.

Rodogno, D. (2012), *Against Massacre: Humanitarian Interventions in the Ottoman Empire, 1815–1914: The Emergence of a European Concept and International Practice*, Princeton: Princeton University Press.

Rodriguez, M. E. (2009), *Under the Flags of Freedom: British Mercenaries in the War of the Two Brothers, the First Carlist War, and the Greek War of Independence (1821–1840)*, Lanham, MD: Hamilton Books.

Roidis, E. (1997) [1895], *Το παράπονο του νεκροθάπτου*, Athens: Periplous.

Rothman, E. N. (2009), 'Interpreting Dragomans: Boundaries and Crossings in the Early Modern Mediterranean', *Comparative Studies in Society and History*, 51 (04), pp. 771–800

Rotzokos, N. (2003), 'Οι εμφύλιοι πόλεμοι. Το ζήτημα της εξουσίας στην επανάσταση', in V. Panagiotopoulos (ed.), *Ιστορία του νέου ελληνισμού 1770–2000. 3ος τόμος. Η ελληνική επανάσταση 1821–1832. Ο αγώνας της ανεξαρτησίας και η ίδρυση του ελληνικού κράτους*, pp. 143–71.

— (2011a), 'The Nation As a Political Subject. Comments on the Greek

National Movement', in P. Pizanias (ed.), *The Greek Revolution of 1821: a European event*, Istanbul: The Isis Press, pp. 151–70.

— (2011b), *Εθναφύπνιση και εθνογένεση: Ορλωφικά και ελληνική ιστοριογραφία*, Athens: Bibliorama.

Roudometof, V. (1998), 'From Rum Millet to Greek Nation: Enlightenment, Secularization, and National Identity in Ottoman Balkan Society, 1453–1821', *Journal of Modern Greek Studies*, 16 (1), pp. 11–48.

Sadat, D. R. (1972), 'Rumeli Ayanlari: The Eighteenth Century', *The Journal of Modern History*, 44 (3), pp. 346–63.

Saitas Y. (2003), 'Η γαλλική αποστολή. Η επιστημονική εξερεύνηση του Μοριά, 1829–1830', in V. Panagiotopoulos (ed.), *Ιστορία του νέου ελληνισμού 1770–2000. 3ος τόμος. Η ελληνική επανάσταση 1821–1832. Ο αγώνας της ανεξαρτησίας και η ίδρυση του ελληνικού κράτους*, pp. 389–400.

Sakalides, G. (2002), 'The Provisioning of Istanbul with Wheat in the Turbulent Times: Yenişehir in Thessaly at the End of the Eighteen Century', *Balkan Studies*, 43, pp. 129–49.

Sakellariou, M. (2012), *Η απόβαση του Ιμπραήμ στην Πελοπόννησο*, Herakleion: University of Crete Press.

Salzmann, A. (1993), 'An Ancien Régime Revisited: Privatization and Political Economy in the Eighteenth-Century Ottoman Empire', *Politics and Society*, 21 (4), pp. 393–423.

Sant Cassia, P. with C. Bada (1992), *The Making of the Modern Greek Family: Marriage and Exchange in Nineteenth-century Athens*, Cambridge: Cambridge University Press.

Sasmazer, L. M. T. (2000), *Provisioning Istanbul: Bread Production, Power, and Political Ideology in the Ottoman Empire, 1789–1807*, PhD dissertation, Bloomington: Indiana University Press.

Schönhärl, K. (2013) 'Fighting the Financial Crisis in Greece: The Privileged Company to Protect Production and Trade in Currants (1905) As International Bank Cooperation', *The Historical Review*, pp. 107–34.

Shechter, R. (2003), 'Selling Luxury: The Rise of the Egyptian Cigarette and the Transformation of the Egyptian Tobacco Market, 1850–1914', *International Journal of Middle East Studies*, 35 (1), pp. 51–75.

— (2006), *Smoking, Culture and Economy in the Middle East: the Egyptian Tobacco Market 1850–2000*, London: I. B. Tauris.

Sheremet, V. (1992), 'The Greek Revolution of 1821: A New Look at Old Problems', *Modern Greek Studies Yearbook*, 8, pp. 41–55.

Shliakhov, O. (2013), 'Greeks in the Russian Empire and their Role in the Development of Trade and Shipping in the Black and Azov Seas (nineteenth–early twentieth centuries)', *The Historical Review 10*, pp. 255–64.

Shusharova, M. (2011), 'A Local View over the War: War Service Functions of the Rumelian Ayans in the Ottoman Empire at the end of the 17th and during the 18th Centuries', in P. Mitev, I. Parvev, M. Baramova, and V. Racheva (eds), *Empires and peninsulas: Southeastern Europe between Carlowitz and the peace of Adrianople, 1699–1829*, Berlin: Lit Verlag.

Sifneos, E. (ed.) (2002), *Soapmaking in Lesvos: A Memento*. Athens: Livani.

— (2004), 'On Entrepreneurs and Entrepreneurship of the Olive-oil

Economy in the Aegean: The Case of Lesvos Island', *The Historical Review*, I, pp. 245–73.

— (2005), 'Cosmopolitanism as a Feature of the Greek Commercial Diaspora', *History and Anthropology*, 16 (1), pp. 97–111.

— (2011), 'Diaspora Entrepreneurship Revisited: Greek Merchants and Firms in the Southern Russian Ports', *Entreprises et Histoire* (2), pp. 40–52.

— (2013), 'Greek Family Firms in the Azov Sea Region, 1850–1917', *Business History Review*, 87 (02), pp. 279–308.

Sigalos, E. (2004), *Housing in Medieval and Post-Medieval Greece*, Oxford: Archaeopress.

Sinareli, M. (1989), *Δρόμοι και λιμάνια στην Ελλάδα, 1830–1890*, Athens: Politistiko Tehnoloyiko Idrima ETBA.

— (2003), 'Το οδικό δίκτυο. Κρατική πολιτική και οδοποιία το 19ο αιώνα', in V. Panagiotopoulos (ed.), *Ιστορία του νέου ελληνισμού 1770–2000. 4ος τόμος. Το ελληνικό κράτος, 1833–1871: Η εθνική εστία και ο ελληνισμός της Οθωμανικής αυτοκρατορίας*, Athens: Elliniki Grammata, pp. 119–30.

Sonyel, S. R. (1991), 'The Protege System in the Ottoman Empire', *Journal of Islamic Studies*, 2 (1), pp. 56–66.

Sotiriou, D. (1991), *Farewell Anatolia*, Athens: Kedros.

Sotiropoulos, D. P. (2009), 'Ελληνική νομαρχία: Ήτοι λόγος περί του ριζοσπαστικός διαφωτισμός. Η γέννηση της ελληνικής πολιτικής σκέψης στις απαρχές του 19ου αιώνα', in P. Pizanias (ed.), *Η ελληνική επανάσταση του 1821. Ενα ευρωπαϊκό γέγονος*, Athens: Kedros, pp. 104–18.

— (2011), 'Helleniki Nomarchia: Discourse on the Radical Enlightenment. The Birth of Modern Greek Political Thought Into the Early 19th Century', in P. Pizanias (ed.), *The Greek Revolution of 1821: A European Event*, Istanbul: The Isis Press, pp. 85–100.

Sotiropoulos, S. (1866), *Τριάκοντα εξ ημερών αιχμαλωσία και συμβίωσις μετά ληστών*, Athens: Franklinos.

Stamatopoulos, D. (2005), 'From Machiavelli to the Sultans: Power Networks in the Ottoman Imperial Context', *Historein*, 5, pp. 76–93.

— (2007), 'Constantinople in the Peloponnese: The Case of the Dragoman of the Morea Georgios Wallerianos and Some Aspects of the Revolutionary Process', in A. Anastasopoulos and E. Kolovos (eds), *Ottoman Rule and the Balkans, 1760–1850: Conflict, Transformation, Adaptation*, Rethymno: University of Crete, pp. 149–66.

Stamatoyannopoulou, M. (1993), 'Déplacement saisonnier et exploitation rurale en Grèce dans la deuxième moitié du XIXe siècle. La cas De Krathis', in S. Woolf (ed.), *Espaces et familles dans l'Europe du Sud l' age moderne*, Paris: Editions de la Maison des sciences de l'homme, pp. 205–13.

Stassinopoulos, Y. (2006), 'Νόμισμα και τράπεζες', in K. Kostis and S. Petmezas (eds), *Η ανάπτυξη της ελληνικής οικονομίας κατά τον 19ου αιώνα (1830–1914)*, Athens: Alexandreia, pp. 379–408.

— (2011), 'The Political Economy of Money and Banking in Greece Before 1914: An Overview', in E. Eldem and S. Petmezas (eds), *The Economic*

Development of Southeastern Europe in the 19th century, Athens: Alpha Bank, pp. 307–34.

Stathis, P. (2007), 'From Klephts and *Armatoloi* to Revolutionaries', in A. Anastasopoulos and E. Kolovos (eds), *Ottoman Rule and the Balkans, 1760–1850: Conflict, Transformation, Adaptation*, Rethymno: University of Crete, pp. 167–80.

Stefanini, I. (1829), *The Personal Sufferings of J. Stefanini*, New York: Vanderpool & Cole.

Stites, R. (2014), *The Four Horsemen: Riding to Liberty in Post-Napoleonic Europe*, New York: Oxford University Press.

Stone, David R. (2006), *A military history of Russia*, Westport, CT: Praeger Security International.

Stouraiti, A. and A. Kazamias (2010), 'The Imaginary Topographies of the Megali Idea: National Territory As Utopia', in N. P. Diamandouros, T. Dragona, and C. Keyder (eds), *Spatial Conceptions of the Nation: Modernizing Geographies in Greece and Turkey*, London: I. B. Tauris, pp. 11–34.

Strohmeier, M. (2010), 'Economy and Society in the Aegean Province of the Ottoman Empire, 1840–1912', *Turkish Historical Review*, 1 (2), pp. 164–95.

Şakul, K. (2009), 'Russo-Ottoman War of 1768–1774', in G. Agoston and B. A. Masters (eds), *Encyclopedia of the Ottoman Empire*, New York: Facts On File, pp. 492–3.

Şenışık, P. (2010), 'Rethinking Muslim and Christian Communities in Late Nineteenth Century Ottoman Crete: Insights From the Cretan Revolt of 1897', *Journal of Modern Greek Studies*, 28 (1), pp. 27–47.

— (2011), *The Transformation of Ottoman Crete: Revolts, Politics and Identity in the Late Nineteenth Century*, London: I. B. Tauris.

Tabak, F. (2008), *The Waning of the Mediterranean, 1550–1870: A Geohistorical Approach*, Baltimore: Johns Hopkins University Press.

Tansu, F. (2011), 'The Greek Community of Izmir/Smyrna in An Age of Transition: The Relationship Between Ottoman Centre-Local Governance and the Izmir/Smyrna Greeks, 1840–1866', *British Journal of Middle Eastern Studies*, 38 (01), pp. 41–72.

Tappe, E. D. (1973), 'The 1821 Revolution in the Rumanian Principalities', in R. Clogg (ed.), *The Greek Struggle for Independence*, London: Macmillan, pp. 134–55.

Tassopoulos, I. (2007), 'Constitutionalism and the Ideological Conversion to National Unity Under the Greek Constitution of 1864', in A. Frangoudaki and Keyder (eds), *Ways to modernity in Greece and Turkey: encounters with Europe, 1850–1950*, London: I. B. Tauris, pp. 9–25.

Teoman and Kaymak (2008), 'Commercial Agriculture and Economic Change in the Ottoman Empire During the Nineteenth Century: A Comparison of Raw Cotton Production in Western Anatolia and Egypt', *The Journal of Peasant Studies*, 35 (2), pp. 314–34.

Theodoridis, G. K. (2003), 'Ένα σύγχρονο κράτος. Η πολιτική οργάνωση του Αγώνα, 1822–1827', in V. Panagiotopoulos (ed.), *Ιστορία του νέου* ελληνισμού 1770–2000. 3ος τόμος. Η ελληνική επανάσταση 1821–1832. Ο αγώνας της ανεξαρτησίας και η ίδρυση του ελληνικού κράτους, Athens: Elliniki Grammata, pp. 125–42.

Theodorou T. P. (1992), 'Η Ρωσία και η επανάσταση της 3ης Σεπτεμβρίου 1843 με βάση έγγραφη των αρχείων της ΕΣΣΔ και τον περιοδικό τύπο εκείνης της εποχής', *Βαλκανικά Συμμείκτα*, 4, pp. 79–90.

Theodossiou, E., T. Grammenos and V. N. Manimanis (2004), 'Theophilos Kairis: The Creator and Initiator of Theosebism in Greece', *The European Legacy*, 9 (6), pp. 783–97.

Theodossopoulos, D. (1999), 'The Pace of the Work and the Logic of the Harvest: Women, Labour and the Olive Harvest in a Greek Island Community', *The Journal of the Royal Anthropological Institute*, 5 (4), pp. 611–26.

Theologou, K. and P. G. Michaelides (2010), 'The Role of Jews in the late Ottoman and early Greek Salonica', *Journal of Balkan and Near Eastern Studies*, 12(3), pp. 307–20.

Theotokas, N. and N. Kotaridis (2006), *Η οικονομία της βίας. Παραδοσιακές και νεωτερικές εξουσίες στην Ελλάδα του 19ου αιώνα*, Athens: Bibliorama.

— (2009), 'Οι θεσμοί οθωμανικής κυριαρχίας και η ελληνική επανάσταση', in P. Pizanias (ed.), *Η ελληνική επανάσταση του 1821. Ενα ευρωπαϊκό γέγονος*, Athens: Kedros, pp. 334–42.

— (2011), 'Ottoman Perceptions of the Greek Revolution', in P. Pizanias (ed.), *The Greek Revolution of 1821: A European Event*, Istanbul: The Isis Press, pp. 265–76.

Toksöz, M. (2010a), *Nomads, Migrants and Cotton in the Eastern Mediterranean: the Making of the Adana-Mersin region 1850–1908*, Boston: Brill.

— (2010b), 'A Migrant-Merchant Family From Mersin: The Mavromatis', in V. Kechriotis (ed.), *Economy and Society in Both Shores of the Aegean*, Athens: Alpha Bank Publications, pp. 337–54.

— (2011), 'Family and Migration: The Mavromatis Enterprises and Networks', *Cahiers De La Méditerranée*, (82), pp. 359–82.

Toledano, E. R. (1982), *The Ottoman Slave Trade and Its Suppression, 1840–1890*, Princeton: Princeton University Press.

— (1998), *Slavery and Abolition in the Ottoman Middle East*, Seattle: University of Washington Press.

Totsikas, A. (2008), *Ελληνική λαϊκή κληρονομία. Εργαλεί και κατασκευές του υλικού παραδοσιακού βίου*, Athens: Armos Publishing.

Triha, L. (2001), *Ο Χαρίλαος Τρικούπης και τα δημόσια έργα*, Athens: Kapon.

— (2009), *Χαρίλαος Τρικούπης. Μία βιογραφική περιήγηση*, Athens: Kapon.

Tuck, C. (2008), 'All Innovation Leads to Hellfire: Military Reform and the Ottoman Empire in the Eighteenth Century', *Journal of Strategic Studies*, 31 (3), pp. 467–502.

Tuckerman, C. K. (1872), *The Greeks of To-Day*, London: Sampson & Low Co.

Tuluveli, G. (2005), 'State and Classes in the Ottoman Empire: Notables in Historical Perspective', *Journal of Mediterranean Studies*, 15 (1), pp. 121–47.

Tzakis, D. (2011), '<<Υποδαυλιζόμενοι παρά Ρωσίας...>> Η συμμετοχή των κοτζαμπάσηδων στην εξέγερση του 1770 στο Πελοπόννησο', in O. Katsiardi-Hering, A. Kolia-Dermitzaki, and K. Gardkia (eds), *Ρωσία και Μεσόγειος. Πρακτικά Α' διεθνούς συνεδρίου. Τόμος B*, Athens: EKPA/Herodotos Publications, pp. 11–31.

Tzanaki, D. (2007), *Δούλα και κυρά. Όψεις εθνικισμού: ρόλοι και συμπεριφορές στην Ελλάδα των ρομαντικών χρόνων*, Athens: Savvalas.

— (2009), *Women and nationalism in the making of modern Greece: the founding of the Kingdom to the Greco-Turkish War*, Basingstoke: Palgrave Macmillan.

Tzanelli, R. (2009), *The 'Greece' of Britain and the 'Britain' of Greece: Performance, Stereotypes, Expectations and Intermediaries in 'Neohellenic' and Victorian Narratives (1864–1881)*, Saarbrucken: VDM Verlag Dr. Müller.

Tzokas, S. (1999), *O Χαρίλαος Τρικούπης και η συγκρότηση του νεοελληνικού κράτους*, Athens: Themelio.

Ursinus, M. (2004), *Grievance Administration (sikayet) in an Ottoman Province*, New York: Routledge.

Varikas, E. (1993), 'Gender and National Identity in Fin De Siecle Greece', *Gender and History*, 5 (2), pp. 269–83.

Varnava, A. (2009), *British Imperialism in Cyprus 1878–1915. The Inconsequential Possession*, Manchester: Manchester University Press.

Veremis, T., and Y. Koliopoulos (2010), *1821 Η γέννηση ενός 'έθνους-κράτους. B τόμος. Η συγκρότηση εξουσίας στην επαναστατημένη Ελλάδα*, Athens: National Bank of Greece.

Vionis, A. K. (2005), 'Domestic Material Culture and Post-Medieval Archaeology in Greece: A Case Study From the Cyclades', *Post-Medieval Archaelogy*, 39 (1), pp. 172–85.

— (2013), *A Crusader, Ottoman, and Early Modern Aegean Archaeology: Built Environment and Domestic Material Culture in the Medieval and Post-medieval Cyclades, Greece (13th–20th Centuries AD)*, Leiden: Leiden University Press.

Vlachopoulou, A. (2007), 'Like the Mafia? The Ottoman Military Presence in the Morea in the Eighteenth Century', in A. Anastasopoulos and E. Kolovos (eds), *Ottoman Rule and the Balkans, 1760–1850: Conflict, Transformation, Adaptation*, Rethymno: University of Crete, pp. 123–36.

Vogiatzakis, Ioannis N. (ed.) (2012), *Mediterranean Mountain Environments*, Hoboken, NJ: Wiley.

Vogli E. K. (2007), <<Έλληνες το γένος>> Η ιθαγένεια και η ταυτότητα στο εθνικό κράτος των Ελλήνων (1821–1844), Herakleio: University of Crete Press.

— (2009), 'A Greece for Greeks by Descent? Nineteenth-Century Policy on Integrating the Greek Diaspora', in D. Tziovas (ed.), *Greek Diaspora and Migration since 1700: Society, Politics and Culture*, Burlington, VT: Ashgate, pp. 99–110.

— (2011), 'The Making of Greece Abroad: Continuity and Change in the Modern Diaspora Politics of a "Historical" Irredentist Homeland',

Nationalism and Ethnic Politics, 17 (1), pp. 14–33.

Von Stackelberg, O. M. (1825), *Costumes et usages des peuples de la Grèce Moderne*, Rome: privately published by the author.

Vyzantios, D. (2006 [1836]), *Babel, or the Local Distortion of the Greek Language*, in B. Trencsényi, M. Kopeček, V. Kechriotis, M. Górny, and A. Ersoy (eds), *Discourses of Collective Identity in Central and Southeast Europe (1770–1945): Texts and Commentaries*, New York: Central European University Press, pp. 138–42.

Walsh, R. (1836), *A Residence at Constantinople during a period including the Commencement, Progress, and Termination of the Greek and Turkish Revolutions*, London: F. Westley & A. H. Davis.

White, S. (2012), 'Climate Change in Global Environmental History', in J. R. McNeill and E. S. Mauldin (eds), *A Companion to Global Environmental History*, Hoboken, NJ: Wiley, pp. 394–411.

— (2013), 'The Little Ice Age Crisis of the Ottoman Empire: A Conjuncture in Middle East Environmental History', in A. Mikhail (ed.), *Water on Sand: Environmental Histories of the Middle East and North Africa*, New York: Oxford University Press, pp. 71–90.

Woodhouse, C. M. (1973), *Capodistrias: The Founder of Greek Independence*, Oxford: Oxford University Press.

Yavuz, M. Hakan, and I. Blumi (eds) (2013), *War and Nationalism: the Balkan Wars, 1912–1913, and their Sociopolitical Implications*, Salt Lake City: The University of Utah Press.

Yiannitsiotis, Y. (2006), *Η κοινωνική ιστορία του Πειραιά. Η συγκρότηση της αστικής τάξης 1860–1910*, Athens: Nefeli.

Yiannopoulos, Y. (2003), 'Τα πολεμικά γεγονότα, Β. Η κρίσιμη τριετία, 1825–1827', in V. Panagiotopoulos (ed.), *Ιστορία του νέου ελληνισμού 1770–2000. 3ος τόμος. Η ελληνική επανάσταση 1821–1832. Ο αγώνας της ανεξαρτησίας και η ίδρυση του ελληνικού κράτους*, Athens: Elliniki Grammata, pp. 103–18.

Yiannopoulou, M. (2007), 'Τα ελαιοτριβεία στη Πελοπόννησο από τον 19ο έως και τα μέσα του 20ού αιώνα', in E. Beneki (ed.), <<*Ο δε τόπος ... ελαιοφόρος>> Η παρουσία της ελιάς στην Πελοπόννησο*, Athens: Bank of Piraeus Cultural Foundation.

Yosmaoğlu, I. K. (2014), *Blood Ties: Religion, Violence, and the Politics of Nationhood in Ottoman Macedonia, 1878–1908*, Ithaca, NY: Cornell University Press.

Zandi-Sayek, S. A. (2012), *Ottoman Izmir: the Rise of a Cosmopolitan Port, 1840*, Minneapolis: University of Minnesota Press.

Zarkia, K. (1997), *Preindustrial Tanning in Greece*, Athens: The ETBA Cultural Foundation.

Zelpos, I. (2011), 'Amateurs as Nation-builders: On the Significance of Associations for the Formation and Nationalization of Greek Society in the 19th Century', in H. Grandits, N. Clayer, and R. Pichler (eds), *Conflicting Loyalties in the Balkans: the Great Powers, the Ottoman Empire and Nation-building*, London: I. B. Tauris, pp. 64–86.

Zens, R. W. (2002), 'Pasvanoglu Osman Pasa and the Pasalik of Belgrade, 1791–1807', *International Journal of Turkish Studies*, 8 (1–2), pp. 89–104.

— (2004), *The Ayanlik and Pasvanoglu Osman Pasa of Vidin in the Age of Ottoman Social Change, 1791–1815*, PhD dissertation, Madison: The University of Wisconsin-Madison.

— (2011), 'Provincial Powers: The Rise of Ottoman Local Notables (Ayan)', *History Studies*, 3 (3), pp. 433–47.

Zgaier, A. (2008), 'Landslides on Agricultural Hillslope Terraces Under Mediterranean Climatic Conditions', *Israel Journal of Earth Sciences*, 57 (3), pp. 249–61.

Zilfi, M. C. (2012), *Women and Slavery in the Late Ottoman Empire: The Design of Difference*, New York: Cambridge University Press.

Index